Sin No More

Sin No More

*From Abortion to Stem Cells,
Understanding Crime, Law,
and Morality in America*

John Dombrink and
Daniel Hillyard

NEW YORK UNIVERSITY PRESS

New York and London

NEW YORK UNIVERSITY PRESS
New York and London
www.nyupress.org

Library of Congress Cataloging-in-Publication Data
Dombrink, John.
Sin no more : from abortion to stem cells, understanding crime, law,
and morality in America / John Dombrink and Daniel Hillyard.
p.   cm.
Includes bibliographical references and index.
ISBN-13: 978-0-8147-1988-6 (cloth : alk. paper)
ISBN-10: 0-8147-1988-0 (cloth : alk. paper)
ISBN-13: 978-0-8147-1989-3 (pbk. : alk. paper)
ISBN-10: 0-8147-1989-9 (pbk. : alk. paper)
 1. Social values—United States. 2. Social problems—Moral and
ethical aspects. 3. Social ethics. 4. United States—Moral
conditions.   I. Hillyard, Daniel, 1962– II. Title.
HN90.M6D65 2007
170.973—dc22   2007026182

For Jerry Skolnick
and Maya, Paul, and Kara (JD)

For my wife, Angela Cuevas
and to the memory of my parents,
Dan and Mary Hillyard (DH)

Contents

Acknowledgments   ix

1   Changing Moralities: Shifts in American Attitudes
and Law in the "Moral Values" Debate   1

2   Painless Prosperity: The Spread of Legal Gambling   31

3   Abortion: Contestation and Ambivalence in the
Long Era of *Roe v. Wade*   53

4   Gay Rights: Beyond Tolerance and Privacy to Equality   93

5   Assisted Suicide: The Road to New Rules of Dying   127

6   Stem Cells: Framing Battles and the Race for a Cure   186

7   Conclusion: To Form a More Purple Union?   225

Notes   257
References   269
Index   311
About the Authors   331

Acknowledgments

Thanks first to Val Jenness as a colleague whose interest in this developing project, helpful comments on an early draft of chapter 1, and invitation to participate in a forum on "Morality Battles" in *Contemporary Sociology* helped advance the development of the themes of the book. Special thanks to Arlene Skolnick for including early formulations of this book in the excellent four-part series on the American family she edited for *Dissent* magazine in 2004 and 2005.

The authors also thank the following colleagues who have given us early comments and advice: Kitty Calavita (for helpful comments on early notions of the work), Gilbert Geis, Ron Huff, Henry Pontell, Richard Perry, Jonathan Simon, Karim Ismaili, Roger Magnusson, Ron Weitzer, Harry Mersmann, Joel Best, Michael Walzer, and the anonymous reviewers of the manuscript for NYU Press. At the University of California, Irvine, Christine Byrd encouraged and placed an opinion article on the Schiavo case.

Dan Hillyard benefited from insightful comments by Southern Illinois University Writing Circle participants Bill Wells, Joe Schafer, Martha Henderson, George Burruss, Matt Giblin, Todd Armstrong, and Gaylene Armstrong. SIU colleagues Jim LeBeau, Joan McDermott, and Jim Garofalo also provided learned advice. Thanks also to Shirley Clay Scott, Alan Vaux, Tom Castellano, Marc Reidel, Bob Lorinskas, and Amanda Mathias

We also appreciate the work of the following student research assistants who have helped on various aspects of the book: at UCI, Sean Geraghty, Matt Udink, Erin Pinkus, Ruby Simjee, Ronald Baldonado, Andrea Galanti, Holly Lam, Michael Borokhov, and Cylia Villegas. At SIU: Sarah Knight, Wendy Goldberg, Mark Gauen, and Steve Sikorski.

We also benefited from the insights of UCI graduate students Glenda Kelmes, Erik Fritsvold, Tomson Nguyen, and Johnny Nhan, who served as teaching assistants for an undergraduate course covering the material in the book, and Glenda Kelmes for her parallel insights on drug policy.

Several other groups have aided in reflection on these issues. These include the students in John Dombrink's spring 2006 graduate seminar on religion and morality, whose comments helped refine some of the final thoughts in chapters 1 and 7: Andrew Peterson, Matt Cleary, Jerome Anaya, Jon Herrick, Katie Nelson, and Steve Sosko. Also important in this way were a 2006 Ghost Ranch Seminar led by Rev. B. Gail Joralemon for crystallizing some issues on health and autonomy; the community at Neighborhood Congregational Church (UCC) in Laguna Beach for demonstrating alternative paths on religion and morality (as did the writings of the late Rev. E. Frank Henriques); and Dr. Ron Miller and his Bioethics Luncheon Group at UCI for fascinating discussions on medical ethics, including an opportunity to view and discuss many of the Terri Schiavo court tapes.

We are grateful to have received guidance from Shane Smith for insight and documents from the 2004 California stem cell campaign, and to UCI vice chancellor Sue Bryant for inclusion in talks about stem cell research. Thanks also to Dave Ferguson, Mary Ann Dombrink-Kurtzman, and Sidney Golub for keeping us competent on stem cell issues; to Eli Stutsman for access for Dan Hillyard to the U.S. Supreme Court for the oral arguments in *Gonzales v. Oregon;* to Bill Eadington at the University of Nevada for opportunities to present versions of the gambling chapter at two of his International Gambling Conferences; and to William N. Thompson of UNLV, Basil Browne, and I. Nelson Rose for their always astute gambling observations. For perspectives on death with dignity, we are thankful for the insights of Ron Koons, Peter Goodwin, Eli Stutsman, Barbara Coombs Lee, John Duncan, and Hannah Davidson.

Other colleagues and friends were helpful with their insights and continuing interest: Paul Eklof, Michael Clark, Tom Vickers, Frank Forbath, Eileen Dunne, Annie Dunne, Kathleen Dombrink, Patricia Dombrink, Jeff Green, Steve Cohn, Paul Freeman, Sam Gilmore, Roger Kempler, Mehdi Zahedi, Chris Green, Joan Politeo, Paul Manfrini, Richard Selin, and Brian and Gloria Dunne. Thanks to those at UCI who have kept other programs at the university working well and from intruding on this project: Rich Steele, Jia Frydenberg, Judy Omiya, William C. Thompson, Margaret Wyvill, Carol Stanley, Juan Lara, Robert Sterling, Esteban Rodriguez, Roy Delgado, Mei-Ling Malone, Dave

Tomcheck, Richard Worcester, C. J. Ellis, Jim Meeker, Robert Boyd, and especially Marilyn Wahlert.

Our deep gratitude goes to Ilene Kalish, our outstanding editor at NYU Press, for once again showing interest in our work and deftly guiding us and this book through the completion and review processes, and to Salwa Jabado, Despina Papazoglou Gimbel, and the copyeditor for their excellent assistance there. And heartfelt thanks to John's family, Maya, Paul, and Kara (and the model of Maya's reports, Paul's essays, and Kara's stories), who offered encouragement and gave John the space and time to monitor seemingly endless developments over the past three years and to plunk away at the keyboard. Dan was encouraged by Angela's abiding patience and support, which always comes with a loving measure of good cheer.

It was Jerry Skolnick who started John on reading John Stuart Mill, and other key works in the law and morality debate, five years before the Moral Majority had even formed. His mentorship and generosity then and during the dissertation process, and through subsequent work on gambling and morality issues, have been crucial. From "Coercion to Virtue" (1968) through *House of Cards* (1978), his discussion of ambivalence in "The Social Transformation of Vice" (1988), to his writings on drug policy and his ongoing course syllabi, several of his key concepts are present as anchors in this study, and we hope we did them and him justice.

1

Changing Moralities
Shifts in American Attitudes and Law in the "Moral Values" Debate

There is a religious war going on in our country for the soul of America. It is a cultural war, as critical to the kind of nation we will one day be as was the Cold War itself.
　　—Patrick Buchanan, 1992 Republican National Convention

It's not blue state versus red state after all, but more like blue urban versus red rural, skyscraper versus church house, Chez Panisse versus Denny's. That is to say, it's all about population density, cultural hub, all about the much-touted "redneck revenge" on the "liberal elite" for unleashing, I suppose, small European cars and artisan cheese and "Queer Eye" and "The West Wing" on them without their express written consent. It is, in short, all about Retro vs. Metro.
　　—Mark Morford, "Down with Fancy Book Learnin': What's It Mean That the Big Cities and College Towns of America All Voted Blue?" (2004)

November 2004: Return to "Values"?

American liberals could be forgiven for thinking that indeed things had turned screwy—or scary—in 2004. Everywhere one turned after the presidential elections of 2004, the Reverend Jerry Falwell was pronouncing the meaning of the election, and why George W. Bush was returned to office. Falwell, who many may have thought had flamed out with his intense and uncompromising conservative religious positions and ubiquitous media role since the Reagan years, was all over the airwaves. One night, he was explaining to Chris Matthews on MSNBC's show *Hardball* the failings of an ad campaign by the United Church of Christ, a liberal Protestant denomination, that depicted a church open to gays and lesbians—insinuating to Falwell that evangelical churches in America were bigoted.[1] Another night he was debating on *Meet the Press* with progressive Christian minister Jim Wallis about the role of religion, politics, law, and society.[2]

The rush to engage Falwell, Dr. James Dobson, and other leading lights of the Christian Right as interpreters of the American public's shift in attitudes related to politics in general and the law and personal morality in particular was a result of one frame the media had quickly placed on the 2004 election results.

This strong theme that was being trumpeted in the media was the importance of "values," the result of exit polls taken on election day: As the *New York Times* reported:

> In the survey, a striking portrait of one influential group emerged—that of a traditional, church-going electorate that leans conservative on social issues and strongly backed Mr. Bush. . . . Bush appealed overwhelmingly to voters on terrorism and to many others on his ability to handle the economy. But what gave him the edge in the election, which he won 51 percent to 48 percent, was a perceived sense of morality and traditional values.[3]

The election results were not necessarily a surprise to those who had worried throughout 2004 whether or not the Democrats had a "church gap." Still, a progressive could be dismayed that such strutting by the Christian Right came so soon after what some progressives referred to as an unusual trifecta in the "gotcha" category of politics: who could have predicted that 2003 would have seen conservative author and former drug czar and cabinet secretary Bill Bennett exposed as an inveterate gambler who lost hundreds of thousands of dollars in video poker in Nevada and New Jersey? Or that conservative radio host Rush Limbaugh would be admitted to treatment with a drug problem centering on illegally obtained painkillers? Or that segregationist favorite and longtime U.S. senator Strom Thurmond was disclosed to have fathered a child with an African American woman?

What had happened?

Was this a sign of the continued vitality of the "culture wars," twenty years after that term had first been used? And maybe this was also a sign of the "stealth" nature of the network of Christian conservatives, a factor especially in previous local elections.

Was this a continuation of the conservative mobilization that had followed the sex scandal of Bill Clinton? Sexual behavior had been a major component of the Clinton era scandals and had contributed in no small part to the right's coalescence on abstinence, zero tolerance, and the ascendance of other traditional values in the broader political debate.

Was this a very specific backlash to the issue of gay marriage, which had been raised by the decision of the Massachusetts Supreme Court in 2003, the Supreme Court antisodomy decision in 2003, and the extralegal marriages performed in San Francisco and other cities in 2004? A spokesman for the National Gay and Lesbian Task Force had commented on how the Supreme Court decision in *Lawrence* offered both promise and peril for those advocating equality for gays and lesbians.[4] Certainly, the image of eleven states easily voting in defense of marriage acts (DOMAs) in November 2004, while not necessarily determinative of the Electoral College outcomes, speaks to this backlash.

Was this a continuing example of false consciousness, as raised so effectively by historian Thomas Frank in *What's the Matter with Kansas?*,[5] that led working-class evangelical Protestants to collaborate in their own economic demise by joining forces with a coalition of corporate power and social conservatives in the Republican Party? As Frank wrote: "As a formula for holding together a dominant political coalition, the backlash seems so improbable and so self-contradictory that liberal observers often have trouble believing it is actually happening." Is there anything that progressives could take heart from in the 2004 results? Something had happened, but what?

This book will argue that there is much more consensus on moderate views among the American public on public policy toward issues of law and personal morality—where the "family values" come into debate. In fact, Americans are more "purple" than "red" or "blue" on many of these values issues. Activists care deeply about such issues—on either side of the debates—and political strategists find ways to use these beliefs to achieve success in political campaigns on the margins. Moreover, over the past thirty years America has incrementally liberalized its laws and attitudes across the range of these issues and has even seen new "combustible" issues emerge (assisted suicide and stem cell research, which are discussed in chapters 5 and 6, respectively). We argue:

1. The importance of the "values voters" was overstated, but they remain a vital force;
2. Americans have a more moderate–and tolerant—approach toward a range of policies in the personal morality area;
3. Not all persons of faith are conservative, but the marriage of secularization and religiosity is a confounding one

In this book, we analyze events and lawmaking across these several arenas of the culture war between 2004 and 2006 and present a counterinterpretation to the "values voters frame" of 2004. We end with an assessment of where America stands in 2007 after a few years of discussion and debate, use and abuse of "wedge issues," and accusations of misplaced emphasis and false consciousness. We also present our thoughts on the nature of lawmaking in this complicated area and how the American consideration of legal changes in the area of "victimless crime" has changed in various ways since the concept was first introduced forty years ago.

We should explain the title of the book. The use of the word "sin" here is meant to convey the complexity and duality of the subjects of law and morality we address inside. In one use of the term, a Catholic priest encourages a penitent in confession (or the now renamed "sacrament of reconciliation") to "go and sin no more," with the understanding that the individual has transgressed and should now try to stay on the straight path. The second sense in which we use the term—and that which cuts against the first use—is in signifying that an activity, like abortion or same-sex relations, is no longer considered a "sin" by many. While ultimately we are not focused on religious changes, we have written a book about the changing of mores and norms, and the changing of laws to follow that societal trend, however contested it has been.

The Importance of the "Values Voters"

The night of the November 2, 2004, presidential election, exit polls—which had already caused havoc earlier in the day by contributing to a prediction of a Kerry victory—began shaping a story line from the election that would be startling to many: that "moral values" was the leading reason given by voters for their reelection of George W. Bush. According to the *New York Times*, "What gave him the edge in the election, which he won 51 percent to 48 percent, was a perceived sense of morality and traditional values."[6] In opening a panel discussion on the topic among reporters, pollsters, and analyst two weeks later, journalist Marvin Kalb framed the discussion by introducing the "now conventional wisdom, raised and debunked at the same time, that moral values, more than terrorism, more than the war in Iraq, more than the economy, was the one issue that mattered most to the people voting for President."[7]

Within a few days, critiques had arisen from political analysts and pollsters, noting that the choice of closed-ended questions from a list had skewed the results, so that "moral values" headed a list of seven choices. (By comparison, an open-ended list elicited a much weaker finding.) Even Michael Barone, a conservative political analysts, allowed as to how, when aggregated, the combination of the Iraq war and terrorism (37 percent) or four leading domestic issues (37 percent) both dwarfed the values item.[8] The Pew Research Center concluded that while "moral values is a top-tier issue for voters . . . the relative importance of moral values depends greatly on how the question is framed."[9]

Andrew Kohut further explained, from data from the Pew Research Center:

> In our post-election survey we did a little experiment. We repeated the question that the exit pollsters used, asking voters to choose from five or six items, including moral values, and in the other half of our sample we asked people on an open-ended basis to tell us what issues were on their mind, and we got quite different answers. In the fixed list column, which is that first column, we got 27 percent mentioning moral values—the most frequently given response, just like in the exit polls. Iraq came second, then economy, then terrorism. But in the open-ended question we just got 14 percent saying anything remotely close to moral values, either moral values itself, social issues such as—one of the social issues such as abortion or gay marriage.[10]

Others commented on the ambiguous nature of all the polls. Adam Nagourney, a political writer for the *New York Times,* observed: "Presidential elections often produce a clear story line, a lesson for losers and winners alike. Not this one, at least not yet. . . . the very ambiguity of the 2004 election results has pushed the party into new sets of arguments. . . . did Democrats lose because they were seen as lax on 'values,' which was the early verdict on the Kerry loss, or because they were seen as weak on terrorism?"[11] Sen. Edward Kennedy later added: "Defeat has a thousand causes, and it is too easy to blame it on particular issues or tactics or on the larger debate about values."[12]

In a listing that approximates the concerns of many of the Christian Right groups, a Catholic group has identified the "five nonnegotiables" —abortion, gay rights, assisted suicide, stem cells, and cloning—for focus in its political activity.[13] However, by most measures, Americans currently:

1. support the key tenets of *Roe v. Wade,*
2. support civil unions for same-sex couples, and oppose a constitutional amendment against same-sex marriage,
3. support suffering patients enlisting doctors to end their life,
4. support research using stem cells to end serious disease, and
5. support legal gambling in many forms throughout the country.

Arenas of Contestation

Abortion

Americans have been consistently supportive of the main tenets of *Roe v. Wade* in polls since 1973, even as the Supreme Court has been reshaped and determined to undercut it. At the same time, polls have captured the ambivalence of many toward the implications of that support or, more appropriately, the limits of that support—such as Medicaid funding, teenage access, and late-term abortions. Still, a November 2004 poll taken for the Associated Press found what many precursor polls had—that most Americans (59 percent in the AP poll) thought that President Bush should choose a nominee who would uphold *Roe v. Wade.*[14]

Gay Rights

While 2004 may be remembered for the political fallout from the raising of the gay marriage issues—in legal decisions, extralegal actions, church pronouncements, and philosophical discussions—the common ground that did exist was downplayed in favor of the contestation that made for better media coverage. According to those measures, a majority of Americans favor at least the establishment of civil unions for same-sex couples.[15] Clearly, only a majority of Americans favor allowing same-sex marriages. At the same time, clearly only a majority of Americans support a constitutional amendment opposing gay marriage (such as the 56 percent in the November 2004 *New York Times*–CBS poll). Taken by itself, the majority support for civil unions is a remarkable figure, especially given that only one state (Vermont) then allowed them, and that they were controversial not so long ago. This trend can be seen as signifying the increasing support among a majority of Americans for a range of legal protections for gays and lesbians, beginning with city and county antidiscrimination ordinances in the 1970s. Only a minority thus embraces a position such as that of U.S. Senator John Cornyn (R-Tex.), who offered this assessment of the classic Millian position on gay marriage, morality, and harm: "It does not affect your daily life very much if your neighbor marries a box turtle. But that does not mean it is right. . . . Now you must raise your children up in a world where that union of man and box turtle is on the same legal footing as man and wife."[16]

Death with Dignity

Gradually, since the 1970s, Americans have supported the ability of a patient to be able to end his or her life when terminally ill—first through withdrawal of treatment, living wills, advance directives, and "do not resuscitate" orders. While this has taken full legal form in only one state—Oregon, where the Oregon Death with Dignity Act was passed in 1994—polls have regularly shown that Americans are consistent in their support for patient autonomy at the end of life. A 2004 Gallup poll found that two-thirds of respondents agree that doctors should legally be allowed to intervene in a situation in which a patient has "a disease that cannot be cured and is living in severe pain."[17] A majority (53 percent) felt that doctor-assisted suicide is morally acceptable. While there is some discrepancy between what level of support is expressly for the act of physician-assisted suicide, or physician-aided death (which is how Oregon reformers have started to rename their approach), the events surrounding the Terri Schiavo case in 2005 illustrated how deeply Americans feel about autonomy in deeply personal and family matters like end-of-life decisions.

Stem Cell Research

While the passing of Ronald Reagan may have stirred the memories and allegiances of conservatives who revered him, the scene of his son Ron Reagan standing before the Democratic National Convention in August 2004 to support the case for expanded research on the use of stem cells to provide advances in the treatment of debilitating disease was at odds with that legacy. Young Reagan, who had witnessed the steady deterioration of his father, afflicted with Alzheimer's disease, spoke strongly about the promise of potential new scientific breakthroughs. His mother, Nancy Reagan, showed her support in a more personal fashion, adding support to Senate efforts to pass a law in 2006.

With the support of newly elected governor, Arnold Schwarzenegger, a pro-choice Republican, California solidly passed a state initiative to invest $3 billion in stem cell research, beyond the parameters of what the federal government would allow. The appeals to the electorate—those in the 1994 and 1997 Oregon assisted-suicide campaigns—found doctors and others asking for the opportunity to cure life-threatening diseases through scientific advances made possible through stem cell research. Polls showed that 60 to 70 percent of Americans favored such research,[18] and fifty-four U.S. senators (including fourteen Republicans) supported softening the federal position. Since California's vote, several other states have begun to frame stem cell opportunities, lest California get too far ahead in germinating such research, and in 2006 Missouri passed a similar law.

Gambling

It may seem unusual for this section to include gambling as an example of a personal morality issue that Americans are not deeply divided over. After all, it has been many years since a majority of Americans considered gambling a serious moral issue, or since laws criminalizing gambling were much enforced. Still, as Guth and colleagues explain, gambling was a social issue raising concern for Protestant ministers as late as 1988.[19]

However, legal gambling has been spreading in the United States since New Hampshire legalized its lottery in 1964, and legal gambling revenues have risen from $10 billion in 1982 to $83 billion in 2005. Now forty-eight states permit legal gambling of at least one form, with only Utah and Hawaii as exceptions (one red state and one blue state, as it is). Two in three Americans reported in 2004 having participated in some form of gambling activity in the prior twelve months.[20]

Gambling still appears on the radar of Christian conservative groups, just not as a high priority. Their efforts have been successful in small campaigns, to prevent the expansion of gambling, but as Bill Bennett's explanations after his vice was revealed indicate, gambling has been fairly well normalized as an unproblematic leisure time activity in America.

Normalization of Victimless Crimes: Movement and Backlash

Many of these events of 2004 had their roots in a shift in social attitudes and legal forms that had been taking place throughout the United States for the prior forty years. Since the early 1960s, when legal scholars and social activists had pressed for reforms in how America treated abortion, gambling, drug laws, and homosexuality, various states had acted to liberalize their laws in the area of personal morality.

It would have been unthinkable (but satisfying) in 1978 for Harvey Milk, the newly elected openly gay supervisor in San Francisco, to think that one of his successors, Mayor Gavin Newsom, would be allowing the city and county of San Francisco to perform same-sex wedding ceremonies in 2004. Milk himself had helped to beat back a state ballot initiative in 1978 that would have prevented gays and lesbians from being employed as K–12 teachers in public schools in California. And Milk might have been heartened to see *Brokeback Mountain* as a candidate for the Best Picture Academy Award for 2005. This normalization, however problematic, has been taking place over these thirty years in the case of gay rights. Its pace slowed or changed during the early years of the AIDS crisis, but it has since accelerated in what historian John D'Emilio terms the fourth stage of gay rights.[21]

Newsom was praised in many circles for his open approach and bravery, and derided in others for running outside the law, as the California Supreme Court would eventually decide. In the context of this book, the retrospective look at his action and the legalization of same-sex marriage in Massachusetts in 2004 provide a context for appreciating the vituperative response of the social conservative Right, and its delight in claiming that acts of "overreach" such as those committed by

Newsom fueled the fire of the values voters, on whose votes they claim the 2004 election turned decisively. This also introduces the theme of rapidity, which we think is key to understanding the social religious Right and its call to man the battlefronts of the "morality wars." To the same extent that Milk would have been surprised to see gay marriage legalized and debated so widely only twenty-six years after his efforts, other groups we focus on in this book are equally dismayed and angered by the changes to culture and morality they see as ascendant in American life.

By 1978, many states and cities were on the cusp of broad changes in how they treated issues of the law's reach and personal morality. In California, for instance, 1978 was the year in which the legislature, in a bill sponsored by then assemblyman Willie Brown, voted narrowly to decriminalize sodomy. It had been only two years since California had acted legislatively to decriminalize the possession of small amounts of marijuana (the Moscone Act of 1976). In this way, California was in the first group of states to change its law, after an active debate in the 1960s and 1970s, about the overuse of the criminal sanction in the drug area.

California had been one of the early states to decriminalize abortion, through a law enacted by former governor Ronald Reagan.[22] Twenty years later, it would be on the forefront of state initiatives and funding to circumvent federal prohibitions on research on stem cell lines from embryonic tissue.

California had also been one of the first states to enact a natural death act in 1976, which also reflected the changing mores of society about the law's reach, in this case in matters related to death and dying. California became the first state to pass "living will" legislation;[23] it was followed closely by other states expanding rights in this most personal of areas. The impetus for that change was certainly different than in the other areas discussed in this book: There was no great opportunity for raising state revenues in times of fiscal crisis, as in the case of gambling. There was no redefinition of an activity as recreational, rather than harmful, as in the case of marijuana use. There was no movement by members of a minority to challenge how society saw them and controlled their personal lives, as in the case of gay rights. Instead, the death with dignity movement was propelled by changes in medicine and specifically in life-extending technology, which led to examples of people dying long, drawn-out deaths in hospital intensive care units, when they might have preferred dying privately at home. These changes fueled the death with dignity movement that began to gain steam with passage of laws like California's Natural Death Act. Even though California would not be the first state to approve assisted suicide (a 1992 measure failed in an initiative attempt), the 1976 law—and the do not resuscitate and withdrawal of treatment options it provided—was part of the general trend in that state toward redesigning criminal law in the areas of personal morality.

These changes were not without their challenges, with the successes generating a backlash that took many forms. Even as gay supervisor Harvey Milk and gay rights were successful in San Francisco, and California was decriminalizing sodomy, the state ballot in 1978 featured an initiative that would have prohibited gays and lesbians from being employed as schoolteachers in the state. Across the country, the Resorts International Hotel opened its doors as America's first legal casino outside of Nevada on Memorial Day weekend of 1978. State lotteries had been expanding since being introduced in New Hampshire in 1964, and would do so through the 1980s and 1990s.

With the opening of Atlantic City in 1978, America seemed poised to become a nation of casino states. Indeed, casino industry analysts—including the new category of Wall Street gambling stock analysts—predicted just that. Although the failure of Florida to join that movement in 1978 seemed to slow down the effort, many observers of gambling thought that the country was ripe for more casinos and even sports gambling. But as James Frey has noted, the many fears about corruption in sports limited enthusiasm for that. However, one form of gambling did boom during this period: state-run lotteries. At the same time, a number of Indian reservations were experimenting with forms of gambling that would grow over the next two decades. But even in 1978, one could discern the ambivalence that characterized gambling legalization.

With the advent of Las Vegas–style gambling in Atlantic City, more than the local gamblers from Newark and Brooklyn were taking notice of the available casino gambling. After *Business Week* trumpeted the value of the newly discovered gambling stocks in a 1978 cover story, Wall Street, which had not been a major player in the growth of Las Vegas gambling, given its roots in organized crime and closely held ownership groups, began taking note.[24]

Indeed, President Jimmy Carter had espoused marijuana decriminalization while campaigning in 1976 and supported it in his first year in office, saying in 1977: "Penalties against drug use should not be more damaging to an individual than the use of the drug itself. Nowhere is this more clear than in the laws against the possession of marijuana in private for personal use."[25]

When one looked across the broad sweep of victimless crimes in 1978, it was not difficult to think that, within a few years, legal treatment of these formerly prohibited victimless crimes would be dramatically changed. We would be buying marijuana at the local drug store, perhaps packaged by tobacco companies under catchy names, as rumors of the time suggested.[26]

One author of this book coauthored an article predicting the wide-scale decriminalization of drugs and other forms of deviance,[27] a prediction that would be found lacking fifteen years later.[28] Ten years after that critique, progressive changes such as gay marriage were emerging, but not without heated contestation.

What was happening in 2004? Was it the ascendance of "value voters" and a backlash to the liberal and tolerant policies of the recent past? What happened between 1978 and 2004 in terms of the legal treatment of abortion, gambling, gay rights, assisted suicide, and now stem cell research?

Soon after the events of 1978, the election of Ronald Reagan as president signaled the ascendancy of a group of conservatives, many of them greatly concerned with changes in areas of American law and morality. From Reagan's election onward, the battle was joined over the status of abortion, and legislative, judicial, and political debates and contests between pro-life and pro-choice activists would come in many ways to define the American social landscape of the 1980s.[29]

Still, looking at the events of 2004 against the background of the preceding forty years of contestation, it would be hard not to agree with Thomas Frank's assertion that, despite the setbacks such as those in 2004, the Right in America has not been able to stop the progress of cultural history.[30] This operates, despite what Kevin Phillips calls the "national Disenlightenment" and "cultural antimodernism" of the social conservative agenda.[31]

The story of this book is therefore not one of evolutionary change throughout those decades. In fact, it is one of extremely contested change, events that earned the term "culture war," which has been widely used from the 1990s forward. This book presents important developments in current American law and policy toward each of the topics covered, both those that are a central feature of the culture wars—

abortion, gay rights, assisted suicide, and stem cell research—and gambling, which is now a normalized and common feature of American life, an accepted form of entertainment. It does so in a comprehensive manner, with each activity analyzed within the context of prior efforts toward normalization and liberalization of criminal laws. Each of the topics is at a different point in terms of such normalization, and each has traveled a unique road to achieve that situation. Some have generated more direct and grassroots response and support, whereas others have followed more corporate, or bureaucratic, or state-sponsored models. Each topic will be examined in depth in a separate chapter: chapter 2, "Painless Prosperity: The Spread of Legal Gambling"; chapter 3, "Abortion: Contestation and Ambivalence in the Long Era of *Roe v. Wade*"; chapter 4, "Gay Rights: Beyond Tolerance and Privacy to Equality"; chapter 5, "Assisted Suicide: The Road to New Rules of Dying "; and chapter 6, "Stem Cells: Framing Battles and the Race for a Cure." Finally, chapter 7, "To Form a More Purple Union?," addresses the questions of political polarization in America, assessing whether we are as "red" or "blue" as suggested by some analysts, and whether it is possible that we are more tolerant, more in agreement, and more "purple" than generally portrayed. Running through each chapter will be a central tension: that American attitudes and laws regarding these victimless crimes are best understood as a process of "problematic normalization."

This book takes a unique perspective based upon extended empirical research in each of the four issues. It does this through examining the framing of issues, creation of social movements, and deploying of strategy in what Edwin Schur has termed "stigma contests."[32]

A major theme of the book is that of the rising level of tolerance or liberalization in each of these fours areas, especially when tracked over the past forty years. There has been a "rising floor" of liberalization, despite the images of polarization and red-versus-blue separation and conflict.

Who wins such contests, and what tactics do they employ? The next sections of this chapter will examine successful and unsuccessful efforts to remove the criminal sanction from specific activities in the United States since the 1960s. We will consider the nature of efforts to initiate reforms, to define constituencies, to mobilize resources, to frame debates, and to connect with public opinion and parallel social movements to achieve cultural change.

The Concept of Victimless Crimes

In his 1859 essay *On Liberty,* John Stuart Mill wrote that all persons should be free to "go to Hell in their own way" and that it is not the business of government to prevent people from doing harm to themselves.[33] Mill's dictum is a classic statement of the principle that the individual citizen is to be protected against unwarranted state control, in a zone of freedom guaranteed by legal rights, a principle that distinguishes the tradition of Anglo-American liberal democracy from all other forms of government.

Over the past several generations, all Western industrial democracies have witnessed remarkable social foment surrounding the question of the boundaries of the private domain of individual autonomy ("liberty interests," in the language of American constitutional law) and the state's right to dictate terms of personal behavior for the common good. The Wolfenden Committee in England can be taken as the most important 1950s critique of the use of the criminal law in this area.[34]

On the American scholarly front, Sanford Kadish has written of a "crisis of over-criminalization,"[35] Edwin Schur has elaborated on the problem of "crimes without victims,"[36] Jerome Skolnick has worried about society's capacity to "coerce virtue,"[37] Gilbert Geis has surveyed the range of activities considered "not the law's business,"[38] and Herbert Packer has sought to delineate the "limits of the criminal sanction."[39] Others have mulled over the bases for legitimate penal intervention in zones of individual privacy. Sir Patrick Devlin, a former British high court judge, for instance, has advocated state intervention in private morality because "society cannot ignore the morality of the individual any more than it can his loyalty; it flourishes on both and without either it dies."[40] Importantly, discussion about vices has revolved not only around issues of right and wrong but also around the issue of the practicality and usefulness of applying criminal law to the private behavior.

In the everyday public arena, these same issues have been framed relatively constantly through debates about the private, versus public, nature of forms of conduct as diverse as euthanasia, abortion, use of substances, sexual orientation, commercial sexual activity, the production and commercial exchange of pornographic materials and drugs, and myriad forms of gambling. All of these, at one time or another, have been characterized as "victimless crimes."[41]

The term "victimless crimes" first gained widespread attention among social scientists when Edwin Schur wrote his now classic book *Crimes without Victims,* a study of the reciprocal relationship between deviance and public policy.[42] Following from previous scholarship by Howard Becker, Erving Goffman, Edwin Lemert, and Frank Tannenbaum,[43] Schur demonstrated how borderline crimes have less to do with the characteristics of behavior than with the social processes by which certain behaviors and people who engage in them are successfully labeled as deviant. Unlike violent crimes against persons and serious crimes against property, borderline crimes involve "the willing exchange of socially disapproved but widely demanded goods or services."[44] This element of consent, Schur averred, "precludes the existence of a victim—in the usual sense of the word,"[45] hence the coinage "victimless crimes."

Victimless crimes are said to lie at the borderline of the criminal sanction for several key reasons. First, there are two types of problems inherent in enforcing such laws. One is that providers and consumers of illicit commodities and services do not perceive themselves as victims; hence they do not call upon law enforcement. This means that police themselves must initiate enforcement, and because of the consensual nature of victimless crimes, the tactics required to catch, prosecute, and convict perpetrators are time-consuming and costly, and they divert police resources from preventing and solving more serious crimes. The second problem with enforcement is its creation of "secondary crime."[46] Illicit markets for drugs, prostitution, gambling, and abortion, when it was illegal, are created and thrive due to the very criminalization and enforcement of these activities. Often these activities are accompanied by more serious crimes, such as assault, battery, theft, burglary, robbery, and even homicide. Moreover, secondary crimes are not limited to civilians: for where there's vice, there's often police corruption.

A second key reason victimless crimes exist at the borderline of the criminal sanction is that they are viewed ambivalently. Cook observes that public attitudes toward victimless crimes are subject to significant changes over time.[47] For example, American views on abortion changed dramatically in the 1850s as the birthrate declined and waves of Catholic immigrants arrived with large families. As Conrad and Schneider explain, up to that time, physicians and midwives commonly practiced abortion before quickening, and the procedure was not associated with any moral, legal, or medical problems.[48] But as the demography of abortion shifted, and middle- and upper-class men grew "anxious about the decline in production of . . . strong, native-born, Protestant stock," the American Medical Association responded with passage of a resolution condemning abortion.[49] That action prompted laws criminalizing abortion across the country. Yet physicians themselves began to challenge abortion laws in reaction to the harsh treatment of women who obtained abortions in the 1940s and 1950s,[50] and by 1973 the movement to decriminalize abortion culminated in *Roe v. Wade.*

In addition to this propensity for temporal ambivalence, Cook explains that public attitudes toward victimless crimes are characterized by lack of consensus at any point in time.[51] McConahay's review of public opinion polls regarding pornography provides a good example: "Pornography is a contemporary problem for a small, but intense, minority of Americans, somewhat of a problem for a larger minority, something to be enjoyed by a larger, less intense minority, and a matter of ambivalence for most Americans."[52] Finally, ambivalence characterizes many individual attitudes, as well. Thus, contemporary attitudes toward homosexuals generally combine tolerance for same-sex relations in private with state-sponsored public disapproval through social shame.[53] Such instances of public and individual ambivalence render borderline crimes unenforceable, said Schur.[54] Quoting Edwin Sutherland he observed:

> Laws have accumulated because the mores have been weak and inconsistent; and because the laws have not had the support of the mores they have been relatively ineffective as a means of social control. When the mores are adequate laws are unnecessary; when the mores are inadequate, the laws are ineffective.[55]

Competition over Relative Moral Standing

In *The Politics of Deviance,* a later book by Schur, he states: "Deviance struggles involve competition over relative moral standing."[56] Competition over relative moral standing involves struggles for power, specifically "the power or resource of moral standing or acceptability."[57] These struggles, or "morality contests" as Schur calls them, are grounded in the sociological perspective that power "is more like a process than an object."[58] This perspective resonates with "one of the dominant sociological frameworks of the last few decades,"[59] namely, the constructionist approach to understanding how social problems, and the deviance associated with them, are collectively defined. Anchored in the constructionist approach, in this book we turn away from the perspective that deviant categories are objective conditions whose magnitude, causes, consequences, and resolutions should be examined. Rather, we examine deviance as subjective definitions—or the activities by which human actors ascribe meaning to social conditions; interpret some conditions as problematic or deviant, and others not; and thereby negotiate the moral order.[60]

As a mode of social subordination, deviance struggles create devalued categories. Devaluation of certain individuals and groups necessarily implies valued status for others. To Schur, "Deviance defining contributes to social cohesion and reinforces the dominant standards in a society by establishing social and moral limits."[61] Thus competitions over relative moral standing, or "stigma contests," as Schur calls them, determine whose rules and standards are legitimated and applied. As a common process at the individual and collective levels, stigmatization—that is, stereotyping, depersonalizing, and devaluing others—works to sustain and reinforce the power of "conformists." In Schur's words:

> In these continuing struggles over competing social definitions, it is relative rather than absolute power that counts most. The power of either side may be subject to change, not only through external causes but to an extent by conscious effort. When people engage in organized political activity on deviance issues they are, in fact, intentionally . . . trying to ensure that a particular balance of power will tip in their favor. . . . Thus, the key to understanding deviance lies not in specific kinds of acts and individuals but rather in this deviantizing process.[62]

Insofar as "victimless crimes" is a polemical concept,[63] the extent to which the criminal law ought to be used as a form of "boundary maintenance" has produced a long course of scholarship and debate. On one side are those who argue that criminalizing immoral behaviors is necessary for maintaining cohesion in civilized societies. The argument on the other side is that issues of morality, while they may be a proper subject for social institutions such as the family, the educational system, and religious tradition, ought to be out of law's reach. The classic statements on each of these positions include this one by John Stuart Mill: "The only purpose for which power can rightfully be exercised over any member of a civilized community, against his will, is to prevent harm to others. His own good, either physical or moral, is not a warrant."[64]

By contrast, Patrick Devlin argued forcefully that as history shows, unless a society enforces a common morality, it is doomed to break down:

> Societies disintegrate from within more frequently than they are broken up by external pressure. There is disintegration when no common morality is observed and history shows that the loosening of moral bonds is often the first stage of disintegration, so that society is justified in taking the same steps to preserve a moral code as it does to preserve its governmental and other institutions.[65]

In its most comprehensive sense, this book presents the "natural history" of attempts to define deviance, specifically the processes through which, and conditions under which, particular deviance categories have developed and changed.[66]

The Paradox: Normalization but Ambivalence

This book presents important developments in current American law and policy toward each of the topics covered, both those that are a central feature of the resurgent "culture wars" or "morality wars"—abortion, gay rights, assisted suicide, and stem cell research—and gambling, which is now a normalized and common feature of American life, an accepted form of entertainment. It does so in a comprehensive manner, with each activity analyzed within the context of prior efforts toward normalization and liberalization of criminal laws. Each of the topics is at a different point in terms of such normalization, and each has traveled its own road to achieve that status. Some have generated more direct and grassroots response and support, while others have followed more corporate, bureaucratic, or state-sponsored models. Each topic will be examined in depth in a separate chapter.

Running through each chapter is a central tension: that American attitudes and law toward these victimless crimes are best understood as a process of "problematic normalization." It is clear that today American society does not enforce policies that mirror the times of Edwin Schur, Herbert Packer, Gilbert Geis, Sanford Kadish, and Jerome Skolnick and their call for liberalization of laws in such areas in the 1960s. Surprisingly, some issues—like drug laws and prostitution—have remained in large part much closer to their 1960 status. Others, like abortion and gay rights, have changed dramatically. Even those persons who were optimistic about liberalization of laws and policies related to gays and lesbians in the 1970s did not predict gay marriages in such a short time. Nonetheless, the issue of sexual orientation, law, and society in the United States is in flux and reflects the ambivalence that Skolnick describes as a key theme in American legal treatment of personal morality issues.[67] Assisted suicide was not even on the radar of the 1960s reformers, and stem cells are a contested issue only because of the scientific breakthroughs of recent years. The full effects of the changes in medicine, dying, and the centrality of privacy and autonomy did not accelerate until after *Roe v. Wade* had taken hold and reproductive rights had been revolutionized.

One paradox is that, despite the growing tolerance and liberalization by Americans across these four issues of personal morality over the past thirty years, there remains a lively and very engaged "morality war" between progressives and religious conservatives, and the "red" versus the "blue." Another paradox is concerned with the related issues of secularization and religiosity. The American paradox is that the United States has clearly secularized over the past forty years, and Americans have changed attitudes regarding personal morality in ways that are at odds with the teaching of major churches. At the same time, America is a decidedly observant nation in religious terms. This is both a societal paradox and a source of tension within the contestation of specific laws and policies. Another paradox is that America has unmistakably limited the law's reach in the area of victimless crime but has stopped short of embracing full legal change in the areas described. We have moved toward new legal forms, but not fully embracing them. We have a checkerboard pattern of laws. A final paradox is that the conservative backlash of the 1980s and the Reagan years slowed, but did not stop, the momentum for these changes in victimless crime laws. Each of these themes contributed to the overall concept of problematic normalization.

The Ongoing "Morality Wars"

Thomas Frank made quite a splash in 2004 with his book *What's the Matter with Kansas?*[68] There he painstakingly and passionately argued for the concept of false consciousness in an attempt to understand the willingness of lower-middle-class voters in Kansas (and elsewhere in America) to forsake their economic interests and embrace the Republican agenda, which promised a return to traditional values at the same time as it supported a corporate business elite restructuring that undercut the ability for many of these same Kansans to make a life for themselves and their families. In Frank's critique, the morality war is represented by a backlash, which is a central feature of the generating power of the conservative movement around such culture war issues such as abortion and gay rights.

Frank describes many features of the morality war. Some groups, like Christian Exodus, point to the level of normalization of formerly sinful or illegal activities that government has increasingly embraced in recent decades: "If you are tired of government-endorsed sin, then stand up and be counted!"[69]

Others, like former House minority leader Tom DeLay, see at the heart of the morality battles the inroads of secular forces—and their supporters in the courts—against those whose morality has religious bases: "'Our faith has always been in direct conflict with the values of the world,' DeLay said. 'We are, after all, a society that provides abortion on demand, has killed millions of innocent children, degrades the institution of marriage, and all but treats Christianity like some second-rate superstition.'"[70] To others, like Focus on the Family head Dr. James Dobson, judicial power is central to their unease:

> You've heard me talk a great deal, especially in the past year, about "judicial tyranny"—the threat that unelected, unaccountable judges pose to our religious liberties, traditional marriage and each human being's God-given right to life. If you've ever struggled to understand why I think this issue is so important, two decisions issued yesterday by the U.S. Supreme Court make painfully clear what's at stake not only for us, but for future generations.[71]

To another social conservative engaged in the morality wars, Gary Bauer (and his organization American Values),[72] secular and liberal forces have advanced in a similar manner:

In a story headlined, "Same-Sex Marriage Battles Escalate," *USA Today* picked up on a point I have been stressing for years—that the militant homosexual movement, in an effort to force its "morality" on the American people, has adopted the most undemocratic method of changing public policy by waging a massive campaign with well-placed, well-timed and well-financed lawsuits in the courts. That is the way liberalism has advanced most of its agenda for decades.[73]

The concern about the reduction of religion in the public square, combined with public ambivalence and feelings about a strict separation of church and state, gives rise to certain efforts to mobilize believers against the de-religionizing of American society. In addition to the courts, of which critique and contestation are intense, few institutions generate as much attention as the public school system.

Increasingly, in the fall of each year, Americans are treated to a debate over the proper limits to celebrating what was traditionally known as the Christmas season. In recent years, with appropriate sensitivity toward American diversity of religion, schools and workplaces have veered toward celebration of non-Christian holidays, to be as inclusive as possible. Religious conservatives become upset when the legal reading of the separation of church and state limits the celebration of Christmas, in lieu of a more generic winter holiday. The 2005 campaign by Rev. Jerry Falwell and Liberty Counsel, with the slogan, "Merry Christmas. It's OK to say it," reflects their legal efforts to fight limitations on references to and the celebration of Christmas. Their targets are especially stores, which may be responsive to boycotts in their busy selling season. On Fox News, Bill O'Reilly's version is "Christmas Under Siege."[74]

Secularization and Religiosity: The Persistent and Variable Role of Religion in America

Our first paradox regards the changing role of religion in American society. The contests over abortion and gay rights in particular have showcased the deep feelings with which many Americans approach the topics included in the victimless crimes category. Denominational groups themselves have been fractured by the issue of ordination of gay clergy and gay officials as mainstream Protestant churches have followed secular society in embracing acceptance of gays and lesbians.[75] The culture war has been a deeply divisive conflict, with fundamental disagreements over issues of morality and religion at its base. One might think that this signifies that America has changed, to the point where those who are churchgoers feel their influence waning. The culture wars then would signify their attempt to keep traditional values in place in American society, against the onslaught of secular and humanist trends.

Political theorist Michael Kazin noted in an article after the 2004 elections, "The United States remains a nation with an evangelical soul, a fact that liberals ignore at their peril." Recent analyses of the 2004 votes emphasize Kazin's point. The Pew Research Center concluded that 36 percent of Bush voters in 2004 were white evangelical Protestants, a significant portion of the base of the Republican Party (a group originally talked about as Reagan Democrats and the focus of Frank's book).[76] At this level, evangelical churches take on the centrality of labor unions or African Americans in the Democratic Party. Part of the backlash against progressive reforms in these four areas is fueled by a concern that such advances—coming from at best a secular approach and at worst an antireligious viewpoint—are undermining the vitality of religion in American society.

The Christian Right became a force of significant impact and attention in the 1990s, as the culture war exploded to include contests over abortion, gay rights, pornography, and changing sexual and cultural mores in general. The Christian Right became a much-used reference in the 1990s to describe groups like the Christian Coalition and an aligned group, the Traditional Values Coalition, and allies like the Moral Majority, Family Research Council, and Focus on the Family.

Ralph Reed, the first executive director of the Christian Coalition, organized it into a potent political force in the 1990s. The Christian Coalition capitalized on the growth in evangelical Protestantism and mobilized the dislike evangelicals had for the shifts in American values and laws, especially regarding victimless crimes and issues of personal morality. During his stewardship—and the growth in the Christian Coalition's power and political influence—the group turned away from what sociologist Jose Casanova describes as the traditional American evangelical apolitical approach, with an emphasis on not being engaged with the material world.[77]

That said, overstating the power of Christian conservatives in the body politic cedes ground that need not be ceded. As UCC minister Madison Shockley commented in the *Los Angeles Times:* "Right-wing fundamentalist Christianity has so dominated the media that many Americans don't believe liberal/progressive Christianity even exists."[78] Shockley's comments resonate with the findings of noted sociologist of religion Robert Wuthnow, who found in a 2000 study: "The perception that religious groups are really only interested in conservative issues is not true. They are not only focused on issues such as abortion or prayer in the schools. Progressive issues do seem to be of enormous importance to people."[79]

Not all Christians are like Rev. Fred Phelps and his "God Hates Fags" campaign.[80] (Phelps is now protesting at the funerals of soldiers from the Iraq War, on the theory that such deaths are attributable to our nation's embracing of homosexuality.)[81] At the same time, we have to recognize that some Christians are like that: Rev. Bob Jones III, for example, wrote the president after the 2004 election: "Don't equivocate. Put your agenda on the front burner and let it boil. You owe the liberals nothing. They despise you because they despise your Christ." The Reverend Donald Wildmon of the Traditional Values Coalition warned California governor Arnold Schwarzenegger that moderate Republicans who are pro-choice, –gay marriage, and –stem cell research should not stand in the way of the Christian Right.[82]

The American paradox is that the United States has clearly grown more secular over the past forty years, and Americans have changed attitudes regarding personal morality in ways that are odds with the teaching of major churches. And yet America is a decidedly observant nation in religious terms, far more so than our European counterparts, even if there is some dispute about exactly how observant. We stand out in our embrace of religion. In a 2003 survey by the Pew Forum on Religion and Public Life, 85 percent of American respondents stated that religion was either "very" or "fairly" important in their lives.[83] Another 60 percent reported attending religious services at least once a month. This level of interest and support extended even to the young, with three of five teenagers reporting that religion was "very important" or "pretty important" to them in a national poll.[84] The poll also found Americans wanting more religion in public life. As Luis Lugo noted in the *Atlanta Journal-Constitution,* "Nearly twice as many respondents say there has been too little reference to religion by politicians (41 percent) as say there has been too much (21 percent). And it's equally clear that those surveyed also want to see religion play a more prominent role in policy-making."[85]

Christian Smith argues that the secularization process—however strong—is characterized more by contest and struggle than by easy evolution. Fundamentalist activism had increased at the same time, and indeed as a reaction to, this same secularism: "American evangelicalism is thriving as a religious movement not despite the forces of secular modernity but in part precisely because of them."[86]

In November 2005, the Anti-Defamation League (ADL) added to this conversation when it released a poll showing that 63 percent of American respondents feel that "religion is under attack," and 53 percent believe that religion is "losing its influence in American life." This same poll found majority support for teaching creationism, alongside evolution, and displaying religious symbols in public buildings, and a near majority supportive of organized prayer in public schools. The numbers for teaching "the biblical story of creation" alongside evolution are enlightening. Fully 56 percent of respondents agreed with that approach, and the number climbs only to 70 percent with evangelical respondents. Nonetheless, nearly half of the respondents (45 percent) agree that "right wing religious leaders are seeking to impose their religious beliefs on everyone else."

ADL director Abraham Foxman, while not denying the complicating nature of these results, offered that it was unfortunate that "those who would like to Christianize America seek to use the concerns reflected in this survey toward goals which would turn America into a very different place than the one that has been so open to all religious perspectives." Foxman lamented, "Too many people . . . [believe] that there should be a fundamental collapse of our traditional church-state barrier."[87]

This book is deeply interested in the effect of the emergence of the New Christian Right, and how that changed the public discussion of legal reform and options specifically for the most contested of the victimless crimes analyzed here: abortion, gay rights, assisted suicide, and stem cell research. We take as our template the enormous investment by the Christian Right in the abortion rights struggle. Meanwhile, the similar but not identical views of American Catholicism, and the positions and effects of mainline Protestant denominations, suggest a struggle that is still taking shape, that has as much to do with the definition of religiosity in the United States as with the state of our laws, and which will continue alongside whatever trends toward what could be called the unique American brand of secularization.

The public discussion of the role of religion in American society since the 2004 election campaign has taken several twists and turns, as we capture in the following chapters. The question of whether America, despite the exceptional religious observance of Americans compared with our Western industrial counterparts, was separating into a political system with one largely religious party and one large secular political party remained open and debated between 2004 and 2007. The implications of this religious identification have great meaning for the societal discussion and lawmaking efforts surrounding the law and morality topics with which this book is concerned.

Partial Normalization

Our second paradox is that America has unmistakably limited the law's reach in the area of victimless crime but has stopped short of embracing full legal change in the areas detailed in this book. Drug laws changed in the marijuana decriminalization efforts of the 1970s, then shifted as America's prison population and the number of drug offenders in prison rose dramatically in the 1980s and 1990s.[88] The decriminalization of sodomy was followed by the widespread passage of antidiscrimination laws affecting gays and lesbians, but the battles over AIDS and the fevered pitch of culture war discussions, from the Christian Coalition, ACT UP, the Moral Majority, the National Gay and Lesbian Task Force, and others kept the contestation alive.

This is the result of complex and countervailing movements, interests, framing, and discussions. The changes over four decades in societal treatment of victimless crime are reflected in the shifting policy responses detailed in this book. The zone of privacy that Mill wrote about has solidified, if not expanded to the limits that have been hoped for by some legal scholars and movement activists.

One of the signs that America has shifted in its moralistic view of personal choices is in the investment sector. Dan Ahrens and others have argued that "booze, bets, bombs and butts" are recession-proof, and wise investments.[89] "Among the areas that appeared to be recession proof were those industries that have been screened out by many investors and especially many of the so-called socially responsible investors as being 'evil': alcohol, tobacco, gaming and defense."[90] Ahrens discusses how gaming stocks as a group had dramatically outperformed the Standard and Poor Index stocks in the late 1990s and early twenty-first century. He offers specific advice on favorite stocks, which by 2004 had grown beyond the original companies with casinos, to a variety of technology-driven stocks that supplied various aspects of the gaming environment. In a sizable bibliography, Ahrens shows that his advice is far from peripheral, citing a variety of stock analysts and business experts who have made similar observations in a range of venues, from ABC, CNN, and CBS, to *Barron's*, the *American Banker*, the *Wall Street Journal*, and *Financial Times*.[91] Others, like *New York Times* columnist William Safire, do not agree, arguing that "sin taxes" are an unwise, perhaps unholy, way for society to attract tax revenues.[92]

In some of the issues—like gambling—legalization has been widespread, and yet without significant grassroots social support. The type of organization and strategy that has typified the abortion rights area is not reproduced in the gambling issue.[93] We did not see gambling advocates marching in the streets, holding placards that read "Slots Now," or conducting nonviolent sit-ins in front of state legislatures. We did not see impassioned pleas for protecting the autonomy of gamblers, nor did we see arguments that the criminalized gambler was unfairly stigmatized.

Instead, gambling legalization has proceeded in a more top-down manner, with states and gambling corporations playing major roles. The reason for legalization has been relatively straightforward—tax revenue and economic development. Although these claims have been contested —indeed, defeated in some jurisdictions—they have propelled lotteries across the nation since the 1960s and riverboat gambling since the 1990s. (Indian casinos have developed from a unique legal framework.)

In the case of gay rights, several social movement groups from the time of the initial gay rights groups of the 1950s, Mattachine Society and the Daughters of Bilitis, bravely and strategically challenged dominant societal conceptions and laws.[94] Today's key groups, like the Human Rights Campaign and the National Gay and Lesbian Task Force, are among many that negotiate the laws and attitudes of a contested yet normalizing American population.

Rising Tolerance, Stalled and Challenged Movements

Our third paradox is that the conservative backlash of the 1980s and the Reagan years slowed, but did not stop, the momentum for these changes in victimless crime laws. This "Reagan interruptus" theme suggests that the events of 2004 should be looked at as a point in the evolution of American law and policy in the social and legal treatment of victimless crimes, from the time of the early articulation of the proper reach of the criminal law by Schur and others.[95] This paradox asserts that the stalling of movements for liberalization in the 1980s was a momentary setback rather than a redirecting of the general trend toward liberalization of laws and policies in American law and society.

The culture wars of the 1980s and 1990s were a result of the advances made in reproductive rights, anti–gay discrimination measures, drug decriminalization, and general changes in gender relations in American society. The urgent call to protect "traditional values" created countermovements specifically designed to thwart the movement toward tolerance and creation of new rights in the personal sphere.

These movements certainly had the effect of curtailing the effectiveness of some forms of liberalization efforts. While the Christian Coalition did not focus on drug laws, it was part of the constellation of issues that formed the "moral decay" its leader preached against. Other portions of what we might call the "rollback coalition," such as those working with First Lady Nancy Reagan,[96] did spend their energy on this. The drug punitiveness of the crack era of the 1980s was facilitated by these groups, to the extent that they slowed the momentum of drug reformers, including even recriminalization of marijuana in some cases.

Some analysts have drawn upon the idea that the Christian Right movement of the 1990s was a cynical play upon certain segments of the American population, those in the lower middle class who placed their social conservatism ahead of their economic needs.[97] There is a strong element in American sociolegal studies that emphasizes the primacy of "symbolic politics."[98] Nonetheless, some of the accomplishments of the countermovement in the culture wars has been the slowing of liberalized laws, the dismantling of reform efforts, and the adoption of oppositional policies. With this is mind, chapters 2 through 5 will take as one line of inquiry the question of how the conservative ascendancy of the 1990s derailed, redefined, or simply masked the liberalization impulses and successes that have been present from the 1960s.

Conclusion: Ambivalence and the Problematic Normalization of Victimless Crime in America

Our fourth and final paradox combines elements of the prior three items, in what might be called the summary paradox. The current state of victimless crimes in America is one of "problematic normalization." We have moved toward new legal forms, but not fully embracing them. We have a checkerboard pattern of laws, in some ways reflecting our federalism and emphasis on states' rights, or on the diversity of our large population and the strength of views of the "blue" America and the "red" America, representing the Democratic and Republican leaning of various states in presidential elections. But is can also be described as a stubborn ambivalence, a stalled movement toward the 1960s clarion call for liberalization, and the enactment of decriminalization laws in the 1970s.

A few years back, toward the end of a year of American national debate over the scope of privacy and the relative seriousness of adultery in the impeachment of President Clinton, Jacob Weisberg wrote in a *New York Times Magazine* cover story:

> You can . . . say that the Lewinsky scandal says something not just about the development of American political morality, but also about American morality in general. A quick survey might leave one with the impression that the 1990's were the decade that Puritanism died. Since Clinton has been President, homosexuality has gained public acceptance; legal gambling has swept the country; pornography has become ubiquitous; and vice has been redefined as disease. Meanwhile, the public has become unshockable about sex and unconcerned about Presidential adultery. These changes imply that traditional morality has receded.[99]

Weisberg goes on to argue that such an implication would be misguided, that what characterizes the American public at the beginning of a new century is instead adherence to strict personal morality but a reluctance to judge the morality of others. By 2005, even this 1999 interpretation may seem overly optimistic. There is no easy "receding" of traditional morality. Perhaps Weisberg captured a moment when the shift in values was generating a backlash that would crest in 2004?

In place of the "five nonnegotiables," it might be better to focus on the three "A's": anxiety, ambiguity, and ambivalence.

While Frank has clearly captured something important in his false-consciousness arguments about Kansas and elsewhere, acknowledging economic anxiety and frustration while critiquing the forms it often takes is a delicate dance. As Arlene Skolnick notes: "But conservatives, following [late Republican strategist Lee] Atwater's advice, also speak to the ambivalence and anxiety most people feel about the bewildering cascade of changes in family life in recent years and its effects on children."[100] The concept of ambiguity could move one to agree with U.S. senator Barack Obama (D-Ill.), who spoke in his riveting speech at the 2004 Democratic convention of a "purple" America, in which elements of red states and blue states would merge (and later gave speeches that described his own religion and the interplay of religion and society).[101] The Reverend Jim Wallis argues for finding common ground. The "values debate should be the future of American politics [but] which values and whose values?"[102]

By January 2005, the Pew Research Center reported that the concerns of most Americans—Republicans, Democrats, and Independents —did not include a concern with "values" such as that which the exit polls indicated.[103] The top domestic priorities chosen were terror defense, the economy, Social Security, Medicare, education, and the military. While 54 percent of the respondents felt that conservative Christians would gain influence in the next four years (as almost an identical number had responded in 2001), only "education" elicited a response in which "traditional values"—as agreed upon by the liberals, conservatives, and the media—played a significant part. Compounding this, a January 2005 poll by the *Los Angeles Times* found Americans "deeply divided over President Bush's performance and priorities." The 2006 elections closed the chapter on this situation, as the Democrats marshaled this discontent, propelling them to control of the House of Representatives and the Senate for the first time since 1994.[104]

As we observe the two hundredth anniversary of the birth of John Stuart Mill, it could be argued that the changes over four decades in law and personal morality suggest that the zone of privacy that Mill wrote about in the nineteenth century has solidified, even if it has not expanded to the limits that have been hoped for by some legal scholars and movement activists. Ambivalence best characterizes the American approach to legislating personal morality. As Jerome Skolnick argues, this concept of ambivalence best characterizes the American approach to legislating personal morality.[105] An optimistic reading of recent events is that changes in laws regulating personal morality have not been rolled back—despite the postelection punditry—but their vitality remains fragile and contested. It is a condition that is neither purely red nor purely blue. The following chapters will demonstrate that.

2

Painless Prosperity
The Spread of Legal Gambling

I told Worm you can't lose what you don't put in the middle, but
you can't win much either.
— Matt Damon character Mike McDermott in *Rounders* (1998)

The Sin City stigma is largely gone. . . . Las Vegas is almost a nation unto itself. . . . Everybody wants to go to Vegas—they want
to go to a show, shop, eat, be entertained. It seems to have a formula that is working and not really showing any signs of slowing
down.
— Tradeshow Week official, 2006 (*Reno Gazette-Journal* 2006,
"Las Vegas: Sin City Still King of Colossal Conventions")

It's never been a moral issue with me. I liked church bingo growing
up. I've been a poker player. . . . I view it as drinking. If you can't
handle it, don't do it.
— Former federal education secretary and drug czar
William Bennett (Oliver Burkeman 2003 "Voice of
Morality Exposed as Chronic Casino Loser")

Introduction: Making Book on Values

When conservative commentator William Bennett was discovered to be
a high-stakes, and often unsuccessful, gambler in 2003, critics and pundits enjoyed skewering Bennett, the former drug czar and education secretary who himself had rarely resisted the chance to act as a leading
warrior in the culture wars of the 1990s.[1] Most of the commentary took
dead aim at Bennett's hypocrisy as the author of *The Book of Virtues*[2]
and as a leading moralist. Critics had a field day with the person who
had written a book entitled *The De-valuing of America*[3] and who had
written elsewhere:

Moral education must involve following rules of good behavior. It must involve developing good habits, which come only through repeated practice. And character training must provide example by placing children in the company of responsible adults who show an allegiance to good character, who demonstrate the clear difference between right and wrong in their own everyday habits.[4]

Liberal commentators exulted in Bennett's gambling problems. Michael Kinsley wrote on *Slate:* "The news over the weekend—that Bennett's $50,000 sermons and best-selling moral instruction manuals have financed a multimillion-dollar gambling habit—has lit a lamp of happiness in even the darkest hearts."[5] To those who claimed that Bennett was a hypocrite, Kinsley disagreed: "It just shows that he's not a complete idiot. Working his way down the list of other people's pleasures, weaknesses, and uses of American freedom, he just happened to skip over his own. How convenient."

There were those, naturally, who seized upon the seeming hypocrisy of the value-laden Bennett with a large gambling habit—such as references to the "Book of Virtues Race and Sport Book."[6] What was less evident in the commentaries and wry salutes to Bennett's fall from grace was what was being implicitly said about the status of gambling in America. Defenders of Bennett argued that the charges of hypocrisy were unfounded, since Bennett has not railed against gambling in his scattershot condemnation of all things amoral in an American society veering from the virtuous path. As one report captured Bennett's distinction: "Mr. Bennett maintained that his condemnation of the sins of society was not incompatible with his gambling."[7]

As Marc Cooper has recently put it: "In today's America, with gambling legal in nearly every state and gambling casinos as common as 7-Elevens, slot machines are themselves nearly as familiar as ATMs."[8] Bennett was found to have been a large gambler, but at a time when gambling has been normalized.

Contemporary Scope: Profitability of the "Normal Vice"

Revenues from legal gambling grew nearly twenty-fold between 1976 and 2000. As one law professor notes, in comparison to legal gambling's $70 billion of revenue in 2000, "The sum total spent on tickets to all movies, plays, concerts, and live performances, plus all sports events, is only about $22 billion per year. Americans are now spending three times as much on gambling as on all other kinds of entertainment combined."[9]

Eugene Christiansen points out that gross legal gambling revenues by 2000 were more than eight times the box office revenues of American films, more than seven times the size of revenue for live spectator sports, and roughly equal to the amount Americans spent on publications of all kind. Gambling's $84 billion in revenues in 2005 represents a growing percentage of the national expenditure on leisure goods, services, and activities.[10] Cooper estimates that Americans now spend on slots five times the amount they spend on movie tickets.[11]

"It's a good way to get out of the house," explained one Philadelphia visitor to Atlantic City.[12] This man captured the normal way in which gambling is treated in contemporary American society. In fact, fully two-thirds of Americans reported in a 2004 Gallup poll that they had gambled in the prior year. And states looking for revenues had increasingly fixed on legal gambling as a relatively painless form of revenue raising. As one California analysts said of a California gambling plan, "It's hard to resist the economics."[13] Gaming expert Bill Eadington notes that part of the attractiveness of gambling as entertainment is that it is more active than passive forms of general entertainment.[14]

Over the last forty years—since New Hampshire legalized a state lottery in 1964—legal gambling has become a common feature in American life. While American society has questioned and reformed laws regarding many "victimless crimes"—those related to drugs, abortion, and gay rights—legalized gambling has eclipsed its counterparts. In 2003, more than $72 billion in legal gambling revenues were generated in the United States, and by 2004, legalized gambling was available in forty-eight states.

New York has expanded its gambling operations to allow video lottery terminals at racetracks. New York governor George Pataki claimed that the estimated $2 billion in funds from the "racinos" would allow New York to satisfy a court order that mandated the state to provide a "sound basic education" for students without a steep tax increase.[15] In the same way that the New Hampshire lottery spurred legalization efforts in other states in the 1960s, fiscal crises in 2004 were leading states to legalize more forms of gambling, as a way of keeping gambling revenue "home."[16] Gambling had separated itself from the other formerly prohibited victimless crimes by its ubiquity and acceptance—what could be referred to as the standout case of gambling, as it has been "uncoupled" from the other vices.

In what has been called the third wave of legal gambling in America,[17] the rollout has been long and steady. Still, legalization proceeded steadily in different forms. In what we have previously referred to as "loophole legalization,"[18] gambling spread in the 1980s in lateral forms, more than the "Las Vegas" model might have predicted following the opening of Atlantic City in 1978. In this model, riverboats proliferated, but not separate Las Vegas–style casino resorts. Eventually Indian gaming expanded in several states, more of its own accord, especially after the U.S. Supreme Court ruling in *Cabazon* and the subsequent passage of the Indian Gaming Regulatory Act by Congress endorsed Indian sovereignty concepts.[19] Indian gaming revenues grew from $5 billion in 1995 to $19 billion in 2004.

The accumulation of these multiple paths of legalization has been to produce legal gambling in the United States that takes many forms and does not depend on any one for its vitality. In the 1950s, what gambling took place in the United States was still illegal. Law enforcement activity and prosecution had been unsuccessful in this decade in limiting illegal gambling, as they had been in the prior two decades. Las Vegas grew from a small desert town with legal gambling in the pre–World War II era to a major world venue for legal casino gambling, in part with the capital of some American organized crime groups.

During this period, juries were reluctant to convict gambling defendants or to give them significant sentences when they did convict them.[20] This was consistent with Geis's observation that gambling as a criminal activity was assigned a very low level of seriousness by Americans.[21] New Hampshire legalized the lottery in 1964, and movement was begun to legalize that form of gambling in other states.

During the 1970s, gambling expanded as legalization efforts for lotteries continued, and legal casinos spread to New Jersey, with a successful statewide vote there in 1976. The Commission on the Review of the National Policy Toward Gambling found support in polls for legal forms of gambling and was an important national forum for consideration of various forms of regulation.[22]

Although a 1978 Florida referendum was turned down, as were several others despite predictions of casino gambling's spread,[23] gambling emerged as a growth stock on Wall Street and a legitimate leisure time activity for Americans. Still, not all forms of gambling succeeded in becoming legal. As James Frey has noted, the many fears about corruption in sports limited enthusiasm for sports betting, which remains the staple of illegal gambling.[24]

By 1982, gross legal gaming revenues in the United States were $10 billion. Of this, about 20 percent was derived from lotteries, 40 percent from casinos (but not including Indian gaming), and the remainder from horse racing, dog racing, charitable games, legal bookmaking, and Indian gaming.

One form of gambling boomed during the 1980s: state-run lotteries.[25] At the same time, a number of Indian reservations were experimenting with forms of gambling, leading to the U.S. Supreme Court ruling in *Cabazon*[26] and the passage of the federal Indian Gaming Regulatory Act (IGRA), two actions that allowed the regulated proliferation of gambling on Indian lands.

By 1996, gross legal gaming revenues in the United States had grown to $47 billion, nearly a 500 percent increase from 1982.[27] Of this, about a third was derived from lotteries, a third from casinos (but not including Indian gaming), and the remainder from horse racing, dog racing, charitable games, legal bookmaking, and Indian gaming.

Normalization

Every winter, whenever a Super Bowl takes place, American journalists and commentators take note of the enormous amount of legal and illegal sport betting that occurs in the United States. But the Super Bowl is a relatively simple event, pitting two teams, after several games to determine the American Football Conference and National Football Conference champions. By comparison, when the sixty-five-team National Collegiate Athletic Association (NCAA) basketball tournament—"March Madness"—takes place, office pools kick into action, with the activity of betting a small amount of money on a favorite team taking over. Organizations estimate that a third of American workers participate in Super Bowl office betting, and that two-thirds of workers have participated in any betting pool.[28] Few would consider these people serious or addicted bettors—although there may certainly be some among them—but the numbers also demonstrate the widespread involvement in gambling, even as an occasional national pastime.

And poker itself—whether in person, online, or being watched on numerous television shows—has emerged as a national pastime with a trajectory similar to NASCAR racing, with the World Series of Poker an annual highlight.[29] News reports of middle-school poker nights can be found along worries over problem gambling by college students. Roger Gros, the editor of *Global Gaming Business,* a gaming industry trade publication, writes in the inaugural issue of *PokerBiz,* his company's nod to the burgeoning poker business:

> Five years ago, we would not have even considered an entire magazine dedicated to the business of running poker rooms. After all, poker was a "dying" game, dwindling down to its core players and failing to match the pace of the overall growth of the gaming industry. But then two remarkable things happened: the debut of online poker, and the huge technological advances in televised poker. Each of these developments brought the excitement and allure of poker to the masses.[30]

Opposition to gambling used to be based on moralistic grounds. As those objections faded, opportunities were presented for forms of decriminalized gambling. And while state-owned forms have proliferated mostly in the lottery areas, the state has been the dominant player in the legalization and operation of gambling. In this way, gambling is demonstrably different from the path the other victimless crimes have taken.

Jerome Skolnick has referred to gambling as the "normal vice," with widespread participation by most sectors of the American population. Professor Howard Shaffer, director of the Harvard Medical School's Division on Addiction, added, "This is the first time that a generation has grown up amid legalized gambling, in a social setting that not only permits but endorses the gambler."[31]

And Frank Fahrenkopf, president of the American Gaming Association, reported that a recent AGA survey of elected officials and community leaders in communities with gambling found "a stunning affirmation—by the most active and engaged people in the community—of our industry's value."[32] Fahrenkopf was pleased to cite support by 79 percent of the respondents that "casinos have had a positive impact on the community" and a similar number considering casinos as "good corporate citizens."

Even the Las Vegas of today is certainly not the Las Vegas of 1978, when Jerome Skolnick's book *House of Cards* came out.[33] In 1978, the national gambling revenues were not yet up to $10 billion annually. With the opening of Atlantic City casinos in 1978, and the attention and respectability given to the gaming industry by Wall Street investment firms, legal gambling was just beginning its expansion in the United States.[34]

Las Vegas itself has continued to grow and evolve with the arrival in the 1990s of the huge, theme-oriented hotel casino. William N. Thompson explains that Las Vegas has gone from a hotel room capacity of 67,000 in 1989, to 105,000 in 1997, to 127,000 in 2005,[35] the result of the emergence of the massive and/or themed casinos like the Mirage, the Excalibur, Treasure Island, New York, New York, the Luxor, the Bellagio, the Mandalay Bay, the Palms, and the new Wynn Las Vegas.[36] At the same time, the occupancy rate for Las Vegas hotels has remained the same, at about 90 percent, undercutting notions that Las Vegas has hit its end of expansion. A Tradeshow Week official said in 2006 that Las Vegas's popularity is not diminishing.[37]

As the author of *Poker Nation* writes: "Vegas turned itself from Sin City to a family destination. They Disneyfied it. People take their kids there. Now it's a place to play golf, go to the strip joints, Lake Mead and the Grand Canyon—and gamble."[38]

Stephen Ives, director of a PBS documentary, writes:

> Was Las Vegas, I wondered, becoming a Mecca for the twenty-first-century American zeitgeist? . . . This nation has always had a paradoxical, if not downright hypocritical, relationship with Las Vegas. It is a city that America has loved to hate but cannot do without. It is the antithesis of the conventional, the established, and the traditional, and despite our false pretenses, we are drawn to it for precisely these reasons. We are a Puritan nation obsessed with sex, a self-proclaimed meritocracy that idolizes wealth, a hardworking, churchgoing, law-abiding people that can't wait to party all night long. Las Vegas is the necessary dark side of our nature, the skeletons in our collective closet, the orgiastic expression of our own irrepressible id. It is our favorite dirty little secret. . . . a place that was once shunned as Sin City and considered beyond the pale of respectable society has now become the epicenter of mainstream leisure.[39]

To him, Las Vegas has become more like America, and at the same time, America has become more like Las Vegas.

According to gaming executive Alan Feldman, the year 1989 was an important one in the development of Las Vegas, and in the gaming industry in many of its global locations. In 2006, to Feldman, the picture of a Las Vegas where the financial viability of a casino resort depended overwhelmingly on only gaming revenues was a "picture as dated as a one dollar blackjack table."[40] By 2005, 55 percent of Las Vegas Strip revenues came from nongaming revenues, a 50 percent decrease in gaming's financial importance from only seventeen years earlier. Feldman called this earlier era the "pre-Mirage" days, referring to casino owner Steve Wynn's evocation of the Mirage, a resort that had the ambience of a Hawaiian five-star resort.

In these ways, Las Vegas has typified how legal gambling in contemporary America has come to represent what Skolnick has referred to as the "normal vice,"[41] with widespread participation by most sectors of the American population. By 2001, when a Gallup poll showed that only 26 percent of Americans saw gambling as an immoral activity,[42] the normalization of gambling had taken place.

Meanwhile, continuing a trend of the last thirty years, few discussions have concentrated on the morality of gambling.[43] In the case of recent concerns, connection with organized crime and the likelihood of political corruption have remained as themes, as have issues of regressive taxation,[44] but they have faded in resonance, while a concern with problem gambling persists at a lower level.[45]

Instead, the normalization of gambling can be represented by the following statement from the director of the California Lottery, touting the social benefits of legal gambling and its contributions to education in that state:

> As the California Lottery turns 18 years old, we can tout the success of having met our mandate of providing supplemental funds to public schools. We are all very proud of the fact that for three consecutive years, the Lottery has contributed $1 billion to public education. As a former teacher, I respect the hard work and contributions of the education community. As CEO of the California Lottery . . . I am proud to lead a team that works very hard on a daily basis to ensure that the mandate of providing supplemental funding to education is achieved.[46]

In addition, one gaming executive sees a more integrated and diversified future for certain aspects of gambling:

Gaming has become almost ubiquitous around the United States, and I believe over time you will see a natural, common sense convergence between what is available in a casino with a wide range of other forms of entertainment. And hopefully what will come with that will be a normalization of gaming in the political environment, as well as the regulatory environment.[47]

Politics, the Law, and Other Forms: Indian Gaming

Indian gaming revenues nationally grew from $5.4 billion in 1995 to $19.4 billion in 2004 to $23 billion in 2005.[48] In 2005, Indian gaming continued to grow at 16 percent, ahead of other commercial gaming forms, including the newly expanding racinos. This increase came from more than 200 Indian tribes, and more than 400 casinos, with a third of the revenues coming from California casinos. Indian gaming now represents a sector that is approaching the non-Indian casino industry in size.

We argue that these developments at first came embedded in an Indian appeal for self-reliance and economic development, amid great poverty. Increasingly, as described in the later section on California, Indian gaming became a symbol of wealth and power. Although states are not rescinding their Indian gaming licenses, they may be seeing the tribes as more normal commercial interests now.

By 2004, a *Los Angeles Times* poll found conflicting feelings among the residents of California regarding the burgeoning Indian casinos—they supported the Indian tribes in their efforts to develop casinos, but hoped for more in the way of tax revenues.[49] How quickly the image of the deserving, poor Indians has changed from the days of the earlier initiatives, to the more recent image in the popular media as described by Eve Darian-Smith:

Native Americans are all now obscenely wealthy and fly regularly to Paris to drink champagne and live the good life. I argue that this public perception is fostering a new wave of animosity by the dominant society toward Native Americans, which is in turn shaping political and legal discourse surrounding regulation of Indian casinos.[50]

There have been significant developments in the legalization and taxation of gambling in California and the twenty-seven other states that have implemented gambling by Indian tribes over the years since 1988. Much of this growth has come from the unique feature of Indian casinos, whose scope is defined by state compacts that are in current renegotiation. At the same time, other states have evolved policy that directly affects competitors to Indian gaming and have made horse racing venues more viable, through the racino model.

This growth has begun to generate questions about legal gambling proliferation that are relevant to its growth and control elsewhere: the background of operators; the promise of economic development; the competition with other forms of industry and leisure; the reliance of the state on it as a revenue source; regressive taxation and the effect of proximity on low-income populations; and the nature and growth of problem gambling, especially among vulnerable populations.

Although California does not boast the largest Indian casinos in the United States (such as Foxwoods and Mohegan Sun in Connecticut), Indian casinos in that state, with $7 billion in annual gross gaming revenue, account for one-third of the Indian casino revenues in the United States. Fifty-five tribes operate fifty-seven casinos, and upwards of 62,000 slot machines, a gradual development from the time when bingo, pull tabs, and table games dominated, in strict accordance with IGRA and the law. With a 20 percent annual increase in revenues, Indian gambling has become a significant presence in California. As one Indian official recently wrote:

> In little more than 30 years, Indian gaming has provided more than 200 tribes the opportunity for self-determination and economic self-sufficiency. Indian gaming has replaced poverty with jobs bringing Indians back to Indian country. It's replaced disease with hospitals, doctors and medicine for our sick and elderly. We've replaced crime and dropouts with new schools and scholarships. And we've replaced despair with hope for a new generation of Indian people. With the help of gaming, tribal governments are beginning to rebuild communities that were all but forgotten.[51]

In 1998, for example, California voters gave strong support to Proposition 5, the Tribal Government Gaming and Economic Self-Sufficiency Act, an initiative that broke expenditure records. Its title and evocative television ads emphasized the central feature of self-sufficiency. That measure was overruled by the courts, but Governor Davis negotiated treaties with an eye toward the vote, and a 2000 initiative to ratify those compacts passed with 65 percent support.

Beginning with the federal Indian Gaming Regulatory Act in 1988, following the U.S. Supreme Court decision in *Cabazon*[52]—a case from California—a regulatory structure has been in place for tribes that operate gambling in the states that permit it. These multiyear "compacts," negotiated with the state through the office of the governor, vary dramatically in the United States, and often within states. In some states, tribes have agreed to give as much as 25 percent of their revenues to states, which have generally afforded their monopolistic positions. A former Interior Department official observed: "When a few states started pushing the envelope, others said they needed to tap that revenue source, too. It's a new era of compacts, with states wanting higher revenue-sharing from the tribes."[53]

In California, these compacts have evolved in a different economic and political environment, and have historically been less generous to the state. Heated discussions of this situation, including during the 2003 recall campaign of Governor Gray Davis, have recently been the norm in California and formed a central issue in the 2004 statewide ballot.

Those recent events—especially in the gubernatorial arena—have indicated that such prior levels of citizen support for Indian gaming in California may now be viewed as qualified. One analyst describes this changing situation:

> Only a few years ago, Californians were so taken with the idea of fairness to Indians that they decisively approved the initiative. . . . But now, thanks to the incredible success of tribal casinos, Indian tribes have been transformed in the public consciousness from victims of historical oppression into just another grasping, corrupting special interest group.[54]

The author continues: "According to this perception, tribes and their members are merely rich opportunists, taking advantage of long-lost tribal affiliations in order to feast on our national obsession with games of chance." As Indian tribes have become major contributors to political parties and campaigns at all levels in California, they have been viewed more skeptically.

In this same vein, attacks on the Indian gaming presence have taken many forms, including environmental concerns. Stand Up for California, an antigambling group, lists this among the several criticisms of individual gaming projects. And at least one television advertisement against Propositions 68 and 70 in the fall of 2004 focused on the effect on traffic that expansion would have. At the same time, as Indian casinos have grown in scope and revenue, they have strategically been supportive of local government needs, paying for police, fire, and emergency services, as with appreciation expressed for one tribe's response to recent fires in the Southern California area.

According to one article, a Proposition 68 consultant said the campaign focused on inequity—tribes amassing wealth while paying "almost nothing" to the state—because market research showed that "resonates with the public. People have seen this sharp increase in gambling and have seen this turn into a multibillion-dollar industry and are somewhat stunned by it. There was an expectation that it would be much more limited than it has been and that they would pay some level of fair share of the cost." Governor Schwarzenegger used similar language: "The Indian tribes in California are not paying their fair share."

Californians seem to be of two minds on Indian gaming. A *Los Angeles Times* poll reported in 2004 that "a strong majority of Californians believes Indian tribes that own casinos should pay more of the gambling revenue to the state." At the same time, an equally strong majority, by a more than two-to-one margin, "have a formidable view of tribes that have casinos and continue to approve of gambling on tribal land."[55] A large proportion—40 percent—of those surveyed reported that they or someone in their family had visited an Indian casino in the preceding year.

Poker Boom

The boom in gambling at all levels in America society has produced cottage industries that assist the novice gambler. If you ventured into the "games" section at a local Borders or Barnes and Noble bookstore, you would find a sizable selection of gambling books. Many of these books explain the various games to be found in Las Vegas casinos, riverboats, or Indian casinos. They include titles such as *The Complete Idiot's Guide to Gambling* and even new titles pitched to online gambling, such as *Complete Idiot's Guide to Online Gambling* and *Winning at Internet Poker for Dummies*.

Interspersed with these how-to manuals are a number of memoirs of the gambling life by men and women of various ages. In *Moneymaker,* Chris Moneymaker—a relatively untested high-stakes poker player with a fortuitous name—details the thrill of moving from a weekend college player to an everyman who won the World Series of Poker, with the appropriate subtitle for his book: *How an Amateur Poker Player Turned $40 into $2.5 Million at the World Series of Poker.*[56]

Poker commentator Phil Gordon addresses this phenomenon:

> It's the only game that normal, everyday people can visualize themselves doing at the highest level. They know they will never be able to hit a Randy Johnson fastball or catch a Joe Montana pass, but they can imagine themselves sitting across from Phil Ivey and going all in. A plumber with marital difficulties can find himself suddenly rich and famous.[57]

In her book *Poker Face: A Girlhood among Gamblers,* Katy Lederer offers a gendered accounting of her growth as a gambler, soaking up the lessons from her upbringing.[58] In another book, Annie Duke, a former psycholinguistics graduate student turned poker player, recounts her ascent, culminating in a $2 million Las Vegas tournament win.[59] Also popular have been books about how young and artful students have worked their nerve and intelligence to beat casinos through various legal but disallowed practices, such as card counting. *Bringing Down the House* recounts the story of MIT card counters who "outsmart" and outplay the casinos in Las Vegas and elsewhere. In an earlier tale, *The Eudaemonic Pie,* Thomas Bass tells the story of Stanford graduate students in physics who set out to predict winning numbers on roulette games, an unexplored area of "counting" approaches to casino gambling.[60]

If you ventured into the once moribund poker area of a major Las Vegas casino, you would find a phenomenon quite different from that of the 1980s. Instead of a sparse gathering of players from various backgrounds, you would find an infusion of young men, since poker has become an attractive game for younger Americans. The American Gaming Association emphasizes this phenomenon in a 2006 report, noting that one-third of Americans aged twenty-one to thirty-nine reported playing poker in a variety of settings the prior year, clearly the most active age-group.[61]

Get to Know Your Slot Machine

Poker combines the elements of skill and chance.[62] It forces you to place your wager—sometimes your "full stack" of chips—on an assessment of whether your opponents did indeed receive a good set of cards in the initial deal, or whether they received additional cards that strengthened their hand in the draw (in draw poker). The popular "Texas Hold 'Em" game has been the focus of poker tournaments and televised poker (which would have been one of your least likely bets even ten years ago). Still, 2005 revenue reports show that the resurgent poker boom accounted for less than 10 percent of casino revenues in Las Vegas. The biggest change in the thirty years since the report of the Commission on the Review of the National Policy Toward Gambling has been the ascendancy of slot machines, which are not your father's slot machines anymore. Slot machines are no longer the mechanical reel models that defined the "one-armed bandit" of decades past, with computerized display and payout mechanisms now dominant. In fact, one new feature of the coordination and control of slot machines is that a casino can now see the payout percentages from a central computer site and adjust them accordingly, something that was unthinkable twenty years ago.

In 2004 in Nevada, even the revenues from one level of machine—nickel slots—were greater than those for blackjack. For the entire category of slot machines, the win was more than twice that of card games and race and sports books.[63]

Only fourteen years earlier, in 1990, the amounts—while much smaller—were about even. In the not too distant past—say 1980—slot machines were of a limited variety. Already by that time, electronic games were beginning to appear and to eclipse the mechanical devices that had been the mainstay of casino slot machine areas. The introduction of progressive slot machines attracted players looking for the big jackpot. By 2005, devices such as the handheld "scratch-off" device were being touted at gaming expositions. Now a player has the opportunity to play on an "I Love Lucy" machine in which players earn bonuses by trying to grab chocolates faster than Lucy in the classic scene of her working on a factory assembly line in the show. The "Star Wars" slot machine seems designed to attract those who have grown up both on the six movies in the series and on the range of video games associated with it.

Problem Gambling and Other Impediments to Normalization

The debate over whether this much legal gambling in the United States is a good thing has focused on several issues, as the debate has also turned in many countries.[64] At the 2003 International Gambling Conference in Vancouver, gambling expert William N. Thompson warned of the social costs of legal gambling: "If Bill Bennett, who had published several books and was a success in life, could be tripped up by poker machines, what about the average Joe?"[65] The issues of problem gambling and of the state taking advantage of those in vulnerable populations make the wide-scale spread of gambling problematic even in its tremendous growth.[66] The American Gaming Association, the trade association for legal gambling operators, has attempted to blunt this potentially negative association by sponsoring its own publications on and efforts to address problem gambling.[67]

Nagging problems persist with this widely accepted activity. There are concerns over problem gambling, youth gambling, and overblown promises of economic development, and still limited legalization in the lucrative area of sports gambling. Focusing on the issue of regressive taxation, Charles Clotfelter and Philip Cook demonstrate that legal lotteries rely on revenues from those at the lower end of the socioeconomic structure.[68] Of course this makes sense: unlike blackjack, lotteries hold out the promise of enormous winnings for a small investment. Critics like Goodman have argued that the expansion of legal casinos is premised on the overblown projections of economic development capacity and state tax revenue.[69] As Reith explains, "The net result of gambling expansion is not so much a dramatic *increase* in wealth as a *transfer* of existing wealth."[70] Goodman adds:

> A state has economic problems, often due to a recession, and introduces gambling. Gambling revenues climb, then taper off, flatten out, and decline. At that point the state introduces some other form of gambling. . . . the trend is always toward more "hard-core" forms of gambling. . . . Where will the states turn next? Now they are concerned about competition from offshore Internet casinos. The states may try to get in on Internet gambling.[71]

The seeds of this ambivalence about legal gambling survive despite the significant growth in legal gambling over the last thirty years and the steady trend toward normalization of gambling in Americans' attitudes and practices. As the National Gambling Impact Study Commission reported in 1999:

> The two principal studies sponsored by this Commission found that the prevalence of problem and pathological gambling in America is troubling. NRC estimates that, in a given year, approximately 1.8 million adults in the United States are pathological gamblers. NORC found that approximately 2.5 million adults are pathological gamblers. Another three million of the adult population are problem gamblers. Over 15 million Americans were identified as at-risk gamblers.[72]

A debate took place over whether the percentage of Americans displaying problem gambling characteristics was a relative concern or an absolute concern. If problem drinking is estimated to affect more than 10 percent of those who drink, then the legal gambling industry should be buoyed by the commission's acceptance of the lower rates offered by various problem gambling studies, including those of the Harvard Center on Addictions.

For example, the Responsible Gaming Association of New Mexico produced a thirty-minute documentary titled *Knowing When to Stop,* which received an industry award in 2005 from the National Council on Problem Gambling.[73] The American Gaming Association has led in this regard for several years with its publication of a booklet, and dissemination to constituent members of supportive materials and training. Bill Eadington, a professor of economics and an international gaming expert, describes the last decade as one in which the gaming industry at first paid lip service to problem gaming, then was reactive in providing programming, and now has reached levels of proactive programming and responsiveness.[74]

Social conservatives were not enamored of the composition and process of the National Gambling Impact Study Commission (NGISC) and attempted to frame the findings as supportive of their concern over problem gambling. One summary from Focus on the Family read as follows:

> The nine-member Commission faced numerous obstacles in its work, the foremost being a united and relentless effort on the part of the gambling industry and its political allies to sabotage the Commission's work. In fact, the gambling industry succeeded in placing three mem-

bers of the Nevada casino industry on the Commission. Another member was appointed to represent Native American gambling interests.

In spite of this, the Commission's final report paints a dark—and often devastating—portrait of the effects of widespread legalized gambling on America's families and communities.[75]

A group of ministers underlined this concern in a 2002 letter to the members of Congress, emphasizing several ways in which legal gambling was rending the social fabric of society:

> The rapid increase in legal gambling opportunities has created a concomitant boom in the number of gambling addicts. . . . Gambling exploits those with the fewest financial resources. . . . Each of us—and the faith communities we represent—could provide countless stories of families shattered by gambling addiction. . . . The gambling boom has made our communities more dangerous places to live. . . . Gambling has become a blight on our nation's cultural landscape[76]

Dr. James Dobson had also been a member of the National Gambling Impact Study Commission. He wrote the following at the end of that commission's work, when he was upset that the NGISC reported a far lower lifetime incidence for problem gambling than for other problem behaviors such as alcohol dependence:

> Clearly, gambling is a destroyer that ruins lives and wrecks families. A mountain of evidence presented to our Commission demonstrates a direct link between problem and pathological gambling and divorce, child abuse, domestic violence, bankruptcy, crime and suicide. More than 15.4 million adults and adolescents meet the technical criteria of those disorders. That is an enormous number—greater than the largest city in this country. When other activities, such as smoking, have been shown to be harmful, the hue and cry for regulations to warn and protect the public has been loud and long. Today, the silence of most of our leaders about the risks of gambling is deafening. It is well past time for a Paul Revere to sound the alarm. Gambling is hazardous to your—to our—health![77]

Other critics, including many psychologists who are concerned with the prevalence of problem gambling behavior among vulnerable populations—notably youth—continue to challenge gambling's easy normalization. Psychologist Jeffrey Derevensky and colleagues, authors of numerous studies, conclude:

> With the continuous expansion of the gambling industry worldwide, more gambling opportunities and types of gambling exist today than in the past. With this increased exposure, more adolescents, already prone to risk-taking, have been tempted by the lure of excitement, entertainment, and potential financial gain associated with gambling.[78]

In March 2005, voters in two populous southern Florida counties went to the polls to consider a ballot measure to allow legal gambling operators there to include slot machines as part of their operation. The latest in a series of "racino" proposals, the Florida attempt came in a state that had balked at expanding legal gambling to include legal casinos in votes in 1978.[79] Proponents of the effort noted that the growth of Indian gaming and the presence of gambling ships that sailed out of southern Florida had spurred local interests to back a measure that would provide some revenues for state education and other needs.[80] As they had in previous campaigns, opponents claimed that Florida's status as a family vacation destination would be sullied by expanded gambling: "That reputation [as a "family-friendly state"] has been endangered by the efforts of the gambling industry to expand gambling throughout the state."[81] Florida governor Jeb Bush added his opposition, calling the measure "false hope" that would bring higher crime and problem gambling to the state. Voters in Florida split on the issue, with those in Broward County (including the Fort Lauderdale area) approving the measure, and those in Dade County failing to do so.

In general, though, social conservatives are not getting much mileage out of their opposition to gambling. Thus, it has not become one of the leading issues in their organizational growth strategies, fund-raising, and public profile. As far back as 1974, when New Jersey considered its first statewide initiative to legalize casinos, research showed that there was a limit on the number of voters who would respond to a religious or moralistic challenge to gambling on its face. Since then, opponents may have couched their opposition in part in moral arguments, but as normalization has taken place, more explicit moralistic opposition usually has not found large, receptive audiences.

Beyond William Bennett's personal story, a more complicated and structural issue arose in 2005 when Jack Abramoff, a lobbyist with strong Republican ties, was charged with and later pled guilty to influencing legislators in Washington, in large part regarding Indian casino issues. At its general level, the Abramoff story was a simple one of quid pro quo corruption. Beneath the surface, the scandal also captured the ambivalence some social conservative leaders feel toward gambling. While the taint of scandal is never one that a political party invites, this particular twist presented the two sides of the Republican coalition in disarray, as powerful Republicans, such as House majority leader Tom DeLay, were seen to be close to a lobbying cause including Indian casinos, which would put them at odds with the sentiments of the antigambling ministers and activists.

Ralph Reed, once the executive director of the Christian Coalition and later an influential Republican Party strategist and corporate consultant, came under attack for work supporting Indian tribes and their efforts to defeat additional gambling in some states. Critics from within the anticasino movement explained their dismay. Said the Reverend Tom Grey of the National Coalition against Legalized Gambling, "When you get paid big money, it's got to be gambling money. Ralph Reed with all his sophistication should have known where the money came from."[82]

Perhaps gambling's beauty is that it can be seen as another defensible issue of freedom from government intrusion in a liberal sense, seen as an acceptable corporate player and industry in a Republican sense, and seen as an acceptable leisure time and entertainment activity by a growing number of Americans. The American Gaming Association lists both Democratic pollster Peter Hart and Republican pollster Frank Luntz as two of its experts. And, while it is a sizable campaign contributor, the gambling industry gives funds relatively equally to Democratic and Republican legislators and office seekers.[83] In some ways, that makes sense, because the Democratic streak of supporting the zone of privacy and avoiding moralistic attacks merges well with the Republican emphasis on keeping government limited in business regulation. As the normal vice, legal gambling takes advantage of both strains of thought.[84]

Gambling Uncoupled

This chapter has presented the case of legalized gambling as the one formerly prohibited vice that has been accepted in most quarters of

American society. One of the goals of this chapter has been to understand contemporary legal gambling in the context of the stalled movement toward drug decriminalization and the gradual change—but continued contestation—of the culture war's central issues, especially abortion and gay rights, and now gay marriage.

How has gambling been normalized—as these other "victimless crimes" have taken a different path, a rockier road, a series of dead ends and thwarted reform?

Legal gambling may have had its skeptics, but little about the slot machine or lottery ticket generated the kind of excitement and antipathy that gay marriage did in 2004. Nor had it drawn the ire of social and religious conservatives in the 1980s, when gay rights repeals were taking place. If the federal government could be accused of turning a blind eye toward AIDS in the 1980s and not aggressively seeking treatment or a cure to the extent that it has for other diseases,[85] the lack of attention paid to gambling was considered a good thing by gambling operators, who desired state support but beyond that minimal intervention. One of the reasons that gambling does not generate a backlash is that it does not involve a critique of the establishment, and does not offer up a new paradigm of gender relations (as abortion does) or sex itself (as gay rights does). It also does not offer ties to contested social movements of the day in the way, for example, that marijuana decriminalization was tied to the anti–Vietnam War protests.

In the cresting of what Nelson Rose has called the "third wave" of gambling legalization, legal gambling advocates may have suffered their occasional setbacks,[86] as gambling did not spread as far and as fast and in as many forms as some industry analysts had predicted. Still, neither did it generate the level of backlash that something like abortion liberalization and then legalization had created. If the backlash of the 1980s against liberal reforms of the 1970s was a key theme—the success of groups like the Moral Majority and the Christian Coalition—legal gambling trod lightly, as it did not offer to change deeply entrenched gender roles (as did abortion) or expand greatly minority rights and freedoms (as did gay rights).

If John Stuart Mill's concern with harm—which later philosophers, such as Feinberg, and social scientists have focused on as a crucial element in considering use of criminal sanction—can be used as a guiding concept in the evaluation of "victimless crime," in gambling it can be seen as receding as a central issue. As mentioned earlier, Geis has commented on the low level of seriousness associated with gambling in its criminalized days.[87] This concept of harm also has been a frame through which normalization—indeed legalization—has proceeded in a fairly uninterrupted process over the past thirty years (admittedly, there could be more sports gambling, more states with full-blown Las Vegas–style casinos, and more Internet gambling, but stay tuned). It is the frame through which prosecutions ceased being made.

Gambling is distinguished from the other formerly prohibited victimless crimes by its ubiquity and acceptance—what could be referred to as the standout case of gambling, as it has been "uncoupled" from the other vices. First, gambling did not challenge existing paradigms. Unlike entrenched bureaucratic issues such as the drug war,[88] changing gambling policies did not run directly against entrenched government entities. In fact, in the preceding era, police and prosecutors embraced de facto decriminalization. Economist Bill Eadington adds: "Gaming organizations have become mainstream in terms of objectives, management practices and corporate strategies."[89]

Also of importance was a second factor: the lack of successful opposition. Legal gambling proposals and initiatives did not mobilize waves of committed, single-issue opponents.

A third item was the lack of a successful antigambling "frame." In some locales and times, the issue was organized crime. In many cases, it was compulsive or problem gambling. Sometimes it would be the overpromise of economic development.

Eadington notes that gaming operators, gaming regulators, and the state by 2006 have paid greater attention to the issue of responsible gaming. To him, "this has increased from lip service to semi-commitment to full commitment." At the hotel where Eadington's most recent international gaming conference was being held (attended by gaming researchers from many countries), three brochures on responsible gambling were included in the hotel's welcome pack. Analysts divide the responses to problem gambling by jurisdictions and operator; these responses include providing informed choice, implementing consumer control, instituting restrictions (like hours of operation), and placing a cap on the number and size of gaming venues.

A fourth issue has been crucial—the positive role of the state and the importance of tax revenues and economic development.

In sum, there may be limits to legal gambling, but not enough to dramatically slow its growth. A Pew Research Center report in May 2006 found a "modest backlash" on attitudes toward the legalization of gambling, suggesting that Americans feel that we have enough gambling now.[90] But fully 70 percent of the respondents said that legalized gambling encourages people to gamble more than they can afford, suggesting a vein of ambivalence in even this very normalized activity. The highest level of support for legalizing gambling as a policy option was for lotteries, approved by 71 percent of respondents. Still, the Pew report concludes: "The negative turn in attitudes toward gambling appears to be driven by concerns that people are gambling too much rather than by any revival of the once common view that gambling is immoral."[91]

In 2006, this perspective also supported arguments that the government is bound to be unsuccessful as it attempts to limit Internet gambling. One of the owners of an online betting service estimates that 8 million Americans participate each year and wager an estimate $6 billion annually.[92] With a prohibitionist federal law passed, this newest possible outlet for gambling may continue to evolve and grow in an unregulated atmosphere, at least as far as the United States is concerned.

This book was completed in 2007, in an America far different from 1964, when New Hampshire legalized the lottery; 1976, when the Commission on the Review of the National Policy toward Gambling issued its report, and New Jersey voters authorized Atlantic City casinos; 1978, when Wall Street discovered gambling stocks; 1987, when the *Cabazon* decision was handed down; and 1999, when the National Gambling Impact Study Commission made its report. Eadington offers the following perspective:

> Twenty years ago, could we have predicted the spread of legalization and hybrids of gaming institutions, the technological advances for slot machines and gaming devices, the reinvention of Las Vegas, and the diversification of entertainment, the emergence of internet and remote gaming; the growth of responsible gaming as an important policy topic?[93]

In a day when lottery tickets are sold at 7-Eleven stores and *USA Today* publishes the winning lottery numbers of thirty-five states,[94] educators and law enforcement support legal gambling, and politicians tout its economic development potential, America may still be embroiled in a culture war over other issues, but gambling is far along the road to full normalization.

3

Abortion ·

Contestation and Ambivalence in the Long Era of Roe v. Wade

Two words. South Dakota. One threat. The risk of losing *Roe v. Wade.*
> —NARAL Pro-Choice America (May 2006)

People in favor of abortion-on-demand never, ever want to use the word "abortion." But if you watch a "pro-choice" rally you'll notice the applause lines always include a "woman's right to choose" and "women's access to health services." To them, abortion is a health service for women. To us, abortion means a funeral service for the preborn baby.
> —Gary Shepard, "It's Going to Get Ugly" (2005)

Perhaps the best summary [of polls] is that a majority of Americans want abortion to remain legal, but their support is quite ambivalent.
> —Carole Joffe, "It's Not Just the Abortion, Stupid" (2005)

Introduction: Supreme Court Vacancies

If the 2004 election were to provide any meaningful spoils for those "value voters" and other foot soldiers of the social and religious conservative movement who helped reelect George Bush, it should come in the form of the nomination and confirmation of Supreme Court justices who would one day soon lead to the overturning of *Roe v. Wade.* In this context, the announced resignation of Justice Sandra Day O'Connor in July 2005 presented a unique opportunity, but also one deeply caught in the context of the ambivalence of American attitudes and government positions toward abortion.

To most, Sandra Day O'Connor was an icon: the first woman on the Supreme Court. A former Arizona legislator and state judge, she was appointed by President Reagan in 1981 to fulfill a campaign promise he had made to choose a woman justice. Her appointment was met with fanfare, and she successfully negotiated the Senate confirmation process, with the issue of abortion on at least a few of the senators' minds.[1]

Throughout her career, Justice O'Connor represented the swing vote in a number of sensitive areas in which the court ruled—affirmative action, display of religion, and abortion prominent among these. On affirmative action, she had usually been resistant to civil rights claims for redress. Typical of this was her vote in minority business enterprise set-aside cases. However, by the end of her tenure she became the author of a 5-to-4 decision supporting the right of the University of Michigan to use race as a criterion in electing its first-year undergraduate class. In typical fashion, in a companion case, she voted to restrict the same university from deploying a quota system in the admission of its first-year law students.

Nowhere was her desire to chart a middle course, or to bring legislative-style compromise to legal issues, more prominent than in her many rulings on abortion throughout her years on the court. One of Justice O'Connor's great contributions was her ability to bring votes with her to support *Roe* in 1992, in a reframing of the legal rights to abortion in *Planned Parenthood v. Casey,* in which a majority of the court affirmed the standing of *Roe* but allowed for a diminution in legal protection, a change in Justice Blackmun's trimester system, and allowance of limitations such as parental consent and a mandatory waiting period that would not have been allowed through a strict reading of *Roe.* After the tenuous nature of *Roe* during the *Webster* case of a few years prior, O'Connor's handiwork was appreciated by many, as she brought along Justices Kennedy and Souter in her opinion.

O'Connor, Kennedy, and Souter, in their draft opinion in *Casey,* described how "for better or worse, *Roe* was an enduring part of the nation's way of life."[2] Speaking that day for the majority, O'Connor stated: "Some of us as individuals find abortion offensive to our most basic principles or morality, but that cannot control our decision. . . . Our obligation is to define the liberty of all, not to mandate our own moral code."[3]

Yet pro-choice advocates were not overjoyed. Kate Michelman, then president of the National Abortion Rights Action League (NARAL), writes, for example, from the perspective of someone hearing the *Casey* decision read in person in 1992:

> As O'Connor spoke, I was both incredulous and ecstatic that the Court would continue to protect women's fundamental right to privacy. Just moments before, we were nearly certain that the right to choose—a liberty on which women's lives depended—would be lost. . . . But as O'Connor continued, it became clear that a compromise that left the shell of *Roe* intact but hollowed out many of its protections was taking shape.[4]

Justice Harry Blackmun, the author of the *Roe v. Wade* decision, was heartened by the "courageous decision" of Justice O'Connor and others to no longer delay ruling on the central thrust of *Roe,* but to support it. However, the fact that it was diminished concerned Blackmun, as did the fervor of those waiting to gain a fifth vote and overturn *Roe.* The day of that 1992 ruling, then Democratic presidential candidate Bill Clinton called a press conference to assert that "the constitutional right to choose is hanging by a thread."[5]

The O'Connor replacement set off an intense lobbying effort for the reshaping of the Supreme Court. As social conservatives vilified O'Connor for her prominent role in abortion cases and her recent votes on affirmative action and gay rights (ignoring her conservative rulings in many other cases), it was clear that much was at stake.

A remarkable finding in a Gallup poll taken soon after Justice O'Connor's resignation found the following:

> When asked specifically if they would want the new justice to vote to overturn *Roe v. Wade* or to vote to uphold that decision, Americans overwhelmingly would want that justice to uphold the decision rather than overturn it. Four in 10 Americans say they would like the court to become more conservative, while 30% would want it more liberal.[6]

If Justice O'Connor's role in preserving a balance in abortion rulings was paramount, then the action initiated by her 2005 decision to retire was one of the most fervent events in the Bush presidency. If the 2004 vote was meaningful to religious conservatives, the payoff would come in the form of the nominee. What that would also demonstrate about the state of American attitudes toward abortion is a major focus of this chapter.

Abortion in an Ambivalent America

If one were to choose a topic that characterizes the most strident disagreement between Americans over issues of personal morality in the last forty years, arguably abortion would top the list. Nonetheless, Americans have been supportive of the main tenets of *Roe v. Wade* in polls consistently since 1973, even as the Supreme Court has been reshaped and determined to undercut it. At the same time, polls have captured the ambivalence of many toward the implications of that support or, more appropriately, the limits of that support—such as Medicaid funding, teenage access, and late-term abortions. Still, a November 2004 poll taken for the Associated Press found what many precursor polls had—that most Americans (59 percent in the AP poll) thought that President Bush should choose a nominee who would uphold *Roe v. Wade,*[7] a level of support matched when Justice O'Connor announced her retirement.

One of the goals of this chapter is to establish the ways in which the morally contested issues of this book—abortion, gay rights, assisted suicide, and stem cell research—differ from gambling. If legal gambling in the United States, as it has increased greatly over the past twenty-five years, represents what Jerome Skolnick has termed the "normal vice," then legal abortion represents quite a different case. Although legal at a national level since *Roe v. Wade* was decided in 1973, it can safely be characterized as one of the most contested and polarizing issues in American public life. This chapter seeks to contextualize, operationalize, identify, explain, and appreciate the ambivalence that is operating in the case of abortion and in several of the other topics of the book. In chapter 7, we will also discuss political scientists who believe that such polarization is overstated.

This chapter focuses on the parallel themes of the great contestation of abortion in the courts, churches, public opinion, and politics, alongside a continuing ambivalence of the American public toward the appropriate laws and policies in this area. This chapter places the current restive state of legal abortion against America's recent history of criminalization, piecemeal decriminalization, legalization through *Roe v. Wade* and the courts (1973), and continuing battles at the forefront of the culture wars since then.

First, it exemplifies the ambivalence that many Americans have about some of the activities analyzed in this book. In fact, Americans are decidedly unsupportive of abortion for "personal" or financial reasons, which according to the Guttmacher Institute and other institutions are the primary reasons American women seek abortions.

Second, support for *Roe v. Wade* remains high, and has done so consistently since the ruling. This came to the forefront during the series of nominations to the U.S. Supreme Court by President Bush during 2005.

Third, abortion remains a vastly important issue to partisans of the pro-life and pro-choice movements. As the Pew Research Center and others have demonstrated, abortion is an issue in which the political landscape is characterized by deeply invested activists on either side, and a middle group of more conflicted, more ambivalent, but not necessarily less informed people.

Roberts, Alito, Miers, O'Connor, and the Meaning of the Middle

Some of the population thinks of abortion as something supported by true believers and chooses to frame them as "pro-abortion" advocates. Following the successful framing by pro-life activists focusing on late-term abortion, these pro-choice supporters are portrayed as going so far as to nearly endorse infanticide, which is the effect of using the frame of late-term abortion. They see the Democratic Party as beholden to these "special interests," or to the "feminazis," as Rush Limbaugh so inartfully describes them: "I prefer to call the most obnoxious feminists what they really are: feminazis. The term describes any female who is intolerant of any point of view that challenges militant feminism. I often use it to describe women who are obsessed with perpetuating a modern-day holocaust: abortion."[8]

At the same time, another large portion of the population thinks of abortion in the frame of women's reproductive health. They articulate "choice" as a key element of modern autonomy and see those who choose to diminish this right as true believers who would go so far as to support turning the clock back to a not-so-distant time when women's lives were ruled by their biological nature.

Given the concerns about privacy and abortion raised in many quarters with the retirement of Justice O'Connor, the hearings for John Roberts were widely watched. Though he was eventually nominated for the seat of the conservative Chief Justice Rehnquist, and thus would not necessarily change the balance of the court as such, any nomination of a justice—and especially the chief justice—focused various interested parties, especially those in the morality wars, on his view of the law and the role of the court.

Ralph Neas of the People for the American Way referred to Roberts as "Antonin Scalia in sheep's clothing."[9] Nan Aron of the Alliance for Justice criticized Roberts across a range of issues:

> In his years of service as a political appointee in the administrations of Presidents Reagan and George H. W. Bush, Judge Roberts also helped craft legal policies that sought to weaken school desegregation efforts, the reproductive rights of women, environmental protections, church-state separation and the voting rights of African Americans.[10]

These issues colored this early exchange on the second day of the confirmation hearings, in an exchange between Roberts and Senator Arlen Specter, the Judiciary Committee chair (Specter is a pro-choice Republican who would ultimately vote for Robert's nomination in committee and on the floor of the Senate):

> SPECTER: Judge Roberts, in your confirmation hearing for the circuit court, your testimony read to this effect, and it's been widely quoted: "*Roe* is the settled law of the land." Do you mean settled for you, settled only for your capacity as a circuit judge, or settled beyond that?
>
> ROBERTS: Well, beyond that, it's settled as a precedent of the court, entitled to respect under principles of stare decisis. And those principles, applied in the *Casey* case, explain when cases should be revisited and when they should not. And it is settled as a precedent of the court, yes.
>
> SPECTER: You went on then to say, quote, "It's a little more than settled. It was reaffirmed in the face of a challenge that it should be overruled in the *Casey* decision." So it has that added precedential value.
>
> ROBERTS: I think the initial question for the judge confronting an issue in this area, you don't go straight to the *Roe* decision; you begin with *Casey*, which modified the *Roe* framework and reaffirmed its central holding.[11]

Democratic senator Patrick Leahy of Vermont, a Judiciary Committee member, differed from half of his Democratic colleagues when he de-

cided to support Roberts based on his presentation of judicial philosophy and self:

> I can only take him at his word that he does not have an ideological
> agenda. For me, a vote to confirm requires faith that the words he
> spoke to us have meaning. I can only take him at his word that he will
> steer the court to serve as an appropriate check on potential abuses of
> presidential power. I respect those who have come to different conclu-
> sions, and I readily acknowledge the unknowable at this moment, that
> perhaps they are right and I am wrong. Only time will tell.[12]

Senate minority leader Harry Reid (D-Nev.) explained that he voted
against Roberts because of the unanswered questions to many issues,
such as precedent affecting *Roe v. Wade* and similar cases: "No one
doubts that John Roberts is an excellent lawyer and an affable person.
But at the end of this process, I have too many unanswered questions
about the nominee to justify a vote confirming him to this enormously
important lifetime position."[13]

Judiciary Committee member Joseph Biden (D-Del.) expressed much
the same reservations during the hearings and eventually voted against
Roberts in committee and on the floor: "We're rolling the dice with
you, judge, because you won't share your views with us. You've told me
nothing in this Kabuki dance. The public has a right to know what you
think."[14]

Eventually, 22 Democrats voted to confirm Roberts, and 22 voted
against his confirmation; he was approved by the Senate on September
29 by a vote of 78 to 22.[15]

The death of Chief Justice William Rehnquist on September 3, 2005,
after a long illness, had caused changes in the nomination plans for the
Supreme Court. President Bush acted quickly to resolve what was then
presenting itself as a significant reshaping of the Supreme Court. Within
days, he moved his nomination of John Roberts, whose confirmation
hearings for appointment as an associate justice were about to begin, to
be the chief justice, replacing Rehnquist.

With the one associate justice seat open—and debate already ongoing over whether it was the "O'Connor seat," and thus a moderate seat
—the president and his advisers mulled over a list of potential nominees, many of whom had been suggested and vetted during the process
leading to Roberts's nomination. When Bush announced his choice for

the open seat, it was met with underwhelming response, some consternation, and rumblings of dissatisfaction among some prominent conservatives and some of the president's social conservative base. In nominating Harriet Miers, a Dallas corporate attorney, former president of the Texas Bar Association, and then his White House counsel, Bush surprised many who were following the lists of suggestions and assessments from the Roberts nomination. With an eye toward gender balance on the court following O'Connor's retirement, the selection of a woman seemed to many to be an attempt to address the "O'Connor seat" issue, but it remained to be decided where Miers's judicial philosophy rested, since she was not coming from the well-published and well-scrutinized federal appellate bench or law school rosters. Into this vacuum would emerge conflicting views of Miers, with conservatives triumphant from the 2004 election worried that Bush was failing to use his mandate to appoint a strong conservative jurist. Although Miers received praise from certain quarters for her devout religious nature, it also became apparent that in her Texas positions she might have been more flexible on women's rights and reproductive freedom than conservatives desired. A barrage of criticism ensued, which led within weeks to her withdrawal of her nomination.

The nomination of Miers was met at first in October 2005 with considerable criticism from social conservatives. Even though important players like Dr. James Dobson and Southern Baptist president Richard Land were called in to shore up the conservative base by declaring their support for Miers, there was an uproar from various elements of the social and religious Right. There was also concern that Miers had made promises about *Roe v. Wade,* implicitly or explicitly, leading to her nomination or to Dobson's support. As a *Wall Street Journal* writer asked,

> What did James Dobson know about Harriet Miers, and when did he know it? One report noted that Dr. Dobson and other conservative leaders got assurance for the idea that Miers would vote to overturn *Roe v. Wade* when they offered their support to her soon after the nomination. The support was orchestrated through a telephone conference call.[16]

Many of the comments—particularly those like Rush Limbaugh's that President Bush had "squandered an opportunity"[17]—can be read as commentary on Bush's inability to capitalize on the mandate of the "moral thrust" of the 2004 election, and the role that "values voters" played in it.[18] Tony Perkins of the Family Research Council said in a statement that he worried that some of Mier's prior actions as a city council member in Dallas were "helping to legitimize the drive of homosexual organizations for power and influence over our public policies."[19]

Conservative activist Gary Bauer cited a 1990-era quote from Harriet Miers and added his own objection to her reasoning about the role of morality in legislation. Miers was quoted as saying: "Legislating religion or morality we gave up on a long time ago. Remembering that fact appears to offer the most effective solutions to these problems."

Bauer's response was as follows: "When millions of 'values voters' went into their voting booths and reelected George W. Bush and sent more conservatives to the United States Senate, I don't think they had in mind putting someone on the Supreme Court who thought legislating morality was a mistake!"[20]

Conservative author Ann Coulter was typically more blunt in discussing Miers on *Real Time with Bill Maher*: "The point is, she's unqualified. Not that she won't vote right. I mean that is the one thing Bush keeps telling us about her, that, you know, he knows her heart. She's not qualified for the position. This isn't like, you know, 'best employee of the month.'"[21]

Former House Speaker Newt Gingrich wrote, in an attempt to mollify critics:

> With the president's knowledge of Ms. Miers, his stated commitment to rebalancing the judiciary and his conservative record—not only in appointing judges but on big decisions in general—conservatives should feel comfortable in taking the president at his word that he has just now delivered another nominee in that tradition.[22]

Former Justice Department lawyer John Yoo, a lightning rod in the first Bush term for his defense of the Patriot Act, suggested in an article, "Opportunity Squandered," that, "according to press reports, [Miers] did not win a reputation as a forceful conservative on issues such as the administration's position on stem cell research or affirmative action."[23] Many vocal supporters of the Bush administration expressed their unease at assuming that Miers's personal religious orientation would result in effective leadership on the Court on issues of extreme interest to them. It did not help matters when Miers was also shown to have written the president expressing admiration for his great brilliance, something even his strongest supporters may not have felt.

From redstate.org, a writer offered an opinion on why Harriet Miers's pro-life credentials were not enough to warrant her nomination to the Supreme Court, where the need is, to antiabortion activists, for someone whose constitutional philosophy, brilliance, and judicial skill would undo *Roe:*

> While it is certainly not a bad thing to be a Republican, an Evangelical, or personally pro-life, this does not mean that Ms. Miers has a judicial philosophy that will lead her to reject the extraconstitutional law-making of *Roe, Doe,* and *Casey.* The vast majority of members of Congress describe themselves as personally pro-life, but are actually opposed to overturning *Roe* or amending the Constitution—including a majority of the members of the Judiciary Committee (and a few names that might surprise folks). Many Texas Republicans—some maintain that list includes the President, who still believes that "the culture" needs to change before such things can happen—fall into this category. In fact, as ludicrous as it may sound, many of the original authors of *Roe* were personally pro-life.[24]

Some critics of Bush's nomination saw in Miers a reflection of the president's own less-than-firm commitment to pro-life principles and the overturning of *Roe.* George W. Bush is the son of a former president whose loyalty to the pro-life cause, coming late in his career, was often suspect. Both the current president's mother and his wife had been known to speak a language of tolerance and moderation on this issue. One pro-life blogger asserted that Miers should be opposed precisely because she shares George W. Bush's weak commitment to the pro-life stance:

> When President Bush says that Miers shares his judicial philosophy, he is not saying that his personal pro-life inclinations extend to overturning *Roe.* Laura Bush vouches for the veracity of this analysis. The pro-choice First Lady says, about *Roe,* "No, I don't think that it should be overturned." When asked about the thinking of her husband, she replied, "I would say, in general, George and I are on the same page on the issue."[25]

This comment echoed the sentiments that Coulter had made earlier in the year:

> Maybe he is an idiot. On the thirty-second anniversary of *Roe v. Wade* this past Monday . . . President Bush told a pro-life rally in Washington that a "culture of life cannot be sustained solely by changing laws. We need, most of all, to change hearts. . . ." Actually, what we need least of all is to "change hearts." Maybe it's my law background, but I think it's time we changed a few laws.[26]

Conservative commentator Tony Blankley wrote about what the conservative wing of the Republican Party hoped for:

> First, withdraw the unfortunate nomination of Miss Miers. Not only is there almost no enthusiasm for her nomination, I have never seen as much outright hostility and even anger at an appointment from a president's own party. Replace her with a highly qualified, full-blooded, proven conservative nominee (any number of his appointments to the courts of appeal will do).[27]

Ralph Neas of the progressive organization People for the American Way reacted to the Miers withdrawal in this way:

> It's an astonishing spectacle. The unelected power-brokers of the far right have forced the withdrawal of President Bush's own Supreme Court nominee, before a confirmation hearing has even been held. President Bush's complete capitulation to the far-right interest groups is astounding. The ultra-right wing dominance of Republican Party politics is complete, and they have dealt a terrible blow to an already weakened President and his administration. . . . Right-wingers are openly saying they elected Bush to put a battle-ready ultraconservative on the court to replace the moderate Sandra Day O'Connor, and they're demanding a new choice—bipartisanship, moderation and mainstream Americans be damned.[28]

Bauer, speaking for one branch of the social conservative movement, offered this admonition:

> The Miers mess will be quickly forgotten if the president now follows-up with a solid, clear conservative whose record is unambiguous. Will

the Left fight such a nominee? Of course it will. . . . All of them worked to elect John Kerry president—not George W. Bush. They don't want him to succeed—they want him to fail. They are desperate to keep their grip on the courts that have forced abortion-on-demand on the country and are trying to force same-sex "marriage" on us now.[29]

Robert Bork, himself a failed Supreme Court nominee, wrote on how the Miers nomination reveals the heart of George W. Bush's commitment to originalism and conservative ideology:

Finally, this nomination has split the fragile conservative coalition on social issues into those appalled by the administration's cynicism and those still anxious, for a variety of reasons, to support or at least placate the president. Anger is growing between the two groups. The supporters should rethink. The wars in Afghanistan and Iraq aside, George W. Bush has not governed as a conservative (amnesty for illegal immigrants, reckless spending that will ultimately undo his tax cuts, signing a campaign finance bill even while maintaining its unconstitutionality). This George Bush, like his father, is showing himself to be indifferent, if not actively hostile, to conservative values.[30]

John Dickerson described the uneasiness among parts of Bush's governing coalition that the Miers nomination had exposed:

Left-wing bloggers may see the Bush administration and its allies as a uniform mass, but like all successful political teams, it's actually a coalition. At the heart of the coalition is an uncomfortable mix between, on the one hand, right-wing intellectuals, including the neoconservatives whose backing for the Iraq invasion has been so important, and, on the other, the evangelicals who turned out in such numbers to vote for a man who boasted that he was one of them. The Bible-thumping armies may carry the elections, but they sometimes make the elites in the Republican Party as uncomfortable as they make Maureen Dowd and Michael Moore. In return, the mega-church attendees are mistrustful of the party's often secular, often not-Christian pundits and wizards.[31]

With Miers's withdrawal, and the causes of it coming from elements of his conservative supporters, the president's next nomination would be much scrutinized by a now-activated base. Issues about nominating a jurist like O'Connor, or even a conservative woman jurist, fell by the wayside as the now-coalesced coalition argued for a strong and tested conservative who would utilize the president's 2004 mandate to draw the Supreme Court in a more conservative direction.

Bush appeared to answer this sentiment with the nomination of appellate court judge Samuel Alito from the Fourth Circuit Court in Philadelphia. A conservative jurist with a long record, Alito had written a dissent on husband notification in *Casey v. Planned Parenthood* when it appeared before his court.

Gary Bauer urged his followers to offer up prayers for Judge Alito at the end of his confirmation process to prevent the agents of "judicial tyranny" from dominating this important process. In a fund-raising letter, the National Organization for Women (NOW) warned that "Samuel Alito is a conservative dream-come-true [who] . . . will most certainly do everything that he can to restrict and dismantle reproductive rights . . . once he is confirmed." A student group organizing against the nomination of Judge Alito graphically warned in a short video that depicted future Supreme Court justices using binoculars and peering at a woman in a hospital bed with her legs up, alongside the caption "Court limits privacy rights." The accompanying text read, "Dick and Jane thought their personal medical decisions, including ones related to reproductive health, were theirs to make—but they thought wrong! In Alito's America they might have help from the government, whether they want it or not."[32] The group's newspaper parody included a mock story from 2009 with "High Court Dramatically Restricts *Roe v. Wade*" as its headline.

In an op-ed piece, former NARAL president Kate Michelman disclosed her personal anguish at trying to secure paternal consent from an estranged husband under a law similar to the one Alito found favorable in his dissenting opinion in the appellate-level review of *Casey v. Planned Parenthood* (1991).

The social conservative group Focus on the Family saw in Alito's nomination the possibility of undoing decades of "judicial tyranny," which they argued had affected not only abortion but a range of religious freedom and other cultural topics as well:

> Greetings from Colorado Springs. In the New Year, are you praying for
> a return to the Christian heritage upon which this nation was founded?
> Are you hoping that prayer will be allowed in public schools and that

the Ten Commandments will be displayed proudly on public property? We believe this may be the year our country's secular trends will begin to be reversed—if Judge Samuel Alito is confirmed to replace retiring Justice Sandra Day O'Connor on the Supreme Court.[33]

Presidential adviser Karl Rove had masterminded getting ballot initiatives aimed at curbing gay marriage on the 2004 ballots in seventeen states, which brought out conservatives who may have been likely to stay home from the poles otherwise. Those votes provided the margin Bush needed to eke out a second victory. Social conservatives expected something in return. First and foremost, that something was a conservative appointment to the U.S. Supreme Court—a conservative who could be counted on to provide the remaining votes needed to overturn *Roe v. Wade*.

In that context, Republican senators questioning Alito during his confirmation hearings appeared strangely at ease, confident, and gentle. Apparently something in Alito's responses to questions regarding whether *Roe v. Wade* is settled law provided the buzzwords Republicans needed to feel confident that Alito was a "safe" pick for the Supreme Court. Democrats, by contrast, seemed increasingly desperate to take down the candidate. At times they pleaded with Alito. They wanted to know why he was so forthcoming with answers to questions on a wide variety of topics yet persistently stopped short—in their eyes—of either confirming or distancing himself from a controversial comment about abortion he had made earlier in his career.

Right at the start, Judiciary Committee chair Arlen Specter asked Alito whether he accepted the legal principle articulated in *Griswold v. Connecticut* that the liberty clause in the Constitution carries with it the right to privacy. Alito responded that he agreed with the result of *Griswold* but would not say that *Griswold* stands for a sweeping right to privacy.

Coming from another angle, Senator Richard Durbin asked Alito whether he believed *Roe v. Wade* is the settled law of the land. Alito responded: "If 'settled' means that it can't be reexamined, then that's one thing. If 'settled' means that it is a precedent that is entitled to respect . . . then it is a precedent that is protected, entitled to respect under the doctrine of stare decisis."

Alito further explained his view that while *Roe v. Wade* is entitled to considerable respect under the doctrine of stare decisis, that doctrine in not an inexorable command. Durbin of course had a different notion in mind: by using the word "settled," Durbin wanted Alito to declare that *Roe v. Wade* is not just precedent but binding precedent.

To explain why he could agree that *Griswold* is settled law but would not say the same about *Roe v. Wade*, Alito declared that while he could believe that there is no realistic chance of the issue of possession of contraceptives ever coming before the courts again, *Roe* remained roundly contested, and on that basis Alito refused to go along with Durbin's view that *Roe* was settled law. Alito said that *Roe* should be accorded a level of greater deference that goes along with a case having been reconsidered and reaffirmed. He noted that *Casey*—the 1992 case wherein a majority of justices wrote joint opinions reaffirming *Roe*'s "essential holding" that prior to viability a woman has a constitutional right to choose to abort a fetus without undue interference from the state—begins and ends with discussions of stare decisis, and on that basis may even be viewed as a precedent on precedent.

Nevertheless, Alito seemed to punctuate his affirmation that stare decisis is not an inexorable command, repeating several times throughout the hearings that if he were to get beyond the analysis of stare decisis, he would approach the constitutional analysis of *Roe v. Wade*'s central holding with an open mind. These and other remarks gave even pro-choice Republicans what they hoped to hear. If, as Alito said, the issue of precedent itself was the beginning and ending point of analysis in *Casey*, the road to a constitutional reanalysis of *Roe* will be through a fresh assessment of the competing arguments regarding stare decisis in *Casey*. And, says Alito, being "settled" means, "If you bring your case before my court, I'm not even going to listen to you; I've made up my mind on this issue; I'm not going to read your brief; I'm not going to listen to your argument; I'm not going discuss the issue with my colleagues. Go away. I've made up my mind," then *Roe v. Wade* is not settled law.[34]

Judge Alito moved through the Senate Judiciary Committee on a party-line vote, and then discussions followed on whether his nomination was radical enough to cause the undoing of a bipartisan compromise to preserve Senate rules, including cloture votes or the filibuster. If the Democrats had wished to do so, they would have risked the vitality of that rule itself. From the leadership came a decision that Alito was not that exceptional radical who exceeded the threshold. Ultimately, he was confirmed by a vote of 58 to 42.

When Alito was sworn in on January 31, 2006, it marked the beginning of the Roberts Court, which, given Roberts's youth, might have a long tenure. Its first chapter is just being written, as Roberts proclaimed in a May 2006 commencement speech that he favors a "minimalist" judicial philosophy, the shape and outcomes of which remain to be seen.[35] Many social conservatives remain hopeful that a change in the court's composition, providing the fifth vote to overturn *Roe,* is imminent. Gary Bauer believes, for example, that

> Washington is already buzzing about the possibility of one more vacancy, which would give the president the opportunity to truly leave behind a court that has clearly been shifted in a conservative direction in the values debate. If it occurs, it will make the Roberts and Alito confirmation battles look like "a day in the park."[36]

Framing Battles

The three Supreme Court nominations provided an unusual window onto the politics of abortion law and policy, with all the associated conflicts. Whether one thinks of pro-life protesters chaining themselves to Planned Parenthood clinics, or even murdering abortion doctors in the names of innocent fetuses,[37] or thinks of women activists locked arm in arm and marching in New York or Washington, D.C., the images of the contest between pro-life and pro-choice are easily recognizable elements of the culture war. While abortion may no longer be a leading issue of concern for most Americans, it nonetheless motivates many on either side of the values debate at times and is part of what sociologist Kristin Luker calls the "constellation of values," which may include gender relations, premarital sex, and equal rights for women.[38]

In the years immediately preceding *Roe,* several states had liberalized their abortion laws, and a movement for abortion law reform was active and widespread throughout the country.[39] Before that, under criminalization, abortion had been an underground activity, still common but controlled in various localized ways. Historian Leslie Reagan describes how abortion took place in the 1950s, as it did in prior decades in the United States, through a network of physicians and community members. Abortion, which had been legalized, tolerated, or criminalized at different points in American history, was characterized by Reagan as being in a repressive phase in the mid-twentieth century. Efforts to liberalize abortion laws were in their early stages. Garrow, Reagan, and Solinger describe the means to which women had to go in the 1950s to obtain abortions. As sexual mores changed, with the accompanying growth in premarital and extramarital sex, abortion again became an important contested crime. Garrow details how advocates for reform—including physicians—argued over the strategic value of calls for reform versus repeal of abortion laws. In the years leading up to the landmark 1973 decision in *Roe v. Wade* to guarantee a woman's right to choose abortion in the first six months of pregnancy, activists and legal reformers were working state by state to reform abortion laws, following successes with laws against contraception.[40]

In the United States, the 1960s were a time of liberalization for abortion laws in several states, the culmination of years of effort. For example, at the time of the *Roe v. Wade* ruling in 1973, seventeen states had passed laws either allowing abortion for any reason (four states) or when necessary to protect the physical and mental health of the mother.[41] Public opinion grew in favor of therapeutic abortion as sexual mores changed and as celebrated examples of denial of abortion in cases of potential deformity engaged American debate.[42] Several states liberalized their laws in the 1960s and early 1970s, with a central feature of the legal reform being the issue of the health of the woman. In some states, it took the form of mental health; in others, physical health.

With *Roe*, the women's movement and legal reformers achieved an unparalleled success, with the trimester system of abortion legalization, dependent on women's choice. The 1973 Supreme Court case, decided by a 7-to-2 majority and authored by Justice Harry Blackmun, represented a watershed event in the development of laws regarding privacy, reproductive rights, and women's rights. *Roe* permitted virtually unfettered access to abortion in the first trimester. During the second trimester, states could regulate but not restrict the provision of abortion. Only in the third trimester did the state interest in the potential life of the now viable fetus become paramount.

Following *Roe*, a backlash in Congress led to the first set of limitations on abortion funding and the growth of a countermovement.[43] The mobilization of single-issue voters and grassroots activists described by Luker and others represented the emergence of the Christian Right in

American politics as we know it today.[44] As Casanova and others note, before then it was customary for fundamentalists and evangelical Christians to choose to be disengaged from the world of politics.[45]

The election of Ronald Reagan as president in 1980 was due in part to his appeal to disaffected blue-collar Democrats, who were conservative on social issues. As Joffe notes: "The so-called Reagan democrats—white workers who switched their allegiance to the Republican Party in part because of 'values' issues such as abortion—were just the first indication of abortion's strong capacity to realign American politics."[46] In the case of abortion, many of these "Reagan Democrats" came from Catholic communities in the industrial Midwest. Reagan sought to reward these constituencies through the appointment of pro-life judges, and the use of "litmus tests" for candidates' positions on abortion were thought to be widespread throughout his administration. One of the results was a series of opinions limiting—if not downright challenging—*Roe v. Wade* through the 1980s, with the 1989 *Webster* decision coming close to overturning *Roe v. Wade*.

As Ginsburg and Risen and Thomas[47] describe, the emergence of direct-action groups such as Operation Rescue brought greater contestation to the abortion issue, one the Christian Coalition built upon as a key organizing issue,[48] thus bringing American fundamentalist religious groups to a new prominence in American politics.[49]

With the Supreme Court decision in *Planned Parenthood v. Casey* in 1992, and the election of Bill Clinton in 1992 and the retirement of an anti-*Roe* vote on the Supreme Court in the person of Byron White, America reached a period of stability regarding regulation of abortion.[50] The pro-life movements splintered into more violent factions and turned their attention toward rebuilding.[51] While federal abortion protections reached a plateau, and state constitutional protections increased access to abortion, the contestation of "partial-birth" late-term abortions eventually emerged and by 2004 reshaped an issue that threw traditional political strategy into disarray.

Culture Warriors in 2004

Abortion was a strong theme in the 2004 presidential election, when Massachusetts senator John Kerry, a pro-choice Catholic, was the Democratic nominee. Bishops in several American Catholic dioceses spoke of their opposition and began a debate over the proper role of the church and politics in this discussion. Some conservative bishops declared that they would not provide Communion or other church sacraments to Kerry or any other pro-choice politician. An extreme position along this line was taken by those bishops who claimed that they would deny the same sacraments to parishioners who supported such candidates. The bishop of Green Bay admonished parishioners, "Don't leave religion outside the polling booth" when voting in November.

During the 2004 presidential campaign, the archbishop of St. Louis, Raymond L. Burke, made headlines when he said he would deny Communion to candidate John Kerry. Staunchly antiabortion, Burke denied Communion to politicians whose support of abortion rights had been blamed for increasing polarization among Catholics. After receiving a crush of media coverage, Burke modified his stance on serving Communion to Kerry, but a few weeks before the election he issued an open letter to St. Louis Catholics, questioning their support for Kerry. Burke wrote that voters must ask themselves "whether it is fair to our unborn brothers and sisters to help put someone in office who will not lift a finger to save their lives because we favor that candidate's position on health-care reform, education, the death penalty or some other issue." Positive positions taken by political candidates, Burke wrote, could not justify their support of abortion, embryonic stem cell research, euthanasia, human cloning, or same-sex marriage. Jeff Smith, a political scientist who observed the election, felt that while Burke probably managed to influence some Catholic voters, others were notably offended, and indeed Smith sensed that Burke may have actually created something of a backlash.[52]

In the abortion examples, members of one activist group attempt to define key attributes of the other. Pro-life activists, for example, often refer to their opponents as "pro-abortion." In one instance, James Bopp Jr., long-standing counsel for National Right to Life, said this about the Planned Parenthood lawyers in a New Hampshire parental notification case (*Ayotte v. Planned Parenthood of Northern New England*): "There is an effort by the pro-choice side to finally capture the absolute right to abortion that they have been seeking." In this way, Bopp's framing of the "absolute right" demonstrates to those who are ambivalent, moderate, or supportive of parental consent laws that their real opponents are unreasonable pro-choice forces, who would extend the rights provided until they trampled on things like the agreed-upon role of the family. In addition, Bopp identified the pro-choice side as "wanting all or nothing," and thus resistant to the types of compromises that might better reflect the will of the American people (especially post-*Casey*).[53]

Judicial Tyranny

Among the many meanings that *Roe v. Wade* has had for America over the years since the Supreme Court ruling was as a flash point for conservative criticism of the overreach of the judicial branch. The Supreme Court had earned some share of enmity in the 1960s when the Warren Court issued a series of pro-defendant criminal procedure rulings and extended other constitutional rights. Chief Justice Earl Warren endured his share of "Impeach Earl Warren" billboards and campaigns in selected regions of the county, as the courts became an active branch in the provision of newly extended rights, especially around contested categories of race and gender. This activist court earned a special place of scorn in conservative circles as critiques of "judicial tyranny" expanded.

When Ronald Reagan took office in 1981, one of the key goals of his Justice Department was to nominate conservative jurists for the federal judiciary, including the appellate courts and the Supreme Court. In the topics under consideration in this book (save gambling), the role of judicial-made law—and critiques of its legitimacy—stands at the foreground in most instances. In the case of abortion, the membership of the Supreme Court has been a sustained focus. Since *Casey*, the cases have focused on differences outside the key provisions of *Roe*—teenage consent or late-term abortion restrictions—and have led to the passage of numerous laws in state legislatures, some anticipating the overturn of *Roe*.[54] Only in 2006 has a facial challenge strategy arisen, in the case of the new South Dakota law.

Because of his vote in *Casey*, and eventually his authorship of the majority opinion in the *Lawrence v. Texas* sodomy case in 2003, Justice Anthony Kennedy, a Reagan appointee once considered a reliable conservative vote, has earned the enmity of the social conservative Right, some of whom regard him as a "traitor" to the conservative legal cause.[55] Justice John Paul Stevens, the oldest liberal judge, and thus closely watched by conservatives for his health status, was criticized for his rulings on gay rights, the focus of chapter 4.

Although he promised in 1975 to leave policy-making on controversial social issues to Congress and the states, Stevens has nevertheless advanced the homosexual agenda from the bench. In 1986 he dissented in the *Bowers v. Hardwick* decision upholding Georgia's anti-sodomy statute, and in 2003 joined the majority in striking down Texas' anti-sodomy statute in *Lawrence v. Texas*. In 1996, he helped strike down Colorado's constitutional amendment prohibiting special rights being granted to homosexuals. Then in 2000 he signed an opinion that would have forced the Boy Scouts to accept openly homosexual scout leaders.[56]

On a related topic, assisted suicide—the focus of chapter 5—Wesley J. Smith's analysis of the 2006 Supreme Court decision in *Gonzales v. Oregon* resonates with the abortion critiques: "Don't confuse the majority opinion with truth. What is really happening is the Court, as it often does in cultural issues, is reflecting elite liberal views, and if nothing else, the drive to legalize assisted suicide is an elite liberal political movement."[57]

Ambivalence

To many, the issue of abortion immediately divides the country into polarized camps of red and blue, stridently pro-life or pro-choice, giving no quarter in debates, but unwilling to consider compromises or moderation. What is more evident, however, is that there has always been an ambivalence among the American public over the years since *Roe,* even as support for the law has remained high, despite attempts to change the Supreme Court composition and generate legislation to limit it. As one analyst explains, "Polls show that most American support legal abortion, yet they also favor some restrictions, particularly after the first trimester."[58] Sociologist Carole Joffe argued that "perhaps the best summary [of polls] is that a majority of Americans want abortion to remain legal, but their support is quite ambivalent."[59]

Political journalist Karen Tumulty adds, in her assessment of the mixed pattern of support, opposition, and ambivalence across the states:

One reason that abortion-rights opponents in Missouri and elsewhere succeed in winning restrictions is that regulations on the procedure generally enjoy broad popular support, even among people who say they want to keep abortion legal. Pollsters says that Americans' views on abortion have shifted relatively little since *Roe v. Wade,* that they have always been complicated and that sometimes they are even contradictory.[60]

As Justice O'Connor's biographer explained about the *Casey* decision:

At the time, the vast middle of America approved of the Court's ruling in *Casey.* Polls showed that 70 percent of those surveyed believed the Court got it about right. As William Schnieder wrote in *The Atlantic* magazine four months after the decision: "The debate over abortion seems to have no middle ground—except in public opinion." He noted that while support for abortion rights has edged upward over the past three years, half the country continues to say that abortion should be legal only "under certain circumstances."[61]

One does not need to agree with journalist William Saletan's position that conservatives have succeeded in shaping the current abortion contests to see the working out of this ambivalence in public opinion, judicial nominations, and legal decisions.[62] Sociologist Todd Gitlin argues that even abortion is not a single-issue veto topic for all voters, finding in his conversations with pro-life Pennsylvanians in the fall of 2004 that they were willing to support a pro-choice candidate in John Kerry because he agreed with their economic issues and displayed egalitarian values.[63] Political commentator E. J. Dionne Jr. adds: "Twenty-five percent of people who think abortion should always be legal voted for Bush. Twenty-two percent of people who thought abortion should always be illegal voted for Kerry. Now, that shows on the one hand a split, but on the other hand some crossing over on that issue."

Support for *Roe* remains at least at the 60 percent level, but this support is not necessarily viewed as being more "liberal." Perhaps *Roe* is now as normalized as Justice O'Connor meant when she said that people had reordered their lives around it. A 2004 ABC News poll found Americans generally favorable toward abortion by a 54 percent to 43 percent margin, while another poll that year found less support, suggesting the importance of the wording, the ambivalence of Americans, and the complexity of the topic.[64]

Writing for the Gallup poll, Lydia Saad identified poll findings around the time of Judge Alito's nomination: "When asked about their preference for changing abortion laws, only 38% of Americans favor making abortion laws more strict; most are generally content with keeping abortion legal, saying the laws should remain the same (39%) or be made less strict (20%)."[65] Ramesh Ponnuru reads these kinds of data differently, arguing that pollsters provide misinformation to the public, and that the routine finding that the public supports *Roe* so strongly is a mistaken conclusion amplified by a liberal media.[66]

Earlier, however, he had cited a report by a colleague that showed remarkable consistency in public support for *Roe* over thirty years:

> Karlyn Bowman, who studies public opinion for the American Enterprise Institute, has compiled poll data about abortion from several years into one handy document. . . . Her conclusion is that public opinion on the issue has been remarkably stable. When Gallup asked whether abortion should be available under all, some, or no circumstances, respondents split 21-54-22 in April 1975. In May 2005, they split 23-53-22. That is impressive stability.[67]

At the same time, Bowman's analysis reflects that, when data are looked at in this way, the largest proportion of Americans believe abortion should be available under "some circumstances" (roughly half of all Americans). These respondents can vary on exactly how limited the circumstances should be, providing encouragement for both pro-choice and pro-life activists.

A Pew Research Center poll and report explains how these views toward abortion vary by religious affiliation:

> While "pro-choice" advocates (those who would impose, at most, just "some limits") outnumber "pro-life" advocates (people who believe abortion should always be illegal or that there should be "many limits") by a narrow 52%-to-48% margin, there has been an eight-point gain for pro-life positions since 1992. Behind those figures lies a sharp division between traditionalists and modernists in each of the three major Christian traditions. Among Evangelical Protestants, for instance, traditionalists are overwhelmingly pro-life (84%-to-16%), while modernists favor the pro-choice position (63%-to-37%). A split also occurs among traditionalist and modernist Catholics and Mainline Protestants, although Catholics as a whole are more "pro-choice" than Evangelical Protestants, and Mainline Protestants are more "pro-choice" still. At

the same time, strong majorities of Latino Protestants, Latino Catholics and Black Protestants favor the "pro-life" positions. Non-Christians and people without formal religious affiliations tend to be "pro-choice."[68]

While there is agreement in many quarters that American public opinion has been steady for years regarding abortion, those involved on the battlefront have fervently desired to reframe the issue so as to move those who are uncommitted or ambivalent or moderate to their side of the debate. Thus, the emphasis on "partial-birth abortion"—a very uncommon procedure—serves to frame the pro-choice side as horrific.

Recently, a pro-life blogger took on California senator Dianne Feinstein's assessment of where Americans stand on abortion. Feinstein, the blogger charged, had slanted her reading of a 2005 ABC News/*Washington Post* poll in asserting that "60% of Americans support *Roe*." The reality of the poll was that 17 percent favored abortion being legal in all cases and 40 percent legal in most cases, while 27 percent responded "illegal in most cases," and 13 percent illegal in all cases.

A 2005 *Los Angeles Times* poll asked the questions differently, and while it had 43 percent of participants responding that abortion should be legal in all (24 percent) or most (19 percent) cases, fully 41 percent believed abortion should be illegal with a "few exceptions"—specifically cases of rape, incest, and to save a woman's life (with 12 percent responding "illegal in all cases"). Naturally, this begs the question of whether some of that 60 percent commonly referenced includes people who want *Roe* to exist because it allows for abortion in those extreme cases.[69]

Californians, as a 2006 Field poll indicated, are among the most pro-choice electorates in the union. According to the directors of the poll, "There has been little change in Californians' consistently pro-choice position about abortion laws over the past twenty years." Fully 71 percent of California's registered voters "want the current U.S. Supreme Court to uphold rather than overturn its *Roe v. Wade* decision should it come up again for review." Not surprisingly, both of California's U.S. senators, Dianne Feinstein and Barbara Boxer, voted against the confirmation of both John Roberts and Samuel Alito, with Feinstein serving on the Senate Judiciary Committee. Interestingly, this also includes a period when the state was reelecting Republican George Deukmejian; reelecting Republican Pete Wilson to the U.S. Senate; electing Wilson, admittedly pro-choice, as governor for two terms; and voting for Proposition 186, to limit services for undocumented persons, Proposition 227, to limit bilingual education, and Proposition 209, to limit affirmative action. What is clear, as sociologist Mark Baldassare has explained in a trend surfacing two decades ago, was the rise of the pro-business pro-choice Republican, someone not represented by the consistently pro-life national Republican Party platforms on abortion.[70] In this way, California resembles other states that have trended blue, if not Democratic, over that time period. Similarly, NARAL lists California at the top of the list of states that would be most likely to quickly and thoroughly reestablish protections similar to *Roe* if it were to be overturned. At the end of this chapter, we will examine differing views of what American abortion regulation would look like in a "post-*Roe*" era.

More polls reiterating the themes of American ambivalence on abortion appeared in 2006, supporting the "abortion gray" theme. In a later section, we will discuss how Democratic groups have argued for embracing this middle ground or third way as a means of turning around recent electoral defeats.

One article reported, "For all the recent tumult over abortion, one thing has remained surprisingly stable: Americans have proven extremely consistent in their beliefs about the procedure—and extremely conflicted in their view."[71]

Political scientist Morris Fiorina presents a strong case, backed up by analysis of electoral and attitudinal data, that Americans are more moderate on a range of issues—including central pieces of the culture war such as abortion and gay rights—than the polarized political elites and media would have us think. To Fiorina, most Americans are "ideological moderates."[72]

Sociologist Dalton Conley identifies the issue:

> Of course, most Americans seem to fall somewhere between these two positions. They support abortion rights, but they are also willing to accept restrictions on those rights. They do not think a fetus is the same as a person, but neither do they think of it as part and parcel of a woman's body like her appendix, a kidney or a tumor. They see a fetus as an individual under construction. Hence the almost universal support for abortion in the case of risk to the mother—why not opt for

protecting life that is already here on earth over something that is still, ultimately, potential?[73]

Law professor Jonathan Turley spoke to this ambivalence when he observed the following about the parental consent or parental notification debate:

> Most pro-choice Americans favor parental involvement in abortions for minors. It is a hard-core minority that resists any and all limitations. Yet, those are the zealots that tend to give money and seek positions in advocacy organizations. The result is that both the pro-life and pro-choice movements tend to be led by the most extreme, not the most representative, voices of their respective constituencies.[74]

Angela Bonavoglia makes a similar point about the "purpleness" of American Catholics:

> While the debate rages, the statistics show that in fact Americans, including Catholics, have begun to settle, clearly with unease on both sides, into a compromised middle ground where the majority favor abortion at least in some circumstances and reject making the procedure illegal. By polarizing the debate even further, using abortion as the litmus test of Catholicity and politicizing the Eucharist, the U.S. Bishops may be enlarging that middle ground.[75]

And the former head of the Bush administration's Office of Faith-Based Initiatives observes that Catholics are political centrists.[76] In this sense, members of the country's largest religion may be solidifying a moderate stance nationally on abortion, rather than leading the charge for dramatic changes.

Competing Frames: Imposing the "Partial-Birth Abortion" Frame

Still, even centrists and moderates and those who are ambivalent can be swayed by a successful conservative framing of the abortion issue, as has happened in the last decade with late-term abortions. There has been a marked ability of the pro-life movement to use its framing of "partial-birth abortion" to force pro-choice activists to defend a practice that a majority of Americans find distasteful. Susan Dominus acknowledges this successful framing: "The right was very dexterous in using partial birth abortion, and I don't think our side had good answers. The media shifted its attention from women's role to the details of this grisly procedure."[77]

George W. Bush's election as president in 2000, plus the shift in party control in the Senate during the 2002 elections, led directly to the enactment of a partial-birth abortion ban in November 2003—the first time since *Roe v. Wade* that lawmakers had succeeded in banning a particular abortion procedure. In May 2004, Senator Sam Brownback and Representative Chris Smith introduced a new bill that would require women seeking abortions at twenty weeks' gestation or later to be informed that a fetus at that age might feel pain, then given the option of accepting or declining—in writing—anesthetic for the fetus. These bills are part of what is "fundamentally an image-manipulation campaign" aimed at ambivalent Americans who think abortion is a woman's private decision yet commonly disapprove of the very reasons women give for seeking abortions.[78]

As Cynthia Gorney explains her compelling essay "Gambling with Abortion: Why Both Sides Think They Have Everything to Lose,"[79] the image-manipulation campaign started when an Ohio doctor and abortion clinic owner, Martin Haskell, presented a paper entitled "Dilation and Extraction for Late Second Trimester Abortion" at a 1992 meeting of the National Abortion Federation. Jenny Westberg, an occasional clinic protester with some experience in cartooning, got hold of Haskel's paper. Westberg is one of many pro-life activists who have managed to infiltrate the mailing lists of organizations like the National Abortion Federation. Westberg decided to write a short article about Haskell's procedure for a small antiabortion magazine in Portland, Oregon. She thought a few illustrations might go nicely with the article.

Westberg's five pen-and-ink illustrations have been seen around the world. They are remarkable for their simple yet compelling depiction of a pair of hands in surgical gloves holding a five-month-old fetus, demonstrating the moment at which the fetus goes limp and dies as the doctor works surgical instruments in and out of its skull. Westberg has said she had no idea her drawings would set off a chain of events that could end up reshaping American abortion law.

At the heart of the pro-life image manipulation campaign is an effort to get those who are ambivalent to look at abortion from the perspective of what actually takes place during the procedure. Gorney claims:

> For two decades the people who frame legal-abortion campaigns in this country had been working assiduously to keep the door to that procedure room shut, redirecting the national attention to the action beforehand and afterward: the *choice* to seek an abortion, the *decision* to have an abortion, the *values* inherent in a society that gives women the liberty to make this momentous decision without interference from the state. They had worried for years that if the general public were forced into a mangled-fetus-versus-women's-autonomy tradeoff, the mangled fetus would win.[80]

Abortion foes have long considered that sensible people who have been willing to tolerate choice in abortion would reconsider upon looking at graphic pictures of aborted babies. But, Gorney explains, "bloody tissue, the ripped-off arms and legs, the fetuses corroded by fluids injected to induce abortion by miscarriage—made for what right-to-life people came to regard as *a collective averting of the eyes*" (emphasis added).[81] Thus, it is the simple, almost cartoonish character of Jenny Westberg's drawings that makes them compelling to look at—and widely reproducible.

The Westberg drawings have been a boon for pro-life litigators, who realized immediately that passage of a law prohibiting partial-birth abortion would put defenders of choice in an inescapable bind. The Supreme Court had never allowed a ban of a particular abortion procedure, and pro-choice litigators were not about to cede ground there.

That, however, put pro-choice leaders in the very tenuous position of having to stand in the public spotlight and defend an undeniably gruesome procedure that ends thousands of healthy pregnancies every year. (In fact, 12 percent of the 1.3 million abortions performed in America are done after the twelfth week of gestation; after about thirteen weeks, a pregnancy is generally too far advanced for simple vacuum aspiration.) Kate Michelman—president of NARAL—admitted she was never confronted with a tougher issue. Michelman wearily recalls a 1995 meeting with NARAL executive vice president James Wagoner: "I remember us sitting in my office and James saying to me: 'Kate—this is a disaster' "[82]

Gorney describes the angst further:

"Silver platter" is another way this sentiment is sometimes expressed, among abortion doctors and abortion-rights advocates, or "gift-wrapped." By this they mean the swiftness, the devastating ease, with which they found themselves ceding their opponents control over the public imagination the month the first Partial-Birth Abortion Ban Act was introduced in Congress, nearly a decade ago.[83]

Pro-choice strategists further acknowledge that they briefly considered walking away from "the appalling gamble of a public fight."[84] The risk, of course, is that if a public fight turns people to considering what goes on in the procedure room, and gruesomeness becomes part of a new legal standard, then all procedures used in tens of thousands of abortions performed after about the twelfth week each year are in jeopardy.

As a legal strategy, Congress's partial-birth abortion ban, which makes the procedure a felony, is having its intended effect. Much of abortion law is written with an eye toward reaching a realigned Supreme Court—one with a majority of justices signaling a willingness to reexamine *Roe v. Wade* once again. The Court has overturned one partial-birth abortion ban already, in 2000, for its failure to include an exception for cases wherein a physician determines the procedure is necessary to safeguard the health of the mother. That was a Nebraska state law, and Congress carefully worded its federal ban to avoid some of the language that the Court ruled was unconstitutionally vague in the Nebraska law.

Congress's ban intentionally omits a health exception, however, and primarily for that reason, federal courts in California, Nebraska, and New York overturned the federal ban in 2003 and 2004. The newly aligned Roberts Court announced its decision to review the California case—on the very day that Justice Samuel Alito joined the Court in February 2006. In June 2006, the Court announced it would also review the Nebraska case. O'Connor was part of the majority in the Supreme Court's 5-to-4 decision to overturn the Nebraska state law in 2000—because it lacked a health exception. Alito, of course, has replaced O'Connor.

As a legal matter, the new cases involving the federal ban will center significantly on whether all abortion restrictions require an exception when the procedure is necessary to safeguard the health of the mother. But the essential backstory is the image-manipulation campaign aimed at the ambivalent masses, and the impact that may have on the future of *Roe v. Wade.*

Democrats Reframe

As the fallout from the perceived resurgence of the religious Right in the 2004 election was unfolding, there was a clear atmosphere of reassessment within progressive circles and Democratic strategy groups. Several analysts and strategists spoke of the belief that the Democratic Party's use of a litmus test for national candidates on the pro-choice position may have been limiting the ability to reach out to centrist voters. Recently defeated Democratic presidential nominee John Kerry advised a group of political activists that the party needed a bigger tent on abortion issues. This followed a campaign in which Kerry's pro-choice stance was attacked by bishops and others in his Catholic faith.[85]

Even as Kerry was arguing for a "big tent" on choice, activists such as Gloria Feldt, the president of Planned Parenthood of America, were calling for greater mobilization. As Feldt wrote: "The passage of the Partial-Birth Abortion Act was the culmination of a long-term strategy by right-wing extremists who have been working ever since *Roe* to take away a woman's right to control her reproductive destiny."[86]

Even New York senator Hillary Clinton, with an eye toward being the first woman nominated by a major party for president, argued for outreach to the pro-life voters in the Democratic Party, even as she argued to keep abortion "safe, legal and rare."[87] Former presidential candidate Howard Dean, on his way to becoming chair of the Democratic Party, offered a similar olive branch: "I have long believed that we ought to make a home for pro-life Democrats. The Democrats that have stuck with us, who are pro-life, through their long period of conviction, are people who are the kind of pro-life people that we ought to have deep respect for."[88]

In this way, as Arlene Joffe and Carole Skolnick, among others, have pointed out, the continued contestation of personal morality issues around the "moral values" debate gained further impetus with the 2004 elections, however overblown initial reports were in attributing the reelection of President Bush to such "values voters."[89]

None of the arguments in one April 2006 appeal letter for funds for the Democratic Party in that year's upcoming election had to do with abortion (or any of the culture-of-life issues). Nor did the emphases in the Center for American Progress or the Democracy Corps. Rather, the focus there was on the failure of the war in Iraq, the issue of corruption in Washington, and economic concerns, including health care.

At the same time, frequent romances of the Democratic Party with more red state politicians such as Virginia's Mark Warner or Montana's Brian Schweitzer may strike some as insincere, in the same way that calls for the Democrats to "get religion" in 2004 appeared to those on the opposite side as posturing. While one could view some of these efforts as the work of a cynical consultant, one would be hard-pressed to read and hear progressive religious figures such as Michael Lerner and Jim Wallis make clarion calls for an engagement on the role of religion in American political and social life, and not see the depth of their belief and commitment.

As with Senator Hillary Clinton's attempt to reframe efforts on abortion, the Third Way's Culture Project offered that the best way to position candidates, given Americans' support for *Roe* and ambivalence about abortion, is to promote the message: "I will work to dramatically reduce the number of abortions in America while protecting personal liberties." It remains to be seen if this attempt will truly capture the "abortion grays" who the Third Way analyzes—or the purplest of Americans. The danger is that it "comes across as defensive, confusing and disingenuous to average Americans." Rachel Laser, of the Third Way Culture Project, writes that the current progressive message on abortion "is perceived as devoid of moral complexity with one that addresses the deeper concerns of many Americans."[90]

Laser adds in a statement that resonates with Senator Clinton's appeal to make abortion "safe, legal and rare": "The fact is the majority of Americans are pro-choice, but the majority of Americans also see something sad in what this procedure does."[91] She concludes that, despite the fact that the "abortion grays" tend to be more pro-choice than pro-life, "strategic initiatives have helped conservatives win 'the battle of reasonableness.'" She advises:

Step #1: Realize that attempting to avoid the issue does not avoid the issue. Step #2: Define yourself as the candidate who will work to reduce the number of abortions, while protecting the right to have one. Step

#3: Define your opponent as seeking to criminalize abortion. Step #4: Have an agenda that finds common ground to reduce abortions.[92]

New Frames, New Battles: The Morning-After Pill and the HPV Vaccine

In the 1960s, the birth control pill revolutionized sexual activity in America. By making sexual activity less likely to lead to pregnancy, the pill allowed a generation of women (and men) to be sexually active with fewer of the consequences faced by their predecessors, especially given that abortion itself was also being sought as a candidate for law liberalization. The success of modern pharmaceutical science allowed a dramatic change in mores and behavior.

Today, another pharmaceutical advance is offering to reshape the face of American contraception, although the battle that is being waged by social conservatives does not even cede the point that it is a contraceptive that is being discussed. To them, the "morning-after pill" is a form of abortion, an abortifacent (even though it blocks implantation, and the American College of Obstetricians and Gynecologists holds that pregnancy begins at implantation, not fertilization). This has resulted in attempts to prevent the morning-after pill, described as "Plan B" in its development, from being available as an over-the-counter drug, as the scientific panels of the Federal Drug Administration have determined.

Plan B, or levonorgestrel (a product of Barr Pharmaceuticals), is referred to as the "morning-after pill" for a reason: it is most effective when used within twenty-four hours after unprotected sex. Although it may work as long as seventy-two hours after intercourse, speed is of the essence. Thus, efforts to slow down the process—requiring doctor visits and prescriptions, for example—render the morning-after pill ineffective.

Key institutional bodies had expressed support for the Plan B approval: the American Academy of Pediatrics, the Society for Adolescent Medicine, and the relevant committees of the FDA, including a 23-to-4 vote for the Plan B option.[93]

The U.S. General Accounting Office (GAO) report on the FDA's handling of the morning-after pill, and political responsiveness to social conservative lobbying, set off a round of commentary on the practice and the process.[94] Senators Hillary Clinton and Patty Murray held up the approval of the interim FDA director as permanent director until the Plan B situation was resolved. In protest, Dr. Susan Wood, the director of the Office of Women's Health at the FDA, resigned, saying: "I saw it as a win-win situation, something that everyone on both sides of the issue could support," given that the abortion rate would drop.[95]

Because the relevant federal bodies have been slow in acting, power devolved to the states and brought about a mixed map of America in which progressive or blue states are moving toward ensuring the right to Plan B, as eight states have already done. Because of the timeliness of the pill, pharmacists are allowed to provide the drug without a doctor's prescription, coming close to the over-the-counter distribution contemplated by the pharmaceutical company and the FDA scientists and panels.

It has been interesting to note how the Internet—both because of its use as the preferred medium of information gathering and because of its speed—can reduce the burden of locating important information for the women involved. Web sites such as EC-help.org direct an inquiring person to a pharmacy in her zip code that has pharmacists ready to dispense Plan B without a doctor's visit in the eight states that allow it.

Social conservatives attempted to stem the dispersal of Plan B in the states in which it was approved. One focus was on the retail giant Wal-Mart. While Wal-Mart was still under pressure from pro-choice groups to loosen its conscientious objector clause for pharmacists, NARAL Pro-Choice America complimented it on its eventual decision to allow its pharmacies to prescribe Plan B: "Many of us never thought we'd be thanking Wal-Mart (of all companies!) but, please, express your appreciation to Wal-Mart for doing the right thing."[96]

The paradox, the working out of which remains to be seen, has to do with the fact that Plan B is presumably most often going to be used by young, single women, who are in fact the primary group utilizing abortion (and contraception, for that matter). While the issues of privacy, autonomy, and women's health constitute the frame used by Planned Parenthood and the pro-choice activists for Plan B, these issues also veer close to the issue of parental consent and underage women, where American public opinion is much stronger against. While not as graphic as late-term or partial-birth abortion, Plan B comes much closer to the disapproval of sex that has run through critiques of abortion and contraception for forty years. This is clearly the direction in which the governors of Massachusetts and other states have gone, in terms of limiting the availability of Plan B. It borrows a page from the classic playbook of the pro-life movement, with its attempts to block access to clinics and to impose a number of waiting periods—in this case beyond the pill's effective period. This is why Dr. Wood's concept of Plan B as a "win-win" development misses the mark, since contraception is at odds with the social-religious conservative strategies and paradigm.[97]

Eventually, the FDA relented. In August 2006 it approved over-the-counter sales of Plan B for women over age eighteen, keeping it as a prescription drug for women seventeen and under.[98]

In the same year, controversy also developed over the Centers for Disease Control's approval of a vaccine against the human papillomavirus (HPV), which can cause cervical cancer. Although the Pap smear procedure is an effective screening mechanism for this for HPV, the vaccine would offer a significant level of prevention.

Clinical reports on the HPV vaccine marvel at its efficacy and describe it as a potential "major public health advance against cervical cancer and other, less common cancers."[99] The chair of the Food and Drug Administration's Advisory Committee on Immunization Practices called the data on efficacy "absolutely stunning."[100]

What concerned social conservatives was the message that the availability—or even requirement—of the vaccine would send to adolescent girls, for whom social conservatives were preaching abstinence as the primary form of birth control. A CDC researcher had told the Advisory Committee on Immunization Practices in Atlanta that for the vaccine to be fully effective, it would probably need to be given to adolescents before they had sex—so health officials have considered giving the vaccine at age eleven, twelve, or earlier.[101]

One examination focused on social conservative activists who oppose childhood vaccination for HPV because it "removes a disincentive to having sex." Some conservatives "have even stated that they would feel similarly about an H.I.V. vaccine."[102]

Bridget Maher of the Family Research Council represented this position when she said: "Abstinence is the best way to prevent HPV. . . . giving the HPV vaccine to young women could be potentially harmful, because they may see it as a licence to engage in premarital sex."[103]

Eventually, social conservatives withdrew their opposition to the vaccine per se and spent their energy on making sure that it was not included in a package of immunizations required for school attendance. The FDA licensed the HPV vaccine in June 2006.[104] At the same time, pro-choice and women's health advocates hailed the fact that the expensive vaccine would be covered for low-income women through an existing government vaccination support program.[105] The state of New Hampshire acted in November 2006 to be the first state to provide the vaccine free for all girls, a development that may be modeled in other states.[106]

It will be interesting to see what the effect of the availability of the morning-after pill will be. One reason that pro-life activists oppose Plan B is not only because it can be easily disseminated and used but also because it blurs the image and shifts the frame closer to the birth control concept, thus making it harder to paint pro-choice people negatively (as partial-birth abortion has). As Page and others have claimed, this reveals the emphasis that social conservatives have on preventing effective contraception.[107]

After Roe? *The Meaning of South Dakota 2006 and Beyond*

The first legislative shot across the bow in the Roberts-Alito era came when the governor of South Dakota signed legislation in March 2006 making that state the only state to be challenging *Roe*. The South Dakota legislature decided to up the ante in challenging *Roe v. Wade*. It took direct aim at *Roe* by passing a law restricting abortion to only those cases involving the life of the mother. It did not even bother to include rape and incest, two categories of exceptions that had been begrudgingly admitted by many social conservatives as a key to attracting moderate support.

The proposed action in South Dakota was draconian by comparison to other states' laws and general American access. But one observer, the author of a recent book about his physician father and abortion providers, argued that South Dakota's action instead codified what had been a steady slide into lack of access there and in similar states over the last decade. Eyal Press echoed the complaints of many in the pro-choice community: 87 percent of American counties do not have an abortion provider.[108] Since 1982, pro-choice advocates note, the number of abortion providers has declined by 87 percent in the country.[109]

A diminishing percentage of abortions are performed in hospitals, with stand-alone clinics the most common provider—and an easier target for protesters. One of the reasons that South Dakota was a likely state to initiate such a facial challenge to existing law was that the lone provider in that state works out of a Sioux City Planned Parenthood clinic, flying in weekly from neighboring Minnesota.[110]

The South Dakota legislature was portrayed as so uncaring as to essentially prohibit abortion except, as one observer said of the comments by a state legislator to a PBS interviewer, with the "Sodomized Religious Virgin Exception":

> A real-life description to me would be a rape victim, brutally raped, savaged. The girl was a virgin. She was religious. She planned on saving her virginity until she was married. She was brutalized and raped, sodomized as bad as you can possibly make it, and is impregnated. I mean, that girl could be so messed up, physically and psychologically, that carrying that child could very well threaten her life.[111]

A South Dakota coalition mounted an effort to have a November 2006 ballot measure to rescind the law. Following the classic framing strategy identified by Lakoff and others, their group was called the South Dakota Campaign for Healthy Families.[112] A committee of the Ohio legislature passed a similar bill in June 2006. Louisiana's governor signed a bill similar to that in South Dakota, although it would take effect only if *Roe* is overturned, one of many such bills.[113] To that extent, the threat posed by laws like South Dakota's stringent 2006 abortion law was used by NARAL and other organizations to broadcast the frame of threat to moderate women of all ages.

Different visions of a post-*Roe* America, some more sanguine than others, have emerged from analysts of varying viewpoints. To Cristina Page, a NARAL official, "the day after *Roe* is overturned, the right to abortion will be threatened, if not quickly made illegal, in no fewer than twenty-one states."[114] To Stuart Taylor it would be a disaster for Republicans, who have been able to engage their social conservative base by sending forward judges to overturn *Roe,* while not losing moderates by actually eviscerating it.[115] To Ramesh Ponnuru, as efforts turned to state legislatures, there would be as much vulnerability as opportunity for Democrats, as pro-life advocates enforced the partial-birth frame.[116] To Jeffrey Rosen, the outcome would be a beneficial return to democracy in the states, a third of which would keep current protections, a third of which would choose to criminalize, and a third of which would have more restrictive laws short of criminalization.[117] To Gorney, "In many ways, the overturning of *Roe v. Wade* would be a loss for the Republican Party. It's much more useful to hold up the decision as a spectre. It serves their interests better. If *Roe* were overturned, it would change things in very unpredictable ways."[118] With more than thirty years of living arranged around the reproductive freedom Americans enjoy, it is difficult to see the clock being turned back, but some states are clearly more interested than others in a return to pre-1973 society.

Justice O'Connor discussed her opinion in *Casey,* according to her biographer: "She explained that although the justices might not agree with *Roe v. Wade,* people had lived with it, reordered their lives around it."[119]

Younger Americans have reached adulthood in an era in which the compromises of *Casey* and the upholding of *Roe* in that decision have been the law of the land. And almost all American women of childbearing age have grown up in the post-*Roe* era. At a practical level—if not a social, philosophical, moral, ethical, or religious level—this can have significant implications. We now have more women than men graduating from medical school, something probably not contemplated even when women surpassed men as law school graduates. Even as there has been a decline in the number of working mothers, the nature of gender roles and the status of women in the work world have changed inexorably.[120]

At the same time, Dominus has argued that the new cohort of young adult women are less likely to consider themselves pro-choice. One argument for this finding is that they are years removed from the struggle of original feminists who fought for the rights enshrined in *Roe v. Wade* regarding reproductive freedom and other feminist issues. According to a CBS poll, the proportion of American women aged eighteen to twenty-nine who answered in the affirmative to the question of whether "abortion should be available to any women who wants one" has dropped from almost 50 percent to 35 percent. In this view, to these young women, abortion

> doesn't have the appeal it had in the seventies—in part because back then, the right to have an abortion was indirectly tied to a woman's right to pursue a career. It was tied to women having all sorts of rights. Now we have those rights! So young women are questioning abortion and looking for other solutions to the challenges that pregnant women and young parents experience.[121]

In this way, pro-choice advocates have to confront the recent inroads their pro-life opponents have made with the partial-birth abortion frame, although they can take some solace in the poll results supporting *Roe v. Wade.*

Which framing attempt will succeed in the battle for the moderates and the ambivalent? Mark Kleiman argues that the combination of effects from the South Dakota law and the Plan B and HPV controversies may present enough of an example of overreach that it could galvanize some support for pro-choice politicians and positions among the purple or gray moderates:

> Is it possible that the combination of the South Dakota abortion law, the Plan B fiasco, and the HPV vaccine scandal can start to convince suburban "security moms" that reproductive freedom is really at risk if they keep voting Republican? How about a nice TV spot with a cervical cancer victim and a scientist in a white jacket explaining that the vaccine is ready but is being held up by bureaucrats and politicians?[122]

Laser and the Third Way Culture Project are in step with Senator Clinton, Joffe,[123] and others when they argue that the South Dakota law provides an opportunity for progressive parties and the pro-choice movement and electoral politics to effectively assert their framing: "We can dramatically reduce the number of abortions in America while protecting personal liberties. The South Dakota abortion ban reveals the conservatives' goal: reducing abortions through criminalization and incarceration."[124]

The November 2006 election provided one clear result: the rejection of the South Dakota abortion ban.[125] NARAL Pro-Choice America celebrated this event: "South Dakotans struck down the draconian abortion ban imposed by anti-choice politicians by a 10-point margin."[126] An ACLU attorney celebrated: "Voters sent a clear message to the legislature that they had gone too far."[127] NARAL also heralded the election of numerous pro-choice congressional representatives among the Democrats elected to the 100th Congress. The election results also had the effect of reducing the attention paid to the November 8, 2006, Supreme Court hearing of the congressional partial-birth abortion bill.[128]

The U.S. Supreme Court ruled in April 2007 on the late-term abortion case involving a congressional ban on certain specific forms of intact dilation and evacuation, which opponents of the practice had termed partial-birth abortion. In a shift from its prior decision on similar state cases, the court ruled 5 to 4 that the congressional ban was constitutional, did not need to provide additional waivers and exceptions, and would stand. Additionally, any state lawmaking that followed the same principles would be allowed.[129] Writing for the five-member majority, Kennedy stated: "The Act, on its face, is not void for vagueness and does not impose an undue burden from any overbreadth."[130]

In her spirited dissent, Justice Ruth Bader Ginsburg (joined by three colleagues) not only disagreed with the majority's conclusions but reiterated her long-standing belief that equality, more than privacy, should be the basis of a woman's right to choose.[131] Not surprisingly, Kennedy was joined in his opinion by recent Bush appointees Roberts and Alito (as well as conservative justices Scalia and Thomas), a situation that made the issue of presidential election and selection of justices a focal point for critics, with an eye on court openings in the term of whoever is elected in 2008.

As might be expected, the reaction from ardent pro-life and pro-choice forces was swift and certain. Gary Bauer expressed, "I am greatly encouraged today. The United States Supreme Court has upheld the 2003 ban on partial-birth abortions! . . . Not only will this ruling put an end to this particularly horrific form of infanticide, but it represents a tremendous victory for the American people. . . . And while we are still a long way from fully restoring the right to life in America, we have succeeded in ending abortion-on-demand at anytime, for any reason, by any method."[132]

NARAL rallied its supporters with a headline stating, "For the first time since *Roe,* this ban makes no exception for a woman's health!" The group later encouraged engagement and action, since "the Court's decision is a perfect example of why next year's presidential election matters so much."[133] Critics also chided Justice Kennedy for basing part of his opinion on the indecisiveness of the pregnant woman, echoing Justice Ginsburg's dissent.[134]

Since it was a physician-chosen procedure that was being foreclosed, the *New England Journal of Medicine* reacted in an editorial and in a lead article that argued against the decision, stating: "The greatest uncertainty of all concerns the continued viability of any right to abortion in all but imminently life-threatening situations," and "with this decision the Supreme Court has sanctioned the intrusion of legislation into the day-to-day practice of medicine."[135]

Candidates for the party nominations of the Democratic and Republican parties, with campaigns forming early for an unusual race with no sitting president or vice president standing for election, responded in a short time as well. Senator Hillary Clinton offered a nuanced opinion: "As the Supreme Court recognized in *Roe v. Wade* in 1973, this issue is complex and highly personal; the rights and lives of women must be taken into account. It is precisely this erosion of our constitutional rights that I warned against when I opposed the nominations of Chief Justice Roberts and Justice Alito." Senator Barack Obama was more direct: "I strongly disagree with today's Supreme Court ruling, which dramatically departs from previous precedents safeguarding the health of pregnant women." Senator John McCain favored the decision, saying, "The ruling ensures that an unacceptable and unjustifiable practice will not be carried out on our innocent children."[136]

A few articles and opinion pieces emphasized the limited nature of the ruling, given the range of abortion procedures and decisions not reached by the court's ruling.[137] Still, with no organized constituency for that reading of the decision, and the fervent statements by those who interpreted the ruling as presaging a change in the court's general reproductive rights approach, it seemed unlikely to be a position embraced in the electoral campaign to follow.

While it is naturally too early to determine how this issue and the role of the Supreme Court will play out over the next few years, it is clear that the *Carhart* decision has the capacity to reenergize the polarizing nature of the reproductive rights debate in this country, as both sides in that debate focus on the possibility of a rollback of the provisions of *Roe v. Wade*.

Even as the abortion debate has raged on throughout the years since the *Roe v. Wade* decision as the primary culture war topic, it was often eclipsed in the last few years by the issue of gay rights, and in particular same-sex marriage, as an issue that got the social religious side talking and acting. It is to that topic, which has shared some institutional opposition with abortion, that we now turn.

4

Gay Rights
Beyond Tolerance and Privacy to Equality

It's not gonna be that way.
> —Ennis Del Mar in *Brokeback Mountain* (2005)

It's time we learn from our mistakes and acknowledge that lesbian and gay Americans . . . speak the vocabulary of marriage, live the personal commitment of marriage, do the hard work of marriage, and share the responsibilities we associate with marriage. It's time to allow them the same freedom every other American has—the freedom to marry.
> —Evan Wolfson, *Why Marriage Matters* (2004)

Your children and grandchildren will be taught that homosexuality is normal and same-sex unions equally valid to heterosexual marriages. So-called "hate crimes" laws will make sure that anyone who objects is silenced.
> —Gary Bauer, American Values

Who cares?
> —Billy Crystal's Aunt Sheila, referring to the imminent marriage of her daughter and another woman, as told in his play *700 Sundays* (Billy Crystal *700 Sundays*, 2006)

Wedding Day in San Francisco

San Francisco has long been regarded as one of America's most liberal cities, so it was little surprise that it was there that the gay marriage debate was turned up a notch in February 2004. Newly elected mayor Gavin Newsom, the favored successor of the popular mayor and former state assembly speaker Willie Brown, and most of the Democratic establishment, had narrowly survived a runoff election against a grass roots–inspired county supervisor and Green Party member. As in Berkeley, the smaller city across the San Francisco Bay, San Francisco politics had often been a case of liberals versus progressives, contests that much of the country would find unusual. Nonetheless, they were real contests, involving key values in the eyes of the combatants, such as over downtown power versus neighborhood interests.

So it was somewhat of a surprise that one of Newsom's first major acts as mayor was a proclamation that same-sex couples would be allowed to marry in San Francisco. Before the California Supreme Court ordered San Francisco to stop marrying same-sex couples on March 11, more than 4,000 had already been issued marriage licenses in San Francisco, a coterminous city and county, acting with its county authority.[1] Lines of applicants snaked around city hall in the rain. Hotels began to market to the San Francisco gay marriage business, offering special packages, and hotels in other cities that were recognizing such marriages, such as Portland, Oregon, followed suit. Meanwhile, in Massachusetts, in anticipation of the first legal marriages there as a result of a state supreme court ruling, hotels readied packages, such as their "Love in the City" offer, specifically aimed at newly married gay customers.[2]

The first couple married in San Francisco had been Phyllis Lyon and Del Martin, seventy-nine and eighty-three, respectively, two women who had been together as a couple for fifty-one years. These longtime lesbian activists had founded America's first lesbian rights group, Daughters of Bilitis, in 1955, and Martin had authored several books and established a reputation as an expert on domestic violence. Together, they were the subjects of an award-winning documentary, *No Secret Anymore* (2003), which one publicity article referred to as "tracing the emergence of lesbians from the fear of discovery to the expectation of equality."[3] Their lives exemplified the crucial history described by Suzanna Walters in which she identifies the importance of the process of gays and lesbians coming from the shadows—the "closet," in common usage—as key to understanding their social and political struggles over the past few decades.[4]

The president of the National Organization for Women referred to the San Francisco decision as a turning point in the fight for equal marriage rights. "The right to civil marriage for same-sex couples is an essential step on the road to full equality," NOW president Kim Gandy said. "Every American, regardless of their sexual orientation, deserves access to the more than 1,000 legal protections and benefits in state and federal law that a legal marriage brings."[5]

It was an apt and moving spectacle to see the marriages taking place in San Francisco's grand city hall, the scene of so much violence and sadness not many years before. It was in city hall that former supervisor Dan White had shot and killed liberal mayor George Moscone and then, separately, Supervisor Harvey Milk, one of America's first openly gay elected officials (as recounted in the documentary *The Times of Harvey Milk*).[6]

California was a good place for an action like Mayor Newsom's, since the state was generally progressive on social issues, even in some otherwise notoriously conservative enclaves, and had passed a landmark domestic partner law in 2003. That bill, AB 205, sponsored by Los Angeles assembly member Jackie Goldberg, provided domestic partners with "nearly all the rights, benefits, and responsibilities granted to spouses under state law."[7] California had inched along in the gay and lesbian rights protection area in the previous decade, lagging behind other states like Wisconsin, which had been the first to adopt a statewide antidiscrimination measure in 1982.[8] By 2004, twelve American states had adopted some form of antidiscrimination measures, including Massachusetts and Vermont. Many cities and counties in California had enacted such legislation in the 1980s. In addition, by March 2004, an estimated 25,000 couples had registered in California as domestic partners.[9]

Polls taken soon after Newsom's actions reflected both the progressive nature of the San Francisco Bay Area citizenry and the changing opinions—and ambivalence and divided loyalties—of the American public. An analysis of thirty years of poll results by the conservative organization American Enterprise Institute in 2004 found a range of growth in popular support of gay rights, even with a majority in opposition to gay marriage.[10] The events surrounding gay marriage in 2004 in the United States would further explore that ambivalence.

As writers Lacey Fosburgh and Frances FitzGerald discuss, San Francisco has been a tolerant and wide-open city, from its past as a port city, influenced by the male influx around the gold rush of the nineteenth century, up to the present. San Francisco is, as FitzGerald quotes Fosburgh, "tolerant of unconventional behavior, tolerant of diversity, it became an outpost 'for everything that was strange and different' and 'a mecca for people who wanted to change their lives, break with the past.'"[11]

But it was not that different from the rest of the United States, where much had shifted regarding sexual orientation and tolerance of homosexuality in the previous two decades. Newsom's initiatives occurred soon after the high court in Massachusetts had ruled in favor of gay marriage in that state, leading to the first wedding on May 19, 2004. And the state of Vermont had pioneered civil unions for same-sex couples.[12] Even though later in 2004 the California Supreme Court would invalidate the San Francisco marriages, the topic of gay marriage was discussed in ways that could not have been contemplated ten years earlier. Meanwhile, other Western countries, such as Belgium, Canada, and the Netherlands, had adopted same-sex marriage laws.

San Francisco had its own notable heritage as a gay rights center over the previous three decades. The city, which was known for attracting and tolerating, even championing, bohemians and beatniks in the 1950s and hippies in the 1960s, claimed a large gay and lesbian community by the 1970s. Frances FitzGerald, in an incisive chapter in her book *Cities on a Hill*, cites an estimate that one in every five adults in San Francisco in 1978 was gay or lesbian.[13]

San Francisco, through its defiance of California state law, had stolen some of the thunder of the state of Massachusetts, where the high court had ruled in favor of gay marriage in February 2004. Moreover, that court, when asked by the Massachusetts legislature whether it would be open to legislative enactment of a Vermont-style civil unions scheme, fired back with a second ruling that set May 2004 as the first date for legal same-sex marriage to take place in Massachusetts. The first gay marriage in Massachusetts took place on May 17, 2004; it was estimated that 1,700 marriages licenses had been applied for in the first month.[14]

Because of the prominence of religious and social conservatives in the coalition that had helped elect him in 2000, President Bush reacted to the twin marriage events by announcing his support for a constitutional amendment banning same-sex marriage, saying: "The union of a man and a woman is the most enduring human institution, honored and encouraged in all cultures and by every religious faith. . . . Marriage cannot be severed from its cultural, religious and natural roots without weakening the good influence of society."[15]

A week before Newsom's actions, a CNN poll had found that Americans ranked the importance of gay marriage for their November vote seventeenth on a list of priorities, far below terrorism, war, and the economy. American debate on this topic flared up, then retreated as a key issue in the early months of the 2004 presidential campaign, as both sides realized that American attitudes toward civil unions, domestic partnerships, and gay marriage were strident in some groups, more nuanced in some cases, and more ambivalent in others, while decidedly not favoring same-sex marriage.

Normalization: Seeing the "Blue" in America

Still, the signs of normalization were also alive in 2004. The Sunday "Style" section of the *New York Times* is an entertaining diversion from the hard-news stories of war deaths, suicide bombings, and congressional conflict. One of its core features is the several-page spread of wedding announcements, complete with photographs, of engaged or recently married couples. Befitting New York, the photos portray individuals of diverse ages and races, though usually with a significant pedigree of family standing or personal accomplishment (or both). Starting in 2002, the newspaper changed its policy to allow same-sex partners to appear in the section. Although the *Times* was not the first newspaper to do so in the United States (reportedly dozens of others had done so as well, although at a much lower profile), this change in the national newspaper of record offered a look into the changing mores of Americans and the normalization of same-sex relationships.[16]

While 2004 may be remembered for the political fallout from the raising of the gay marriage issue—in legal decisions, extralegal actions, church pronouncements, and philosophical discussions—the common ground that did exist was downplayed in favor of the contestation that made for better media coverage. According to those measures, a majority of Americans favor at least the establishment of civil unions for same-sex couples.[17] Clearly, only a minority of Americans favor allowing same-sex marriages. At the same time, clearly only a minority of Americans support a constitutional amendment opposing gay marriage (such as the 56 percent in the November 2004 *New York Times*–CBS poll).[18] Taken by itself, the majority support for civil unions is a remarkable figure, especially given that only one state (Vermont) at that time allowed them, and that they were controversial not long ago. This trend can be seen as signifying the increasing support among a majority of Americans for a range of legal protections for gays and lesbians, beginning with city and county antidiscrimination ordinances in the 1970s.

Even as there has been a definite growth in tolerance on gay rights issues since 1973, there has also been a resulting backlash that has activated the conservative religious movement and led to specific opposition to legal advances. Gay rights has become the equivalent of abortion for social conservatives, who use it to rally supporters, raise funds, and show electoral and legislative (and boycotting) success in various states. For example, in 2004, eleven states voted on definition-of-marriage acts in the November election. In 2006, Alabama became the twentieth state to approve a defense of marriage act (DOMA). In 2006, eight additional states voted on such initiatives, including a first-time defeat of a DOMA ballot initiative in Arizona.[19]

Anti–Gay Rights Sentiment: Reds in Full Flowering

It would be easy to picture the anti–gay rights movement as being religiously inspired and obsessed. Leaders of the movement themselves would bristle at that conceptualization, however, and offer that they are the "pro-family" movement, in a nation in which an institution as central and sacred as the traditional family is under attack by the courts, the media, libertine activists, and the forces of modernity. Still, whatever the support for this movement in America, it has managed to be successful in a number of arenas.

Many of the groups rallying around the traditional family banner are themselves religious groups aligned with American evangelical and fundamentalist Protestant churches. Key participants in this sector include Gary Bauer and his American Values organization, the American Family Association, the late Reverend Jerry Falwell, the Christian Coalition, Renew America, Focus on the Family, Liberty Counsel, the Family Research Council, the Arlington Group, and Justice Sunday. A statement of the Traditional Values Coalition is representative:

Homosexuality, Bi-sexuality, Transgenderism, and Other Deviant Sexual Behaviors: The Bible clearly condemns all sexual behaviors outside of marriage between one man and one woman. Homosexual behavior is explicitly condemned in both the Old and New Testaments as an abomination and a violation of God's standards for sexuality. We oppose the normalization of sodomy as well as cross-dressing and other deviant sexual behaviors in our culture.

An organization committed to the reversal of gay identities in gays and lesbians—the "ex-gay movement"—adds further framing on the "life-style choice theme: "Homosexuality is a frivolous and malleable life-style choice."[20]

One writer from Dr. James Dobson's Focus on the Family answers the question of "What do gays really want?"

While winning the right to marry may be the "crown jewel" of the gay-rights movement, what homosexuals really want is for homosexuality to be declared normative, natural and God-ordained. Their deepest desire is that homosexual behavior would no longer be sin. At its core, the homosexual *zeitgeist* seeks to destroy God's created intent for sexuality and the family while deconstructing the *imago dei* that humans bear— male and female—on the Earth.

Truly an epic battle is being waged both in the spirit and the flesh. As Bible-believing Christians, we are being called to defend one of the most fundamental principles of God's created order—marriage between one man and one woman. In love and compassion, we must reflect God's heart on the matter and commit to fully engage those in the public arena who seek to declare "good" that which God calls "evil."

Lon Mabon, a leader of the Oregon Citizens Alliance in a 1994 campaign for an anti–gay rights initiative, expressed his sense of what troubled him—what sociologists call "problem consciousness"—in this way: "We're going to lose America as we know it." His wife added: "You're not going to take this culture another inch down that road."[21]

The director of the Family Foundation of Virginia put it this way: "This is about so much more than two individuals who might love each other but don't happen to be a man and a woman. . . . This is about redefining an institution that has been a bedrock of society for all of history."[22]

Gary Bauer represents this position well:

The American people do not see traditional marriage as a partisan issue. The people—Republicans and Democrats alike—overwhelmingly oppose same-sex "marriage." Unfortunately, for many liberals same-sex "marriage" is a litmus test issue, and the militant homosexual-rights movement has a lot of money.[23]

Even Justice Scalia talks about the "product of a Court, which is the product of a law-profession culture that has largely signed on to the so-called homosexual agenda."

> Gay-marriage proponents use the language of openness, tolerance and diversity, yet one foreseeable effect of their success will be to usher in an era of intolerance and discrimination the likes of which we have rarely seen before. Every person and every religion that disagrees will be labeled as bigoted and openly discriminated against. The ax will fall most heavily on religious persons and groups that don't go along. Religious institutions will be hit with lawsuits if they refuse to compromise their principles.[24]

Tying in with the anti–gay rights initiative language of "no special rights," religious conservative critics like the American Family Association's Donald Wildmon argue that gay activists in America are over-emphasizing their "suffering" and are, indeed, doing much better financially than their heterosexual counterparts:

> The spokesman says . . . "We must cut off the suffering." That is, the homosexual suffering. You know, I saw yesterday how much—how much money the homosexual community has. I mean, good gracious, the average homosexual makes four times more than I do. . . . I mean, they're not—these people are not in poverty or hurting or denied or anything else.[25]

Focus on the Family also refers to "today's 'gay-affirmative' culture."[26] At a more provocative level, also referring to the pattern of normalization, conservative author Ann Coulter complained about the movement from invisibility and oppression for gays and lesbians to visibility and celebration of equality: "As Pat Buchanan said, homosexuality has gone from 'the love that dare not speak its name' to 'the love that won't shut up.' "[27] Coulter was in part referencing the national attention paid to the film *Brokeback Mountain,* depicting the lives of two sheepherders in a definitely less hospitable place and time than the Hollywood of 2006.

While *Brokeback Mountain* received critical reviews and support of the Academy of Motion Picture Arts and Sciences, nominated for best picture and earning an Oscar for best adapted screenplay, social conservative critics pointed to its popularity as a thin creation of the media elites,[28] emphasizing exactly what sort of influence the cultural elite in the cosmopolitan blue states had:

> I've never watched the Golden Globes, but it's apparently an awards show that honors the contributions of homosexuals in film. Or maybe it honors films about homosexuals. Anyhow, it definitely has something to do with gay people and it was on last night. Felicity Huffman won best actress for playing a transsexual in Transamerica, a movie that has grossed $506,000 (I didn't omit any zeroes) after 46 days in theaters. Philip Seymour Hoffman, who was excellent as a gay man in Boogie Nights, won best actor for playing gay author Truman Capote in the biopic Capote. After more than 100 days in the theaters, Capote has grossed $13,266,000. Brokeback Mountain, a film about gay cowboys, won best drama and earned Ang Lee the best director nod. Despite free publicity on par with The Passion of the Christ, Brokeback Mountain has not broken the bank. It's taken in $32,088,000 after 39 days. The rest of the world might think we're all gay from watching our movies. They would discover that we're not if they saw all the empty seats.

Decrying the inroads into attempts to promote the "gay agenda" in the macho world of cowboys (apparently including sheepherders), a social religious spokeswoman complained that *Brokeback Mountain* subverted a sacred American symbol. "Their major agenda is to make this normal," said Janice Crouse of the group Concerned Women for America.[29]

Beyond being neutral or nonjudgmental in matters of sexual orientation, these groups also perceive the state as adapting policies that support and indeed privilege gay orientation, including in educational matters. In 2006, the California legislature passed a bill that would require K–12 textbooks to acknowledge the contributions of the gay and lesbian community and movements for equality. In California and elsewhere, "ex-gay" groups have been petitioning to have their perspective aired, claiming that failing to do so would be a form of discrimination.[30]

Family policy expert Arlene Skolnick also identifies this critique as one aimed by social conservatives at the deterioration of the "traditional" family, with all its elements of patriarchy. These same critics argue for greater primacy of the two-parent family and place many of the ills of modern American society at the feet of our marriage practices—with same-sex marriage set aside for now:

> Their argument is, we live in a "post-marital," "post-nuclear family" society. Marriage has disappeared as a cultural ideal. A "culture" or ideology of liberation and self-fulfillment, originating in the 1960s and sustained by the liberal elite, has spread throughout the society, leading to the disintegration of the two-parent family and the desertion of their children by vast numbers of men. Single parenthood, or "fatherlessness," whether it occurs in the inner city or the suburbs or through divorce or out-of wedlock birth, is a tragedy for children, and a catastrophe for the rest of society. It is the direct cause of our worst individual and social problems: poverty, crime, violence, delinquency, drug and alcohol abuse, school failure, teenage pregnancy, welfare dependency. In short, it is the number one domestic problem facing the country, because it drives all the rest.[31]

It is this level of perceived deterioration that piques conservatives like Senator Rick Santorum, who says:

> We have laws in states, like the one at the Supreme Court right now, that has sodomy laws and they were there for a purpose. Because, again, I would argue, they undermine the basic tenets of our society and the family. And if the Supreme Court says that you have the right to consensual sex within your home, then you have the right to bigamy, you have the right to polygamy, you have the right to incest, you have the right to adultery. You have the right to anything.[32]

As with so many issues, the concept of the slippery slope is utilized in this same-sex marriage case. Gary Bauer articulates his version of the slippery slope argument against gay marriage:

> The Senate Judiciary Committee will soon begin debate on a federal marriage protection amendment. We got another unfortunate reminder recently of why this amendment is so necessary. Parents in Lexington,

Massachusetts, are up-in-arms over a teacher's decision to read the fairy tale book "King & King" to her second grade class. The story is about a prince who cannot find "true love" until he meets another prince!

This is the future of public education in America, and it is one more example of how same-sex "marriage" impacts all marriages. Your children and grandchildren will be taught that homosexuality is normal and same-sex unions equally valid to heterosexual marriages. So-called "hate crimes" laws will make sure that anyone who objects is silenced. The unintended consequences of this radical social experiment are already coming to light. The pro-polygamy movement is gaining steam and credibility with every defeat for traditional marriage. In the wake of legislation legalizing same-sex "marriage" in Canada, an official government report actually recommended repealing Canada's laws against polygamy![33]

In part, Bauer, Santorum, and their colleagues were reacting to the 2003 Supreme Court decision overturning state sodomy laws. While it would pale in comparison to the same-sex marriage level of debate and division, the 2003 decision began the events of the current era as far as gay rights and their backlash are concerned.

The Supreme Court and Lawrence *(2003)*

A sheriff's deputy had burst into John Lawrence's living room while Lawrence and Tyron Garner were having sex. The deputy was called to Lawrence's apartment by a neighbor who later admitted to falsely reporting an armed man had entered the apartment. After the deputy determined that no weapons disturbance had occurred, he turned and arrested Lawrence and Garner for "deviant sexual intercourse." The two spent the night in jail and were subsequently convicted.

Lawrence and Garner appealed their convictions, arguing that since the Texas law applied to same-sex couples only, it violated their rights to equal protection. Their claims were denied on the basis that all such claims were precluded by *Bowers v. Hardwick*,[34] a case wherein the U.S. Supreme Court ruled that the Constitution confers no fundamental right upon homosexuals to engage in sodomy.

The Supreme Court granted Lawrence and Garner's petition to hear their case, saying it would consider three issues: whether the petitioners' conviction violated their guarantee of equal protection under the Fourteenth Amendment; whether their conviction violated their interests in liberty and privacy protected by the Fourteenth Amendment; and whether *Bowers v. Hardwick* should be overruled.

Writing for the majority, Justice Kennedy first considered how the Court in *Bowers* had defined the issue to be decided in that case. He found it troubling that in *Bowers* the Court assessed only the very narrow question of whether homosexuals have a fundamental constitutional right to engage in homosexual sodomy. This narrow view of the constitutional question before the Court in *Bowers* "misapprehended" and "failed to appreciate" the scope of the liberty interest asserted in that case, said Kennedy. For just as it would demean married couples, it demeans homosexuals to define their rights merely in terms of a right to have sexual intercourse. Intimate expression, said Kennedy, "is but one element in a personal bond that is more enduring."

The majority opinion in *Lawrence,* written by Justice Kennedy, was surprising in its reach. Rather than taking a narrower approach, which many predicted (and which fellow justice Sandra Day O'Connor took) and striking down those state laws that prohibited same-sex sodomy, the court majority went further. Writing for the majority, Justice Kennedy restated what he had said in *Casey* regarding the autonomy of persons making these decisions:

> These matters, involving the most intimate and personal choices a person may make in a lifetime, choices central to personal dignity and autonomy, are central to the liberty protected by the Fourteenth Amendment. At the heart of liberty is the right to define one's own concept of existence, of meaning, of the universe, and of the mystery of human life. Beliefs about these matters could not define the attributes of personhood were they formed under compulsion of the State.[35]

Lawrence reversed a decision the Court had made seventeen years earlier in *Bowers v. Hardwick* (1986), in which a narrow majority had rejected claims that private, consensual same-sex relations were protected under privacy rights similar to those that governed conception and abortion, flowing from *Roe v. Wade.* Justice O'Connor, in her separate concurring opinion, "took pains to demonstrate that overturning a law that sent consenting adults to jail for their private sexual behavior did not imply recognition of same-sex marriage."[36]

Gay activists hailed the decision as "magnificent." Before the decision, many in the gay community disagreed about what would be the most favorable basis for a Court decision striking down the Texas law. Some thought it would be more empowering if the Court ruled that the right to privacy protects all adults who engage in consensual sex, including gays and lesbians. Others argued that a ruling on equal protection grounds would send a message that moral sentiments alone are not a rational basis for state laws that discriminate on the basis of sexual orientation. Many were delighted that Justice Kennedy made it clear that the Court avoided basing its decision on equal protection grounds, for the very purpose of sending the message that states cannot simply "fix" laws that discriminate against same-sex participants merely by discriminating equally against different-sex participants. The Court's decision to ground its opinion in privacy rights guaranteed by the Fourteenth Amendment was read as a careful strategy to make the opinion wider rather than narrower.[37]

Lawrence was clearly not the *Roe v. Wade* of the gay rights movement. Although sodomy laws were important in fifteen states, and as a symbolic issue in all fifty states, by 2003, gay marriage had already assumed the lead as the top gay rights goal.

Much had happened in the years since *Bowers* in terms of American society and homosexuality, but it had happened along a timeline of a struggle for equality and antidiscrimination through law. David Richards has written that *Lawrence* was remarkable because it came at a time when everyone agreed that the Supreme Court had become more conservative.[38]

The Road to Marriage: History of Gay Rights

Since the 1950s, most Western countries have either decriminalized sexual orientation or reduced enforcement activities attendant to it. Yet sexual orientation, whose behavioral components are considered by some as a "lifestyle liberty," remains a controversial topic. Attempts to sway legislatures to decriminalize homosexual activity often are countered by opponents' attempts to link homosexuality to a naturally heightened propensity to molest children—that is, to introduce a victim into a discussion of a victimless crime—and to identify homosexuality with a public health menace, the AIDS epidemic.

D'Emilio breaks the gay rights movement into several eras: (1) the pre-Stonewall era (1950s–1969), (2) the Stonewall era (1970s), (3) the post-Stonewall/AIDS era (1980s), and (4) the modern era (1993 to present).[39] In the pre-Stonewall era, D'Emilio identifies the theme of legal reformers as "Give us a hearing." Action depended upon individuals and institutions that were neither gay nor gay-friendly. Society was hostile, arrests commonplace, and invisibility for gays and lesbians was the norm. To D'Emilio, "Gays and lesbians were not setting the terms in which their lives were discussed or understood."

According to Michael Smyth,[40] throughout this period, discussions of homosexuality were especially prone to portray homosexuals as "sick," or mentally ill. Of the forty-three articles on homosexuality that appeared in *Time* and *Newsweek* from 1946 through 1968, 79 percent drew on the "sick" script. Smyth elaborates:

> In "The Case of the Elusive Euphemism" (*Time*, 7/22/66), homosexuality was conflated with a "psychopathic personality" and "Homosexuals Can Be Cured" (*Time*, 2/12/65) identified homosexuality as an "emotional maladjustment stemming from reactions to childhood experiences." In "The Abnormal" (*Time*, 4/17/50), in which homosexuals were discussed in the same breath with "fire-bugs" and kleptomaniacs, homosexuality was described as a curable, symptomatic disorder that can be treated with psychoanalytic psychotherapy.

In his autobiographical work *Cures,* historian Martin Duberman vividly describes the main approach of this era. Duberman recounts his years of therapy, in which the goal was his "heterosexual adjustment," the shifting of his same-sex attractions, and his cooperation in trying to be cured or "fixed."[41]

At the same time, reformers began the brave struggle of working for equality for gays and lesbians. In 1951 the Mattachine Society—the first modern gay rights organization—was founded. Organized as a secret society and with a membership of 2,500 within two years, the society sponsored discussion groups and founded the magazine *One*. Daughters of Bilitis, founded in 1955 as the first lesbian organization, produced a publication called the *Ladder*. Both of these organizations had gone national by the 1960s. From the late 1950s to 1968, gay rights activists protested police harassment, brought lawsuits defending their right to congregate, became active in local politics in New York and San Francisco, and protested employment discrimination in Washington.

Mattachine founders were the first to conceptualize gays as a legitimate minority within a hostile mainstream culture. Urvashi Vaid depicts this viewpoint as a "profound redefinition of homosexuality."[42] While few gays embraced the minority concept during most of the 1950s and 1960s, it became a focal point of the gay rights movement in 1969. Vaid explains that this change "moved homosexuality from the domain of illness and sociopathic deviance and into the public domain of civil rights," thus marking a pivotal point in the history of gay rights activism. Specifically,

> The minority group framework located gay and lesbian people within a long liberal democratic tradition of ethnic, racial, and cultural minorities. Gay and lesbian people were like immigrants who came to America and made a home, but had to overcome prejudice and irrational fears along the way. We urged society to see us as it saw the Irish, the Jews, or any other ethnic or racial minority.[43]

The "Stonewall" era is generally considered a dividing mark in American gay rights history, following a protest and altercations with police at a gay bar in New York City. After Stonewall, and simultaneous with other protest and liberation movements in the United States, D'Emilio describes a new image of gay activists—those more willing to be confrontational and stand up to authority. The themes changed, in his terms, to "Here we are." Insistence and indeed defiance were themes, and reformers stressed a dual commitment to coming out and building community. Many local antidiscrimination laws were passed in this era,[44] although few states followed with comprehensive legislation.[45]

Several gay rights legal reform agendas advanced in the 1970s, from the challenging of sodomy laws—many were decriminalized in the 1970s—to the passage of antidiscrimination ordinances. During the 1970s and 1980s, numerous municipalities and counties passed antidiscrimination measures.[46] Repeal efforts became a commonplace area of contestation, from the time of the celebrated Dade County effort of the late 1970s.[47] The initial successes with antidiscrimination ordinances generated such countermovements, as D'Emilio explains and Smyth illuminates with his depiction of the rise of a "predator" image for the now less-invisible gays and lesbians:

Articles reporting on Anita Bryant's "Save Our Children" crusade accounted for many of the instances in which homosexuals were discussed as predators. . . . In general, Bryant's grievance centered on a Dade County, Florida ordinance that forbade discrimination against homosexuals in areas such as housing, jobs and public accommodation. Such ordinances, Bryant claimed, would mandate the hiring of homosexual teachers, who would be inclined to lead impressionable youth into a life of sodomy and abominations against god. The Dade County ordinance, *Newsweek* reported Anita as saying, was an attempt to "legitimize homosexuals and their recruitment of our children (*Newsweek*, 4/11/77, p. 39)."[48]

In the post-Stonewall period, AIDS become both a reason for mobilization and a change in circumstances that demarcated an era, in D'Emilio's terms. "Leave us alone" was the dominant theme to him, along with a more oppositional "Get out of our bedroom and our psyches."[49] Goals of the reform movements included eliminating disease classification; repealing sodomy statutes; adopting civil rights protections; and preventing violence, with the assistance of law enforcement. Groups like ACT UP and authors like Larry Kramer were aggressive and vocal on lack of AIDS funding.

This 1980s era saw the full flowering of Christian Right opposition. Vaid offers a view that advocating for a distinction between homosexual culture and the dominant culture has the effect of further alienating gays and lesbians, attracting more hostility toward them. Vaid observes that this disagreement between gay radicals and gay conservatives persisted into the 1970s, with the "far more moderate course for legal and political legitimacy" being the viewpoint embraced by the political wing of the movement.[50]

Smyth also locates the emergence of another theme in his newsmagazine inventory, that of dangerousness:

Throughout the article, male-on-male sexuality is portrayed as an innately dangerous, destructive and ultimately doomed proposition. In "Leather Fringe," S&M aficionados—and, in fact, homosexuals in general—are depicted compulsively wandering through a dark and dangerous urban landscape in search of the bizarre sexual thrills they endlessly crave. Danger, according to the article, is the leather scene's *raison d'etre*—and an element of homosexual cruising in general. Danger is depicted in the article as a prerequisite of homoerotic arousal.[51]

Although many gays and lesbians were members and leaders of the antiwar movement, as well as the movements for race and gender equality, at least two factors hindered the success of homosexual rights. One was that too many gays and lesbians kept their sexual preferences secret for fear that revealing them would be counterproductive to the other causes they fought for. The other was the threefold problem of how to convince large numbers of people to get politically active, how to narrow the diverse interests of homosexuals into a unified policy objective, and how to transform the decentralized nature of the movement into coordinated efforts.[52] These conditions persisted through the 1970s and well into the 1980s.

The era also includes the unsuccessful U.S. Supreme Court case of *Bowers v. Hardwick*. In the 1980s, gay rights became a key focus— along with abortion—for the Christian Coalition as it sought to mobilize conservative and religious forces against growing tolerance in American sexual practice, attitudes, and laws.

With the emergence of the AIDS epidemic in the early 1980s, a good deal of the energy aimed at expanding this front of civil rights protections was directed at providing support for persons with AIDS, especially through activism by groups such as ACT UP (and its slogan "Silence = Death") and for pushing for medical attention, societal concern, and federal funding in that arena.

With all these changes by 2005, gay rights—and the normalization of same-sex relationships—remained a key issue for social and religious conservatives.

Frank Rich of the *New York Times,* commenting on the protracted and intense struggle over the Senate's confirmation of Bush judicial nominees, and potential change in the use of the filibuster, references this when he writes: "Those were the dark ages [1950s], but it isn't entirely progress that we now have a wider war on gay people, thinly disguised as a debate over the filibuster, cloaked in religion."[53]

The years 2003 and 2004 were important ones for gay rights in the United States, featuring the 2003 ruling by the U.S. Supreme Court in *Lawrence v. Texas* that states like Texas could not have laws which prohibited sodomy and the first legal same-sex marriage in Massachusetts in May 2004. These shifts—"sea changes" in Griffiths's term[54]—were unforeseen in the heated central days of the culture wars over victimless crime and morality in the United States.

In the major opposing case to rights expansion in other "privacy" areas, *Bowers v. Hardwick*, decided in 1986, the U.S. Supreme Court held in a split decision that a statute such as Georgia's prohibiting sodomy could be upheld despite the expectation of privacy in one's own bedroom established by *Griswold* two decades earlier in a contraception case, and extended in *Roe v. Wade* in 1973. Bowers appears as a counterexample to our hypothesis regarding the general removal of consensual adult sexual activity from the purview of the criminal law.

Some have observed that the necessity of allocation of scarce economic and social resources to the fight against AIDS arose at a time when gay rights became a rallying point for fundamentalist religious groups and conservative activists. Moral entrepreneurs like California's Reverend Louis Shelton and his Traditional Values Coalition have become commonplace lobbyists against attempts by public entities such as school districts to discuss sexuality, abortion, AIDS, and other issues in an educational setting.[55]

D'Emilio's final era began in 1993 and continues to the present. The year 1993 is a useful point of demarcation, since it is when Bill Clinton took office and immediately undertook, through executive order, the "Don't Ask, Don't Tell" policy toward homosexuality and the armed services. D'Emilio identified "We want in" as a key theme of this era. In this period, effective action requires allies. To D'Emilio, it was important that gays and lesbians were "no longer framed as monsters."[56]

There are successes and defeats in this era as well, at the ballots, in the legislatures and in the courts.[57] Gay activists heralded the defeat of Oregon's Measure 9, which would have equated homosexuality with pedophilia and bestiality, and prevented the state or local entities from enacting laws covering antigay discrimination, or describing homosexuality as an acceptable lifestyle. Gay activists also bemoaned the passage of Amendment 2 in Colorado, which rescinded municipal laws against gay and lesbian discrimination, but responded positively to the *Romer v. Evans* 1996 United States Supreme Court decision which overturned that law.[58]

By 1999, homosexual practices by consenting adults were decriminalized in many U.S. jurisdictions. In 1998, however, nineteen states retained either same-sex or sex-neutral sodomy prohibition, which is the situation the *Lawrence* case would address in 2003.[59] At national and regional levels, despite whatever progress might have been made through the passage of the many municipal, county, and state antidiscrimination ordinances, the power of antigay violence and the use of homosexual rights as an organizing point for the religious Right (and the secular Right) have represented the power of notions of vice in concert with other forms of bigotry and resentment.

Key issues, in D'Emilio's view, are connected to core societal concerns such as family, school, and work. Reformers sought recognition of domestic partnership, legalization of same-sex marriage, right to parent, adopt, foster, custody, workplace equity, and recognition of equality in school curricula. (Not surprisingly, all these terrains are where the contests continue to take place with social conservatives and the Christian Right.) To D'Emilio, if there is a "gay agenda," as opponents claim, the agenda includes repeal of sodomy laws; removal of disease classification; elimination of discriminatory provisions; fair representation in media; due process of law/enforcement; hate crime enactment and enforcement; and recognition of family relationships.

Once we enter an era in which gay rights were becoming more recognized, some of the arguments turned toward the approval of "special rights"[60] and the arguments that gays and lesbians had exceeded the rights "granted" to them under the civil rights model and were being too "pushy," advancing a "gay agenda." As early as 1982, activists and analysts such as Dennis Altman were looking for such parallels in the civil rights movement and trying to determine the efficacy of assimilationist approaches, versus more aggressive movement impulses.[61]

While San Francisco's mayor Gavin Newsom was clearly going beyond the existing law in California, he was challenging the law in one of a handful of American states that had incrementally expanded rights for gays and lesbians over the past ten years. Even Republican governor Pete Wilson had signed a statewide antidiscrimination ordinance that prohibited discrimination in employment and housing. The next governor, Democrat Gray Davis, further expanded this position when he signed bills that expanded domestic partnerships.

New York Times columnist Frank Rich places the remarkable present in the perspective of the gains and losses of reformers over twenty years:

The AIDS epidemic, in retrospect, made same-sex marriage inevitable. Americans watched as gay men were turned away at their partners' hospital rooms and denied basic rights granted to heterosexual couples coping with a spouse's terminal illness and death. As the gay civil rights movement gained a life-and-death urgency, the public started to come around, and it has been coming around ever since, at an accelerating rate. As recently as 1993, the year Tom Hanks did his Oscar turn as an AIDS victim in "Philadelphia," fewer than a dozen Fortune 500 companies offered domestic partners health benefits and even a city as relatively progressive as Atlanta erupted over extending them to its employees. That now seems a century, not a decade, ago: today even Wal-Mart is among the nearly 200 such companies offering these benefits, and even a conservative city like Cincinnati is contemplating the repeal of antigay legislation, passed in 1993, that may be hindering its ability to recruit businesses.[62]

The landmark events of 2004 have kept the societal consideration and legal treatment of gays and lesbians at the forefront of national discussion, even in a time of war and economic challenges.

Whether *Lawrence v. Texas* has helped or harmed the modern fight for lesbian and gays rights remains to be seen. What is certain is that the case set off a firestorm of citizen petition drives and legislative amendments seeking to ban gay marriage.

Religion and Gay Rights

We acknowledge that gay rights generates an intense level of opposition from social conservative religious Americans and their fundamentalist churches. While we will devote significant space to understanding the underpinnings of the reaction, and describing the contours and ramifications of it, some attention must also be paid to the more complex attitudes and reaction among the members and officials of mainline Protestant churches and the Catholic Church.

Although the fundamentalists are certainly compelling, there is little reason to paint the opinions of people of faith in this area with the brush of Rev. Fred Phelps and his "God Hates Fags" campaign. Religion in America, and the influence of religiosity and church membership and attendance on social and political attitudes, is certainly not monolithic. The multidimensional nature of this relationship includes a range of conservative persons and their churches, a good-sized moderate sector of centrists, as well as a third tier of progressives or "modernists."[63]

We will demonstrate that there has been a range of institutional issues related to gay rights among the mainline Protestant churches in the United States. In addition, we will present the views of American Catholics—who nearly mirror the general American public in many of these measures—based on the findings of various polls, and the reactions and pronouncements of the official church, in a series of documents dating from the late 1970s.

The Catholic Church, since the selection of Pope John Paul II in 1978, has steered a decidedly conservative course on homosexuality. Indeed, it has included homosexuality in its "culture of life" argument, along with abortion, euthanasia, stem cell research, and the death penalty. In 2006, Pope Benedict XVI announced that the primary enemy he would focus on was not war or poverty but secularism.[64]

In 2003, with the Vermont legislature considering the civil union bill that it eventually would pass, the Vatican issued the following statement:

> Homosexual unions are totally lacking in the biological and anthropological elements of marriage and family which would be the basis, on the level of reason, for granting them legal recognition. Such unions are not able to contribute in a proper way to the procreation and survival of the human race. . . . Homosexual unions are also totally lacking in the conjugal dimension, which represents the human and ordered form of sexuality. Sexual relations are human when and insofar as they express and promote the mutual assistance of the sexes in marriage and are open to the transmission of new life.[65]

The Catholic pronouncements halted what liberalization had been taking place in the Church during the 1970s and positioned the hierarchy against groups like Dignity, which strove to keep a gay and lesbian voice inside the church. At the local level, bishops were instructed not to be welcoming to pro-gay Catholic groups like Dignity, which objected to the policy:

> Dignity felt called to a prophetic stance, which, simply said, is to be honest about the matter. After nearly twenty years of ministering to hurting Catholics, Dignity members were aware of the harm that the

Church's repeated condemnation of homosexuality does to individuals. One statement from a pope or bishop can throw devout gay Catholics back into guilt and self-deprecation that they may have spent years trying to overcome.[66]

Specifically responding to the Catholic Church's pronouncements during the height of the AIDS crisis, the Dignity web site explained:

What did people find harsh and uninformed in that 1986 Vatican letter? It backed away from the prevailing ethical opinion that a homosexual orientation is morally neutral and called it "an objective disorder." Whatever this is supposed to mean, it suggests that gay people are sick, despite massive evidence to the contrary in medical, psychological, and sociobiological research.

As if blaming gay people for the AIDS epidemic and ignoring their heroic—and virtually solitary!—efforts to stem it, the letter said: "Even when the practice of homosexuality may seriously threaten the lives and well-being of a large number of people, its advocates remain undeterred and refuse to consider the magnitude of the risks involved."

Regarding gay-bashing it read: when gay people seek to "protect behavior to which no one has any conceivable right, neither the church nor society at large should be surprised when other distorted notions and practices gain ground, and irrational and violent reactions increase."

As for securing the civil rights of gay people: "The bishops should keep as their uppermost concern the responsibility to defend and promote family life"—as if lesbian and gay children, sisters, brothers, fathers, or mothers were not part of family life.[67]

The American Catholic bishops also expressed their strong support in 2006 for the federal marriage protection amendment, to be discussed at the end of this chapter.

In 2006, Pope Benedict XVI issued a proclamation that those with active homosexual inclinations were to be barred from seminaries, and thus from ordination into the Catholic priesthood. The *Los Angeles Times* reported that this ruling was Benedict's first since ascending to the papacy and reflected his ongoing concern with the tides of secularism: "This is the first major instruction to be issued by Pope Benedict XVI, and the fact that it focused on homosexuality reflected the German pontiff's concern over morals he sees eroded by Western secular culture."[68] Many saw his proclamation as a partial response to the priest sexual abuse scandals that have received much attention in the United States since the 1990s.

Then there are conservative evangelical Protestant churches for which the gay rights issue is less debated, but the work against secular forces occupies an inordinate amount of their time. Gary Bauer writes of the commonality of views among evangelical organizations on marriage:

> But we must not lose sight of the fact that the pro-family movement has come together in an unprecedented way in recent years. Our movement consists of a tremendous and growing coalition. We are finding new friends—particularly among African-American pastors—in our efforts to preserve normal marriage as the union of one man and one woman.[69]

Michael Cromartie, the director of the Evangelicals in Public Life project at the Ethics and Public Policy center, suggested that there is "a kind of ambivalence just beneath the surface of opposition to same-sex marriage, even among people of strong religious convictions."[70]

While many of the signatories were evangelical ministers, the following document from 2006 did cut across some denominational lines, as a statement of the Religious Coalition for Marriage:

> For millennia our societies have recognized the union of a man and a woman in the bond of marriage. Cross-culturally virtually every known human society understands marriage as a union of male and female. As such marriage is a universal, natural, covenantal union of a man and a woman intended for personal love, support and fulfillment, and the bearing and rearing of children. Sanctioned by and ordained of God, marriage both precedes and sustains civil society.[71]

One of the ways in which the Republican Party has tried to make inroads into an African American community that votes overwhelmingly Democratic is to focus on black churchgoers, who tend to be more conservative than other African Americans. One focus has been on black pastors, who have been courted in a series of events. While the outcome has not been sizable, there have been enough changes in the population to affect the vote in a closely contested state, such as Ohio in the 2004 presidential election. In one instance, it was an African American pastor in the state of Washington who led the charge against Microsoft and other local companies because of their support of a bill in the state legislature prohibiting discrimination in housing, employment, and insurance on the basis of sexual orientation.

There are elements of the African American community that are not enamored of the use of the civil rights concept by gays and lesbians, feeling that the difference in their status is significant. One Maryland pastor notes:

> Gay rights is not an extension of the civil rights movement simply because there's no choice involved in our blackness. I think there is an amazingly militant group of gays who have made it their point to say, "We're going to be out; we're going to be visible"—that's their choice.[72]

One analyst writes that there are a very few liberal Protestant churches for which the issue of equality for gays and lesbians has been decided "in favor of equality." Primary among these is the United Church of Christ, with the inclusive imagery of its "God Is Still Speaking" campaign and its process of authorizing "open and affirming" churches. The ad campaign by the United Church of Christ that depicted a church open to gays and lesbians insinuated to Rev. Jerry Falwell that evangelical churches in America were bigoted.[73]

Left in the middle are a number of mainline Protestant churches, which have moved slowly in this area over the last decade, with many experiencing schisms over the issue. While these churches are generally liberal, they have been beset by issues related to gender and sexual orientation for the past decade.[74] As the morality war has heated up, they have been increasingly drawn into controversies over ordination of ministers, consecration of bishops, and sexual orientation.

The Methodist Church, for example, held an unusual trial for a lesbian minister who had crossed the line and declared that she was sexually active with her partner, an infraction against the church's code.[75]

The Episcopal Church is still in flux, considering the decisions of churches in the American part of the worldwide church to allow for the ordination of gay priests and, as in the case of the Rev. Gene Robinson in 2003, bishops. The top official of the Episcopal Church in America retired in 2006 following a nine-year term marked by controversy over sexuality and religion. He was replaced by a progressive bishop from Nevada, who favored ordination of gay bishops.[76] But then three conflicting events took place. First, following the selection of the bishop, the American Episcopal Church passed a resolution to go slow on the ordination of gay bishops, so as not to cause strain within the world-wide Anglican communion.[77]

More conservative churches in the Episcopal fold have sought to dis-associate from their church and instead join more conservative ranks, such as those of the African Church, where the Anglican Communion has grown even as it has declined in the developed world.[78] As one ac-count explains:

> The worldwide Anglican communion of 77 million people faces a seri-ous possibility of schism over the issue of homosexuality. Anglican lead-ers from the developing world, led in large part by Archbishop Akinola, have objected bitterly to the 2003 ordination of an openly gay bishop by the Episcopal Church of the United States of America, and to the Anglican Church's blessing of same-sex marriages in Canada. Many church leaders from Africa, Asia and Latin America think that tolerance of gays is a repudiation of biblical orthodoxy, seeing it in light of a se-ries of disputes with the Western arms of their faith over the last 35 years, notably the ordination of women.[79]

Second, one diocese challenged that plan with the announcement that it intended to ordain a gay bishop soon.[80] Third, the archbishop of Can-terbury, the titular head of the Anglican Communion, announced that he was planning to ask member churches to agree to limit each church's autonomy, a decision that could compel the American Episcopal Church either to follow a direction it did approve of or to act at some level of resistance or schism.[81]

The Era of DOMAs: Social Conservatives against Normalization

The bumper stickers on sale at one of the social conservative Web sites say it well: "Marriage is one man and one woman." While liberals and gay activists may assert that this is code for bigotry, one could also ar-gue that it could not be more clear what subject it is addressing. The rallying cry is used in support of "defense of marriage acts" (DOMAs) in the states, which are laws defining marriage in that way. Specifically, these laws—and we also have a federal DOMA passed in 1996 and signed into law by President Clinton—prevent the recognition of any marriage from another state that is anything but that of "one man, one woman." DOMA initiatives have been passed in twenty states, and several more passed in 2006. Republican strategists have made good use of the laws in the past several years, winning at the state level in those states that passed DOMAs in 2004, with the exception of Oregon.

As one group supporting DOMAs in Virginia describes its stance: "va4marriage is a non-partisan, grassroots project of concerned citizens, pastors, community leaders, and like-minded organizations united together to preserve the bedrock of Western Civilization in Virginia, namely, traditional marriage as a lifelong union between one man and one woman."[82] To avoid being accused of bigotry, DOMA campaigns tend not to single out gays and lesbians, choosing to emphasize instead that they are only "protecting marriage."

Still, Rev. Louis Sheldon's Traditional Values Coalition (TVC) prominently features a link on its Web site for "Ministry and Counseling Resources for Those Struggling with Same-Sex Attractions and Other Gender Identity Disorders."[83] The TVC also has heralded a proposed ballot initiative for the special election in California in November 2005, called the Civil Rights for Families Initiative, which would do the following:

> Require schools to give parents/guardians written notice no more that 15 days and no less than 10 days in advance of any presentation, lecture, or lesson on homosexuality, bisexuality, trans-sexuality.
>
> Require schools to obtain written consent and permission from a parent or guardian that it is allowable to have their child take part in such presentations, lectures, lessons, etc. (Students who do not have parental permission will not be penalized but will be given another form of study worth equal credit.)
>
> Prohibit any teaching on homosexuality, bisexuality, trans-sexuality and other topics to grades 1 to 6.

To critics, "DOMAs are sneaky: They don't mention lesbians and gay men. If Americans think about same-sex marriages at all, they're torn between the basic American belief that 'fair is fair,' and the gut sense that 'marriage has always been this way.' DOMAs appeal to the latter idea."[84]

Much of the energy of gay rights activists has been directed at challenging the slew of DOMAs and anti–gay marriage laws that have been proposed every two years in state elections. As the South Carolina Equality Coalition explains in its effort against a 2006 initiative in that state:

> What this amendment really says: No matter how many years they build a life together, regardless of the children they raise together, gay and lesbian families would be denied any form of legal recognition, rights, responsibilities, and protections available to all other South Carolinians.
>
> Should this amendment pass, the people of our State will, in effect, constitutionally relegate South Carolinians—and their children—to second class citizenship.[85]

With the debate of 2004 on gay marriages quieted for a time, as both sides assessed their own power and vulnerabilities, one state acted in early 2005 to follow the Vermont route and allow civil unions for same-sex couples.[86] In Connecticut, it was a Republican governor who signed the bill. In many ways, Connecticut could be viewed as a likely state to follow Vermont's lead: it is politically moderate to liberal, is a blue state with two Democratic senators, and has a history of supporting gay rights legislation. The bill in question, modeled after Vermont's civil union bill, marked the first time that a legislatively enacted civil union bill had become law, or even moved as far as the governor's desk without court prodding. The Massachusetts experience had been brought about by a state supreme court ruling, and Vermont's legislature acted only after a similar high court ruling.[87]

The movement of the Connecticut bill through the legislature signaled a shift in the politics of gay marriage, as pragmatic considerations were paramount after the 2004 events. As one report noted, there was support forthcoming from Republican legislative circles in the state, but still a reluctance from leading gay rights groups, who had hoped for a fuller gay marriage law at some point. A *New York Times* editorial captured the sentiment when it noted in support of the bill that, while not perfect, it represented an advance, saying, "It's an important step in supporting the stability of gay families, and one that should not be dismissed because it does not take us right to the end of the road: marriages recognized beyond a single state's borders."[88]

The conservative religious group Focus on the Family organized a grassroots effort to demand up or down votes on gay rights in selected states in 2006. Its print ads depicted an Iraqi voter, with her thumb inked after participating in the democratic process. The ad asked why Americans were being denied this same democratic right in voting the various DOMAs and "super-DOMAs" (which the National Gay and Lesbian Task Force defines as legislation that bars any kind of recognition of same-sex couples) up or down. "Iraqis have the right to vote. Why don't Iowans?"[89] Even as U.S. Senate debate on the federal marriage amendment went on, the executive director of the Human Rights Campaign was pleased that negotiations had staved off several possible similar bills from rising to initiative status in 2006.

Conclusion: A Purple America or an Issue Still Burning?

As stated before, while 2004 may be remembered for the political fall-out from the raising of the gay marriage issues (in legal decisions, extra-legal actions, church pronouncements, and philosophical discussions) the common ground that existed was downplayed in favor of the contestation that resulted in better media coverage. According to those measures, a majority of Americans favor the establishment of civil unions for same-sex couples, while only a minority of Americans favor allowing same-sex marriages. Clearly, at the same time, only a minority of Americans support a constitutional amendment opposing gay marriage (such as the 56 percent in the November 2004 *New York Times*–CBS poll).[90]

In 2005, the Gallup organization interpreted its poll as showing that Americans are increasingly tolerant but ambiguous about homosexuality:

> Just as voters see abortion and embryonic stem cell research differently, they also make distinctions between non-traditional marriage and gay rights. Overall, voters split 55%-to-45% in favor of the proposition that marriage should only be allowed between men and women. But people agree with the statement "Homosexuals should have the same rights as other Americans" by a 57%-to-28% margin.[91]

A poll taken by Peter D. Hart Research Associates in 2006,[92] while the federal marriage amendment was nearing consideration, found a strong majority of Americans not in favor of the amendment and listing it as the lowest of several possible priorities for Congress to act on in the last few months of the 109th Congress.

With the 2004 election over, and President Bush and a Republican Congress reelected, the same-sex marriage issue receded for many, while it stayed alive in the pronouncements and strategies of social conservatives and gay and lesbian rights organizations.

Social conservative organizations continued into 2006 to bemoan the scant attention paid to the same-sex marriage topic in the Congress and by the president. Gary Bauer noted to the readers of his American Values group that the president had failed to take the opportunity of his 2006 State of the Union address to support the congressional effort to define marriage as only between a man and a woman. Dr. James Dobson of Focus on the Family agreed with Bauer:

> The threat to marriage has never been more brazen, and as the debate intensifies, we must step up our efforts to defend the foundational institution of our nation. Already, we are daily confronted with the fact that traditional marriage in a given state or region is never more than one federal judge away from being declared unconstitutional, and of course, the U.S. Supreme Court represents the greatest concern. That very issue will be decided in coming months for future generations. It is our duty to make certain that the outcome is determined by the people and their representatives rather than unelected, unaccountable judges. Our answer is found in the federal Marriage Protection Amendment. We desperately need what the MPA will readily accomplish: the traditional definition of marriage placed beyond the reach of all judges—directly in the U.S. Constitution.[93]

Prominent American Catholic cardinals signed a petition in April 2006 in support of a constitutional amendment against gay marriage, an issue for which the American public, and Catholics as well, does not have fire in the belly:

> Marriage is particularly important for the rearing of children as they flourish best under the long term care and nurture of their father and mother. For this and other reasons, when marriage is entered into and gotten out of lightly, when it is no longer the boundary of sexual activity, or when it is allowed to be radically redefined, a host of personal and civic ills can be expected to follow. Such a point has always been

stressed by the world's great monotheistic religious traditions and is, to-day, increasingly confirmed by impeccable social science research.

Therefore, we take the unprecedented stand of uniting to call for a constitutional amendment to establish a uniform national definition of marriage as the exclusive union of one man and one woman. We are convinced that this is the only measure that will adequately protect marriage from those who would circumvent the legislative process and force a redefinition of it on the whole of our society. We encourage all citizens of good will across the country to step forward boldly and exercise their right to work through our constitutionally established democratic procedures to amend the Constitution to include a national definition of marriage. We hereby announce our support for S.J. Res.1, the Marriage Protection Amendment.[94]

Later in 2006, Carol Bauer offered her critique of the potential problems for senators in Washington who failed to embrace the amendment:

Frustration with elected officials is on the rise among the American public. The electorate senses that Congress is unwilling to tackle tough issues of the day head-on in ways that will be truly effective. At the same time there is a growing feeling that politicians are most interested in staying in power. With critical mid-term elections just months away, this unsettled political dynamic could have disastrous consequences.

The Federal Marriage Protection Amendment to the U.S. Constitution is slated for a vote in the full Senate the first week in June. . . . Too many senators continue to say that such an amendment at the federal level is premature, and instead they want to rely on each state to make its own decision on this issue. The folly of that thinking is amazing.

Many are deeply disappointed that the president has not chosen to aggressively fight for this amendment, which he campaigned on, instead leaving the airwaves to carry the views of those like Mary Cheney, who does not support the Federal Marriage Protection Amendment.[95]

In a newspaper report that week, another social conservative leader expressed a similar opinion. According to Joe Glover, president of the Family Policy Network: "We don't believe them anymore. Bush twice made a big deal out of marriage. But once he gets in that big cushy office, you don't hear a peep out of him about marriage."[96]

Within the week, Senator Bill Frist, then still hoping for social and religious conservative support in his prospective 2008 presidential run, articulated the need for a focus on the federal marriage protection amendment:

HOST: . . . Are gay marriage and flag burning the most important issues the Senate can be addressing in June of 2006?

FRIST: . . . When you look at that flag and you tell me that right now people in this country are saying it's okay to desecrate that flag and to burn it and to not pay respect to it, is that important to our values as a people when we've got 130,000 people fighting for our freedom and liberty today? That is important. It may not be important here in Washington where people say, well, it's political posturing and all, but it's important to the heart and soul of the American people. . . . Why marriage today? Marriage is for our society that union between a man and a woman, is the cornerstone of our society. It is under attack today.[97]

This followed by a few days Frist's statement on the Senate floor, where he proclaimed, "I basically say, Mr. Vice President, right now marriage is under attack in this country. . . . And we've seen activist judges overturning state by state law. . . . And that is why we need an amendment to the Constitution."[98]

Proponents of the amendment, such as Focus on the Family, stressed that support for their cause was not a conservative impulse, and thus one that self-professed moderates in the morality wars, like newly elected Senator Ken Salazar (D-Colo.) and others they targeted, should support: "Sen. Salazar from the beginning has portrayed himself as a moderate. . . . Marriage is not a conservative or a right-wing issue. It's a common-sense position to support marriage."

The week of the Senate vote, President Bush called together leaders of the social conservative movement in an event to signal his support for the FMPA, saying, "Changing the definition of marriage would undermine the structure of the family. . . . Marriage is the most fundamental institution of civilization, and it should not be redefined by activist judges."

The debate over the FMPA, held over two days in June 2006, recycled many of the arguments about the protection of the family by supporters of the amendment, and charges of emphasizing unimportant subjects by opponents, like Senate minority leader Harry Reid and assistant minority leader Richard Durbin in a spirited colloquy. As expected, FMPA supporters did not receive the necessary 60 votes to stop debate. Remarkably, they gained only a single vote from a prior consideration of the FMPA and lost the votes of John McCain and several moderate Republicans (a second time), as well as those of Judiciary Committee chair Specter, Judd Gregg of New Hampshire, and maverick senator Chuck Hagel (absent to travel with the president). The 49-to-48 vote was symbolically important, since it demonstrated that the FMPA would not have passed even on an up-or-down vote.

Republican Party chair Mehlman suggested that John McCain's sentiments against the FMPA were a sign of the Republican's big tent approach.[99] In an ad in *USA Today,* Focus on the Family chastised both Senator Clinton and Senator McCain for their upcoming votes on the amendment.[100]

Whatever its symbolic value, the FMPA galvanized supporters and opponents. The National Gay and Lesbian Task Force presented arguments for mobilizing its members and readers to "care about the FMA":

> At the Task Force, we're sick and tired of being used as a political punching bag by the right-wing. Aren't you? If this amendment passes: Discrimination against same-sex couples will be enshrined for generations; We will lose the potential for civil unions, domestic partnerships, even partner insurance benefits; The right-wing extremists will learn they can get away with demonizing us—and they'll find new ways to hold us back.[101]

The importance the general public gave to the FMPA, as indicated by the 2006 polls, was much less. Polls show that the salience of the same-sex marriage issue has diminished since its heights in public discussion in 2004. And even gay rights advocates, as in the Human Rights Campaign poll of May 2006—in which 25 percent supported marriage, 40 percent supported civil unions, and 33 percent were for no legal recognition—see a tolerant American polity.

A Pew report in March 2006 found a decline in Americans' opposition to gay marriage, adoption, and military service. As the authors report, in sentiment directly in concert with the themes of this book, "Public acceptance of homosexuality has increased in a number of ways in recent years, though it remains a deeply divisive issue."[102]

Social conservatives encouraged using a New Jersey Supreme Court ruling on same-sex marriage in the final stretch of the 2006 campaign to rally Republican voters, and President Bush used the issue in his stump speech of the final days, saying in one Georgia district: "For decades, activist judges have tried to redefine America by court order. Just this last week in New Jersey, another activist court issued a ruling that raises doubt about the institution of marriage. We believe that marriage is a union between a man and a woman and should be defended."[103] However, not only did such emphasis fail to provide a winning turnout of voters, it appeared to discourage swing and moderate voters. Eventually, the New Jersey legislature passed legislation that made it the third state in the country (after Vermont and Connecticut) to enact civil union recognition for same-sex couples.[104]

Despite the passage of several more DOMAs in November 2006, indications are that the "gay marriage card" may have run its course as a national political organizing issue.[105] The rejection by Arizona of a DOMA law, making it the first state to do so (even the reliably "blue" state of California has passed a DOMA), drew much notice from progressives and analysts.[106] The New Jersey ruling, mandating that the state's legislature pass at least some equivalent of civil union protection for same sex-couples, should lead to another state on the still-small list of those providing same-sex union equality of some form.[107]

Opposition to gay marriage has fallen since the high levels during the 2004 presidential election. "Strong opposition" to gay marriage moved to a new low, particularly "among seniors, Catholics and non-evangelical Protestants." A Gallup poll from the same time places a significant cohort effect on these data. It notes that the eighteen- to thirty-nine-year-old cohorts believe at a majority level that "gay marriage should be legally valid," and at a 62 percent level that "homosexuality is an acceptable alternative lifestyle" or that "homosexual relations should be legal."[108] This support drops off by a third when the next older cohort is measured—forty- to forty-nine-year-olds. One can conjecture what this means. There can be a familiarity in the youthful cohorts with multiple lifestyles, blended families (or what Arlene Skolnick calls "fragmented families"),[109] children born outside of marriage, and the diminution of marriage as an institution per se. The youngest of these express a strong majority view of childbearing outside of marriage being acceptable, and in favor of cohabitation, a trend that has been steadily increasing for two decades.[110] They have certainly grown up in an era in which being gay and lesbian—and identified as such—is more normalized than in prior generations. The forty- to forty-nine-year-olds came of age in the Reagan years of the 1980s, and the AIDS crisis probably affected their views of gays and lesbians (back when the Gallup question: "Do you think homosexual relations between consenting adults should or should not be legal?" dropped from a plurality to a decided minority).[111]

Still, even as it appeared to decline as an issue for most Americans, it could be argued that in 2006 same-sex marriage had replaced abortion as a leading issue for social conservatives. As Arianna Huffington reported:

> Evangelical leaders insist they know how gay marriage affects their voters—they'll stay home if politicians don't push for the FMA. "It's the one issue I have seen that eclipses even the abortion issue among Southern Baptists," says Richard Land, president of the Ethics and Religious Liberty Commission of the Southern Baptist Convention.[112]

It is unclear what Harry Hay, who founded the Mattachine Society in the 1950s and died in 2002, would have said about the Massachusetts decision, the FMPA, the growth of DOMAs, and the popularity of the television show *Queer Eye for the Straight Guy.* He did not live to see the Massachusetts Supreme Court ruling on same-sex marriage or the Supreme Court decision in *Lawrence,* but the movement he helped found was moving in these directions in his later years.

In the end, data from younger cohorts suggest that we may be entering an era in which they, as well as many of their elders, share the opinion expressed by Billy Crystal's aunt in his play *700 Sundays*—"Who cares?"[113] Some people and organizations do care, rather intensely, but the data suggest that, DOMAs aside, their efficacy may be on the wane, and their pull on a more moderate America less gripping.

The issue of assisted suicide certainly did not threaten to resonate at the level of same-sex marriage. Nonetheless, it regularly appeared throughout this period as one of a set of issues collected under the "culture of life" construct or, in the case of one author, the "party of death,"[114] espousing cultural and legal changes that include abortion, same-sex marriage, stem cell research, and assisted suicide. It is to that last topic, as the third in our set of "culture of life" issues, that we now turn.

5

Assisted Suicide
The Road to New Rules of Dying

If I can't tell the difference between my baby daughter and a bag of groceries, God forbid, and if my only movements and expressions are random and involuntary, I'd rather not hang around, thank you.
—*Los Angeles Times* columnist Steve Lopez (2005)

This is my body. I don't need you. I don't need government. I don't need any church playing politics with my choices, with my life. If I'm terminally ill, I'll decide how and when and in what way I will end my life.
—"Faces," 1994 reformer ad in Oregon repeal campaign

If nothing else, the drive to legalize assisted suicide is an elite liberal political movement.
—Anti-euthanasia activist Wesley Smith (Smith 2006a)

Terri Schiavo and American Attitudes toward Death and the Law, 2005

The images of Terri Schiavo, who for fifteen years had been in a persistent vegetative state, and the battle between her husband and her parents over whether to have her feeding tube and hydration terminated, transfixed America in the spring of 2005. As film clips were vigorously interpreted as showing her responding either voluntarily or involuntarily to external stimuli such as light and sound, Americans held what could be considered an extraordinary electronic town meeting for two remarkable weeks in 2005 on a subject—death—that until then had generally been discussed reluctantly and in private.

Schiavo had collapsed in her home in February 1990 during the early morning hours, and her heart had stopped temporarily, depriving her brain of oxygen. Four months later, in June 1990, a Florida court appointed her husband, Michael Schiavo, as Terri's guardian. Michael Schiavo sued his wife's physician and the hospital, claiming that they had failed to diagnose her condition. The doctor settled out of court, agreeing to pay Terri Schiavo's husband $250,000. In November of that year, Michael Schiavo also won a malpractice suit for close to $750,000 for Terri's care, as well as about $300,000 for himself. It was then that infighting between Michael Schiavo and Terri's parents, Bob and Mary Schindler, commenced.

In May 1998, Michael Schiavo filed his first petition to have his wife's feeding tube removed. Terri's parents objected. The court appointed another guardian for Terri, and in December the new guardian concluded that Terri was in a persistent vegetative state. More court battles ensued. On February 1, 2000, Florida circuit court judge George Greer ruled that Terri would have chosen to have the feeding tube removed, and he issued an order permitting removal. The Schindlers appealed the determination, and in March, Judge Greer suspended his order, which blocked the removal while Terri's parents exhausted their appeals. The case proceeded on up to the U.S. Supreme Court, which declined to consider the case, and on April 24, 2001, Terri Schiavo's feeding tube was removed for the first of three times.

In response, the Schindlers filed a civil suit claiming that Michael Schiavo had perjured himself in testimony regarding Terri's feelings and attitude toward life support. Another judge ordered the feeding tube to be reinserted two days after it was removed. Over the next two years the civil suit wound its way through the Florida appeals process, until September 2003, when Judge Greer granted a second order for removal of the feeding tube.

The Schindlers then sought review in the federal courts, and Florida governor Jeb Bush inserted himself into the dispute by filing a brief in federal court supporting the Schindlers' efforts to block removal of the feeding tube. On October 10, 2003, a federal court judge ruled that the federal court lacked jurisdiction to consider the case. Five days later Terri Schiavo's feeding tube was removed a second time.

Just six days later, the Florida Senate passed an emergency bill known as "Terri's Law," which granted authority to Governor Bush to order the reinsertion of Schiavo's feeding tube. Governor Bush followed up with an executive order to have the tube reinserted. Michael Schiavo responded with a lawsuit challenging the constitutionality of "Terri's

Law." In May 2004, county court judge Douglas Baird ruled that the law was unconstitutional. Governor Bush appealed the decision, but later that summer the Florida Supreme Court unanimously upheld the lower court's ruling. After an unsuccessful attempt to have the case reheard, Governor Bush appealed the case to the U.S. Supreme Court. In late January 2005, the Supreme Court denied review of the case.

In late February 2005, Judge Greer set March 18 as the date when Michael Schiavo could have Terri Schiavo's feeding tube removed again. Raising the volume in the escalating stigma contest, Randall Terry, founder of the pro-life group Operation Rescue, held a news conference with the Schindlers and commenced vigils protesting the tube's removal. On March 16, a Florida appeals court denied a request to block the removal. The next day the Schindlers again sought relief from the U.S. Supreme Court; once again the Court decided not to intervene. On the day set for removing the feeding tube, members in both houses of Congress sought to block the removal, but state court judge Greer rejected these attempts. Terri Schiavo's feeding tube was removed for the third time.

A media encampment outside Terri Schiavo's hospice fueled dueling news conferences between the Schindlers—including Terri's brother and sister—and Michael Schiavo. Federal lawmakers saw an opportunity to put a face—Terri's face—on the culture of life versus culture of death divide. On March 19, the U.S. Senate passed special emergency legislation allowing Terri's parents to move their daughter's case into federal court. The extraordinary move triggered the reinsertion of Terri's feeding tube. More extraordinary still, President Bush cut short a vacation to fly to Washington after midnight on March 21, just to sign the legislation. Bush said in a statement after signing the bill: "In cases like this one, where there are serious questions and substantial doubts, our society, our laws, and our courts should have a presumption in favor of life."

The bill had passed the House by a vote of 203 to 58 during an emergency Sunday session that lasted past midnight. On the Republican side, 156 house members voted for the measure, 5 voted against it, and 71 did not vote. Of the Democrats, 47 voted in favor, 53 voted against, and 102 did not vote. The Senate approved the bill Sunday in a voice vote.

Carl Hulse, a reporter for the *New York Times,* stated, "The fevered Congressional intervention in a single individual's health crisis is being driven in significant part by powerful political forces" being played out at Terri Schiavo's bedside.[1] Republicans, said Hulse, saw an opportunity to stake a further claim about the "the culture of life" so important to religious conservatives. Democrats, on the other hand, availed themselves of the chance to appear more moderate on such issues.[2] Citing Congress's willingness to stay past midnight on the eve of its recess and to bypass standard hearings and review, Hulse declared that there was "little question that this matter would not have risen so far and so fast in Congress" were it not for legislators' own ambitions and constituencies.[3]

Republican supporters denied suggestions that political motives lay behind the last-minute maneuver. "When a person's intentions regarding whether to receive lifesaving treatment are unclear, the responsibility of a compassionate nation is to affirm that person's right to life," said the chairman of the House Judiciary Committee, James Sensenbrenner (R-Wis.). "In our deeds and public actions, we must build a culture of life that welcomes and defends all human life." Those Democrats who opposed the bill said it is better to leave such issues to family members and state courts. "Today, congressional leaders are trying to appoint Congress as a judge and jury," said Representative Jim Davis (D-Fla.). "If we do not draw the line in the sand today, there is no limit to what democratic principles this Congress will ignore or what liberties they may trample on next."[4]

Michael Schiavo said he was outraged. His lawyer, George Felos, said of Congress's involvement in the controversy: "It was odious, it was shocking, it was disgusting and I think all Americans should be alarmed."[5] Felos had words for Democrats, as well. "If they don't stand up for Terri Schiavo, they deserve to be the minority party," Felos told reporters.

Some Democrats were also dismayed. "Congress is turning the Schiavo family's personal tragedy into a national political farce," said Representative Henry A. Waxman of California. California senator Dianne Feinstein added: "We change the nature of all these things to put this in the political arena."[6]

After Congress held its unusual and dramatic eleventh-hour session —what bioethicist Arthur Caplan has called the "Palm Sunday Compromise"[7]—the case went to a federal judge in Florida, who ruled against imposing an injunction to reinsert the feeding tube. Terri Schiavo's parents appealed that ruling to the Eleventh Circuit Court in Atlanta, which affirmed the lower court ruling. A plea for an en banc rehearing of the case also failed, and the parents appealed to the U.S. Supreme Court, where the media was fixed on a literal 11:00 p.m. submission on Wednesday, March 23. The next morning the Supreme Court announced in a terse statement that it was not accepting the case for review. Eyes then turned once again to Florida, where Governor Jeb Bush and the State of Florida were attempting to take control of Terri Schiavo through another legal approach. Those efforts were also rebuffed by the state judge who had overseen the case over the years.

Provoking the critique of social conservatives who felt that "judicial tyranny" was the major culprit in so many of the battles of the culture war, Terri Schiavo's fate rested in the courts, rather than the Congress or the Florida state house. From March 21 to March 30, the Schindlers' last hopes were raised and dashed again and again as federal judges at every level rejected or refused to consider their claims. On March 31, thirteen days after her feeding tube had been removed, Terri Schiavo died.

What the Schiavo Case Represents

When the Republican Congress, the White House, and the governor of Florida voiced strong objections to removing the feeding tube of Terri Schiavo, then inserted themselves into the legal battle, most pundits believed that politicians had the deep support of most Americans (and their fervent Republican base). Certainly Democratic National chairman Howard Dean and Democratic congressional leaders must have reached a similar conclusion, given their general silence during the debate on this matter.

But after weeks of national attention and discussion and several court rulings, we know that Americans were far more supportive of Michael Schiavo's efforts to have his wife's feeding tube removed than originally presumed. Pundits may express surprise; however, the public reaction is not surprising to we who study death, dying, and the law in the United States.

One of the consistent results we found when researching the topic for our book *Dying Right: The Death with Dignity Movement,* was that American attitudes about death and dying have changed in the thirty-one years since California passed the first Natural Death Act in 1976.[8] For example, around the country, public support for the statement "A person has the right to end his or her life if this person has an incurable disease" increased steadily from 38 percent to 61 percent between 1977 and 1996.

In Oregon in 1994—and in 1997, when a repeal vote was turned back—proponents of a carefully drawn Oregon Death with Dignity Act (ODDA) permitting physician-assisted suicide were connecting with widely held sentiments regarding personal autonomy and the intrusiveness of medical intervention at the very end of life. Americans have been expressing the desire to die at home, not in hospitals, and to decide when to decline treatment, refuse resuscitation, and withdraw tubes and machines, since medical advances have made the end of life an often protracted and medicalized event.

With hindsight, it may seem easy to make conclusions about the Schiavo case, but it is clear now that many analysts and politicians underestimated the ways in which the American public has evolved on the issues of death and dying. The consistent poll numbers from a variety of sources are an indication that, as the Pew Research Center's Andrew Kohut has observed, "On life-and-death issues, support for moral values among Americans must contend with a deeply held pragmatism."[9]

Analysts on all sides have commented that, beneath its sadness and contestation, the Schiavo case at least has generated a national conversation about death and dying. We have indeed witnessed an amazing American conversation, about personal wishes and gut-wrenching family decisions involving end-of-life care. What the intense national discussion of March 2005 demonstrates is that, below the radar of politicians, political strategists, and analysts, the evolution of values has slowly but surely come through the many conversations that have taken place in family kitchens, hospital hallways, and church offices over the last thirty years. The changes have come in an America that is clearly more reflective, more protective of personal autonomy, and yet still very religious—an America more moderate and "purple" than was widely assumed at the beginning of the national debate over Terri Schiavo's fate. Arthur Caplan, a leading ethicist and the director of the Center for Bioethics at the University of Pennsylvania, expressed this sentiment when he called that the Schiavo episode "an important case in that it has commanded an inordinate amount of attention. They [politicians] are fighting the consensus that has been entrenched for at least a decade."

Said one analyst:

Today, most deaths occur in institutions and as a result of a decision about medicine or technology. The idea of letting nature take its course has fallen by the medical-technology wayside. Each day, about 460 people die in Florida, many by someone's decision—respirators removed, dialysis stopped, feeding tubes clamped, antibiotics refused.[10]

MSNBC reported how the politics of the Schiavo case intertwined with the ethical considerations: "But the case also has broader implications for long-running debates about euthanasia and abortion, with Republicans characterizing their support for her case as a 'right-to-life' issue. A one-page, unsigned memo circulated among Senate Republicans at the time characterized it as 'a great political issue' that had the potential to energize the party's 'pro-life base.'"[11]

The editors of the *Wall Street Journal* wrote: "Another judge might look differently today on Mr. Schiavo's right-to-die claims given his apparent incentives to be rid of the burden of a severely disabled wife."

The national Democratic Party and leading politicians, meanwhile, also either did not have a sense of the Republican overreach on the Schiavo case or did not want to object and be seen as the "party of death."[12] Democratic Party chair Howard Dean did not offer any official argument, nor did Senate minority leader Harry Reid. Senator Hillary Clinton did not fly back from New York to vote on the congressional bill on Schiavo.

Former Reagan speechwriter Peggy Noonan wrote in the *Wall Street Journal* of Republican politicians' responsiveness to evangelical members of their party's base: "The Republicans are in charge. They have the power. If they can't save this woman's life, they will face a reckoning from a sizable portion of their own base. And they will of course deserve it. This should concentrate their minds. So should this: America is watching."[13] Noonan also characterized the "opposition" as being personified by Terri Schiavo's husband only:

On the other side of this debate, one would assume there is an equally well organized and passionate group of organizations deeply committed to removing Terri Schiavo's feeding tube. But that's not true. There's just about no one on the other side. Or rather there is one person, a disaffected husband who insists Terri once told him she didn't want to be kept alive by extraordinary measures. He has fought the battle to kill her with a determination that at this point seems not single-minded or passionate but strange. His former wife's parents and family are eager to care for her and do care for her, every day. He doesn't have to do a thing. His wife is not kept alive by extraordinary measures—she breathes on her own, is not on a respirator. All she needs to continue existing—and to continue being alive so that life can produce whatever miracle it may produce—is a feeding tube. It doesn't seem a lot. So politically this is a struggle between many serious people who really mean it and one, just one, strange-o. And the few bearded and depressed-looking academics he's drawn to his side.[14]

Religious conservatives like Gary Bauer proclaimed that the Schiavo case was the opening salvo in a battle of the culture war that needed to be fought: "We're on the cusp of a really gigantic national debate about life and advances in medicine . . . that touches in a very important way in the whole debate on the sanctity of life, and it will encourage voters to believe that it is something Republicans feel strongly about."[15] However, others worried that Senate majority leader Bill Frist, a conservative and a physician who at the time was interested in the 2008 presidential race, may have "overplayed his hand" by offering medical advice,[16] and others feared that the congressional action would alienate those who did not favor such use of government power.[17]

One of the other pro-life figures who reappeared in the Schiavo case was Randall Terry, who had come into American consciousness as the leader of Operation Rescue in the 1980s and 1990s.[18] Terry had fallen into disrepute as he evolved during the post-*Casey* Clinton years as an advocate of abortion clinic violence. He accompanied Terri Schiavo's parents at a press conferencing the day after the congressional vote.

In a letter to state legislatures posted on the Web site of his organization, the Society for Truth and Justice, Terry wrote: "Over the past 40 years, the most sweeping (and most Americans believe the most repugnant) changes on America's political and ethical landscape have been forced upon us by the courts."[19]

Surrounding the case was a national spectacle in which news stations and talk radio stations and blogs—the watercoolers of the twenty-first century—devoted enormous amounts of time to coverage of breaking news, legal analysis, and public assessment. A CBS News poll showed that 82 percent of Americans felt that Congress should not have gotten involved, and 66 percent supported the removal of the feeding tube. Few analyses spoke to the state of American public opinion on this matter. In doing so, the analysts, and the activists, underestimated the ways in which the American public has evolved on the issues of death and dying.

Analysts observed that there was a possibility for overreach by Republicans, fresh from their 2004 victory.[20] Even death with dignity advocates such as Dr. Timothy Quill—prominent physician, author, and plaintiff in the 1997 U.S. Supreme Court physician-assisted suicide case —have displayed dismay at how the Schiavo case became a media spectacle: "Distortion by interest groups, media hyperbole, and manipulative use of videotape have characterized this case and demonstrate what can happen when a patient becomes more a precedent-setting symbol than a unique human being."[21]

In the midst of the debate, National Public Radio (NPR) aired a show depicting the views of various religions toward end-of-life issues. For a Muslim commentator, the issue turned on the question of just how a life is defined: is a permanent vegetative state still life, as we understand it? A Jewish expert noted that the issue turned on whether food and hydration was considered nourishment or medicine. If it was considered medicine, and the patient was not heading toward a cure, Jewish teaching would allow its removal. A spokesperson for the U.S. Catholic Conference depicted the feeding issue as one on which Catholic teaching was clear—it should remain. The NPR reporter noted that "very few policies are clear-cut and universally held in this debate."[22]

Further adopting the frame of secularism versus religion, FoxNews commentator Bill O'Reilly depicted the Schiavo debate as an example of the schism between "secular and Christians" in America, failing to note that 60 percent of Catholics and 60 percent of Protestants supported the removal of the feeding tube.[23]

Operation Rescue, part of the "Voice for Terri" coalition, wrote in a lengthy explanation of the case on the organization's Web site, that "many Americans don't realize that Terri is NOT being kept alive against her will. She is NOT being kept alive by 'extraordinary means.' And she is NOT in a 'persistent vegetative state.' She's simply disabled, and needs *proper* care just like any other severely disabled person."[24] "What kind of a nation are we becoming?" asked columnist Nat Hentoff.[25]

Politicians eventually began reading and responding to the poll results, and muting their opposition to a process and outcome that the American public overwhelmingly supported. As the Schiavo case drew to an end, politicians were spinning their prior moves and reassessing their actions. Some conservative analysts supported the president, stating that he at least paid attention to the Republican Party's Christian conservative base. Political commentators tried to figure out who had benefited from these actions.[26]

While Democrats did not boldly critique the proposed congressional action in the Schiavo case, the American public responded in the opposite direction. The findings of an ABC News poll, taken directly after the congressional action, found that a sizable 70 percent of respondents believed that Congress's intervention in the Schiavo case was inappropriate. A significant majority (63 percent) supported the removal of Schiavo's feeding tube, and fully two-thirds (67 percent) thought "the elected officials trying to keep Schiavo alive are doing so more for political advantage than out of concern for her or for the principles involved." With such substantial numbers, that majority naturally included large numbers of Republicans (61 percent) and Catholics (63 percent) who agreed with the statement.[27]

With the death of Pope John Paul II—which involved no removal of life-sustaining equipment—following within days, the national spotlight faded and the national discussion subsided, in part because Republican activist politicians realized that the American public had not agreed with their dramatic intervention. As one might predict, there were rallying cries against activist judges from those like House majority leader Tom DeLay. The Senate scheduled hearings, which were held a week after Ms. Schiavo's death, but which were low-key and not fired up with the type of testimony and attention one would expect if a true case was being made. Senator Mike Enzi, chair of the Senate's Health and Education Committee, mainly used the forum as a chance to encourage Americans to sign living wills, even though his few persons who testified were speaking to the issue of the severely brain damaged person and his or her capability and rights.[28] At the same time, at least some were worried about legislation from the House of Representatives, such as the Incapacitated Person's Legal Protection Act, which Doug Ireland describes as requiring "federal courts to intervene at the request of any family member or loved one if a state court 'authorizes or directs' the withholding of food or life support when there is an alleged dispute over the patient's wishes."[29]

Conservative analyst David Brooks placed a different emphasis on the Schiavo polls. In his view, Americans were displaying their conservative bent:

First, there's the Terri Schiavo case. Republicans charged boldly forth to preserve her life and were surprised by how few Americans charged along behind them. Fewer than a third of the American people opposed removing her feeding tube.

Being conservative, most Americans believe that decisions should be made at the local level, where people understand the texture of the case. Even many evangelicals, who otherwise embrace the culture of life, grow queasy when politicians in Washington start imposing solutions from afar, based on abstract principles rather than concrete particulars.[30]

After the Schiavo autopsy in June 2005, there was a sense of finality. When the autopsy found a severely limited brain, the expectant result for those who had seen her years of vegetative state and decline, there was general consensus that all had gone the best way.

But not all acquiesced—or read the polls. Senator Frist—who perhaps lost his position as leading candidate for the support of the religious Right in Republican primaries in 2008—had been chastised and ridiculed for his long-distance "diagnosis" of Ms. Schiavo's opportunity for recovery, which he made from watching a video supplied by her parents and supporters during the battle over her feeding tubes (or what one analyst later called Frist's "telemisdiagnosis").[31] When the autopsy was released, Frist tried to backpedal on the diagnosis, but the damage had seemingly been done. Frist was sensing the emergence of other conservative voices and competitors, like Rick Santorum, Sam Brownback, George Allen, and Mitt Romney, the Republican governor of Massachusetts, some of whom were interested in pursuing the 2008 Republican presidential nomination.

Governor Bush kept going on the Schiavo story, promising an investigation into any criminal activity having to do with her injury. He relented only when a state investigative body concluded that there was no criminal wrongdoing.[32]

Ten months after his wife's death, Michael Schiavo married. He started the Terri PAC, fully named Political Action to Restore Personal Freedoms and Individual Rights. When he announced plans for a book, Nat Hentoff countered claims that the book was, in a publicist's words, the "seminal case in the right to die with dignity story." Instead, wrote Hentoff, "This is the seminal case for whether euthanasia for the seriously disabled becomes embedded in the American way of death."[33]

When published in 2006, Michael Schiavo's *Terri: The Truth* continued dueling, now with the Schindlers' book and their opposing web site.[34]

In the year after Terri Schiavo's death, almost fifty end-of-life bills were proposed in twenty-three states.[35] Analysis by Compassion and Choices, the organization that grew out of the Oregon and Washington initiative experiences, showed that a large number of these proposals were modeled after a national right-to-life model bill that would in effect roll back portions of what had been a national consensus on dying and the law since the 1970s.

The Blue Way: The Importance of Autonomy

Where had the impetus and rationale for the natural death laws, the death with dignity movement, and the Oregon Death with Dignity Act come from? And what was it saying about us as Americans in the year of Terri Schiavo?

For much of the last half of the twentieth century, medical practitioners shunned death and dying, treating it as a failure of medicine. The overriding goal became to cure. High-tech medicine was the means to that end. Hospitals replaced homes as the place where death occurred. For many, dying was now accompanied by acute, chronic illness. Once those changes in what has been called the locus of dying took place, they coincided with a movement for autonomy in the dying process, which mirrored struggles for reproductive freedom and led to legal reforms from the time of the 1976 California Natural Death Act onward. The changes in Oregon took place in the context of a sea change in how Americans felt about autonomy and dying. There was a remarkable growth in American support, from 38 percent to 61 percent between 1977 and 1996, for the statement "A person has the right to end his or her life if this person has an incurable disease."[36]

The movement that resulted in the California law and those of the other states that soon followed furthered sentiment expressed two decades earlier in England, when British jurisprudential scholar Glanville Williams argued in 1958 for legal reform of euthanasia laws as a way of preventing cruelty to patients and to relatives. Williams anticipated the arguments by physicians Timothy Quill[37] and others who would lead physician movement for assisted suicide reform in the United States in the 1990s when he wrote: "If the doctor honestly and sincerely believes that the best service he can perform for his suffering patient is to accede to his request for euthanasia, it is a grave thing that the law should forbid him to do."[38]

Williams's sentiments did not have many parallels in the American legal reform movements, though the decriminalization of suicide itself did take place in the United States and other Western nations. But another significant societal change was taking place—where and how people died.

The example of the civil rights movement in the 1960s and 1970s inspired other groups to press for rights grounded in the notion of liberty. Whereas equal rights activists pressed claims for political access, visibility, and legitimation, civil liberties groups pushed for self-determination, political autonomy, and individual choice. Whereas the former emphasizes inclusion in the civil affairs of society, the latter stresses freedom to act outside the values and customs of the mainstream. One movement to successfully adapt to the nature of rights claiming, developed in the 1960s and 1970s, was the right-to-die movement.

In the late 1930s, efforts to present legislation permitting voluntary euthanasia—which had been pursued primarily by elite academics in the behavioral, natural, and social sciences—never attracted a bill sponsor. Those efforts were further immobilized by the human atrocities committed by Nazi Germans in the 1940s. But rapid advancements in end-of-life care beginning in the 1950s created wholesale changes in where people died (in hospitals instead of in homes) and causes of death (slow degenerative illnesses such as cancer and heart disease). These changes aroused concern among patients, families, and physicians suffering through prolonged dying, which is the dark side of life-sustaining medical technology. Buoyed by the successes of rights claimants in the 1960s and 1970s, advocates of a right to die took aim at legal reform.

The example of abortion law reform that took place throughout the 1960s—relying as it did upon changing social mores about sexual relations, women's roles, the appropriate responsibilities of physicians, and the influence of religious organizations—has provided a rights framework for right-to-die advocates making claims favoring patient autonomy. As medical innovation has given way to the institutionalization of death, patients have demanded greater parity in the physician-patient relationship, including the right to die on their own terms; physicians have struggled to preserve a level of nobility and autonomy based on expertise in the practice of medicine; and the state has had to adopt new ways for physicians to enforce the state's interest in preventing killing.[39] These changes closely parallel changes in the patient-physician-state relationship that accompanied shifts in pubic opinion and legal reform efforts in the abortion rights context.[40]

From 1976 and the landmark court decision that gave Karen Quinlan's parents the right to disconnect her ventilator, through 1998 and the airing of a videotape on *60 Minutes* showing Jack Kevorkian giving a lethal injection to a fifty-two-year-old man with Lou Gehrig's disease, the country was engaged in serious debate about the limits of physician-aided dying. Beginning with the nation's first living will statute in 1976, laws were created to address issues of treatment withholding and withdrawal, advance directives, surrogate decision making, and the symbolic value of artificial nutrition and hydration. Until Kevorkian leaped onto the scene in 1990, however, the strategies and rhetoric of right-to-die reformers stopped short of seeking to decriminalize assisted suicide or more direct forms of euthanasia. But in a series of citizen ballot initiatives in Washington (1991), California (1992), Oregon (1994), Michigan (1998), and Maine (2000), mainstream reform seekers worked hard to pass laws that would permit physicians to aid patients in hastening death when it was imminent. Reformers were successful only in Oregon, although in most of the other states the votes were very close. In 1996, the group that pressed for ballot measures in Oregon, Michigan, and Maine convinced two federal circuit courts of appeal to strike down state laws prohibiting assisted suicide; however, those decisions were overturned in two unanimous decisions by the U.S. Supreme Court the following year. Jack Kevorkian was convicted of homicide and imprisoned in 1999, and the right to die had fallen off the national agenda until the Schiavo case.

Right-to-die reform efforts reflect the earlier debates over the proper use of the criminal law in the regulation of gambling, drugs, prostitution, and abortion in two ways besides their grounding in rights consciousness. One centers on the fact that these illegal activities occur frequently in spite of the law. As Dr. Timothy Quill tellingly demonstrated in a 1991 *New England Journal of Medicine* article detailing how he had prescribed a lethal dose of painkillers to help a terminally ill woman commit suicide, physicians often aid their dying patients.[41]

This recognition that "it happens anyway" gives rise to the reformers' claim that only by bringing into the open what occurs now in secret are regulation and oversight truly possible. In other words, reformers argue, preventing the economically marginalized from being pressured into dying against their will; avoiding a slippery slope to more active or involuntary forms of euthanasia; thwarting an erosion of trust and good care in the patient-physician relationship—these goals are *more* likely to be assured of success if certain forms of physician-aided dying are decriminalized in certain circumstances. In this way, some of the claims by proponents of reforming assisted suicide laws reflect the realities of modern life that proponents of decriminalizing gambling, drugs, prostitution, and abortion claimed in earlier debates about the proper use of the criminal law in regulating morality.

A third way the claims of right-to-die reformers have reflected claims in prior debates about law and morality is in their focus on the principle of harm reduction. As with the reform of marijuana possession laws in the 1970s, which was pursued largely for the purpose of lessening the impact that a felony conviction had on individuals in the demographic group that was breaking the law by using marijuana, right-to-die advocates have sought to reduce the harm that criminalization of physician-aided dying has brought about. Examples cited by reformers include prolongation of the dying process, which impacts not just dying patients but also their families and other caretakers; the prospect of beneficiaries being denied life insurance payments in the event a patient's hastened death is ruled a suicide (a rare occurrence); and the inability of poor dying patients to obtain the same assistance that paying patients may be able to negotiate "with a wink and a nod."[42]

Here again, the history of illegal abortion provides a close parallel. As Leslie Reagan amply demonstrates, laws criminalizing abortion did not reduce the prevalence of abortions; however, they dramatically increased the prevalence of injuries and deaths associated with the procedure.[43] Thus the decriminalization of abortion is a solid example of legal change wherein there was some recognition that extending the criminal law to regulate moral choices can make matters worse.[44] Likewise, proponents of physician-aided dying have claimed, the failure to decriminalize more proactive measures that physicians could use to ease the dying process makes dying worse for the vast majority.

One statement by an amicus brief on behalf of reformers in the 2005

Gonzales v. Oregon case is representative of this emphasis on growing public support for the option of assistance in dying:

> The Attorney General's claim that the practice is "universally condemned" is similarly plainly wrong. Polls, legislative consideration, the debates being conducted in the medical and ethics journals, and the many amici briefs filed with the court in support of our clients all demonstrate that there is very large and growing support for the availability of the option of a humanely hastened death for the terminally ill facing an imminent death that often involves excruciating and intractable pain, as well as loss of functioning and dignity.[45]

Seeing Red: Against the Taking of Life

Opponents of assisted suicide have generally framed their objections in two ways. The first involves religious claims that life is sacred and only God should determine the timing and manner of death. The National Right to Life Committee and the U.S. Conference of Catholic Bishops, whose members are the active Catholic bishops in the United States, as well as several of their state affiliates, have been major parties in the controversy since 1991. In that year a small group of citizens in the state of Washington introduced the first state ballot initiative seeking to permit physicians to provide assisted suicide and active euthanasia as medical services. Had the initiative passed, Washington State would have been the first and only place in the world where the intentional killing of patients by physicians had been formally decriminalized.[46] The initiative failed, 51 to 49 percent.

In March 2004, the Vatican issued an opinion declaring that feeding tubes are not medical treatment and therefore cannot be withheld from permanently unconscious patients. A few days later, Pope John Paul II agreed, saying that removing feeding tubes from unconscious patients constitutes "euthanasia by omission." The pope's pronouncement has caused confusion within hospitals operated by the Catholic Church in the United States. Many hospital administrators, however, are choosing to follow the "Ethical and Religious Directives for Catholic Healthcare Services" outlined by the U.S. Conference of Catholic Bishops. Those guidelines define artificial nutrition and hydration as medical treatment, removal of which the guidelines permit. Leaders of the Catholic

Healthcare Association called for discussion among bishops and Catholic health care providers.

In earlier remarks, the pope had been clear in the Catholic Church's position:

> Above all, society must learn to embrace once more the great gift of life, to cherish it, to protect it, and to defend it against the culture of death, itself an expression of the great fear that stalks our times. One of your most noble tasks as Bishops is to stand firmly on the side of life, encouraging those who defend it and building with them a genuine culture of life. . . . The introduction of legalized abortion and euthanasia, ever increasing recourse to in vitro fertilization, and certain forms of genetic manipulation and embryo experimentation are also closely related in law and public policy, as well as in contemporary culture, to the idea of unlimited dominion over one's body and life. . . .
>
> Euthanasia and suicide are grave violations of God's law (cf *Evangelium Vitae,* 65 and 66); their legalization introduces a direct threat to the persons least capable of defending themselves and it proves most harmful to the democratic institutions of society. The fact that Catholics have worked successfully with members of other Christian communities to resist efforts to legalize physician-assisted suicide is a very hopeful sign for the future of ecumenical public witness in your country and I urge you to build an even broader ecumenical and inter-religious movement in defense of the culture of life and the civilization of love.[47]

The Catholic Church's involvement in 1991 in Washington consisted of raising money to fight the initiative and rallying Catholic voters to vote against it. In parishes across the state, clergy preached against the initiative, and church members and officials stuffed inserts into church bulletins and sent flyers home with parochial schoolchildren with a message that implored:

> We are confronted here with a violation of the divine law, an offense against the dignity of the human person, a crime against life and an attack on humanity. Phrases such as "mercy killing," "rational suicide," and "aid-in-dying" or "death with dignity" should not be allowed to obscure the fact that euthanasia is killing an innocent human being. It is morally wrong. No civilized society should condone it.[48]

In Oregon in 1994, Roman Catholic sources provided more than 75 percent of the $1.5 million raised to challenge passage of the ODDA, including $300,000 in collections from church members. A bishop and an archbishop from dioceses in Baker and Portland instructed their priests to preach against the ballot proposal one week, then collect money a week later to defeat it. The Oregon Family Council distributed 200,000 copies of a voters guide to members in 1,600 churches. The measure's proponents charged, "This politicking from the pulpit clearly shows our opponents' intention to promote Catholic religious doctrine by influencing Oregon voters."[49]

The second way opponents have framed their stance is by claiming that legalizing assisted suicide would result in systematic abuses against the sick and vulnerable. A key message in ads and other voter appeals was that the proposed law lacked effective safeguards: doctors would become killers, contrary to their oath to fulfill the role of healer; methods for predicting the imminence of death are fallible; family rights would be violated; a slippery slope would be created, leading to court judgments ordering lethal injections when patients cannot swallow medication; people may kill themselves to avoid financial burdens; and depressed patients will be at risk.

Richard Doerflinger, deputy director of the Secretariat for Pro-Life National Activities, U.S. Conference of Catholic Bishops, has prepared policy statements and testified before Congress, the National Bioethics Advisory Commission, and the National Institutes of Health (NIH) on ethical issues involving abortion, euthanasia, and human embryo research during his twenty-one year career with the bishops' conference. Doerflinger's comments from his testimony before Congress on behalf of the conference in 1999, capture his view and that of his organization:

> When we accept assisted suicide as a "good enough" solution for these patients, we preach a counsel of despair to all terminally ill patients. We tell them that we find it easier to kill them than to find ways to kill their pain. By rejecting the "quick fix" of assisted suicide, however, we reaffirm to ourselves and to the medical profession that these patients have lives worth living, and that they deserve real solutions for the pain, depression and isolation that they may experience.[50]

James Bopp Jr. is a leading pro-life lawyer in death and dying cases; his law practice includes biomedical issues of abortion, foregoing and withdrawing life-sustaining medical treatment, and assisted suicide. Bopp has served as a member of several committees, including the President's Committee on Mental Retardation, the Congressional Biomedical Ethics Advisory Committee, and the NIH Human Fetal Tissue Transplantation Research Panel, and was also appointed by President Ronald Reagan to the White House Conference on Aging. He is the general counsel for the National Right to Life Committee, president of the National Legal Center for the Medically Dependent and Disabled, special counsel for Focus on the Family, general counsel and state treasurer for the Indiana Republican Party, and a member of the Bush-Cheney '04, Indiana Campaign Leadership Team. It was Bopp who won the initial injunction against the ODDA.

Sometimes those opposed to assisted suicide law reform take more profane approaches, such as that of conservative radio host Rush Limbaugh. In 2005, Limbaugh reacted to the *Gonzales v. Oregon* oral arguments by lampooning the use of the ODDA to change the prescribed manner of dying in Oregon, offering this inelegant reference to more tried-and-true methods of suicide: "If people want to kill themselves, there are ways of doing this. A six pack, and a hose, and go sit in your car, and wave sayonara."[51]

Wesley J. Smith, author of *Forced Exit: The Slippery Slope from Assisted Suicide to Legalized Murder* (1997), argues that legalizing euthanasia or assisted suicide would be a disaster for the disabled, the critically ill, and the indigent. The death of a friend who checked into a hotel room and committed suicide using the Hemlock Society's method of overdosing and suffocating oneself with a plastic bag piqued Smith's activism on the subject. Since then, Smith has worked closely with the International Anti-Euthanasia Task Force to write and speak on the dangers of legalizing euthanasia and assisted suicide.

In Smith's view, there can be no compassion in euthanasia without cruelty. Legalized murder is practically inevitable when society allows any form of complicity in death. The only possible result is calamity. Just as with euthanizing animals, argues Smith, euthanizing people will result in killing not just the sick but also the abandoned.

Smith derides supporters of physician-assisted suicide for drawing parallels between choice in assisted suicide and choice in abortion, claiming that using abortion to bootstrap assisted suicide arguments is disingenuous because the debate is still fluid. As evidence of this fluidness Smith points to the fact that even though pubic opinion polls suggest that there is strong support for seeking physician assistance in controlling the timing and manner of death, support generally plummets when ballot referendums and other concrete opportunities to officially sanction physician-aided dying occur.

Smith examines the Dutch experience and warns of an impending "slippery slope," a common argument of anti–assisted suicide reformers: "Once we accept the killing of terminally ill patients . . . we will invariably accept the killing of chronically ill patients, depressed patients, and ultimately, children."[52] He draws an analogy between attitudes of assisted suicide supporters and the attitudes expressed during the pre-Nazi and Nazi periods in Germany. That arguments for physician-assisted suicide "are presented in warm tones of compassion or the bland prose of scholarly dispassion does not make them any less dangerous," Smith concludes.[53]

Smith is a prolific writer whose articles concerning assisted suicide and stem cell research appear frequently in *National Review Online* and the *Weekly Standard*. Founded by William F. Buckley and considered to be one of the most influential political publications in the country, the *National Review* was very popular in the Reagan administration. The *Weekly Standard*—an American neoconservative magazine edited by William Kristol and Fred Barnes, and owned by Rupert Murdoch's News Corporation—is reported to have achieved the same status in the Bush White House, with Vice President Dick Cheney's office alone receiving a special delivery of thirty copies.[54] *National Review* editor Ramesh Ponnuru has recently published his attack on autonomy and the "culture of death," entitled *The Party of Death*.[55]

Smith penned many articles on the Terri Schiavo case. In his view, Michael Schiavo's eventual decision to start a new family while still married to Terri amounted to marital abandonment, which alone should have been enough to remove Michael as Terri's guardian. The judge's failure to do so was one of many judicial failures in the case, Smith said. He said the mainstream media "cherry-picked facts" on account of a bias in favor of Michael. Smith's criticisms had been driven by his firm belief that the videos of Terri showed she was eager to please when a doctor asked her to open her eyes, and she exhibited happiness, as well, when her mother entered a room and when music played.[56] Smith was bitterly critical of Florida bioethicist Bill Allen's view that because Terri exhibited a complete lack of awareness, she was not a person. Such thinking is not a fringe view in bioethics, Smith charges, and it could lead to human experimentation, lethal injection, and organ harvesting. Smith implores: "Know this: There is a direct line from the Terri Schiavo dehydration to the potential for this stunning human strip-mining scenario's becoming a reality."[57]

Smith has also written on the subject of Oregon's assisted suicide law, which we discuss at length later. In his view, the Oregon law is "a prescription for anarchy," in that theoretically there could be fifty separate state laws regulating how drugs are used in assisted suicide practice.[58] Smith agrees with former attorney general John Ashcroft's determination that the federal government has the authority to enforce federal law regulating medical practice in the states, and that there is a long history of the federal government acting in this way. As we explain later in this chapter, the Supreme Court agreed that under the commerce clause, Congress is empowered to write legislation that affects state medical practice, but to date it has not authorized the attorney general to determine which medical practices are or are not legitimate.

Of course, former attorney general Ashcroft, the son and grandson of Assemblies of God ministers, himself typifies the views and attitudes of a "classic red" opponent of assisted suicide law reform. Strongly conservative and deeply religious, in his book *Lessons from a Father to a Son* Ashcroft tells how he arose every morning to "the magisterial wake-up call" of his father's prayers.[59] A generation later, Ashcroft the son—himself a nonsmoker and nondrinker—was one of the first senators to suggest that President Bill Clinton's wrongdoings in the White House might warrant impeachment.

Ashcroft rose through the political ranks in his home state of Missouri, first as state auditor beginning in 1973, then as attorney general for two terms spanning 1976 to 1984, then two terms as governor from 1985 to 1993, and finally a single term as U.S. senator from 1995 to 2001. He supported the death penalty and established a firm record of opposition toward gun control, abortion, and gay rights. Nearing the end of his Senate career, the conservative Christian Coalition rated Ashcroft at 100 percent, while the environmentalist League of Conservation Voters and the left-leaning National Organization for Women each rated him at zero.[60]

With backing from social conservatives, Ashcroft briefly considered a run for the presidency in the year 2000. He decided instead to focus on a Senate reelection campaign. His opponent—then Missouri governor Mel Carnahan—was killed in a plane crash shortly before the election.

At the time, polls showed Ashcroft ahead, but the lieutenant governor's announcement that he would appoint Carnahan's wife to serve in her husband's place if Carnahan won the election moved voters to elect Carnahan by a slim margin—giving Ashcroft the unenviable distinction of being the only U.S. senator ever to be defeated by an opponent who had passed on.

Soon after, in December 2000, president-elect George W. Bush nominated Ashcroft to be U.S. attorney general. During Ashcroft's confirmation hearings in the Senate, most Democrats opposed the nomination on account of Ashcroft's prior opposition to desegregation and abortion. Ashcroft was narrowly confirmed, however, by a vote of 58 to 42.

On November 6, 2001, Ashcroft authorized federal drug agents to revoke the prescription privileges of physicians who prescribed federally controlled drugs for use in assisted suicide—taking direct aim at Oregon's physician-assisted suicide law. Along with social and religious conservatives seeking to undermine or even abolish the Oregon law, Ashcroft contended that any official sanction of assisted suicide is immoral. His action may have helped to mollify some conservative groups who were frustrated with the administration's standstill on abortion issues and the president's decision only months earlier to compromise and support some research on embryonic stem cells.[61]

Ashcroft's action reversed a Clinton administration policy allowing the Oregon law to stand. An Oregon doctor, a pharmacist, and several terminally ill patients joined state attorney general Hardy Meyers to challenge Ashcroft's move. The challengers won rulings against Ashcroft in a federal district court and a federal court of appeals. In a willful last move, Ashcroft petitioned the U.S. Supreme Court to review the case on behalf of the Bush administration, filing the petition on November 9, 2004—the very day Ashcroft resigned. We discuss the Supreme Court's ruling in the case later in this chapter.

The Oregon Death with Dignity Experience, 1994–2007

The only American state currently permitting legal physician-assisted suicide, Oregon has been as active as any state with the use of citizen initiatives, and had indeed pioneered them. Oregon had decriminalized marijuana, and Portland was a progressive and livable city with a significant gay and lesbian population. It had been one of the first states to grant women suffrage early in the twentieth century. So it was appropriate that Oregon stepped out from the rest of the United States in 1994 when it passed America's first assisted suicide law. After court review, and an unsuccessful repeal vote, the law went into effect late in 1997.

On March 27, 1998, an Oregon woman in her eighties who was near death from breast cancer legally ended her life with barbiturates supplied by a physician. Another fourteen persons would join her in utilizing the Oregon Death with Dignity Act in its first year of operation.

The Oregon woman was the first person to die under the provisions of the ODDA, a 1994 law passed by voter referendum. The ODDA provides a safe harbor from criminal and civil law for family members, counselors, and physicians who help competent adults with less than six months to live end their lives with prescription drugs. The law also protects patients from fraud and coercion. The Oregon Death with Dignity Act is the world's first law of its kind.

The ODDA was drafted by attorneys in consultation with interested health care professionals and became effective on October 27, 1997, after three years of failed court challenges and an unsuccessful repeal effort. While these challenges were pending, the Oregon Health Division —the agency charged with overseeing and regulating ODDA practices —produced a list of requirements for physicians to follow. According to the Oregon Health Division, the attending physician has the following responsibilities:

1. to determine whether the patient has a terminal illness, is capable, and has made the request voluntarily;
2. to inform the patient of his/her diagnosis and prognosis, the risks and probable result of taking the prescribed medication, and the feasible alternatives including comfort care and pain control;
3. to refer the patient to a consulting physician for confirmation of the diagnosis and determination that the patient is capable and acting voluntarily;
4. to refer the patient for counseling if, in the opinion of either the attending physician or the consulting physician, the patient may be suffering from any mental disorder, including depression, causing impaired judgment;
5. to request that the patient notify next of kin (the patient does not have to comply); and

6. to offer the patient the opportunity to rescind the request at any time.[62]

Over the years since the ODDA took effect, it has not been much used. From 1998 through 2005, the Oregon Health Division reported in 2006, it has been used in 246 cases, with 80 percent of those resulting from terminal cancer diagnoses.

Gonzales v. Oregon: *The Federal Interest*

Even as the ODDA was being reviewed in federal courts between 1994 and 1997, congressional Republicans were strategizing how to use their authority to curtail the Oregon law. Their efforts to pass legislation that would have criminalized physicians' prescribing of pain relief for terminal patients met the resistance of organized medicine and national hospice groups, which feared that much physician prescribing that took place under the auspices of "standard medical practice" (or what legal philosopher Ronald Dworkin and the *New York Times* editorial page referred to as a "wink and a nod" between a well-heeled patient and his or her physician) would then be subject to scrutiny and prosecution.[63]

A second avenue was a policing response, when the director of the Drug Enforcement Administration (DEA) argued the federal Controlled Substances Act (CSA) regulated such physicians and their "non–medically authorized" prescription of scheduled drugs for patients to end their lives. With the Democratic Clinton administration and Attorney General Janet Reno feeling otherwise, that approach did not threaten the operation of the ODDA at that time.

That was to change when, five months after Bush took office, his administration sought to challenge the Oregon Death with Dignity Act. In June 2001, Attorney General Ashcroft asserted his authority to revoke the prescribing privileges of physicians who prescribe drugs to assist patients in suicide. The state of Oregon and a physician and a pharmacist with practices in Oregon challenged the interpretive rule in the U.S. District Court for the District of Oregon. The court held the interpretive rule invalid and blocked it from being implemented. Ashcroft and others appealed. The court of appeals sided 2 to 1 against Attorney General Ashcroft, and the Bush administration appealed the case to the U.S. Supreme Court.

In a 2-to-1 ruling in May 2004, the Ninth Circuit Court of Appeals confirmed a lower court ruling that Ashcroft had no authority over Oregon's assisted-dying law. Ashcroft had argued that Oregon's law permitting physicians to prescribe a lethal dose of medicine in certain circumstances contravenes the federal CSA. In a 2001 directive, the attorney general ordered that physicians prescribing lethal doses of drugs in compliance with the law should have their prescription licenses revoked. But, said the judges, "The attorney general's unilateral attempt to regulate general medical practices historically entrusted to state lawmakers interferes with the democratic debate about physician-assisted suicide and far exceeds the scope of his authority under federal law." Commenting on the Court's ruling, the president of the country's leading right-to-die organization stated, "The opponents who remain at this point after six years of success in Oregon are really moral opponents."[64]

Before the Court was the question of whether the attorney general is permitted to construe the federal CSA (21 USC 801 et seq.) and its implementing regulations (specifically 21 C.F.R. 1306.04) to prohibit the distribution of federally controlled substances for the purpose of facilitating an individual's suicide, regardless of a state law purporting to authorize such distribution. In essence this question required a determination of the proper scope of the attorney general's authority under the CSA. More specifically, it called for the Supreme Court to determine whether Congress intended to empower the attorney general to address the state-authorized and duly regulated medical practice of physician-assisted suicide. We provide some general background on the CSA and its implementing regulations to put this query into perspective. We follow that brief description with some of the claims propounded in friend-of-the-court briefs provided to the justices by parties with a variety of interests in the case. That is followed by our firsthand account of the oral arguments before the Court, which took place on October 5, 2005.

The CSA is a complex regulatory scheme that controls how prescription drugs are manufactured, distributed, and dispensed. Congress enacted the CSA as Title II of the Comprehensive Drug Abuse Prevention and Control Act of 1970. These policies, which were aimed at conquering drug abuse, were enacted during the first campaign in the "war on drugs," launched by President Richard M. Nixon shortly after he took office in 1969. They centralized law enforcement and provided more tools to combat national and international traffic in illicit drugs. Specifically, the CSA is aimed at preventing the diversion of legitimate drugs into illicit channels. The CSA and its implementing regulations strictly regulate registration requirements, production quotas, labeling and packaging, drug security, and record keeping.

Although physicians' prescribing practices fall under state authority, physicians must register with the DEA and comply with the provisions of the CSA. The CSA provides criminal penalties for physicians who dispense controlled substances beyond "the course of professional practice or research" (21 USC 802(21)), as well as for revocation of the DEA drug registrations of physicians who have engaged in criminal conduct or in other "conduct which may threaten the public health and safety" (21 USC 823(f)(5)). The act provides the attorney general with broad authority to promulgate "rules and regulations . . . relating to the registration and control of the manufacture, distribution, and dispensing of controlled substances" (21 USC 821), and "any rules, regulations, and procedures which he may deem necessary and appropriate for the efficient execution of his functions" under the CSA (21 USC 871(b)).

When the CSA was implemented in 1971, the Bureau of Narcotics and Dangerous Drugs (the predecessor of today's DEA) issued a regulation requiring that a prescription for a controlled substance "must be issued for a legitimate medical purpose by an individual practitioner acting in the usual course of his professional practice" (21 C.F.R. 1306.04(a)). In 2001 Attorney General Ashcroft asked the Office of Legal Counsel (OLC) at the Department of Justice to determine whether a prescription for a drug to assist in an individual's suicide as contemplated under Oregon's Death with Dignity Act is a valid prescription under the CSA and the implementing regulation requiring prescriptions to be issued for a legitimate medical purpose. On June 27, 2001, the OLC issued a memorandum stating that "assisting in suicide is not a 'legitimate medical purpose' that would justify a physician's dispensing controlled substances consistent with the CSA." Ashcroft adopted the OLC's analysis and, on November 9, 2001, published an interpretive rule in the *Federal Register* stating that "assisting suicide is not a 'legitimate medical purpose' within the meaning of 21 CFR § 1306.04," and therefore "prescribing, dispensing, or administering federally controlled substances to assist suicide violates the CSA."[65] Under the rule, physicians who prescribe controlled substances pursuant to the ODDA risk having their DEA registrations revoked. When Ashcroft resigned and was replaced by Alberto Gonzales as attorney general in 2005, the case became known as *Gonzales v. Oregon*.

Amici Curiae

Friend-of-the-court briefs were filed to support each side in the case. Although the issue of the propriety of assisted suicide was not here before the Court, as it was in *Washington v. Glucksberg* and *Vacco v. Quill* eight years earlier, many organizations used the opportunity of having the controversy again before the Court to champion their political and moral views.

Physician-assisted suicide gravely concerns many people with disabilities, and the Oregon law has provided a focal point for the disabilities rights movement. One highly visible group—Not Dead Yet—got its start fighting against assisted suicide and euthanasia around the United States and in other parts of the world. The Supreme Court cited the group's amicus brief in *Washington v. Glucksberg,* and the group gathered a small force of supporters outside the Court building during oral arguments in *Gonzales v. Oregon.*

Many of the nation's leading organizations representing people with disabilities joined with Not Dead Yet in a brief urging the Court to uphold the attorney general's determination that prescribing controlled substances for assisted suicide is not a legitimate medical purpose under the CSA. Groups advocating this view included ADAPT, which has been a plaintiff in numerous civil rights lawsuits and is one of the key organizations that helped enact the Americans with Disabilities Act; the Center on Disability Studies, Law, and Human Policy at Syracuse University, whose studies have included the history of the treatment of people with disabilities in America, as well as images of disability in the media and popular culture; and the National Council on Independent Living, which represents more than 700 advocacy organizations whose independent living philosophy holds that "people with disabilities have the right to live with dignity and appropriate supports in their own homes, participate in their communities, and control and make decisions about their lives, regardless of the degree of disability."

These and other related organizations aver that assisted suicide laws deny people with disabilities the same legal protections against suicide as others without disabilities. In doing so, they say, such laws represent "the ultimate legal judgment" that lives with disabilities are not worth living, as well as distracting from other solutions such as improved treatment, community-based health care, and other measures stressing the enhancement of independence, personal fulfillment, and dignity.[66] Other groups that signed on to this position included Self-Advocates Becoming Empowered, the Center for Self-Determination, the Hospice Patients Alliance, the Society for Disability Studies, TASH (formerly the Association for Persons with Severe Handicaps), *Mouth* magazine, the National Spinal Cord Injury Association, and the World Institute on Disability.

Disability groups opposed to the Oregon law outnumbered supporters six to one. The only two groups to submit amicus briefs supporting the law were AUTONOMY, Inc., and the Cascade AIDS Project, both of which are headquartered in Oregon. They agree with opponents of assisted suicide that autonomy and self-determination are the cornerstones of the disability rights movement. But unlike opponents, they assert that autonomy and self-determination include a wide range of end-of-life choices. Their view of people with disabilities is not one of potential victims needing protection from a biased society. Rather, they stress how the personal circumstances of people with disabilities vary substantially, and they focus on those whose unbearable suffering in their final days of terminal disease "is depriving them of the personhood they have worked so hard to achieve."[67] This has been the minority view in the disability rights movement, however.

Four more briefs supporting the Ashcroft directive were filed on behalf of a range of groups which argued that assisted suicide is incompatible with medicine's aims to prevent illness, to heal, and to alleviate pain. Joining in the brief were the U.S. Conference of Catholic Bishops; the Catholic Health Association of the United States, which is composed of more than 2,000 nonprofit Catholic health care systems, sponsors, facilities, health plans, and related organizations; the bishops from the California, Oregon, and Washington State Catholic Conferences; and the Lutheran Church–Missouri Synod. Stressing the fact that physician-assisted suicide is criminal in virtually all states, these groups argued that providing patients with lethalities "does not become 'medicine' simply because the perpetrator is a doctor, the patient is terminally ill, or one state has decided to rescind its own criminal penalties for the act." Obliterating the distinction between treating pain and assisting suicide, they claimed, could negatively impact pain management and palliative care. Indeed, they added, distinguishing assisted suicide from treating pain and keeping the former illegal "has led to significant improvements in palliative care and in the ability of physicians to care for dying patients."[68]

The National Association of Pro-Life Nurses, Physicians for Compassionate Care Educational Foundation, and the family-centered organizations Focus on the Family and the Family Research Council propounded similar claims in other briefs. Describing itself as a voice for the pro-family movement in Washington, D.C., the Family Research Council joined with James Dobson's nonprofit religious corporation Focus on the Family in observing that the American Medical Association (AMA) condemns physician involvement in assisted suicide precisely because it contradicts widely shared and long-standing views of the medical profession. Americans United for Life, the oldest pro-life legal organization in the country, argued further that physician-assisted suicide is unnecessary for the treatment of pain in terminally ill patients. On the contrary, the group claimed, what causes terminally ill patients to suffer are "unwarranted fears, untrained health care professionals, and uninformed patients."[69]

Claims similar to these were stated in a brief filed by five religious organizations, the Christian Medical Association, the American Association of Pro Life Obstetricians and Gynecologists, the Union of Orthodox Jewish Congregations of America, the National Association of Evangelicals, and the Christian Legal Society. Citing the Supreme Court's alignment in *Glucksberg* with the AMA's position that "physician-assisted suicide is fundamentally incompatible with the physician's role as healer" (521 U.S. at 731), the brief concluded that "the Attorney General has taken an eminently reasonable position that facilitating suicide by overdose is not a legitimate medical purpose for which federally controlled substances may be used."[70]

Senators Rick Santorum, Tom Coburn, James N. Inhofe, Jim Demint, Christopher S. Bond, Larry Craig, Judd Craig, and Sam Brownback joined with Representatives Steve Chabot, Chris Smith, Jack Kingston, John Shimkus, Joseph R. Pitts, Henry Hyde, Mark Green, Todd Akin, Roscoe Bartlett, Jeff Miller, Steve King, Thomas Petri, Mark E. Souder, Peter King, Paul Ryan, Virgil H. Goode Jr., Gene Taylor, John N. Hostettler, and Ralph Hall in a brief supporting the U.S. government's case. The senior senators and representatives among the group served in Congress when the CSA was amended to include the authority under which Ashcroft acted in this case. Additionally, Brownback and Hyde have conducted and participated in hearings on the subject of assisted suicide. The elite group argued that the attorney general's interpretive rule is consistent with the CSA's legislative intent, and that it represents "a reasonable response to the DWDA."[71] The National Legal Center for the Medically Dependent and Disabled rendered similar claims, noting the clear trend in American legislatures, voter referendums, state courts, and the U.S. Congress rejecting the notion of using controlled substances for assisting in suicide. Their brief concluded: "If the Oregon DWDA is an experiment in the laboratory of the states, it is an experiment that has failed."[72]

Like the brief from members of Congress focusing on the attorney general's authority under the CSA, about a half dozen additional briefs focused more squarely on the legal issues actually before the court. They stressed Congress's intent to establish a comprehensive regulatory scheme and warned of the potential difficulties in administering the CSA if individual states are permitted to follow the path that Oregon has taken.

The Catholic Medical Association, for instance, charged that Oregon's position "renders the national design of drug approval incoherent and federal enforcement subject to the dictates of state authorities."[73] Oregon's assertion of authority to determine what is a legitimate medical purpose could potentially result "in fifty different sets of accepted purposes," asserted the brief for the International Task Force on Euthanasia and Assisted Suicide.[74] A brief submitted by the Pro-Life Legal Defense Fund and the Legal Center for Defense of Life, two not-for-profit corporations that provide pro bono legal services for the protection of human life, and the group University Faculty for Life, a multidisciplinary association of academics who promote scholarship on various topics in medical ethics, including euthanasia, faulted the state of Oregon for unilaterally trying to "opt out" of federal regulation. In their view, opening the door for permitting state action like that in Oregon would "create an impracticable system of administrative law by establishing a precedent for future opt-outs."[75]

A final brief in this group offered the interesting proposition that upholding the lower courts' decisions favoring Oregon in this case would effectively immunize physicians from federal control so long as state law authorizes the particular practice.[76] This claim obviously cuts against the state of Oregon. Yet, as will be seen later in this chapter, Oregon's senior assistant attorney general made precisely this claim during oral arguments before the justices—a move that appeared to surprise many.

Overall, briefs opposed to Oregon's assisted suicide law averred that the Justice Department's position is fully consistent with the widely held view that physician-assisted suicide is not commensurate with the practice of medicine in the traditional sense. Furthermore, the Court should not establish a precedent that would render ineffectual Congress's intent to centralize the regulation of prescription drugs. A Court ruling along these lines would also protect vulnerable populations and reject the notion that lives with disabilities are not worth living.

Supporters of the Oregon law refuted the above claims nearly point for point, addressing issues of medical practice, mental impairment and choice, the rationale behind Attorney General Ashcroft's directive, the scope of the Controlled Substances Act, and the authority of a single state to experiment with presently unpopular protocols in end-of-life care.

A brief submitted by fifty-four physicians, attorneys, and professors who address issues of medical ethics in their work argued that in limited cases, physician-assisted suicide meets the demands of sound medical practice. For physicians whose practices include ongoing care for mentally competent, terminally ill patients, they claimed, the ability to provide assistance in hastening death "is in some cases essential to effective end-of-life medical care"[77] Without this possibility, they claimed further, physicians may indeed be forced to abandon their patients just as death approaches. Never abandoning a patient "is an important and long-standing principle of medical ethics";[78] hence, in some circumstances providing requested assistance in dying fulfills a physician's obligation to address a patient's needs fully. On these grounds, the group concluded, the attorney general's belief that a physician's role is confined to curing or preventing disease or repairing injury "reflects a fundamental lack of understanding of contemporary medical practices and ethics."[79]

A group of mental health professionals submitted a similar argument. Identifying themselves as an ad hoc group of individual social workers, psychologists, and psychiatrists and related professional groups working as academicians, private practitioners, agency clinicians, administrators, and consultants with relevant training and experience concerning terminally ill patients' decision-making capacity, the "coalition" called the Justice Department's assumption that patients who want to hasten death must suffer from impaired judgment "erroneous."[80] Another group—this one composed of health law professors at American law schools—added a similar claim: that arguments which claim the Oregon law poses a risk to the poor, to the poorly educated, to the disabled, or to incompetent, terminally ill Oregonians "are grounded in ideology, not facts."[81] More starkly, those writing under the auspices of the American College of Legal Medicine charged that the attorney general's attempt to assess the legitimacy of physician-assisted suicide "constitutes a unilateral, uninformed, and politically-motivated action."[82] The determination of what constitutes "legitimate medical practice" must be informed by medical expertise, the brief added, and that is the purpose of leaving the determination to the states and to the secretary of Health and Human Services. If upheld, the brief writers concluded, "the opinion of a single administrative official" could retard the ability "to ensure a pain-free and dignified end of life."[83]

A group formed by a diverse array of fifty-two religious organizations, leaders, and scholars as well as advocates of religious liberty also opined that the attorney general "did nothing more than impose his unilateral moral and policy views on the people of Oregon."[84] The group of clergy, organizations, and theologians from a wide range of faiths, including the United Church of Christ, the Unitarian Universalist Association of Congregations, Reform Judaism, the Episcopal Church, the Catholic Church, and various humanist organizations argued further that "freedom of personal and religious choice" includes the freedom to determine whether physician-assisted dying fits with one's own religious and spiritual beliefs. They reminded the justices that steadfast opposition to physician-aided dying is not a universal view among all faiths, religious organizations, or religious leaders. By contrast, "Numerous faiths, religious organizations, and religious leaders strongly support physician-assisted dying as an entirely legitimate and moral choice by which the terminally ill can hasten their impending death with dignity and integrity."[85] The states, the brief concluded, should be permitted to honor the various religious and spiritual views of their citizens, and that is the course that Oregon voters have properly taken.

These claims were rendered in more concrete terms in a brief submitted by surviving family members of deceased loved ones who had hastened their deaths—some positively, others not. "The individual experiences present the Court with the emotional resonance of dying with and without physician assistance to hasten the process," the brief's writers began.[86] Eight of the deceased had access to controlled substances prescribed under the ODDA; the remaining eleven did not. Survivors in the first group spoke around the themes of control, peace, dignity, and being surrounded by children, spouses, clergy, and other close family and friends. The other group told of tragedy. In one instance a man shot himself in bed while his wife lay sleeping in another room. In another a son was prosecuted for helping his father suffocate himself with a plastic bag. Several other stories were even more extreme, but in all of them, the deceased were terminally ill, and they were not suffering from depression. The tragedies, the brief asserted, illustrate the consequences of denying people the freedom to choose a lawful, dignified death. The ODDA, the authors argued, "reduces the tragic consequences that flow from violent suicides, from failed attempts to commit suicide, from subjecting compassionate family members who assist in suicide to criminal liability, and from prolonging physical and emotional suffering of terminally-ill patients." A poem at the end of the brief imparted a stark contrast to claims that the ODDA poses a particular threat to disabled, depressed, or otherwise vulnerable people. The poem, titled, "Come Death," was written by Norma Davis, who exercised her option under the ODDA in July 2001:

> walk toward me
>
> in your flower-printed silk
> and fine mossy velvet or
> in your impeccably tailored
> black suit
>
> come in all your perfection
>
> extending your hand
> and saying your name
>
> draw me toward you as my close friends do
> hold me elegantly still
>
> in dance position
> then waltz me away
>
> glancing over your shoulder once
>
> and with the smallest gesture
> let them know how much
> I liked to dance[87]

The remaining briefs submitted to support the Oregon law took sides on legal issues. Several asked the Court to take notice that Congress enacted the CSA for the purpose of controlling drug trafficking and abuse, and to declare the Ashcroft directive beyond the act's scope. Several members of Congress representing the people of Oregon advanced that claim. They included Senator Ron Wyden and Representatives Earl Blumenauer, Peter DeFazio, Darlene Hooley, and David Wu. Each has led efforts against federal attempts to preempt the Oregon law, although not all support physician-assisted suicide personally.

Along with the fifty-four physicians, attorneys, and professors involved in medical ethics discussed earlier, the American Public Health Association (APHA) had the same take. Founded in 1872, the APHA represents a broad array of health providers, educators, policymakers, and health officials inside and outside government and educational institutions. While the APHA claimed it does not take a position on the wisdom of Oregon's law, the group did share its concern that the Ashcroft directive could have a broad impact on health practices and policy. The CSA, the group insisted, has been Congress's means of creating a closed distribution system to circumvent the "nationally important, but discrete public health problem" of drug trafficking and abuse.[88] By going beyond that authority, the Ashcroft directive portends the unintended consequence of deterring physicians from providing adequate pain care. "These deterrent effects are of special concern because inappropriate *undertreatment* with controlled drugs, and inadequate pain relief for those who are terminally ill, are recognized to be public health problems of the first order," the brief asserted.[89] Moreover, failure to enjoin the Justice Department from executing the directive against the Oregon law could only lead to similar assertions of authority, making "pursuit of similar administrative declarations of 'illegitimacy' the first resort—and the pull and haul of the lawmaking process the Constitution contemplates, a distant second choice."[90]

The Cato Institute's Center for Constitutional Studies also pointed to issues of democracy and shared authority. Authors of the brief described the institute as being dedicated to "the idea that the U.S. Constitution establishes a government of delegated, enumerated, and thus limited powers."[91] They stressed that administrative agencies are less democratic than Congress, and less democratic yet than the ballot initiative process followed twice in the case of the Oregon Death with Dignity Act. Thus the Ashcroft directive, they declared, should be categorically disfavored because it is an instance of an agency seeking to "supplant or undermine the outcome of direct democracy at the state level."[92] Similarly, a brief filed by a group of nine law professors argued that unless it is clear that Congress, "the most democratically accountable branch," made a conscious effort to make state-authorized physician-assisted suicide a federal crime, or gave the attorney general power to do so, time-honored rules of statutory interpretation strongly counsel against the interpretation in the Ashcroft directive. To the contrary, argued this group of law professors who teach and write about statutory interpretation, administrative law, legislative process, and federalism, "the text, structure, and purpose of the CSA make plain that Congress did not intend to displace the States' traditional authority to regulate medical practice within their borders."[93]

The law professors' brief concluded with the observation that in *Washington v. Glucksberg* the Court observed: "Throughout the Nation, Americans are engaged in an earnest and profound debate about the morality, legality, and practicality of physician-assisted suicide."[94] Ashcroft's actions would bring that "earnest and profound" debate to an end, the professors declared, hence the Court should reject the directive and permit the people of the states to explore different approaches to end-of-life care.

This sentiment was echoed in several of these amicus briefs favoring the ODDA, including one signed by eighteen medical groups such as the American Academy of Pain Management, the American Geriatrics Society, the Oregon Hospice Association, the American Academy of HIV Medicine, and a coalition of individual distinguished professionals engaged in pain, palliative, and elder care. In addition, the American Civil Liberties Union, which represented the petitioner in *Cruzan v. Missouri Department of Health*[95]—the Supreme Court's first case addressing hastened death—said that insofar as the opinions in *Washington v. Glucksberg* "provide a general outline of the circumstances in which obstructing access to physician-assisted suicide would have constitutional implications," by upholding the Ninth Circuit's injunction against the Ashcroft directive the Court could avoid having to confront the constitutional question in the future.[96]

Finally, given the Court's invitation to state experimentation in *Glucksberg,* and in answer to opponents' claims that Oregon resists the prevailing opposition to physician-assisted suicide among all other forty-nine states, a brief submitted by attorneys general of the states of

California, Mississippi, Missouri, and Montana as well as the District of Columbia asserted that "a value consensus among the States regarding medical matters is not a measure of the validity of any one State's legislative policy."[97]

Oral Arguments

The Supreme Court heard oral arguments in the case on October 5, 2005. Hundreds of spectators began lining up at 4:00 a.m. for a chance to get into the chamber where the nine justices hear arguments. Adding to the draw was the chance to observe the new chief justice, John G. Roberts Jr., who just two days earlier had filled the seat of the late chief justice William H. Rehnquist. Solicitor General Paul D. Clement commenced the arguments on behalf of the U.S. Department of Justice. The thirty minutes of questioning focused mostly on three issues. The first issue centered on the nature of physician-assisted suicide and whether that practice falls under the ambit of the CSA. The second involved the dual questions of whether the government's position in this case was consistent with its position in *Washington v. Glucksberg,* and what the impact of a judgment in favor of the government would be on the practice of physician-assisted suicide in Oregon. The last issue involved the question of whether a judgment for the government would subject states' laws to the vicissitudes of changes in the attorney general's office.

The issue of the relevance of the CSA to physician-assisted suicide focused the justices' attention on the purpose behind the CSA when Congress enacted it. Justice Souter expressed his opinion that the purpose of federal regulation of drugs has been to stop drug pushing and drug abuse, as those terms are used "in the conventional sense."[98] This, Justice Souter asserted, "simply cuts against" the federal government's assertion that the CSA grants authority to the attorney general to determine the medical legitimacy of physician-assisted suicide. Implicit in Souter's observation seemed to be the notion that physician-assisted suicide, whether from the patient's side or the physician's, does not constitute drug abuse or drug pushing. Clement responded that Congress's concern about drug abuse extended beyond abuse per se to its harmful effects, such as suicide and overdoses. Justice Souter, however, distinguished between suicide that is "a result of the kind of dementia that comes from drug abuse" and suicide "under the circumstances that

we're talking about within the limits of the Oregon law."[99] Clement offered that when Congress enacted the CSA it had not had physician-
assisted suicide in mind because it would have been unthinkable at that
time. Nevertheless, he continued, to him it seemed "odd" that a Congress concerned about suicides would be neutral or indifferent about using federally controlled substances "for the express purpose of inducing
a lethal overdose."[100]

Justice Breyer joined Justice Souter in expressing his view that the essence of Congress's concern has been narcotics addiction. Breyer asked
Solicitor General Clement to address what the Oregon law has had to
do with that. Clement responded that Congress's recent application of
the CSA to address the problem of GHB—one of the so-called date-
rape drugs—is evidence that its attention is "broader than a narrow focus on diversion or a narrow focus on addiction."[101] Souter countered
that Clement's GHB example addressed the problem of using a drug to
hurt unsuspecting people, perhaps for the purpose of facilitating a violation of the law. That seems "worlds away from what we're talking
about here," Souter declared.[102] Clement apparently understood Justice
Souter to imply that unlike victims who are given GHP surreptitiously,
patients consume drugs prescribed under the Oregon Death with Dignity Act voluntarily. Clement had time only to reply that the Controlled
Substances Act is "a very paternalistic piece of legislation" that does not
contemplate allowing people to make their own judgments about risks
to their health.[103]

The second set of issues addressed during Clement's argument involved questions about the government's position in this case and its implications for the Oregon law. Justice Ruth Bader Ginsburg first wanted
to know how the government's position in this case squared with its position in *Washington v. Glucksberg*, the 1997 case wherein the Supreme
Court rejected a claim that Washington's ban against assisted suicide violated a liberty interest protected by the Fourteenth Amendment's due
process clause. Reading aloud from documents in the *Glucksberg* case,
Justice Ginsburg offered that the government, at that time, said, "State
legislatures undoubtedly have the authority to create the kind of exception to assisted suicide fashioned by the court of appeals. There is
every reason to believe that State legislatures will address the urgent issues involved in this case in a fair and impartial way."[104] Ginsburg read
from another passage, which said, "There is no indication that the political processes are malfunctioning in this area." Ginsburg then asked

whether the government was rejecting that position in the present case. It appeared that Justice Ginsburg found it contradictory that in the present case the United States challenged a state's authority to legislate in the area of physician-assisted suicide, whereas in *Glucksberg* the United States argued as amicus curiae on behalf of Washington State lawmakers and their right to regulate the very same area. Solicitor General Clement replied that two conditions distinguish the Oregon case from *Glucksberg*. One is that *Glucksberg* was a constitutional matter. By that the solicitor general apparently meant that the litigants who challenged the state law in *Glucksberg* were seeking a *Roe v. Wade*–type ruling that would have broadly circumscribed the right of state legislators to act at all. It made sense, Clement seemed to imply, that in that case the United States argued that the democratic system worked fine, and thus the Court did not need to constitutionalize the issue, and effectively remove the states from the debate and evolving policy. By contrast, the Oregon case is one wherein the state scheme explicitly interferes with federal government's mandate to uniformly regulate the dispensing of controlled substances. Said differently, Clement appeared to stand by the government's position in *Glucksberg* supporting the important role of the states in determining assisted suicide policy, but he distinguished the Oregon case as one wherein the state played its role in a way that usurps federal authority.

To buttress that distinction, Solicitor General Clement reminded the Court that the attorney general's interpretation of the CSA as it applies to the Oregon Death with Dignity Act "does not purport to foreclose the issue of assisted suicide."[105] By that Clement appeared to mean that a Court ruling favoring the United States in the present case would not negate the Oregon Death with Dignity Act; it would instead only require physicians to prescribe drugs or other substances not scheduled in the CSA. Justice Souter responded that in practical terms the attorney general's interpretation does undermine the practice in Oregon because using scheduled drugs is the way to administer the law sensibly. Justice Ginsburg added that patients and others said in their briefs to the Court that scheduled drugs are much less upsetting from the patient's point of view. Here Clement introduced Jack Kevorkian into his argument, noting that Kevorkian was a proponent of methods that did not include scheduled drugs. (Indeed, Dr. Kevorkian at first used potassium chloride and later switched to carbon monoxide.)

In comments to news organizations outside the court after the hearing, defenders of the Oregon law rebuffed Clement's courtroom invocation of Kevorkian and stressed their claim that the practice of physician-aided dying in Oregon differs profoundly from Kevorkian's former practices. We have noticed many distinctions in our own research. To name a few, many of Kevorkian's subjects died in the sole presence of Kevorkian himself, with no friends or family present. Many of the deaths Kevorkian assisted took place in unusual places, like hotel rooms, campgrounds, and even the back of Kevorkian's Volkswagen bus. Kevorkian characteristically followed up the deaths he assisted with grandstanding and taunts at law enforcement. He crusaded against the law, often claiming that it is no more necessary or appropriate for physicians to seek legal authority to practice aided dying than it is for them to seek authorization to perform heart surgery. While we neither praise nor criticize Oregon's regime allowing doctors to participate in hastening the deaths of Oregon patients—nor for that matter do we judge the actions of Dr. Kevorkian—we appreciate why some observers sitting in the Court, and perhaps some or all of the justices, simply disregarded Clement's mention of Jack Kevorkian.

A third set of questions posed to the solicitor general explored the possibility that the federal government's interpretation of the CSA could produce arbitrary outcomes. Justice O'Connor introduced the issue with a question about whether an attorney general opposed to the death penalty could pull the registration of a doctor who provided drugs to facilitate a state execution. More to the point, Justice O'Connor reminded Clement that former attorney general Janet Reno had determined that the Oregon law did not contravene the CSA. In fact, the history of this litigation demonstrates the problem of unpredictability. In 1997 the DEA administrator, Thomas A. Constantine, declared that delivering, dispensing, or prescribing a controlled substance with the intent of assisting a suicide is not a legitimate medical purpose, and would hence be a violation of the CSA. A few months later, Attorney General Reno exercised her authority over the DEA and declared instead that the CSA did not prohibit the use of controlled substances to facilitate physician-assisted suicide in a state wherein that practice is lawful. The fact that John Ashcroft reinstituted Constantine's interpretation just a few years later pointed to the problem for physicians who could not predict what the CSA was going to mean. When O'Connor reminded Clement about Reno's prior ruling in 1998, Clement shot back, "And the prior administrator of the DEA before that had our position."[106] That, observed

Justice Souter moments later, produced the rather "bizarre result" wherein the determination whether a state may or may not authorize assisted suicide "can flip back and forth—as has happened in this case."[107] Referring back to Justice O'Connor's inquiry about the attorney general's authority to de-register a physician involved in an execution, Justice Souter suggested that this "bizarre result" occurred only if one made the erroneous assumption that a federal scheme to combat the problem of drug pushing and drug addiction contemplated the unrelated issues of executions and assisted suicide.

With that, Clement's time expired and the Court turned to its questions for Oregon's senior assistant attorney general, Robert M. Atkinson. The topics ranged primarily from the U.S. attorney general's statutory authority under the controlled substances regime to the precise social problems Congress intended to address under the CSA. The first discussion centered on what happens under the regime of the CSA when state law authorizes a medical practice that the attorney general purports to be a violation of federal law. Atkinson rendered the puzzlingly unorthodox claim that if a prescription violated state law in one state but not another, the CSA authorizes the attorney general to enforce the act only against the state wherein the prescription is illegal. In other words, it was Atkinson's contention that a medical practice may violate federal law only if it violates state law. This argument seemed to stand the relationship between the states and the federal government on its head: under the preemption doctrine any federal law trumps any conflicting state law. The preemption doctrine derives from the supremacy clause in Article VI of the U.S. Constitution, which states that the Constitution and the laws of the United States "shall be the supreme law of the land . . . anything in the constitution or laws of any state to the contrary notwithstanding."

Atkinson's claim about the state-federal relationship under the Controlled Substances Act rested on a subtle understanding of the CSA's history. That history, said Atkinson, shows that Congress's concern was the states' failure to enforce existing state laws, not how they were defining legitimate medical practices. What Atkinson seemed to be saying here is that back when Congress enacted the CSA in 1971, states enforced their own drug laws inadequately, hence Congress stepped in and created a centralized federal regime, which authorized the attorney general to step in and enforce federal law when state enforcement of state drug laws was lax. Taking the analysis one step further, Atkinson was arguing that the attorney general had no authority to invoke the CSA in states that had their drug laws under control. With respect to the state of Oregon, the Death with Dignity Act authorized physician-assisted suicide and the state duly regulated the practice, hence, the argument goes, the attorney general had no claim to step in.

To buttress this analysis, Atkinson asserted that never has an attorney general attempted to de-register a physician whose prescription practices were in compliance with state law. He stated: "And what you're seeing here in the Attorney General's claim of authority, for the first time, is rules that are not addressed to controlled substances, *per se,* but to medical practices," and that is authority that Congress never contemplated giving to the federal government. The second part of this analysis asserts that what Attorney General Ashcroft had in mind when he stepped in to oppose the Oregon Death with Dignity Act was a claim of authority to interpret what constitutes a "legitimate medical practice." That authority—to determine the legitimacy of particular medical practices—is entirely different from the authority to intercede in cases wherein a state fails in its efforts to enforce its own laws. This is a subtle legal argument that appeared to catch the attention of several of the justices. Justice Kennedy, for example, appeared to challenge Atkinson by pointing to 21 USC Section 821, which states, "The Attorney General is authorized to promulgate rules and regulations . . . relating to the registration and control of the manufacture, distribution, and dispensing of controlled substances." Kennedy stated he believed this section authorized precisely what Attorney General Ashcroft had done. Again Atkinson stressed his position that even the language Justice Kennedy pointed to did not authorize the attorney general to determine the legitimacy of particular medical practices. Instead, Atkinson argued, it showed that Congress intended far more narrowly to authorize the attorney general only to promulgate uniform rules such as requiring physicians to use a prescription system to dispense drugs—not to authorize "a single unelected federal official to decide, in his sole and apparently unreviewable discretion, that this medical practice, of which he disapproves," may be banned.[108]

At another point in the state of Oregon's argument, Assistant Attorney General Atkinson appeared to take nearly everyone in the courtroom by surprise, judging from the reactions in the audience and on the bench. Justice Breyer seemed keenly interested in getting Atkinson, and earlier Clement, to allow that the subject of physician-assisted suicide falls outside the ambit of the Controlled Substances Act. As many court observers are aware, oral arguments before the Supreme Court are more than the justices listening to the attorneys argue their cases. They are, in addition, a conversation among the justices, wherein questions are posed to the attorneys to elicit comments, claims, and retorts that the justices are making to one another. Justice Kennedy makes this point in the film on the Supreme Court shown hourly in the Court's visitors' gallery. Accordingly, courtroom observers in the Oregon case could recognize that Justice Breyer and Justice Scalia had staked out opposing positions in the case and that Breyer, especially, yearned for Atkinson, or even Clement, to acknowledge a distinction between physician-assisted suicide, on one hand, and narcotics addiction, on the other. It is widely recognized in the media that Breyer's wife counsels young cancer patients. Breyer, then, may be particularly sensitive to claims that draw parallels between physician aid in dying and drug abuse, as observers could see in his repeated efforts to ply Oregon's attorney to argue that point. Atkinson's responses, however, appeared to bewilder several of the justices, even as that fact played into Justice Scalia's strong opposition to physician-assisted suicide.

Justice Breyer asked Atkinson to suppose that a state authorized physicians to prescribe morphine for recreational use. What would be the authority of the U.S. attorney general to intercede in that situation? And how is the Oregon regime different? What caught many by surprise was Atkinson's reply that the attorney general could *not* intercede if the state had determined that prescribing morphine for pleasure was a legitimate medical practice. Atkinson's claim was consistent with his argument that Congress contemplated federal intervention only when states failed to enforce their own laws. "No matter what?" asked Breyer, somewhat incredulously. "You're going to say your case turns or falls—you win or lose—depending on whether I accept that [the attorney general] could not stop a doctor from becoming, in effect, a conduit to a group of drug dealers by saying, 'I think recreational use is part of my medical practice'—that would be up to the state?"[109] "Yes," Atkinson answered. Justice Scalia interjected: "And if the state allowed it, the federal government would have to allow the drugs to be used for that purpose, you're saying." Atkinson granted that there would be some limits, but he confirmed that this was his argument. That seemed to back Scalia's warning that holding for Oregon in this case would open the door for all the states to enact drug laws that conflict with the Controlled Substances Act.

Justice Ginsburg, who earlier had appeared to be fully aligned with Oregon's position in the case, expressed disbelief and asked Atkinson to confirm his position, which he did. Chief Justice Roberts asked Atkinson to affirm his position. Atkinson confirmed it again. Justice O'Connor asked Atkinson to confirm his position yet again and added, "How about steroids for bodybuilders? Can the Attorney General find that that's drug abuse?" Atkinson said no, not if it is permitted and regulated by state law. Many courtroom observers stirred in their seats.

Outside the Court, shortly after the oral arguments, Kathryn Tucker, the attorney for the patient respondents in the case, informed the media that Atkinson should have conceded that the U.S. attorney general would have the authority to intercede if a state passed a law condoning the prescription of morphine for pleasure. We would add that to many people, dispensing morphine for pleasure would appear to constitute little more than state-sanctioned drug dealing. Thus, Atkinson's claim that the attorney general would not be authorized to take action if a state deemed such practices to be legitimate seemed entirely at odds with the CSA's regulatory scheme. Moreover, this is what gave worry to Justice Kennedy and others like Wesley Smith about the potential for a "slippery slope." That is, permitting Oregon voters to create what many see as a perfectly appropriate use of controlled substances to control the conditions and timing of impending death could lead to a patchwork of state and federal regulations.

Atkinson's responses clearly aggravated Justice Breyer, who even went so far as to suggest the argument he wanted Atkinson to proffer. "Far be it from me to suggest an argument that you don't want to make," Breyer implored, but the physician-assisted suicide law passed in Oregon "doesn't seem to have much to do with the purpose of the Act."[110] Several times Breyer had expressed his view that Congress enacted the CSA to deal with the problem of narcotics addiction. Justice Souter appeared to want to step in and save some of the state's presentation. Souter asked if Atkinson agreed that to win the case all he needed is for the Court to accept the premise that Congress meant to authorize the attorney general to interfere with the practice of medicine, but to go no further than preventing doctors from prescribing recreational drugs or catering to pushers. Atkinson said he agreed but added, "We think it's clear, from examining the statute, that Congress intended to retain and respect the historic powers of the states to define legitimate medical practices."[111] One could not be sure whether Atkinson was accepting Souter's premise that the CSA authorized the attorney general to interfere with the practice of medicine, and it appeared that he never got the point of distinguishing physician-assisted suicide from drug abuse and addiction. What can be said for Atkinson, however, is that he never wavered from his essential argument that it is for the states and the states only to determine which medical practices are legitimate.

Before Atkinson's time ran out, Justice Stevens, apparently communicating his position to the other justices, asked, "Isn't your point in this case that Congress hasn't really spoken to the issue to which the Attorney General has spoken?"[112] Atkinson agreed and added that the earlier supposition about states enacting laws permitting physicians to dispense morphine to make people happy was erroneous in light of the fact that Congress assumes that states will act responsibly and not enact such laws. Chief Justice Roberts interjected that "in 1971 Congress didn't assume the states were going to pass legislation for use of drugs to assist with suicide, either."[113] Atkinson agreed but added that Congress knew that medical practice evolves, citing acupuncture and Botox as examples of accepted medical practices that were unheard of thirty years ago. Justice Scalia objected that Atkinson offered examples of practices intended to keep people alive; yet, "Assisting people to die is something of a totally different category."[114] Atkinson disagreed and pointed to *Cruzan,* do-not-resuscitate orders, and living wills as examples of accepted medical practices focused on end-of-life issues. He reminded Scalia and the other justices that Oregon had done precisely what the Court invited the states to do in *Glucksberg.*

The final word came from Solicitor General Clement, the petitioners' attorney, who had reserved time for a rebuttal argument. Clement reiterated his point that it is perfectly legitimate to read the CSA and assume that "a Congress that was profoundly concerned with overdoses, with suicide, with drug abuse, precisely because of the debilitating effect on people's lives," would not be equivocal about the incidence of states using controlled substances in physician-assisted suicides. He added that the Court's decision in *Gonzales v. Raich*—wherein it ruled against medical marijuana laws in California and nine other states—made it clear in his view that the relevant factor to consider is not the class of activities that a state decides to decriminalize but, rather, the class of activities that Congress decides to regulate. In the present case, then, the determination of whether state or federal law prevails must be viewed from the perspective of the federal government's power to regulate controlled substances, rather than the state's rights to determine which medical practices are legitimate. Clement closed with the observation that the Oregon Death with Dignity Act is like no other law in that it authorizes doctors to prescribe controlled substances but not to administer them. What becomes clear about this feature of the law, Clement concluded, is that "Oregon is not regulating medicine, it's purporting to basically take a federal regulatory regime that allows doctors the ability to get at schedule 2 substances."[115]

Summary of the Oral Arguments

What seemed likely to weigh most on the Court was the concern that a ruling in favor of Oregon might hinder the Department of Justice in the orderly execution of the CSA. Justice Kennedy, who appeared to be the most ambivalent of the nine justices, expressed that what made the case difficult for him was the concern that if the Court ruled in Oregon's favor, the states could "overtake the federal regime." While Solicitor General Clement said he did not want to overstate his case, a ruling for Oregon "at least creates the potential for there to be a lot of holes in the regime," he said.[116] Demonstrating his own ambivalence, on the other hand, Kennedy pointed to language in the CSA that says provisions of the act shall not displace the judgment of the medical community. That reading would seem to favor the state of Oregon, since undoubtedly a ruling for the Department of Justice would displace the judgment of Oregon physicians who participate in assisted suicide.

Kennedy's ambivalence made it difficult to predict where he might come down in the case. Kennedy's concern about the potential for a "slippery slope" also seemed to concern Chief Justice Roberts, who appeared more openly skeptical of Oregon's claims than all but Justice Scalia did. Given Scalia's use of the term "killing" to describe the practice in Oregon, Scalia appeared destined to vote with the Department of Justice. On the other side it seemed clear that Justice Breyer would distinguish the Oregon practice from Congress's intent to address narcotics addiction and the diversion of legal drugs into illicit channels. Justices Stevens and Souter appeared set to read the CSA narrowly and conclude that although Congress can declare physician-assisted suicide unlawful under the CSA, it has not done so. Justice Ginsburg appeared to be wholly sympathetic to dying patients and the utility of using controlled substances to hasten inevitable death. So did Justice O'Connor, who had expressed support for the right of citizens and lawmakers in individual states to experiment with physician-assisted suicide and even medical marijuana.

The Court's Ruling

On January 17, 2006, the Supreme Court ruled 6 to 3 in favor of the state of Oregon, allowing the Oregon Death with Dignity Act to continue. The opinion was issued in Sanctity of Human Life Week, observed then because of the anniversary on January 22 of the 1973 *Roe v. Wade* decision. Justice Kennedy wrote the majority opinion, which was joined by Justices Stevens, O'Connor, Ginsberg, Souter, and Breyer. Chief Justice Roberts and Justice Thomas joined Justice Scalia in dissent. Justice Thomas had a bit more to say in a second dissent. The majority opinion began with former chief justice Rehnquist's observation in 1997 that "Americans are engaged in an earnest and profound debate about the morality, legality, and practicality of physician assisted suicide."[117] That political and moral debate, the Court observed, gave rise to the dispute between the Oregon litigants and former attorney general John Ashcroft. Nevertheless, this dispute is easily resolved by adhering to a narrow if not mundane application of fundamental principles of statutory interpretation. In this way, the Court made it clear that its holding did not represent a watershed moment in the moral and legal debate over physician-assisted suicide. Indeed, it is fair to conclude from the majority opinion that the Court could be disinclined to overrule a congressional decision to grant the attorney general the kind of authority he assumed erroneously under current federal law, or to criminalize physician assisted suicide itself. The Court thus assured, at least obliquely, that Congress has a rightful role in this earnest and profound debate.

Central to the Court's holding is the conclusion that Congress's main objectives in enacting the CSA in 1970 were combating drug abuse and controlling both legitimate and illicit traffic in controlled substances. The fact that the CSA criminalizes the unauthorized manufacture, distribution, dispensing, and possession of substances classified in any of the act's five schedules is critical to determining the attorney general's statutory authority to criminalize medical practices permitted under state law. If Congress intended to add the power to make particular findings on scientific and medical matters to the attorney general's law enforcement powers, it is reasonable to expect that power to have been made explicit. Instead, the power to make inherently medical decisions is reserved for the states in language in the CSA which states that "No provision . . . shall be construed as indicating an intent on the part of Congress to occupy the field in which that provision operates . . . to the exclusion of any State law on the same subject matter which would otherwise be within the authority of the State" (21 USC § 903). The attorney general's power to enact implementing regulations and to issue directives interpreting those regulations cannot exceed his authority under the statute. That is what the attorney general did here, the majority concluded: He issued an interpretive rule that would effect "a severe restriction on medical practice" and subject physicians involved in such practice to felony conviction under a federal law designed narrowly to combat drug abuse and addiction.[118] Specifically, the Court said:

> The Attorney General has rulemaking power to fulfill his duties under the CSA. The specific respects in which he is authorized to make rules, however, instruct us that he is not authorized to make a rule declaring illegitimate a medical standard for care and treatment of patients that is specifically authorized under state law. . . . The Attorney General's authority to . . . establish controls against diversion . . . do not give him authority to define diversion based on his view of legitimate medical practice. . . . The Interpretive Rule . . . purports to declare that using controlled substances for physician assisted suicide is a crime, an authority that goes well beyond the Attorney General's statutory power.[119]

The Court explained further that it stood to reason that if the attorney general's claim of authority to decide what constitutes an underlying violation of the CSA were correct, his power to criminalize the actions of physicians whenever they engage in conduct he deems illegitimate would be unrestrained. Yet given Congress's painstaking efforts to describe the attorney general's limited authority under the CSA, Kennedy wrote, it would be anomalous for Congress to have given him, just by implication, authority to declare any entire class of physician activity a criminal violation.

The Court turned next to the federal government's contention that Congress itself impliedly criminalized physician-assisted suicide in the provision of the CSA that requires drugs used in medical practice to be dispensed pursuant to written prescriptions. The prescription requirement necessarily implies that drugs shall be made available to patients for legitimate medical purposes only, the government claimed. The CSA therefore calls for anterior judgments about the terms "medical" and "medicine." In this light, it is eminently reasonable for the attorney general to conclude that physician participation in suicide is incompatible with a healing or curative art. That view is embedded in the ancient teachings of Hippocrates, as well as the positions of the AMA and other prominent medical organizations, the federal government (federal funds cannot be used to pay for items and services when the purpose is to facilitate or assist in facilitating a person's death by suicide, euthanasia, or mercy killing), and the policies of the forty-nine states whose citizens and lawmakers have not endorsed physician-assisted suicide.

As the Court examined this claim, it is particularly significant that the majority grounded resolution of the government's case in former chief justice Rehnquist's contention that the debate about the morality, legality, and practicality of physician-assisted suicide should be governed by democratic processes. Rehnquist's contention tolerates competing understandings of medical practice. Certainly it is reasonable for the attorney general to embrace the widespread view that purposely hastening death belies a physician's role as healer. Nevertheless, that is but one reasonable understanding of medical practice, and the CSA's overall scheme to battle drug abuse does not require every state to adhere to it. The majority concluded that rather than stretching to reach a holding that prescriptions for assisted suicide constitute drug abuse, the Court should read the prescription requirement to mean more reasonably that in order to prevent addiction and recreational abuse, patients must use controlled substances under the supervision of physicians, who in turn must not peddle such substances to patients who crave them for these prohibited purposes.

In summary, the majority opinion explains that the CSA presupposes state regulation of medical practice. Accordingly, the ODDA limits the practice of dispensing controlled substances for assisted suicide to terminally ill patients whose attending physicians are licensed by Oregon's Board of Medical Examiners. These physicians are required to provide prognoses, give information about alternatives such as palliative care and counseling, and ensure that patients are competent and acting voluntarily. Second opinions from other registered physicians are also required. All the physicians involved must keep detailed records of their actions and submit them for inspection. In short, Oregon's medical regime does not simply decriminalize physician-assisted suicide but is instead an example of the state regulation of medical practice that the CSA presupposes. While there is no question that the federal government can set uniform national standards in matters of health and safety, the structure of the CSA conveys Congress's unwillingness to cede medical judgments to an executive official who lacks medical expertise.[120]

Most of Justice Scalia's dissenting opinion details fine points of administrative law regarding the degree of deference the Court should give to the attorney general's interpretation of the CSA—particularly his authority to declare that physician-assisted suicide is not a legitimate medical practice. The final paragraph of the dissent reveals a posture in the case that may strike some court observers as being at odds with Scalia's originalist view of the Constitution and the Court's role in interpreting it. At the end of the opinion Scalia avers that prescribing drugs to produce death is surely excluded from any reasonable construal of the term *"legitimate* medical purpose." Thus, Scalia supposes, the majority opinion may rest on a feeling that the subject of assisted suicide is none of the federal government's business. It is easy to sympathize with that view, Scalia concedes, because deterrence of assisted suicide is not one of the powers conferred on the government under the U.S. Constitution. Nonetheless, he observes, the enumerated powers also do not include the power to prohibit the recreational use of drugs or to discourage drug addiction. The implication, of course, is that the majority's assertion that the CSA is limited to combating drug abuse is no more authoritative than the attorney general's construal of the term "legitimate medical purpose."

Congress does, however, have some power to protect public morality, says Scalia, through its power to regulate interstate commerce. He cites two examples—one involving a ban against interstate shipment of lottery tickets, another involving interstate transfer of women for immoral purposes. Likewise, Scalia concludes, it is unquestionably permissible for Congress to use the federal commerce power to prevent assisted suicide, and there is no doubt that Congress has done that in the CSA.

Finally, Justice Thomas wrote a separate dissent critiquing the majority's opinion, comparing it with the Court's medical marijuana decision in *Gonzales v. Raich* just seven months earlier. Thomas protested that in each case the Court was presented with the same constitutional principles, hence the Court's decision to strike down a California law permitting the use of medical marijuana calls for striking down the Oregon law in this case. The fact that Thomas dissented in *Raich* and thus would have upheld the law in that case provides a mildly ironic twist to his dissent in the Oregon case. Of course, the majority in the Oregon case is quick to make a distinction: whereas California's medical marijuana law concerned a drug that Congress has deemed to have no lawful medical purpose, Congress does allow the drugs Oregon doctors prescribe under the state's assisted suicide law to be used in medical practice generally. Thus in *Gonzales v. Raich* the Court held that Congress's power to regulate interstate commerce includes the power to determine, or to authorize officials in the executive branch to determine, whether specific drugs have any lawful medical purpose at all. In those instances the CSA authorizes the attorney general to enforce such prohibitions. According to *Gonzales v. Oregon,* however, once Congress or its designee permits specific drugs to be used lawfully in medical practice generally, then under the CSA's present scheme the attorney general is not authorized to determine how such drugs may be used, save for to combat drug abuse and addiction in the conventional sense.

Responses to the Court's Ruling

Attorneys and other officials associated with the plaintiffs in the case praised the decision, and urged lawmakers in other states to move forward with efforts to replicate the Oregon law. Editorial writers for the *Oregonian,* the state's highest circulation daily newspaper, continued to express the view that Oregon's assisted suicide law raises not only profound moral questions for gravely ill people and their physicians and families but also ethical questions for the state itself. Nevertheless, the editorial stated, "These questions don't give the federal government the right to barge into the bedrooms of dying patients . . . or the attorney general to play doctor."[121] Oregon's U.S. senator Ron Wyden praised the Court's decision and vowed to continue to fight tooth and nail against any congressional attempt to overcome it. U.S. representative David Wu, also from Oregon, said the majority's opinion recognized the

American value of self-determination. The Department of Justice issued a public statement expressing disappointment with the Supreme Court's decision and reiterating its commitment to enforcing federal drug laws and ensuring that drugs are not diverted to unlawful uses.[122]

A lawyer for the National Right to Life Committee, the nation's largest pro-life organization, reiterated that organization's position that drugs should never be used to kill people, and said the Court's decision sets a dangerous precedent for people whose disabilities or illnesses threaten their lives or health.[123] Likewise, the National Catholic Bioethics Center issued a press statement asserting that physician-assisted suicide violates human dignity and God's gift of life, and expressing its agreement with Justice Scalia's conclusion that the term "legitimate medical purpose" must surely exclude prescribing drugs to produce death.[124] An official speaking for the 17,000-member Christian Medical and Dental Association agreed, stating that killing is not a legitimate medical purpose and warning that the majority opinion teeters toward ethical mayhem. In a similar response, the president of the Southern Baptist Ethics and Religious Liberty Commission said the majority refused to see the Oregon law as involving the healing arts in death therapy.[125] Other organizations that issued statements include the Culture of Life Foundation, Concerned Women for America, and the American Center for Law and Justice. Anti-euthanasia advocate Wesley J. Smith placed the ruling in *Gonzales v. Oregon* into the context of the judicial tyranny theme that applies for social conservatives across rulings like *Roe, Lawrence,* and *Goodrich:* "Don't confuse the majority opinion with truth. What is really happening is the Court, as it often does in cultural issues, is reflecting elite liberal views, and if nothing else, the drive to legalize assisted suicide is an elite liberal political movement."[126]

Limits on the Spread of Assisted Suicide Laws

Since Oregon had allowed the first legal assisted suicide in 1998, other American states began to contemplate similar laws. The diffusion that has taken place to date with assisted suicide laws does not resemble the path of abortion (and the liberalization laws that spread in the years immediately before the *Roe v. Wade* decision). Michigan voted on an ill-framed initiative that was poorly campaigned for in 1998—and few would have placed the "Reagan Democratic". social conservative state on a list of those that would likely pass such legislation. In 2000, Maine came close on an initiative but eventually voted it down.[127]

Strong support for reform of assisted suicide law was displayed by Californians in a 2005 poll.[128] California's Field poll reported: "Consistent with previous Field Poll measures taken during the past twenty-five years, large majorities of Californians continue to endorse the concept of doctor-assisted suicide and say that they themselves would want this option if they were terminally ill and expected to die within six months."[129] Remarkably, this includes 64 percent of Republicans and 65 percent of Catholics.

Strong levels of public support had preceded the 1992 defeat of the California assisted suicide initiative as well.[130] DiCamillo explains the loss in 1992, as the second state to consider physician-assisted suicide, as a result of low awareness of the issue. The year 1992 was also a presidential election year, along with the unusual situation of having two U.S. Senate races, and, as often characterizes California ballots, numerous other propositions clamoring for attention. Oregon reformers would also point to an uneven campaign effort and to the specific issue of doctors being allowed to give shots to patients (that was missing from the ODDA, which thus gave greater emphasis to the autonomy of the dying person).

In March 2006, a Field poll also showed that 70 percent of Californians supported the elements of assisted suicide as presented in the bill pending before the California legislature.[131] The problem with the poll, as opponents of death with dignity legislation would point out, is that it conflates the already available relief through medication—the "morphine drip" or terminal sedations—with the express writing of prescriptions for drugs to actively assist suicide, as is the case with the Oregon Death with Dignity Act. However, when specifically faced with an existing bill or actual initiative, experience has shown that the framing of specific antireform advertisements and funding and assembling of an active coalition can neutralize that nascent support. It remains to be seen whether the Schiavo experience and the *Gonzales v. Oregon* ruling have combined to create in at least one state the conditions for passage of a law similar to Oregon's.

Few states had moved legislation through their state legislatures, with California having gone the farthest when it moved a bill partway through the 2000 legislature. In 2006, a bill that had cleared the state assembly in 2005 ended in the Senate Judiciary Committee.[132]

Anti–assisted suicide activist Wesley J. Smith expressed his pleasure:

> A diverse coalition of political strange bedfellows—made up of pro life advocates, disability rights activists, advocates for the poor, and medical professionals—defeated AB 651, which would have legalized Oregon-style assisted suicide in California. Given the size and importance of California, a law permitting assisted suicide in the Golden State would have boosted the euthanasia agenda throughout the country, and indeed the world.[133]

Vermont was also moving on a bill in 2006, but it died in committee.

The Oregon sentiment and *Gonzales* decision have not translated into pervasive support for physician-assisted suicide, and even in particular cases where it did, state legislation or court decisions permitting the practice have not been forthcoming. It may well be that widespread attention to the battle for passage of the ODDA, to reactions by Congress and the Bush administration to the ODDA, and to the court battles that ensued for more than a decade have prompted widespread changes even under the current regime of medicine and the law. When citizens' groups first began organizing ballot initiatives to change the rules of dying back in the early 1990s, it was easy to tap into the personal angst that many people share when thoughts about institutionalized death and dying arise. But as a result of the activities of the death with dignity movement, today there is greater institutional attention to palliative care and training of physicians and other health personnel on matters related to dying. Alongside these changes, there is greater public familiarity with patients' rights, and increased participation of individuals and families in decisions concerning end-of-life care, including do-not-resuscitate orders, health care powers of attorney, and scattered use of living wills.

The continuing opposition of the AMA and other professional organizations toward physician-assisted suicide is further reason why assisted suicide laws have not spread. Only about one in ten physicians say they would be willing to prescribe medication to hasten a patient's death under current legal constraints. That number rises to only about one in three when physicians are asked if they would do so if it were legal. While these numbers tend to be higher for specialists who are most likely to treat patients with terminal illnesses, polls indicate that this willingness decreases as physicians become more familiar with aggressive measures for treating pain.[134]

In relation to these findings, even physicians who are willing to engage in aggressive measures to ease the process of dying are leery of inviting the greater government attention and scrutiny to their medical practices that could result under a regime to regulate assisted suicide. For these reasons and more, the organizational line persists: physicians ought not to be purposefully involved in bringing about the deaths of patients, and the profession will be harmed if laws permitting such practices are passed.

Thus, given advances in end-of-life care, and the continued reluctance of most physicians to practice assisted suicide, there is very little incentive for lawmakers to entangle themselves in life politics, as many of them learned in the Terri Schiavo case.

On the other hand, Schiavo's lesson against government entanglement in family life-and-death decisions also suggests conditions under which public attention may translate into passage of assisted suicide or other euthanasia laws. If a high-profile controversy caught national attention—as in the 1976 case of *In re Quinlan,* wherein hospital officials blocked the request of a patient's parents to disconnect the patient's ventilator, or the 1990 case of *Cruzan v. Director, Missouri Department of Health,* wherein a state supreme court blocked the request of a patient's parents to terminate the patient's artificial nutrition and hydration—lawmakers in numerous states could react and pass laws permitting physician-assisted suicide. This possibility is one of the significant reasons for assisted suicide reformers to maintain active organizations with mailing lists of grassroots supporters.

After November 2006

The period between the November 2004 and the November 2006 elections did not see any state advance an assisted suicide measure to a voter initiative, or forward legislation to a governor's desk for signature —although a California bill passed one house of the legislature before failing in the other house in 2006, and would fall short in 2007.

Right-to-die or end-of-life legal issues were certainly mentioned in the aftermath of the 2006 elections. While the primary determinants of the Republican losses in the House of Representatives and the United States Senate were due to disapproval of the Bush administration's Iraq war policy, and while the 2006 event of a Republican congressman's resignation over a sexual scandal that had been treated less than urgently by those in charge certainly had an effect, there was still frequent mention of the administration's overintrusive effort to prolong the life of Terri Schiavo in 2005.

Writing in a book that expanded several of the themes of disagreement with the religious Right he had introduced in two *New York Times* op-ed pieces, former U.S. senator John Danforth thought the Schiavo case was central:

> That the federal government could intervene in the Schiavo case was a threat to all the families who had seen their loved ones suffer through terminal illness. It was a threat to people who were terrified that their own lives might someday be artificially extended in nightmarish circumstances. It was a threat to some of our most heartfelt values. It was Big Brotherism in the extreme, an exercise of the raw and awesome power of the federal government.[135]

Political analyst Mort Kondracke—certainly no progressive—concluded in a postelection analysis: "The exit polls also suggest that revolt took place this year against the right's infusion of religious dogma into politics, as in the effort to keep brain-damaged Terri Schiavo alive and Bush's veto of expanded federal funding for embryonic stem-cell research."[136]

Former congressional leader Republican Dick Armey complained that "Republican lawmakers have taken up such issues as flag burning, Terri Schiavo and same-sex marriage."[137] A Republican political activist, trying to rally her party around a new moderate message, argued that the excesses of the 2004–2006 period were consequential:

> You can't spend six years opposing everything from life saving stem cell research to contraception, and expect moderates to continue to support you. The final straws for most in the moderate majority were the bone thrown to the far right with the veto of stem cell research and injecting big government in the middle of the Terry [sic] Schiavo battle, both of which imposed personal, religious and moral beliefs on the American people.[138]

The Meaning of Gonzales v. Oregon

Legally, the Court remained consistent in its view that Congress has authority to regulate physicians' prescribing practices. If Congress wants to criminalize physician-assisted suicide, it could. If Congress wants to grant power to the attorney general to prohibit assisted suicide, it could. Will Congress act to prohibit physician-assisted suicide? Not any time soon, given the public's reaction to congressional involvement in the Terri Schiavo case.

Could it be that the Terri Schiavo affair marked a turning point in the culture wars? Many of those who are "purple" probably viewed the Schiavo case as an example of how extremist the religious Right's influence on public policy could be. The culture wars were muted as a theme in the 2006 elections. That muting seemed to begin around the time of the Schiavo case.

After Schiavo and *Gonzales,* the ODDA would seem to be safe from further attack. *Gonzales* enshrines the ODDA as a legitimate medical practice. It leaves the future of physician-assisted suicide to the judgment of public opinion. In all, *Gonzales* preserves a fine balance between the doctor-patient relationship, state regulation of medical practice, congressional power to regulate the prescription drug trade, and the power of the courts to say what the law is.

Culturally, people do not want to suffer beyond a certain point, and they need to trust their doctors. The ODDA has been instrumental in getting physicians to treat death and dying differently. Palliative care and hospice are becoming the norm. Legal devices such as health care powers of attorney and do-not-resuscitate orders are honored routinely. The world of end-of-life care has changed dramatically since the time Oregon doctor Peter Goodwin said "it felt as if my blood nearly froze" the first time a patient asked him for assistance in dying.[139] *Gonzales* preserves the new status quo.

Moral Pragmatism in Law and Medicine

Our main argument has been that following forty years of legal change in the policy arenas of gambling, abortion, and the treatment of gays, among others, Americans are less likely to turn to the criminal sanction as a means to control personal morality. Legal developments governing physicians' involvement in ending patients' suffering and hastening death have manifested this trend and extended it. Social movement claims around "a right to die with dignity" have followed 1960s- and 1970s-style rights claims, where clearly an old morality rooted in what are sometimes called "Judeo-Christian values" has been challenged by a new morality marked by an increased individualism.

In opposition since the 1990s, the Christian Right has added assisted suicide to its tremendous political activity around abortion and gay rights. Framing the conflict as a battle between a culture of life and a culture of death, compromise has been rejected as directly devaluing ideological and programmatic goals. The operating styles of extremists have differed from the styles of most people. The issues attended to have often not been the issues that interest most people. The appearance of polarization has resulted from the extremes being overrepresented and the center underrepresented in the political arena. We have argued that as with gambling, abortion, and gay rights, polarization in the politics of death and dying is limited largely to a political class of activists and party candidates.

At the same time, the center has not embraced privacy and autonomy in all matters in which patients seek to end suffering and hasten death. Patients need to trust physicians. Physicians need to protect the nobility of their profession. People who are dependent and vulnerable need state protection from manipulation and abuse. Thus, along with laws and ethical standards concerning criminal battery and informed consent, legal and moral proscriptions against assisted suicide and homicide preserve and safeguard these and other needs. And among most people outside the political class of activists and party candidates, considerations of law and policy have been marked less by polarization over criminal sanctions and judgments involving personal morality than by ambivalence about safeguarding individuals and allowing them choice.

In earlier chapters we described various models of law and social change, or paths taken toward decriminalizing "victimless crimes." In the case of gambling, decriminalization has occurred as states allowed casino gambling and established lotteries to increase state revenues. In the case of abortion, decriminalization has been a function of identifying a woman's decision to terminate her pregnancy as an aspect of liberty constitutionally protected against undue state interference. In the case of gay rights, decriminalization has granted equal liberty interests in relation to personal decisions in intimate, private, adult relationships.

In this chapter we have described a fourth model of law and social change: the establishment of safe harbors in state legal codes.

The prime example is the state of Oregon. Contrary to what is sometimes reported, assisted suicide is still a crime in Oregon. What the ODDA does is establish a rigorous set of procedures that patients, physicians, pharmacists, and others must follow in order to secure immunity from criminal and civil liability. Although Oregon is still the only state where competent, terminally ill patients may obtain a prescription for a lethal dose of medication to hasten death, safe harbors in state criminal homicide and assisted suicide laws are not unique to that state. Natural death acts in every state have the same effect: following procedures pertaining to do-not-resuscitate orders, living wills, and medical powers of attorney renders medical personnel and others immune from criminal and civil liability. The same results follow from the Supreme Court's holding in *Vacco v. Quill* that states may permit palliative care which may have the foreseen but unintended "double effect" of hastening a patient's death. (The Court also recognized, without condemning, the related practice of "terminal sedation," in which patients are maintained in a drug-induced coma while they die as a result of food and liquids being withheld.) While reports of prosecutions or malpractice lawsuits resulting from physician involvement in end-of-life care have been rare, the theoretical possibility of such liability has led to a lot of end-of-life civil litigation and clarifying legislation. The resulting safe-harbor provisions, loosely defined, manifest and extend the national trend toward reining in the criminal sanction in contested areas of personal morality.

Protest by religious and social conservatives against right-to-die legislation has slowed but not stopped the trend. Because most people are ambivalent about safeguarding individuals and allowing them choice, an effective antireform strategy has been to argue that specific reform proposals will not adequately protect dependent and vulnerable people from bad-acting family members, physicians, or cost-conscious insurance providers. Years of litigation seeking to block or undermine the death with dignity law in Oregon stalled efforts to pass similar laws in other states as policymakers waited to see how the challenges would be resolved. What was finally most significant about *Gonzales v. Oregon* was the Supreme Court's determination that rather than simply decriminalizing assisted suicide, Oregon has limited its exercise in a carefully crafted statutory regime that exemplifies the state regulation of medical practice. Under current federal law, that leaves every state free to develop its own response to the needs of dying patients.

In the Terri Schiavo case, the religious Right lost credibility in the illusory divide between a culture of life and a culture of death, taking along the president and some in Congress, including presidential hopefuls for 2008. That spectacle tainted debate on human embryonic stem cell research—the subject of the next chapter—where moral pragmatism had already begun to split social and religious conservatives.

Religious or not, Americans have always been pragmatic about abortion, and now many abortion opponents support stem cell research. Reillustrating our theme of ambivalence, Americans value human life, *and* they have a strong faith in the potential of science and medicine. Thus the political Right has had its greatest success in thwarting gay marriage, which social and religious conservatives are not necessarily interested in for themselves. However, as with access to a sympathetic physician, one is less inclined to come out strongly against something one may have a pragmatic reason for wanting oneself.

6

Stem Cells

Framing Battles and the Race for a Cure

I have never seen in my career a biological tool as powerful as the stem cells. It addresses every single human disease.
—Dr. Hans Keirstad, *60 Minutes* (2006)

Prop 71 was a thinly veiled, and successful attempt by scientists, actors, and some members of the media to create a constitutional right to embryonic stem cell research and human cloning. One of the most disturbing parts of Prop 71 is the fact that it allows for the cloning of human beings to be used for destructive embryonic stem cell research.
—Diane Vargo, "Connecting the Dots: Stem Cells and Human Cloning" (2005)

I just don't see how we can turn our backs on this. . . . We have lost so much time already. . . . [Stem cell research] may provide our scientists with many answers that for so long have been beyond our grasp.
—Nancy Reagan (2004)

A State Steps Forward

In 2006, one American state battled to consider an emerging scientific policy direction over which many in the country were conflicted. The issue was the state funding of stem cell research, important because the Bush administration in 2001 had blocked the use of federal funds for research on the promising scientific development, on the grounds that destruction of embryos, a central concern of the pro-life movement, was necessary for stem cell research advances.

In one television advertisement produced and run by the reformers, a

7-year-old boy appears with his mother. With seeming resignation, the boy reveals that he found out when he was four that he has juvenile diabetes. The boy's mother says:

> Stem cell research seems to hold hope and promise for a cure. How do you look at anyone with cancer, or Parkinson's, or a spinal cord injury and say we're going to walk away from hope? How do I look my son in the face and tell him we're going to give up hope. I can't.[1]

What was remarkable was that this electoral event was not taking place in California, which had passed a similar initiative in 2004. Nor was it in New Jersey, which was moving in a similar direction, or any of another handful of blue states that were also considering it or moving forward. The 2006 electoral battle was in the "red" state of Missouri, which had voted for George W. Bush in 2000 and 2004. Missouri also had famously been a test case state against *Roe v. Wade* in the 1980s.[2]

Missouri was the home of John Ashcroft, the former conservative U.S. senator and later the attorney general who attempted to shut done the Oregon Death with Dignity Act. By all accounts, while it kept leaning "red," it was a battleground state, where Democrats and Republicans vied for electoral success with national implications. Missouri was known as a bellwether state, where many of America's policies were debated. It had a mix of urban and rural residents, a racial mix (although without many Latinos or Asians), blue-collar and white-collar workers, significant Catholic and evangelical populations, and good colleges and universities. The Missouri reformers were acting to be the sixth American state to fund stem cell research, at a time when seven other American states had passed laws to prevent stem cell research from being undertaken in their state.

The issue has created controversy around the country. California, Illinois, Washington, Wisconsin, Connecticut, Massachusetts, New Jersey, and Rhode Island have passed laws either protecting stem cell research or allocating funds for it. Meanwhile, Iowa, Indiana, Michigan, Arkansas, North Dakota, South Dakota, Nebraska, and Arizona have banned embryonic stem cell research or limited funding for it.

The Missouri initiative would provide support for basic scientific research that would go beyond existing early research using only embryonic stem cells, many in excess from fertility clinics, stipulating the potential next step in therapeutic application. In a procedure scientists call "somatic cell nuclear transfer," an adult skin cell or a cell taken from another body part is inserted into an egg from which the nucleus has been removed. Scientists stimulate the egg to grow in a lab dish; five days later they obtain the developing stem cells, which are a genetic match to the donor cell. Scientists believe that they can use the procedure to study the progression of genetic diseases, and that someday they may derive therapies for these diseases and also use stem cells to repair damaged nerves, organs, and other tissues. Somatic cell nuclear transfer is one of many lab procedures that involve cloning; to distinguish that sort of cloning from cloning that results in a full-term infant, supporters of the procedure and most of the mainstream media have adopted the term "therapeutic cloning." Critics say the procedure is unethical and disrespects life. "All life is worthy of respect," said Larry Weber, executive director of the Missouri Catholic Conference. "There is no exception for life, even when it is created in a laboratory."[3]

In September 2005, the Missouri Coalition for Lifesaving Cures, a group of more than sixty business interests, universities, and patient and medical organizations, began a petition drive to put a measure on the 2006 ballot that would amend the state constitution to guarantee that stem cell research, therapies, and cures allowed under federal law also are permitted in Missouri. The measure would also prohibit attempts to create an infant through cloning, which is known as "reproductive cloning."

The proposed amendment was backed by a coalition of medical research institutions, patient advocacy groups, and business leaders who say medical researchers need protection from repeated efforts in the state legislature to criminalize embryonic stem cell research. More than 40,000 individuals joined the coalition in its first three months.

William Neaves, president and chief executive officer at the Stowers Institute for Medical Research in Kansas City, said concern over the possibility of criminal prosecution caused researchers to turn away from Missouri and delayed plans for major expansion of the institute. The Stowers Institute was founded by cancer survivors Jim and Virginia Stowers. The Kansas City facility, funded by the Stowerses' own fortune, includes a $300 million laboratory with state-of-the-art equipment for 200 scientists who are recruited worldwide. The Stowerses had planned to build a second 600,000-square-foot facility but backed off after state senator Matt Bartle vowed to press his fight to grant legal protection to human embryos. The couple spent millions more in contributions to the initiative campaign.

Annually in Missouri, $658 million pours into the state through federal grants for life science research and development, placing the state at eleventh in funding provided by the National Science Foundation.[4] Shedding the state's reputation for being slow with scientific progress is a priority of state leaders. The executive director of the Missouri Biotechnology Association indicated that many companies in the state's biomedical industry compete for the best talent.[5] She worried that lawmakers' willingness to criminalize any stem cell research would send an antiscience message. There was also the fear of losing biotech jobs and research dollars to the growing number of states that are rewriting their laws and offering their own research grants.

In August 2005, Illinois governor Rod Blagojevich sent letters to Missouri scientists, personally soliciting them to move their research across the state border. Harvard's Kevin Eggan, one of *Popular Science* magazine's "Brilliant Ten" for the year 2005, recruited by Stowers in 2004 and working in a secret lab to create embryos from cells donated by people with Parkinson's disease, is wary of working in Kansas City while the threat of becoming a felon looms over researchers doing work like his. Eggan's contract could bring him to Missouri if the ballot measure passed.[6]

One of the television advertisements aired by the reformers focused on this issue of state competitiveness. Dr. Maureen Dudgeon, an associate dean from the Kansas City University of Medicine and Biosciences, says in the ad:

> It would be heartbreaking to know that cures were available to people all over the United States but not available to the citizens of Missouri. The stem cell research initiative very simply allows Missouri scientists, Missouri physicians, and Missouri citizens to pursue, prescribe, and benefit from potential cures that would be available to every other citizen in the United States.[7]

In Missouri, the opponents of the initiative to ban stem cell research called their group Missourians Against Human Cloning, emphasizing in their statements the slippery slope from stem cell research to therapeutic cloning to reproductive cloning.

Missouri Right to Life, the Missouri Baptist Convention, and the Missouri Catholic Conference all denounced somatic cell nuclear transfer. The state has one of the most vigorous and influential pro-life movements in the nation. For these groups, the debate over destroying human life in the name of scientific research is a natural extension of the abortion battle.

One line of argument in Missourians Against Human Cloning materials stated: "This amendment creates an atmosphere of false hope," since no treatments have come from stem cell research yet. One radio advertisement produced and run by the initiative's opponents was a product of their attempt to try and stop the movement at that point:

NARRATOR: Everyone has an automatic routine for signing their name.
LESLIE: I'm Leslie. When I sign a birthday card I automatically draw a heart over the "i" instead of a dot.
NARRATOR: You're very careful about how you sign, yet some Missourians aren't careful about what they sign. They impulsively signed a petition to change the constitution to allow human cloning and other unethical medical procedures. Think before you sign.
LESLIE: You mean the heart I draw might stop a heart from beating?
NARRATOR: Think before you sign.[8]

As with other campaigns, this one had elements for everyone. The "parade of horribles" approach focused on the prospect of human reproductive cloning, of Dolly the sheep and of brave new world possibilities. The obstruction of proven research emphasized that the activists did not oppose medical research or cures, and that they felt that investment in such wild-eyed and unproven methods would take away from steadier investment in existing research, in a zero-sum fashion.

The proposed ballot initiative to safeguard stem cell research in 2006 had the support of more than 60 percent of Missourians in polls early on, and the issue has complicated matters for Republican senator Jim Talent, who faced strong opposition from Democratic state auditor Claire McCaskill in his 2006 reelection bid. The religious Right had indicated that it finds this law more important than Talent, and urged him to oppose it, which he did in May 2006.[9]

Talent was in the position of losing support from evangelicals if he came out in favor of embryo research. "If he doesn't take a clear position on the pro-life side, it's going to hurt him, no question about it," said Campaign Life Missouri's director, Sam Lee. "People are just not going to work for him."[10] In line with other antiabortion activists, Lee also said that killing the stem cell initiative was more important than re-electing Talent. But if Talent opposed the research, he stood to lose support from those in the business community who might back him financially, said Max Skidmore, professor of political science at University of Missouri–Kansas City.

The issue has divided Republicans, pitting former first lady Nancy Reagan and Senate majority leader Bill Frist against President Bush and religious conservatives. Reagan and others are hopeful that stem cells cultivated from cloning a patient's own cells could lead to cures for diseases such as Alzheimer's, from which former president Reagan suffered for years. Pro-life conservatives counter that cloning a patient's cells and dissecting the stem cells results in taking a human life, since the procedure creates human embryos that must be killed when they are just days old to harvest the stem cells. "It splits libertarian, free-market Republicans from social conservative Republicans," said Mathew Crenson, a political analyst at Johns Hopkins University in Maryland.

Some prominent pro-life Republicans, concerned with the economic impact of losing medical researchers in Missouri, threw their weight behind efforts to keep all forms of stem cell research in the state. Governor Matt Blunt supported the proposed constitutional amendment.

Meanwhile, Blunt attempted to use other actions and statements to demonstrate that he remained staunchly pro-life, despite his backing of the stem cell initiative. In November 2005, for example, he championed a bill to allow pharmacists to refuse to dispense the "morning-after pill."

Former Republican U.S. senator John Danforth appeared in TV commercials supporting the measure, saying in an ad for the reformers: "My entire voting career I voted pro-life, and that is exactly why I favor this initiative. I believe in saving human life."[11] In a March 2005 op-ed for the *New York Times,* Danforth had charged that "the only explanation for legislators comparing cells in a petri dish to babies in the womb is the extension of religious doctrine into statutory law."[12]

Business leaders—who would like the Republican Party to exemplify a "big tent" approach—favored the initiative and split with their frequent partners, the religious/social conservatives.

The *St. Louis Post-Dispatch* reported early in November 2005 that the bishops of four dioceses that make up the Catholic province of St. Louis directed their parish priests to convey from the pulpit the church's position on embryonic stem cell research and its opposition to the research and cures initiatives. Using the first Sunday of Advent to kick off the campaign to keep Catholics from signing the petition, the bishops also asked every Catholic parish to hold an educational event to discuss the issues surrounding embryonic stem cell research in the state. "The whole purpose is to educate the public that this coalition wants to amend our constitution to give free rein to do whatever scientists want to do with our embryos," said Molly Kertz, director of the St. Louis archdiocese's Respect Life apostolate. In a letter to his priests dated November 10, Archbishop Raymond Burke told them: "In order to avoid Catholic voters succumbing to the false promises and statements made by this initiative's proponents, it is important that voters in our parishes receive appropriate scientific, moral and ethical information."[13]

As directed, priests around the state delivered a variation on the same homily painting embryonic stem cell research as evil and instructing Catholics not to sign the petition. "The similarities of the arguments behind the destruction of life by the Nazis and the use of human embryos [for stem cell research] are scary," Reverend Smith told hundreds of worshipers at a morning Mass at St. Peter's Catholic Church, across the street from the state capitol. "Human embryos are not potential human beings. Human embryos are human beings with potential," John Weaver, deacon of Sacred Heart Catholic Church in Columbia, told worshipers Sunday. Rev. Michael McDevitt also spoke of the need to balance the interests of patients and the lives of human embryos. "Our hearts should go out to the people who are ill, but there has to be other means than destroying life," McDevitt told more than 150 parishioners attending Saturday Mass at St. Agnes Cathedral in Springfield. "Human life is a gift from God."[14]

Archbishop Burke had announced the Catholic campaign against the initiative in the weekly newspaper of the Archdiocese of St. Louis. In a November column, the archbishop urged Catholics to be vigilant in promoting the respect for human life, "safeguarding the life of every brother and sister from the moment of inception to the moment of natural death." Burke instructed Catholics that to sign a petition favoring the initiative is to promote the culture of death that tragically besets the nation and constitutes cooperation in the destruction of human lives at their very beginning. Because of its size and appearance, the archbishop explained, the human embryo can be described in various ways that distort the most fundamental truth that at every stage of development, a human being—whether zygote, blastocyst, embryo, fetus, infant, adolescent, or adult—is an integral being structured for maturation along its proper time line. "Apart from the question of whether stem cells obtained through the destruction of human embryos is, in fact, an effective treatment for illnesses or physical impairment, it is never morally justified to do something intrinsically evil to accomplish some good," Burke declared. Quoting from Pope John Paul II's encyclical *Evangelium Vitae,* Archbishop Burke reminded Catholics of the church's position that "the use of human embryos or fetuses as an object of experimentation constitutes a crime against their dignity as human beings who have a right to the same respect owed to a child once born, just as to every person." The archbishop implored Catholics that they not only should oppose any legislation or amendment to the Constitution of the state of Missouri but also must work for legislation and constitutional guarantees directed to respect for the inviolable dignity of innocent human life.[15]

Surveys of Catholic attitudes toward stem cell research show mixed results, depending on the wording of particular questions. In 2004, Peter D. Hart Research Associates polled believers from various religious denominations and found that 54 percent of Catholics favored stem cell research, while 29 percent opposed it. The percentage of Catholics who favored the research was only slightly lower than the 59 percent of mainline Protestants who also responded favorably. By contrast, just 34 percent of evangelicals said they favored the research. The Hart Research Associates poll, however, did not distinguish between embryonic stem cell research and adult stem cell research. As with polls soliciting public opinion about abortion, people respond more favorably to a broad question asking simply whether they support stem cell research than they do to questions containing more specific information about the source of stem cells or the source of funding for stem cell research. For example, a 2004 poll by the Pew Forum on Religion and Public Life found that 55 percent of Catholics said it was "more important to pursue stem cell research than to not destroy embryos," up from 43 percent in 2002. But in May 2005, the Catholic bishops sponsored their own poll and found that just 36 percent of Americans support "federal funding" of embryonic stem cell research, while 52 percent opposed federal funding.[16]

Staunchly antiabortion, Archbishop Burke had made headlines during the 2004 presidential campaign when he said he would deny communion to candidate John Kerry, a pro-choice Catholic. Burke upped the ante when he warned that is a sin to vote for any candidate who supported abortion rights. The *St. Louis Post-Dispatch* said the crush of media coverage "immediately made Burke a national player." After Burke had left Wisconsin to be installed as archbishop in St. Louis, a priest there wrote a letter to the editor of a local newspaper saying the former bishop had increased polarization among Catholics, particularly by denying communion to politicians who support abortion rights. Burke later modified his statement about denying communion to Kerry, but in October—less than five weeks before the election—he issued an open letter to St. Louis Catholics. He wrote that positive positions taken by political candidates could not justify their support of abortion, embryonic stem cell research, euthanasia, human cloning, or same-sex marriage. Voters must ask themselves, he wrote, "whether it is fair to our unborn brothers and sisters to help put someone in office who will not lift a finger to save their lives because we favor that candidate's position on health-care reform, education, the death penalty or some other issue."

The reformers sought to blunt some of this religious opposition through one advertisement of their own, featuring an African American minister:

> When there is nothing left that the medical establishment can do, we in the faith community say all we can do is pray. I'm excited when there's the possibility that we can discover medicines that can save lives. I will vote for the stem cell initiative with the hope that the people of Missouri can move forward.[17]

A spokesman for the Missouri Democratic Party described Republicans as "beholden to both deep-pocketed donors and a right-wing base," and said that on the stem cell issue these supporters are pulling politicians in opposite directions.[18] Sam Fox, a St. Louis businessman with deep financial ties to Missouri Republicans, said different views are to be expected on account of the Republican Party being a "big tent."[19] That was also the view expressed by national Republican Party chairman Ken Mehlman, who worked to sidestep media questions about Republican divisions by focusing attention on topics on which Republicans agree.[20]

But many foot soldiers in the culture wars are wary of the big-tent view. During the GOP's annual Lincoln Days conference, a Republican ward committeewoman from Kansas City spoke about her disappointment with Blunt's support for embryo research and confided that she hoped for a Republican challenger to run against Blunt in the 2008 gubernatorial election. She said it is no less necessary for Republican leaders to oppose embryonic stem cell research on moral grounds than it is for them to oppose abortion. That issue, she said, is what she and conservatives like her will be thinking about when they finally decide if they would vote for Talent.[21]

Stem Cell Research Emerges as an Issue

This chapter examines the emergence of a new medical breakthrough that is poised on the divide of two deeply held cultural precepts: belief in the potential of scientific discoveries to fight disease, and beliefs about embryos and the sanctity of life. As the possibilities of stem cell breakthroughs have excited Americans, they have galvanized conservative religious groups, which have attempted to reproduce their efforts against abortion. This chapter examines the tensions between these deeply held beliefs, the ambivalence of key actors, and the framing of appeals for support among an interested American public as states act to circumvent federal limitations on research. The discussion will frame this debate, analyze the appeals and actions in California and elsewhere, and follow the growth of this new phenomenon.

On August 9, 2001, in a prime-time television address to the nation, President George W. Bush announced his much-anticipated decision regarding federal funding for stem cell research. By executive order, and in a policy first, the president reaffirmed existing prohibitions against harming or destroying human embryos but authorized federal funding for research on existing stem cell lines—"where the life-and-death decision has already been made."[22] The president's compromise embraced both widespread enthusiasm for the potential to treat a broad range of disabilities and diseases, and deep concern that destroying human embryos devalues human life. Mixed reactions, even among pro-life leaders, began a new chapter in the decades-long debate concerning the propriety of using taxpayer dollars to support human embryo research.

Overview of the Stem Cell Controversy

Debates concerning embryonic stem cell research are part of a larger controversy concerning whether federal funds should be used to support research in which human embryos are destroyed. Many people who view embryos as persons object to such research on the grounds that it devalues human life. Of course, taxpayer support is vital to scientific research—raising the thorny issue of the propriety of funding research strongly opposed by many citizens on moral grounds:

> To this point, the federal government has pursued a policy whereby it does not explicitly prohibit embryo research but does not officially condone it, encourage it, or support it with public funds. This approach has allowed the political system to avoid banning embryo research against the wishes of those who believe it serves an important purpose, while not compelling those citizens who oppose it to fund it with their tax money.[23]

The controversy stretches back to *Roe v. Wade,* the Supreme Court decision that for antiabortion activists raised the specter of experimentation on aborted fetuses. In the immediate aftermath of *Roe,* a temporary moratorium backed by Congress forbade federal funding of clinical research using aborted fetuses or living human embryos. In 1979, after considering the recommendations of the national Ethics Advisory Board (EAB), the Department of Health, Education, and Welfare (DHEW, the precursor of today's Department of Health and Human Services [DHHS]) decided against offering funds for human embryo research. The DHEW decision came on the heals of massive lobbying against the EAB's conclusion that, subject to certain restrictions, research involving in vitro fertilization (IVF) techniques and human embryos was "acceptable from an ethical standpoint."[24] Bonnicksen reports that nearly a hundred members of Congress and thousands of antiabortion protesters turned the EAB's endorsement of embryo research into "a pariah attached to the politically dangerous issue of abortion," effectively foreclosing federal sponsorship of all research involving human embryos.[25]

Conscious failure to renew the EAB's charter in 1980 created a de facto moratorium that lasted throughout the administrations of Presidents Ronald Reagan and George H. W. Bush. Both presidents, fearing further entanglement in the abortion debate, rejected pressure to abolish a DHEW regulation requiring EAB review of research proposals involving human embryos.[26] Their inactions left intact a peculiar requirement that proposals undergo a review process that in fact did not exist. In 1993, however, President Clinton worked with Congress to pass the NIH Revitalization Act, which contained a provision to rescind this requirement. The following year President Clinton and the NIH paved the way for funding research involving surplus embryos from IVF procedures. Once again, however, pro-life forces mobilized en masse, and in 1995 Congress blocked Clinton's effort.

President George W. Bush inherited the stem cell controversy from the Clinton administration. In the wake of an announcement in 1998 that a team of U.S. scientists had become the first to isolate and culture stem cells from human embryos,[27] debate concerning the propriety of federal funding for embryonic stem cell research escalated, as researchers speculated about the potential for using embryonic stem cells to treat a broad range of disability and disease. Clinton's response was to adopt a DHHS interpretation that federal law permits funding for research involving embryos that have been destroyed in previous research financed with private funds. President Clinton then adopted a set of NIH guidelines for funding such research, but he left office before the guidelines could be promulgated. President Bush took office and decided to review the Clinton guidelines. That review culminated in the president's announcement of his new policy on August 9, 2001.

The 2001 policy authorizes federal funding for research using stem cell lines derived prior to August 9, 2001. In the eyes of the president, the announcement raised the thorny question of when one can benefit from a prior immoral act. A three-part rationale was offered in a 2004 report published by the president's council established under the new policy. First, the report states, by restricting funding to cell lines derived prior to a designated date, the president had avoided cooperation in future harm. Second, since the embryos from which the cell lines were derived were destroyed prior to that date, the president had not abetted their destruction. Finally, by firmly disavowing further destruction of embryos ("We do not end some lives for the medical benefit of others" —a point the president repeats frequently), the president reaffirmed the underlying moral principle. Thus, the report explained, the president's policy met the conditions of noncooperation, nonabetting, and reaffirmation of the principle.[28]

Protest groups on either side of the controversy nonetheless interpreted Bush's policy in terms of its political underpinnings and implications. Favorable reactions characterized the president's compromise as "an effort at a principled solution," a "Solomonic compromise," and "an elegant solution to a thorny issue." Unfavorable characterizations called it "a crafty dodge of a difficult ethical issue," "a political splitting of the difference," and a move calculated to "please all, satisfy none."

Critical Events Change Prevailing Patterns of Institutional Politics

For nearly three decades, federal policy governing human embryo research was dominated by the threat of mobilization by antiabortion activists. As Andrea Bonnicksen observes in her book *In Vitro Fertilization: Building Policy from Laboratories to Legislatures,* "For a politician, the best way to deal with a political thicket is to do nothing, which is what happened."[29] John Fletcher agrees; in a 1999 treatise on stem cell policy for the National Bioethics Advisory Commission, Fletcher reported that throughout the 1980s and beyond—and influenced primarily by abortion politics—Congress "became hostile to science at the beginning of life and substituted what it could legitimately control, i.e., by imposing bans on federal funding."[30] In this political context, and because "traditionally, the potential beneficiaries of embryo research were a compact segment of the population,"[31] clinicians, researchers, and infertile couples who attempted to mobilize support for embryo research were effectively locked out of the policy process.

However, critical events in the late 1990s created opportunities to mobilize a movement and challenge prevailing policy. One set of events occurred in the field of stem cell research. In 1998, researchers at the University of Wisconsin and at Johns Hopkins University announced that for the first time, human embryonic stem cells had been derived from and sustained in lab cultures. Hailed as the scientific "Breakthrough of the Year" by the journal *Science,* the changing science of stem cells created an opportunity to reframe the costs and benefits of human embryo research.

Two more critical events also made international headlines. The first was the cloning of Dolly the sheep by Scottish scientists in 1997; the second was an announcement in early 1998 of plans by a rogue Chicago physicist to open an international chain of human cloning clinics. In response to each event, Congress and the White House proposed policies seeking to distance the federal government from human cloning. Unwittingly, they also threatened to criminalize a large swath of research—including research on embryonic stem cells. Together, these proposals and the changing science of stem cell research changed the pattern of institutional politics surrounding human embryo research. These changes created new opportunities among patient advocacy groups, medical societies, and the biotechnology industry for mobilizing around a range of grievances.

Earlier claims about the number of people who might benefit from embryo research were generally expressed in terms of those affected by infertility. From 1988 to 1995, that number was on average about 2.1 million women per year.[32] By comparison, one estimate put the number of diabetes, Alzheimer's, and Parkinson's patients who might benefit from stem cell therapy at 24 million.[33] Another estimate that also took into account caretakers and other affected individuals put the number as high as 125 million.[34] Proponents of the research successfully reframed the costs and benefits of the research, countering opponents' moral claims regarding the status and value of embryos as human beings with their own claim that it would be immoral *not* to proceed with research that could impact millions.

Mobilization Alters Calculations of Institutionally Oriented Actors

The debate shifted from funding and regulatory agencies to the more overtly political forums of Congress and the White House.[35] In a complete departure from previous politics, sympathetic legislators—many of whom had personal experiences with suffering and loss—involved professional associations, patient advocacy groups, and scientists in the policymaking process. For example, senators leading the fight against criminalization met with representatives from the National Bioethics Advisory Commission, the NIH, the American Society for Reproductive Medicine, the Biotechnology Industry Organization, the Department of Health and Human Services, and the Food and Drug Administration.[36]

Hundreds of related constituencies formed coalitions and sent letters to Congress protesting the criminalization of lab procedures. Capturing the overall sentiment, a letter from the American Association for the Advancement of Science—the world's largest multidisciplinary scientific association—stated:

> Congress should consult with leading researchers in genetics and other areas of the life-sciences in crafting language so that . . . laws do not impede important research that . . . can yield great benefits, for example, in increasing agricultural production, generating new products through biotechnology, finding cures for genetic disorders, and reducing the costs of pharmaceuticals.[37]

Bonnicksen writes that with such letters the embryo research "debate now began more distinctly to encompass values relating to scientific freedom and commercial interest."[38]

Others focused on the "moral imperative" to proceed with funding. In one example, three dozen Nobel laureates sent a letter to President Clinton and all members of Congress urging that federal funds for embryonic stem cell research would allow for peer review, public oversight, and assurances that "the research will be of the highest quality and performed with the greatest dignity and moral responsibility."[39]

Research advocates also used patients' personal stories to lobby Congress for support. In an article in *Science* titled "Patients' Voices: The Powerful Sound in the Stem Cell Debate," the leader of thirty-six national nonprofit organizations operating under the banner Patients' Coalition for Urgent Research explained, "The stories of patients and family members . . . put a human face on the promise of biomedical research."[40] High-profile celebrities like Mary Tyler Moore, Michael J. Fox, and the now-deceased Christopher Reeve bolstered the effect.

Marginal Positions and Criticisms Reach a Broader Audience

Increased public awareness of the issue paralleled increased media attention until—by the summer of 2001—the controversy had catapulted to the top of media, public, and policy agendas. The number of survey respondents who reported they were following the issue rose to more than half. Sixty percent of those polled responded that the issue was "very important" or "somewhat important." Moreover, an independent

CBS News poll showed majority support for funding embryonic stem cell research among Protestants, Catholics, Republicans, Democrats, and independents. The only group that opposed the research consisted of those who also responded that abortion should always be illegal.[41]

Meanwhile, proponent and opponent coalitions stepped up their protest strategies. In one example, the president of the American Life League exclaimed, "If the President approves any support, he will no longer have the right to call himself a pro-life president."[42] On the other side, however, Senator Orrin Hatch—a staunch pro-life leader who earlier led a fight to block funding for fetal tissue research and also once championed a constitutional amendment to outlaw abortion—wrote a letter to the president insisting that "proceeding with this research is in the best interests of the American public and is consistent with our shared pro-life, pro-family values."[43]

Enhanced external scrutiny of stem cell policy and the policy process called for President Bush to address the broadening audience. Officials inside the White House conjectured that Bush could draw on the controversy to instill a public perception that he had considered the issue thoughtfully. Republicans and Democrats outside the White House said Bush's decision would signal either a dogged allegiance to the right or a willingness to embrace a more centrist position on the political spectrum. Whether Bush reached his compromise "from opportunistic calculus or reflective soul-searching" is unimportant, for purposes of this analysis. "In either case, the policy process and product [were] altered."[44]

Thus critical events in stem cell research changed a thirty-year pattern of institutional politics—opening up crucial opportunities for extrainstitutional mobilization. A broader audience came to embrace positions and criticisms formerly on the margins. As the possibility for more volatile mobilization increased, the president followed many in Congress who altered their calculations of the costs and benefits of reforming funding policy for embryo research. The key change was opportunity to renegotiate the ideological balance around prevailing policy and policy processes. Particularly, policy proposals seeking to criminalize key research empowered a new set of actors—those who previously had been excluded from policymaking—who became mutually recognized as legitimate actors in the policy process. Meyer's conjectures about how changes in pubic policy affect the development of challenging movements are borne out in this case study. The next step is to look for how movements channel political opportunity in order to influence public policy.

Institutional and Extrainstitutional Strategies of Influence

One account emphasized how deliberative the process was: "Everybody Bush knows—as well as thousands he doesn't—weighed in with their opinions."[45] In February, a group of eighty Nobel laureates signed a letter to the president urging him not to block federal funds. It was believed to be the largest collection of Nobel signatures ever sent to a president. In March, the American Society for Cell Biology, the Juvenile Diabetes Foundation, the Parkinson's Action Network, Harvard University, the University of Wisconsin, Washington University in St. Louis, the Association of American Medical Colleges, the Christopher Reeve Paralysis Foundation, and the Biotechnology Industry Organization, among others, formed the Coalition for the Advancement of Medical Research and hired a lobbyist with strong Republican connections to more effectively discuss the scientific promise of stem cell research with the administration. The presidents of the Council on Education, the National Association of State Universities and Land-Grant Colleges, and the Association of American Universities, as well as the presidents or chancellors of 112 research universities, signed a similar letter. In July, six former assistant secretaries for health sent Bush a letter urging him to support federal spending for embryonic stem cell research. These letters were in addition to others from professional societies, disease advocacy groups, a group of ninety-five member of Congress, and the American Association for the Advancement of Science.[46]

Several prominent Republicans broke with party ranks and lobbied the president hard. Senator Orrin Hatch, who has two nieces suffering from diabetes, asked Bush to join him with other leading pro-life, pro-family Republicans such as Strom Thurmond, Gordon Smith, and Connie Mack "to lead the way for this vital research."[47] Former senator Mack was particularly outspoken. He made passionate pleas for federal funding in commentaries for the *Washington Post* and *Wall Street Journal*. Moreover, he stressed that he was advocating for funding stem cell research as "a pro-life Republican."[48] Tony Mazzaschi of the Association of American Medical Colleges said on National Public Radio's Morning Edition that "the growing number of Republicans supporting federal funding of stem cell research placed 'tremendous pressure' on Bush, who already was contending with division among his own advisers."[49] Others also noted, however, that the prominence of Republican supporters such as Hatch and Mack offered Bush some political cover for shifting ground on his campaign pledge.

In midsummer, Republican senator Arlen Specter, an outspoken proponent of the research, declared that public interest had risen to "avalanche" proportions. "It's just overwhelming," he said.[50] Nevertheless, polls showed that depending on how pollsters framed the issue, many Americans could be swayed either way. For example, in a poll sponsored by the Juvenile Diabetes Research Foundation, respondents were asked whether they favored the funding of stem cell research using "excess" human embryos "donated" to research "to cure diseases such as diabetes, Parkinson's, Alzheimer's, cancer, heart disease, arthritis, burns, or spinal cord problems." Sixty-five percent responded yes. Conversely, a poll sponsored by the National Council of Catholic Bishops asked respondents whether "your federal tax dollars" should be used to fund "experiments" on "live" embryos that will be "destroyed in their first week of development." In that survey, 70 percent of respondents said they oppose such research.

The finding that strong wording of questions affected respondents' opinions is interesting for what it reflects about how movement activists mobilize public and political support. [51] In a related study of the stem cell debate, Nisbet and his colleagues analyzed more than 1,000 news articles and press reports appearing between 1975 and 2002 in national newspapers, on national news broadcasts, and on National Public Radio.[52] They found that the strategy in which activists define or "frame" issues in moral and ethical ways and draw public attention to their respective claims plays into journalists' need to narratize the policy world. Thus a shift in coverage dominated by science writers, to coverage dominated by political reporters, and the attendant shift from technical frames to strategy and conflict frames, paralleled a shift in policy decision making away from administrative contexts to the more politically overt forums of Congress and the White House.[53] By pushing moral definitions of the stem cell controversy into the media, activists increased their potential of having a say in the president's funding policy.

Routing Efforts to Define the Bush Presidency

President Bush announced his stem cell compromise on prime-time television a month before the terrorist attacks of September 11, 2001, at a time when the new administration was seeking to convince the nation that Bush was up to the job. White House officials had observed that the stem cell controversy could be the defining issue of Bush's presidency.[54] Bush's prolonged rumination was "a way of signaling that he could engage issues that mattered at a level commensurate with their importance," said one analyst. "The stem-cell debate offered the chance to show that he was thoughtful, earnest, tireless—in short, worthy of holding the title of President of the United States."[55]

For these reasons, stem cell research was discussed frequently in the new Bush White House. The president spent months meeting with doctors, ethicists, lawmakers, religious leaders, abortion foes, and health activists. He debated the issue with advisers, read everything on the topic that went across his desk, and surprised many by soliciting views at social gatherings and agonizing over the controversy in public.[56] "Almost everyone in the White House, well, he asked your opinion at one point," said Karen Hughes, the president's White House counselor.[57] Karl Rove said about the president that the decision whether to fund embryonic stem cell research was "no less important than a decision to commit troops to war."[58]

Rove, worried about the Catholic vote, led a White House group opposed to spending federal money for the research.[59] The administration had already begun thinking about Bush's 2004 reelection race, and Roman Catholics were viewed as a crucial voting bloc.[60] Other Republican advisers agreed and said permitting embryo research would not win over enough moderates; hence, Bush should adhere to his campaign promise and protect his conservative base. Still others contradicted those worries and advised Bush that appearing to play to social conservatives represented the more serious political danger. "If he goes and refuses to use stem-cell-research—if he bans it—then I think he will look more rigid and inflexible than he wants to," one Republican strategist said.[61]

As one *Washington Post* staff writer put the apparent dilemma, Bush could choose to stand by his campaign pledge to block all stem cell research and risk alienating moderates, much as President Clinton had alienated conservatives in 1993 with his policy on gays in the military. Or he could go ahead and fund embryonic research and risk aggravating conservatives in the way the elder Bush did in 1988 when he broke his pledge not to raise taxes.[62] Other analysts felt Bush could safely decide either way, so long as he articulated his reasons well.[63]

Signaling a possible compromise, speculation that Bush might authorize funding for research using the thousands of frozen embryos stored in in vitro fertilization clinics had been widespread.[64] A similar policy introduced a month earlier by Senator Bill Frist was believed to be a trial balloon for the White House. Frist's pro–stem cell, anticloning position set the political limits of what Bush could do, "allowing pro-lifers to accept the former without assuming that the latter would follow."[65] Reportedly, this was the policy favored by Tommy Thompson of the DHHS, Vice President Dick Cheney, Chief of Staff Andy Card, and White House counselor Karen Hughes.[66]

As governor of Wisconsin, Thompson—a Catholic and abortion foe —had praised the University of Wisconsin researchers who grew the world's first culture of human stem cells. In mid-June 2001, Thompson let on about the possibility of a compromise in the works, saying, "I think there is an answer there that we are all working on that is going to allow research to continue with some moderations, but one that will be hopefully satisfactory to the various views that are very polarized at this point."[67] Two months later, Bush's "Solomonic" plan was revealed.

President Bush, who is opposed to abortion and believes that life begins at conception, had stood with those who equate the destruction of embryos in research with the ending of human life by abortion. But he was deluged with calls and letters from scientists, disease victims, and activists who say that embryonic stem cell research holds great promise for treating diseases such as Alzheimer's, Parkinson's, and diabetes. They played into worries and doubts surrounding Bush's first months in office, intensifying the pressure on Bush to temper pro-life values and politics with ones that were pro-hope and pro-science. As a presidential candidate, Bush had declared opposition to taxpayer support for research that involves the destruction of live human embryos.[68] Thus, his compromise authorizing federal funding for research on existing stem cell lines "where the life-and-death decision has already been made" can be seen as at least a partial conversion.

Making Continued Vigorous Opposition Unattractive to Each Opposing Side

To some observers Bush sought above all else to craft a stem cell research funding policy that would preempt either side in the stem cell controversy from more volatile mobilization.[69] Starting with a very narrow policy output, Bush limited the stem cell research that could be funded to only sixty or so stem cell lines already available worldwide. One writer who characterized Bush's compromise as "wonderfully adroit, at least in the short term," said:

> By allowing funds for research on the small number of already existing stem-cell lines but denying money for any work with stem cells derived from embryos destroyed in the future, he positioned himself in the narrow political space that allowed him to claim he had not stood in the way of promising medical investigations. At the same time, he could insist that he had kept his promises to the Republican right, which abandoned his father after the elder Bush broke his no-new-taxes pledge.[70]

The president also appropriated some of the rhetoric from each side in the debate, which had the effect of dampening the strength and urgency of particular movement claims. For example, after Pope John Paul II urged Bush to oppose research involving human embryos, Bush spoke of "the need to balance value and respect for life with the promise of science, and the hope of saving life."[71] Two months later, this appropriation of central movement claims was extended to explain Bush's decision to permit funding for research on existing stem cell lines: "It allowed you to balance the hopes of research against the moral imperative that the government should not be funding the destruction of human life," said a senior White House official.[72] By invoking key tenets of each opposing side to substantiate his compromise position, Bush effectively foreclosed the option of vigorous protest as a strategy of influence.

Rhetorical appropriation also had the impact of stigmatizing some of the more virulent protest aimed at the administration. Antiabortion groups, of course, had wanted the president to sustain the thirty-year prohibition against any funding for embryo research. At a briefing in Washington, D.C., a week before the president announced his compromise, the American Life League, a pro-life educational organization, had called on President Bush to ban the use of both federal and private funds for embryonic stem cell research. The group's president, Judie Brown, claimed it had an "inside scoop" that the president was considering a compromise. Brown exclaimed, "If the President approves any support, he will no longer have the right to call himself a pro-life president."[73]

Yet Bush's oft-repeated exhortation against promoting science "which destroys life in order to save life" effectively marginalized such claims in the eyes of many—particularly in light of strong support from prominent pro-life senators. Similarly, on the other side of the debate, President Bush's embracement of advances in science and medicine that improve human life—particularly the strong support he expressed for aggressive federal funding of research on umbilical cord, placenta, adult, and animal stem cells—dampened some claims about a political agenda to interfere with scientific advancement.

Another important factor in institutionalizing movement concerns is "official recognition of movement groups or individuals within a policy domain."[74] To demonstrate the significance of this factor in this case study, it bears emphasizing again how significant President Bush's conversion was in the broader history of politics and policy surrounding human embryo research.

As discussed previously, throughout most of the 1980s and 1990s, the fear that many policy actors had of being tied to the abortion debate had the effect of locking the small number of people who might benefit from embryo research out of funding policy decisions. All this changed precipitously in the late 1990s after researchers at the University of Wisconsin succeeded in culturing stem cells derived from human embryos. This achievement overlapped with policy responses to other prominent news events surrounding animal and human cloning. The outcome was that many policy actors embraced the reframing of costs and benefits of embryo research, and suddenly patient groups and researchers had a prominent place in congressional debate.

Of course, President Bush could have changed all this—and for some time he seemed destined to. Hence his decision to include groups and individuals associated with disabilities and disease within the relevant policy domain marks a significant turnaround in the three-decade-long controversy over fetal tissue and embryo research.

On the other side, Bush did not disappoint pro-life leaders with his choice of who to lead the advisory panel created to oversee his compromise plan. "We give three cheers to his choice of advisors," a *Christianity Today* editorial proclaimed following the president's televised announcement.[75] The president chose Dr. Leon Kass, from the University of Chicago, who along with Daniel Callahan, cofounder of the Hastings Center, is said to have been pivotal in reinforcing "Bush's growing conviction that he should not fund research on newly extracted stem-cell colonies."[76] Kass was well known for his outspokenness and moral skepticism concerning reproductive technology. The significance of Bush's choice to head the panel is evident in reactions from those who lamented it. In one commentary titled "Irrationalist in Chief," a writer for the *American Prospect* said: "Kass has cornered the market on Revelations-style prognostications about the threat of 'dehumanization' through assisted reproduction."[77]

Of course, none of this is to say that either side obtained all that it wanted from the president's policy. On the contrary, each side settled for something substantially less than its preferred outcome. Moreover, the president's compromise significantly altered the terms of the debate, as well as political opportunities to mobilize protest.

Policy Reforms Fracture Coalitions

Bush's compromise produced a "sudden and stark division" in the normally unshakable coalition against abortion.[78] Characterized as a split between pragmatists and purists, and one that surprised even pro-life leaders,[79] the opposing comments were delivered at dueling news conferences. Pat Robertson, founder of the Christian Coalition, described the compromise as "an elegant solution to the thorny issue of stem cell research." A spokesperson for the National Right to Life Committee characterized the organization as "delighted." Moral Majority founder Jerry Falwell agreed, as did James Dobson, founder and president of Focus on the Family.[80] "We were pleasantly surprised," said Focus on the Family's bioethics analyst.[81]

But Richard Doerflinger, spokesperson for the U.S. Conference of Catholic Bishops, expressed surprise at the positive reactions, saying it appeared that the president found it morally acceptable to experiment on embryos "if the killing has already been done." Doerflinger's disappointment was shared by conservative Christian groups, including Human Life International, the Traditional Values Coalition, and the Family Research Council. Others were more disdainful. Speaking on behalf of the conservative public policy group Concerned Women for America, Wendy Wright exclaimed that it is as horrible to conduct research in which embryos are killed deliberately as it is "that gold fillings were taken from the teeth of Holocaust victims."[82]

Proponents of embryonic stem cell research were also divided over the president's policy compromise. Some offered positive comments. "This is the best that could have been asked for given the forces that surround this issue," said an analyst at a bank that specializes in biotechnology. "It allows a degree of freedom to operate in this important area but at the same time is sensitive to groups who have differing views."[83] Patient advocates and researchers who had feared the president might shrink from fierce opposition by antiabortion forces expressed relief. "No one four months ago would have thought the president would come out this way," said Carl Feldbaum, president of the Biotechnology Industry Organization. "The president's decision is a major step forward for patients and the biotechnology industry," he said. "Our only quibble is placing a limit on the number of cell lines." Shirley Tilghman, a molecular biologist and head of the federal panel that authorized funding under the Clinton administration, agreed.[84]

Others, by contrast, expressed disappointment and anger. "We are saddened that President Bush failed the leadership test and cast a shadow on the hopes of patients and the promise of science," said the leader of the patient advocacy group Coalition for Urgent Research.[85] "It would be like Congress telling Bush they'll fund his defense budget, but only if he uses World War II armaments," an embryonic stem cell researcher at Harvard Medical School exclaimed. Yet while bioethicist Arthur Caplan of the University of Pennsylvania complained that the president "basically came up with a ban in sheep's clothing," Shirley Tilghman called the president's compromise "a good first step."[86]

Thus, the compromise President Bush fashioned created "an equilibrium point that made extra-institutional mobilization and continued vigorous opposition unattractive to each opposing side."[87] Key to the Bush administration's success was a narrowly defined policy output, official recognition of previously excluded movement groups within the policy domain, and placement of at least one key movement actor in a bureaucratic position.

California Takes the Lead, 2004

If November 2004 was to be remarked upon as the "value voters" election, one in which red state values exerted their dominance over cosmopolitan blue staters, it would make sense that California would be an exception to this trend, whatever its explanatory power. As has been its practice, California used the initiative process to consider a ballot measure in 2004 that would commit $3 billion in state funding for research utilizing stem cells, thus circumventing the federal ban. The campaign that was mounted framed its appeal to the logical point of the promise of scientific breakthroughs, and the potential for cures for ravaging disease. The televisions ads featured a mix of approaches and voices. In one ad, cancer researcher and Nobel laureate Paul Berg of Stanford University described the potential passage of the initiative as a "clarion call to science. We're going to carry on this research under strict ethical guidelines, with the prospect that we'll be able to cure serious human diseases from discoveries made in this kind of research." A neurosurgeon in another ad spoke specifically of the diseases that could be affected, such as diabetes, Parkinson's disease, and stroke.[88] The campaign also used the celebrity of actors Christopher Reeve, paralyzed in a riding accident and active in supporting research of nerve regeneration, and Michael J. Fox, suffering from Parkinson's disease. In one of Fox's two ads, he stated that the ballot measure was "endorsed by over 70 medical and patient organizations, the largest coalition of this kind ever formed to support a ballot measure."[89] Governor Arnold Schwarzenegger, who had defined himself as a social moderate in campaigning the prior year, came out in support of the measure, saying, "I hope it will win so that eventually 10 years from now or 15 years from now, people will be safe from those terrible illnesses."[90] Schwarzenegger also touted the economic development effects of supporting California's vibrant biotechnology sector and advancing past other states that had not yet committed to such an approach. This perspective was later validated when, after the November 2004 vote, several other states began legislative action to remain competitive with California in the stem cell research area.[91]

The International Society for Stem Cell Research offered support: "Stem cell based therapies have the potential to alleviate suffering for millions of Americans. Proposition 71 offers Californians the opportunity to take an active and proactive role in determining the kinds of treatment that will be available to them and their children."[92]

Even with conservative religious groups listing stem cell research as one of their political priorities, funding for the opposition to the ballot measure was severely overmatched. In the end, those responding to polls and voting saw the ability to cure disease—a central precept of contemporary life—as far more important than any ethical concerns about the generation of embryonic tissue or fiscal concerns about the state's support of a particular industry. Admittedly, California was a significantly pro-choice state. The 2006 Missouri vote demonstrated that the stem cell issue truly raises new issues and cleavages in the pro-life coalition, and that the 2004 California vote did not merely reflect the leanings of yet another blue state.

Obstacles to the easy implementation of the new California stem cell law arose fairly quickly, from both predictable and not so predictable sources. The pro-life forces, which had been underfunded and ineffective in their opposition to Proposition 71, filed suit challenging the constitutionality of the new law. The National Association for the Advancement of Preborn Children argued that *Roe v. Wade* did not apply, because of the nature of the process. Other lawsuits had been field against the Independent Citizens' Oversight Committee, both by pro-life legal groups and by taxpayer groups, which followed the two strands of the unsuccessful opposition campaign.[93] Although the suits did not ultimately prevail, they slowed down the implementation of the California initiative, at the same time as other states have begun to follow California's lead.

Support in the Polls Nationally

It was a sign of the elevation of the cultural discussion on stem cell research that *Parade* magazine devoted a cover story to it in July 2005. Accompanying the story were the results of a poll, showing the American public to be in strong support of stem cell research. The same magazine, distributed weekly in 340 Sunday newspapers, had information for the curious public on *American Idol* winner and singer Kelly Clarkson and reported on the comings and goings of other celebrities of the moment, but it occasionally also focused on a serious issue like the promise of stem cell research.

The 2005 poll done by Charlton Associates for Research!America, and reported in *Parade,* found that 58 percent of American respondents were either strongly in favor or somewhat in favor of stem cell research, as opposed to 29 percent responding otherwise.[94] The poll was in keeping with others done by Research!America, finding strong support by Americans for research with the potential of advancing health care. Other polls of the past few years have reported similar findings. A Pew poll found the following:

> Culture wars divide virtually every religious group in America, but not every issue is a battleground. While there continue to be deep divisions over abortion, for instance, there is a fairly broad consensus that embryonic stem cell research should not be prohibited. And while disagreements over same-sex marriage or civil unions are substantial, there is widespread support for gay rights.[95]

Conservatives decry what they see as media bias, skewing of the polls, and low respondent knowledge of the scientific and ethical issues at stake.

In reviewing some of the polls that have been done on stem cells and similar technologies, the Center for Genetics and Society notes regarding a 2002 poll from Johns Hopkins University and the Pew Charitable Trusts, "The public's knowledge about these technologies is not keeping pace with the steep growth in genetic science. Only 18% of respondents were able to correctly answer 6 or more of the 8 knowledge questions."[96]

With this knowledge as background, the seemingly contradictory nature of the following two poll results may be more understandable. In November 2001, a CNN/USA Today/Gallup poll reported that 54 percent of respondents reported approval to the question "Do you approve or disapprove of cloning that is not designed specifically to result in the birth of a human being, but is designed to aid medical research that might find treatments for certain diseases?" (41 percent disapproved). Around the same time (August 2001), an ABC News poll found only 33 percent of respondents answering "legal" to the question "Do you think human cloning for medical treatments should be legal or illegal in the United States?" (63 percent answered "illegal"). A similarly high percentage (68 percent) expressed favor for "the government allowing scientists to do therapeutic cloning research to produce stem cells for treating life-threatening diseases" in a poll by the Coalition for the Advancement of Medical Research, involved in stem cell research. Consistently strong majorities—as high as 90 percent—disapprove of reproductive cloning, that is, cloning "designed specifically to result in the birth of human being."[97]

Another poll showed an increase in support for stem cell research after the death of Ronald Reagan (who had suffered from Alzheimer's disease), the speech by his son to the Democratic National Convention, and the statement of former first lady Nancy Reagan. A poll done for the advocacy group Results for America soon after the death of former president Ronald Reagan found 74 percent support among respondents, including 64 percent of self-described conservatives, and a remarkable 62 percent among evangelical Christians. Fully 80 percent of the respondents cited Mrs. Reagan's credibility on the issue, while numerous analysts spoke to her impact.[98] Just before her husband's death in 2004, Nancy Reagan had addressed attendees gathered at a fund-raiser for the Juvenile Diabetes Research Foundation and stressed the urgency of the need for promising stem cell research.[99]

Reds against the "Party of Death"

The combatants in the morality wars have attempted to frame the debate in the stem cell research area in ways similar to yet also different from the other morality war battles described in this book. For proponents, the primary frame has been finding cures for Parkinson's disease, juvenile diabetes, and a range of other serious and degenerative illnesses. Witness the ad from the 2006 Missouri campaign:

> For babies who are struggling every day, the hope on the horizon for them and for their families is stem cell research. It is critical that all stem cell research be permitted in Missouri. The focus of the initiative is on finding cures. As a physician, I urge every parent to support the Missouri stem cell initiative.[100]

Nowhere in the argument for allowing funding for the creation of stem cell lines have there been the type of autonomy arguments made in the cases of abortion, gay rights, or assisted suicide. The benefit is not to one individual but to potentially anyone who might need such intervention. As Skocpol has argued, it is precisely these types of "universal appeal"—anyone could find themselves in need of such medical intervention, or have someone in their family in need—that have the greatest degree of success, all things being equal.[101]

Certainly, there are some arguments in favor of the economic generative power of the biotech sector and companies that would be involved. These points have been salient in arguments about scientific brain drain —both nationally and globally. Although they may be useful as arguments to elites—legislators and opinion shapers—they have not been utilized in the reformers' appeals in the two campaigns to a great extent.

When we look at the other side, we see a number of reasons expressed for opposition, given the nature of the funding of campaigns in the two initiatives to date. Not all of these points are utilized in the advertisements. However, all are used, singly or in concert with others, in written articles and testimony given by opponents.

In general, there have been a number of major themes to this opposition: (1) stem cell research involves the killing of embryos; (2) the promise of cures is overblown; (3) it leads to cloning, following the slippery slope; (4) there are alternatives; (5) the biotech industry is pushing it and will profit from it; and (6) scandals characterize the fast-and-loose nature of the enterprises.

Among the opponents of stem cell research, there is no lack of florid language for their own conceptions of what the slippery slope of embryonic stem cell research will lead to. There are numerous references to "scientists playing God," to "fetal farms," to staving off "the evils of the Brave New World."[102] Ponnuru sees the web connecting liberal policies in stem cell research along with the other topics of this book: "The party of death started with abortion, but its sickle has gone from threatening the unborn, to the elderly, to the disabled; it has swept from the maternity ward to the cloning laboratory to a generalized disregard for 'inconvenient' human life."[103]

In several cases, the writers include those who have been notable in their arguments against abortion or assisted suicide (such as Richard Doerflinger of the U.S. Conference of Catholic Bishops). Because of the link with the destruction of embryos in any embryonic stem cell research program, this is a natural affinity. There are those like Ponnuru who see these topics as cut from the same cloth. Indeed, the slippery slope that Smith and others see in one or another of these topics, Ponnuru sees cutting across all these "culture of life" issues, a concept advanced by Pope John Paul II and others.[104]

Doerflinger criticizes the various polls for understating where the embryonic cells come from.[105] Pro-life conservatives assert that harvesting the stem cells results in taking a potential human life.

One of the enduring themes of those opposing stem cell research has been that of overblown promises. For example, the U.S. Conference of Catholic Bishops, in an analysis comparing the promises of stem cell research with the lack of effective treatments and cures to date, uses this slogan: "Let's fund promising medical research that everybody can live with." In that way, it does not appear to be antiresearch and anticure, but anti-pie-in-the-sky technology.

Focus on the Family critiqued the California stem cell effort for disguising certain intents and for misleading the voters of California:

> The authors of Prop 71 purposefully confused the issue by prohibiting "human reproductive cloning" which they define as the creation of a human being "for the purpose of implanting the resulting product in a uterus to initiate a pregnancy." Less well-known is that Prop 71 also creates the right to cloning for destructive embryonic stem cell research. Except, in this instance it is called by its scientific name: somatic cell nuclear transfer.[106]

In general, Focus on the Family and other groups accuse the reformers of muddying the waters with their shading of terminology. This is especially important because the voter knowledge is low on this issue and thus malleable, particularly in a direct democracy campaign. The Focus on the Family critique continues:

> Often, words such as "nuclear transfer" or "somatic cell nuclear transfer" are used because they are less well-known than the more controversial term "cloning." In addition, the description used to explain the mechanics of embryonic stem cell research is often distorted to include somatic cell nuclear transfer (cloning) as well. Blurring the lines by utilizing more technical terms makes it easier to use the guise of embryonic stem cell research to advocate human cloning.[107]

When faced with the possibility of a pro–stem cell research bill coming to his desk in the near future, President Bush in 2005 attempted to get the "cloning" frame centrally reconfigured, as he fought to explain his first potential veto: "I'm very concerned about cloning. . . . I worry about a world in which cloning becomes accepted."[108]

The approach of groups like Focus on the Family has been to refrain from demonizing the science, or from suggesting that people are wrong for wanting cures for these diseases; instead, they emphasize that adult stem cells are a good alternative: "Focus on the Family opposes stem cell research that destroys embryonic humans. . . . Today, researchers are successfully treating patients with Parkinson's disease, multiple sclerosis, heart damage and spinal cord injuries using non-embryonic stem cell sources."[109] Elsewhere, the organization alleges that American media are selling the hope of cures dependent upon embryonic stem cell research only, and ignoring the promise of adult cells.[110]

Social conservative opponents often talk about the issue of stem cell research (often framing it as cloning) being oversold by "venture capitalists." This appeal did not have much effect on the California Proposition 71 campaign. This approach has the potential to cause strain within the Republican Party's electoral coalition, since the party depends on both social conservatives and entrepreneurs for its vitality, a balancing that can be at risk when various parts of the social conservative agenda are promoted or ignored.[111]

A South Korean cloning scandal in 2005 threatened to undercut some of the American public support for stem cell research, but it appears not to have done so. The scandal turned on fabricated evidence that was presented internationally and published in a leading journal and also raised issues of egg donation policy.[112] Possibly the American public is assured by the extent of regulations about American stem cell research put into place by the National Academy of Science.[113]

The director of congressional affairs for the Family Research Council tried to put a feminist spin on the South Korean scandal: "This is a huge concern not only to conservatives, but to a lot of women's rights groups as well—that women would begin using their bodies in a new way for financial gain."[114]

In an interesting twist on the feminist support for abortion, some feminists have viewed the stem cell issue as one in a series of incursions into female autonomy, and have sponsored events like "Hands Off Our Ovaries" in March 2006, a coalition of women to campaign against exploitation of women in biotechnology (which comes from a different strand of thought than the pro-choice "Keep Your Rosaries Off My

Ovaries").[115] The California professor who is associated with the group has a record of research and involvement in genetic testing and eugenics, coming from a progressive viewpoint. Admittedly, there may not be much in her "constellation of values" that she and the conservative religious groups have in common. But like feminists and conservative Christians of an earlier time promoting laws restricting the sale of pornography,[116] both are concerned with the issue of stem cell research.

Professor Diane Beeson articulates her beliefs and road to this position from other opponents:

> Perhaps the biggest factor in making me appreciate pro-life people has been their attitude toward disability and their rejection of eugenics. . . . When I was younger I believed the confident predictions of the geneticists that selective abortion was merely a temporary solution; within a few years we would have cures for all these conditions and we would not be practicing prenatal eugenics. The fact is the cures haven't come, but the eugenic functions of reproductive genetics have expanded. . . . I have watched prenatal diagnosis become the primary tool for preventing the birth of human females throughout the world. . . . This shows how reproductive technologies tend to be used to reinforce existing power arrangements. . . . While we are all being dazzled with the promises of high tech medicine many people's health is declining because we aren't taking care of the basics. We are offering more and more expensive interventions to fewer and fewer people. This feeds inequality and undermines democracy.[117]

When she appeared before the California legislature in 2004 as part of the pro-choice alliance against Proposition 71, Beeson testified: "We support public funding of stem cell research, including embryonic stem cell research, provided it is conducted responsibly, with appropriate transparency and oversight," values she concluded were not sufficiently provided for in the California initiative.

The Purple Path: Polls and Senate Compromises

Still, as Americans polled on the subject of stem cell research remained consistently supportive, it made sense that there would be movement in the Republican Party to diverge from the social conservative base on this issue. With the support offered by Nancy Reagan in 2004 for the California initiative and with the scathing op-ed piece by former Missouri senator John Danforth in the *New York Times* in 2005, there appeared to be a counterweight of influential Republican voices to promote this specific issue. In his article, Danforth criticized other high-profile Republicans for yielding to the pressure of religious power blocs in the Schiavo case, characterizing congressional involvement in private decisions and the effort to empower a federal court to overrule a state court as departures from Republican principles. Danforth said that regardless of religious motivations, all Americans have a right to try to influence political issues, but he scorned the present Republican responsiveness to church activism. He cited advocacy of a constitutional amendment to ban gay marriage and opposition to embryonic stem cell research as further examples that "Republicans have transformed our party into the political arm of conservative Christians."[118]

These elements contributed to a situation in 2005–2007 in which the Bush administration found itself faced with a potential veto of a bipartisan congressional bill advancing stem cell research. The split that emerged in the Republican Party in 2005 over stem cell research was manifested in the passage of a bill in the U.S. House of Representatives and support by important members of the Republican Party in the Senate. Although the bill was delayed until the 2006 session, it was clear that several leading Republican figures were willing to break from the social conservative base in their own party and reflect the poll support among the American public for extended stem cell research.

Chief among these has been Senate majority leader Bill Frist (R-Tenn.), who changed directions and announced support for a liberalized House bill in August 2005, couching his support in a distinction between stem cell research and abortion: "I am pro-life. I believe human life begins at conception. . . . I also believe that embryonic stem cell research should be encouraged and supported."[119]

Former first lady Nancy Reagan praised Frist:

> Every day that goes by without cures is another day that families watch their loved ones suffer. . . . Embryonic stem-cell research has the potential to alleviate so much suffering. Surely, by working together we can harness its life-giving potential. Thank you, Dr. Frist, for standing up for America's patients.

Representative Mike Castle, who was a major supporter in the House, was pleased, saying of Frist, "His support is of huge significance."[120]

In an editorial, the *New York Times* praised Frist for his speech:

> Mr. Frist—the transplant-surgeon-turned-lawmaker who was last seen catering to religious organizations by questioning whether Terri Schiavo was really in a persistent vegetative state—showed courage and common sense yesterday by endorsing a bill to expand federal financing for embryonic stem cell research.[121]

Frist's critics among social conservatives saw his change of heart as an act of betrayal and of political opportunism and warned him not to depend on their support for the 2008 Republican presidential nomination. Some pointed out Frist's expressed conflicts, while criticizing him for "falling under the spell of the 'cures' argument," and for believing the "hyped hope of Nancy Reagan and Ron Reagan, Jr., with their siren call for 'cures' that trump the claims of tiny embryos."[122]

Frist was criticized on a Family Research Council Web page, which said that he was capitulating to the "biotech lobby." The FRC explained that it was "extremely disappointed to see what we consider a crucial moral lapse on this critical issue. The end never justifies the means. Seeking cures for patients is an admirable goal but it must never come at the expense of other human lives." Conservatives also pointed to Senator Edward Kennedy's praise of Frist as a sign of a bad decision. Dr. James Dobson was quick in his criticism: "To push for the expansion of this suspect and unethical science will be rightly seen by America's value voters as the worst kind of betrayal—choosing politics over principle."[123]

In his thirty years in the U.S. Senate, Republican Orrin Hatch of Utah certainly has not been criticized for his liberal orientations. Solidly pro-life, Hatch wielded his power as Judiciary Committee chair strongly during the Supreme Court nomination battles of the 1980s and 1990s and many contested nominations to the lower bench. His "cross-examination" of Anita Hill in the Clarence Thomas nomination hearings still rankles liberals.

Hatch, who also strongly supported the federal marriage protection amendment in 2006, took the lead in the Senate in 2001 on stem cell research. Therefore, it was not surprising that he emerged as a prime

Senate sponsor of the Human Cloning Ban and Stem Cell Research Protection Act of 2005. Hatch argued:

> If you think back and remember when Jonas Salk discovered the polio vaccine—and I realize I'm probably one of the few here old enough to remember that—but remember what a revolutionary step that was, to be able to stop ravaging diseases before they hit their victims. It led to a whole new way of practicing medicine and paved the way for the vaccines and treatments that we take for granted today.
>
> I believe we are on the verge of a similar step, a new generation in medical research and treatment, thanks to the incredible potential of stem cells.[124]

It was Hatch, one of fourteen Republicans who were sponsors of the Senate version of the bill to allow federal funds to be used for stem cell research, to whom former first lady Nancy Reagan addressed a letter in 2006, urging the Senate to move the 2005 bill forward:

> It has been nearly a year since the United States House of Representatives first approved the stem cell legislation that would open the research so we could fully unleash its promise. For those who are waiting every day for scientific progress to help their loved ones, the wait for United States Senate action has been very difficult and hard to comprehend.[125]

Senator Frist indicated that the bill would be brought forward in July 2006, so that it could be considered before the adjournment of the Congress for the 2006 elections.[126]

Why the Stem Cell Issue Does Not Resemble the Abortion Issue

A struggle continues in the social conservative camp to make an electoral wedge issue out of stem cell research, but it seems to have little traction. With a vote coming up on the Senate floor over stem cell compromise in 2006, Focus on the Family analyst Amanda Banks spoke to the rift between social conservatives and entrepreneurs/economic conservatives on this issue and explained its potential political ramifications: "It's a wedge issue, in that it separates the true pro-lifers from the compromisers. Whenever the vote comes, whether it's this year, next year or a later date, we'll be very attentive. If it is voted upon before the election, I think it will be a top-tier issue in the '06 elections."[127]

Some conservatives had even suggested that the stem cell issue in 2006 could be the equivalent of gay marriage in 2004 as an organizing issue for conservatives. Missouri was one test of that view. The prevailing wisdom by June 2006 was that the issue would help Democrats and moderate Republicans, such as those who broke party ranks to support a bipartisan bill in 2005 to overturn the Bush administration's ban on federal funding for stem cell research.[128]

This was further signified when Senate minority leader Harry Reid brought up stem cell research as one issue overlooked by the Bush administration as it claimed the centrality and importance of the federal marriage protection amendment:

> The scientific community cries for help. They believe dread diseases such as Alzheimer's, Lou Gehrig's, Parkinson's, and diabetes could be moderated and prevented. But President Bush emphatically says no to allowing scientists to study and research the healing powers of stem cells. He refuses to keep hope alive for the suffering people of our great country.[129]

Will scandals like the Korean research case have an effect on American attitudes and progress in this field? Observers like the editorial staff of *Scientific American* argued that those scandals did not derail the scientific searches for breakthroughs in that field:

> Embryonic stem cell (ESC) research is no less promising today than it was before Hwang's deceit was revealed; most investigators continue to believe that it will eventually yield revolutionary medical treatments. That no one has yet derived ESCs from cloned human embryos simply means that the science is less advanced than has been supposed over the past two years.[130]

If social conservatives complain that the stem cell research boom has been fueled by venture capitalists, they are also jabbing at their coalition partners in the current Republican Party. As Pew research demonstrates, these "entrepreneurs" share some common belief patterns with their social and religious conservative coalition partners, but clearly not all, and clearly not with the same vehemence. If libertarianism is the split in the coalition, then stem cell research has provided a window into the fragility of the coalition.

The Meaning of Events in 2006: California, Washington, D.C., Missouri

Missouri passed its stem cell bill in 2006, in a close vote, but in a crucial vote in a "red state." While California was the first out of the gates in the post-Bush state support of stem cell research, as well as being the first among equals of the several states providing state funding for the research, the rollout was anything but fast. Soon after the 2004 vote, a series of lawsuits slowed the implementation of the California initiative. A trial court judge ruled against the lawsuit, but appeals went on. The Independent Citizens' Oversight Committee (ICOC) was formed as the guiding body for the California Institute of Regenerative Medicine (CIRM), the primary body through which stem cell funds and policy flow. The institute also had to contend with discussion of property rights, and state legislative inquiries into whether researchers were properly protecting women as egg donors, and by late 2006 was moving ahead with private funds for research support in labs and universities across the state.

Meanwhile, other states eyed California's lead in the stem cell research area and sought to surpass it. In December 2006, New Jersey acted to pass a smaller funding bill than California. Nonetheless, the legislator who drafted the bill claimed, "What edge California thought they had, they've lost it."[131]

While President Bush's veto of the Castle legislation on stem cell research could not be overridden in the 109th Congress, he still was forced to issue the first veto of his presidency. Democrats seized on the scene of moderate Republican support in the two houses, alongside popular support, to make stem cell issues an undertone issue in the 2006 campaigns, tying it together with the government intrusiveness theme that the Schiavo affair had begun. In no place was that more apparent that in Missouri, in which the presence of the state initiative made the issue more than an undertone.

One of the more odd but emblematic matchups of the final days of the 2006 election campaign was the seemingly head-to-head duel between actor Michael J. Fox and conservative radio host Rush Limbaugh on the need for stem cell research. Fox, who has been battling Parkinson's disease, had replaced the late Christopher Reeve as a notable public figure doing ads earlier for the Missouri stem cell campaign. Fox filmed a commercial in October 2006 backing Democratic Senate candidate Claire McCaskill, who supported the Missouri stem cell initiative (and who later would be elected by a slim margin, ensuring the Democratic control of the U.S. Senate). In that ad, the visibly affected Fox exhorted voters: "What you do in Missouri matters to millions of Americans. Americans like me."

Within a day after the ad began running, Limbaugh critiqued it by claiming that Fox either "didn't take his medication or was acting." According to Limbaugh, "Michael J. Fox is allowing his illness to be exploited and in the process is shilling for a Democrat politician."[132] Limbaugh added that this situation mirrored the exploitation of Christopher Reeve in a similar vein for earlier stem cell debates. Fox's ad was shown during the first game of that year's World Series, which included the St. Louis Cardinals. Another ad, featuring an actress and even a baseball player participating in the World Series, aired later in the World Series, an unusual mix of sports and politics.

The Fox-Limbaugh interplay spoke to one of the underlying issues of the stem cell debates—that of compassion. While similar forces competed over reproductive rights, by 2006 that issue had turned to a discussion solely of the autonomy of women, from the emphasis on compassion and autonomy that had characterized early discussions of liberalization and legalization. One reason we argue that support for stem cell research in American had reached greater heights than abortion rights is that it framed an issue on which there was greater understanding and support—finding cures to ameliorate debilitating and potentially fatal diseases. On the other side of the debate, anti–assisted suicide activist Wesley J. Smith lamented:

The worst news of the year was the narrow passage by Missouri voters of Amendment 2—which legalized human cloning for biomedical research in what some now refer to as the "Clone Me State." Making matters more frustrating, the constitutional amendment pretended to "ban the cloning of a human being," which was false from a scientific perspective, and the Missouri courts permitted the false assertion to be made, anyway.[133]

Still, summarizing what seemed to be the trend in American politics, Pam Solo and Gail Pressberg, authors of a book on stem cell research, concluded:

> What is the message here? There is a growing and grassroots demand for action at the federal level on stem cell research. This is a core lesson of the 2006 mid-term election: People want this research to go forward and politicians will be rewarded for taking a clear and unambiguous stand on the issue. This reflects the fact that stem cell research is not a "right" or "left" issue—it is something that mainstream America wants to see happen.[134]

This sentiment was echoed in statements by Senator Hatch on the Senate floor in the 2007 stem cell research bill debate: "I believe history will judge us very harshly if we allow this great opportunity to pass us by." Hatch was one of several Republican senators who supported the 2007 bill despite expectation of a presidential veto. As Hatch explained to the *New England Journal of Medicine*: "I believe that being pro-life is more than just caring for the unborn—it's caring for the living as well. And this type of research is the most promising research in the history of the planet, and it ought to be followed though."[135]

Solo and Pressberg's emphasis above on developments in the social and political views of the "mainstream" of American society toward often contested issues of law and morality provides the entry into a fuller discussion of the state of American thought, presented in our next and concluding chapter.

7

Conclusion

To Form a More Purple Union?

Now that values voters have delivered for George Bush, he must deliver for their values. The defense of innocent unborn human life, the protection of marriage and the nomination and confirmation of federal judges who will interpret the Constitution, not make law from the bench, must be first priorities, come January.
—Michael Skube, "We're Saved. You Lost. Now What?" (2004)

We believe voters are open to an even bolder statement—no more debates about changing abortion and gay marriage, either way; no more constitutional amendments; and no more Terri Schiavo all-nighters for 2 years, until Congress does something about high gas prices and American jobs.
—Stan Greenberg and James Carville, "Getting Heard: Points of Engagement for a Change Election" (2006)

Americans are closely divided, but we are not deeply divided, and we are closely divided because many of us are ambivalent and uncertain, and consequently reluctant to make firm commitments to parties, politicians, or politics. We divide evenly in elections or sit them out entirely because we instinctively seek the center while the parties and candidates hang out on the extremes.
—Morris Fiorina, *Culture War? The Myth of a Polarized America* (2005)

Introduction: Polarization and the Importance of the "Values Voters" Revisited

The resolution of American morality contests surrounding the issues of the preceding chapters, especially in the 2004–2006 period, has been the focus of this book. In this conclusion, we consider the meaning of these events in several ways. In each section, and overarching the discussion in each, we place our analysis of the morality contests in the context of other scholars who have examined other moral contests.

In the first section, we return to the constructs presented in chapter 1 to consider the role of ambivalence, moderation, and "purpleness" in a time and place where analyses of the dichotomy of "red" versus "blue" and the concept of polarization have been the norm. Sometimes, this dichotomy has been driven by media and political analysis accounts. Often, it has been the result of the self-styled goals of organizations involved in the very morality contests, where the concept of a middle ground has not been a rallying cry.

Second, we consider the meaning of these events—including polarization hypotheses—for sociolegal theory. Specifically, we present our analysis of how personal attitudes and legal norms have changed in a more progressive direction over these part thirty years, amid—and sometimes even outside—the contours of the fervent morality contests.

Finally, we assess how the midterm elections of 2006 provide a countermotif to the values voters frame of the 2004 elections. We conclude with observations about the future vitality of the values voters construct and the culture war to shape American political discourse.

One of the key issues of the analysis of morality contests over the past forty years in the United States has been the question of their use as "wedge issues" to separate voters from their economic and community concerns. Since 1980, the ascendancy of the social and religious conservative movement has framed a number of personal morality issues as ripe for social and political agendas. Scholars have analyzed why these issues have emerged, how they have been utilized, and how the focus on these morality contests has been a misplaced debate within American society.

One key explanation for the ascendancy of social and religious conservatives and their vitality in these morality contests has been the concept of false consciousness, which has been used in recent years to describe the current contours of American morality contests.

Thomas Frank deservedly made quite an impact in political circles in 2004 with his book *What's The Matter with Kansas?* In that work he painstakingly and passionately argued for the salience of the concept of false consciousness in a well-developed attempt to understand the willingness of lower-middle-class voters in Kansas (and elsewhere in America) to vote against their economic self-interest by focusing on morality contests and embracing a Republican agenda.[1] While these events—extending the effort to convert the "Reagan Democrats" in 1980—promised a return to "traditional values," at the same time as it supported corporate business elite restructuring that undercut the ability of many of these same Kansans to make a life for themselves and their families. Bill Moyers echoes this when he asserts that a "cultural holy war" serves to "camouflage" the economic interests that underpin this movement.[2] Frank puts his own distinctive cast on the red-blue dichotomy:

> The antagonists of this familiar melodrama are instantly recognizable: the average American, humble, long-suffering, working hard, and paying his taxes; and the liberal elite, the know-it-alls of Manhattan and Malibu, sipping their lattes as they lord it over the peasantry with their fancy college degrees and their friends in the judiciary.[3]

These contests affected the development of public attitudes and social policies in other ways. In one way, overemphasizing the morality contests at the expense of other domestic and foreign policy issues caused many to see them as a distraction from more serious public policy. This view is expressed by progressives like Arlene Skolnick, who observe that the excessive focus on moral values diverts attention from important matters of foreign policy, economy, and justice that affect Americans:

> The culture war, with its focus on hot-button issues like gay marriage, end-of-life decisions, and obscenity on television, to name the most recent examples, crowds out discussion of serious social problems. . . . If we truly want to solve the nation's social problems, we need a drastically altered discourse about moral values and about the role of government in sustaining the health and security of parents and children. At various times in the past several decades—in the late 1970s, the early 1990s—it seemed as if the country was on the brink of another cycle of progressive reform, to address not just family issues but the social and economic contexts in which they are rooted. Each time, the moment was lost to a new round of ideological warfare. Still, it seems inevitable that a new political consensus will one day emerge, because a politics based on myth, nostalgia, and denial is unsustainable.[4]

One blogger captures this in a pithy way with his evocation of "Weapons of Mass Distraction."[5] E. J. Dionne argues how this focus on morality issues distracts us:

The result is a strained, dysfunctional, and often dishonest political dialogue based on symbolic utterances. Hot-button questions that rally particular sectors of the electorate—and draw listeners and viewers to confrontational radio and television programs—pre-empt serious distortion of what ails American society.[6]

Then-senator Rick Santorum (R-Pa.) followed Frank with a book, *It Takes a Family: Conservatism and the Common Good*.[7] While its title and argument seem closely aimed at Hillary Clinton's *It Takes a Village*,[8] it can just as well be read as a response to *What's the Matter with Kansas?* More than the merely economic issues Frank emphasizes, Santorum argues, *this* is what really matters: moral capital is just as meaningful, if not more so, than mere financial capital. Preserving cultural capital is just as important to Santorum as protecting jobs and an economic base in a changing economy.

In a rebuke to the thinking of those like Frank, Santorum adds: "I believe these voters decided one of the most crucial elections in recent times in favor of President Bush and the Republicans because they see these values issues as a bigger problem in their lives than either terrorism or the economy."[9]

To Santorum, the media missed the impact of the values voters in the 2004 election, in part because they did not know what to look for. Santorum begins his book with a depiction of the malaise of election day 2004, when "the simple truth is . . . everything is not well in America."[10] He speaks of an election in which "values voters . . . can feel in their bones that something is wrong, and they sense that the institutions dominated by liberals are a big part of the problem."[11]

If America can be viewed as a highly polarized country, separating into blue state latte drinkers and red state NASCAR fans, then Santorum is one of the reddest cultural warriors. Santorum represents a new breed of aggressive polarizing senator, changing the tenor of agreeable clubbiness of the Senate after his years in the Newt Gingrich–led U.S. House of Representatives after 1994. In fact, one of Santorum's 2006 appearances was as one of several speakers decrying liberal "judicial tyranny" on "Justice Sunday III" in January 2006, an event broadcast on Christian radio and television, taking place a day before the opening of nomination hearings for Samuel Alito for the U.S. Supreme Court.

Santorum has come to represent the morality wars in extremis. He himself has famously been quoted for his strong views against gay rights and gay culture, key to his "moral ecology" sentiments in *It Takes a Family*:

> If the Supreme Court says that you have the right to consensual (gay) sex within your home, then you have the right to bigamy, you have the right to polygamy, you have the right to incest, you have the right to adultery. You have the right to anything. . . . Every society in the history of man has upheld the institution of marriage as a bond between a man and a woman. Why? Because society is based on one thing: that society is based on the future of the society. And that's what? Children. Monogamous relationships. In every society, the definition of marriage has not ever to my knowledge included homosexuality.[12]

As might be expected, there is some focus in the Santorum book on ways in which the policies he recommends would improve the lives of those of his Pennsylvania constituents who struggle with the effects of poverty (an inclusion that was not enough to propel him to reelection in 2006). To be sure, his approach offers a critique of social liberalism in material settings as well, in attempts to extend the concept of "compassionate conservatism."

A tour of classic Santorum dicta lucidly represents some common features found in some American religious conservative groups such as the Family Research Council, the Christian Coalition, Concerned Women for America, Focus on the Family, American Values, and the Traditional Values Coalition. To Santorum, individualism is insidious— liberalism is inevitably "atomized."[13] The family, "not the individual, is the fundamental unit of society." Santorum denies changes in American morality and forms as though they were a disease spread through some contagion model that his policies can now address through some version of quarantine (home schooling; efforts against Hollywood; rails against the diversity of the American family that Pepper Schwartz, Arlene Skolnick, and sociologists of the family have depicted).[14] To Santorum, "Strong families are the seedbed of virtue."[15] "Family, faith, and civic involvement" are the building blocks of the American dream.[16] "Education factories" are producing the "new Progressive,"[17] no doubt one reason Santorum's six children have been homeschooled.

Santorum raised an issue germane to this book when he responded to an interviewer's question that he was indeed attempting to "legislate morality": "When you're going to allocate funds for contraceptive services, are you legislating morality? Of course you are. Now the question is, what moral code are you applying?"

As we have argued in the previous chapters, the American public at large has not embraced this strident vision of moral decline and the need for societal redirection. However, even as we reject the values voters construct, we do not accept an interpretation that America has embraced the opposite position, as have the Dutch, for example.[18] The next section details an alternative interpretation, in which we comment on a prominent debate in the field of political science.

The Meaning of a Purple Path

In the previous chapters, we have argued that the American public is more "purple" on issues of law and personal morality than most commentators or politicians of "red" and "blue" states assume. By many measures, Americans support *Roe v. Wade* but are concerned with its overuse and with teenage access. Buried under the acrimony of the 2004 national discussion on same-sex marriage is the fact that although Americans balk at gay marriage itself, they appear to support civil unions for same-sex couples and oppose a constitutional amendment against same-sex marriage. And that issue has even cooled off since then,[19] although the U.S. Senate consideration of the federal marriage protection amendment in 2006 kept it alive. And even while Americans are willing to allow suffering patients to enlist a doctor's assistance to end their life, an increasing number support stem cell research aimed at ending serious disease, and several states are strategizing to follow California's lead into funding stem cell research, to circumvent federal funding restrictions.

Stanford professor Morris Fiorina is a mainstream political scientist best known for a series of studies on the operation of Congress. In *Culture War?* he argues that we Americans are more "purple"—or less polarized—across even the issues presented as the most polarizing, such as abortion and homosexuality. His classic statement appears early in that book:

> Americans are closely divided, but we are not deeply divided, and we are closely divided because many of us are ambivalent and uncertain, and consequently reluctant to make firm commitments to parties, politi-

cians, or politics. We divide evenly in elections or sit them out entirely because we instinctively seek the center while the parties and candidates hang out on the extremes.[20]

In his two chapters on abortion and homosexuality—two pillars of the culture war that were key venues for the 2004 election—Fiorina argues that even these "wedge" issues prove not to be as divisive when examined more closely. He uses considerable data on preferences and voting to support his hypothesis that it is political elites who are increasingly polarized, rather than average Americans. Such elite polarization has led to political party structures, platforms, congressional representatives (such as Santorum), and presidential nominees who offered only a polarized choice to voters who might prefer a more centrist menu.

Fiorina explains how we got to the state he describes: "Elites have polarized, but the public opinion data reviewed in chapters 2–5 provide little reason to believe that elites are following voters. Rather, they are imposing their own agendas on the electorate."[21]

According to Fiorina, the decline in material incentives for political participation and the increased importance of money in modern campaigns ushered out 1950s political professionals and replaced them with a generation of issue activists and candidates whose ideological commitments run deeper than they did a generation ago. No longer is compromise seen as a means to achieving material goals; rather, compromise "directly devalues" the ideological and programmatic goals of those with policy and ideological motivations.[22] Democrats evolved from the 1950s party of economic liberalism to the 1980s party of lifestyle liberalism, as they had to redirect their interests toward middle-class activists who had money to support candidates. Republicans, needing voters more than money, turned to religious Right groups as a way of overcoming Democratic majorities. A preoccupation with winning elections and gaining power for the good of one's party was replaced by political "purists"—whose rejection of compromise "provides good copy and footage" for a media dependent on people who express deep issue commitments "in loud chants and strident rhetoric."[23]

Further compelling the enlistment of activist energy and resources in support of party candidates was the "new social regulation" of the 1960s and 1970s.[24] "No one can count the expansion of government as measured in total number of restrictions, regulations, and permits, or in the different areas of life in which government began to operate,"

Fiorina argues.[25] This expansion in the scope of government enlarged the demand for government support of activists' views, further narrowing party agendas and helping to explain why the effort at polarization continues.

Finally, at about the same time that motivation for political participation became ideological, and the pubic sector expanded into new spheres of life, changes in American politics gave rise to a significant participatory turn. The changes included a transformation of the nomination process, open meetings, recorded votes, enhanced judicial review, open bureaucracy, and a proliferation of local government bodies. They created, in Fiorina's words, an "advocacy explosion," as thousands of new citizens' groups organized and engaged in political activity.[26] Citizen participation and influence were enhanced by a surge of propositions between 1960 and 2000, by polling, which sensitized politicians to citizen reaction to their actions, and by communications technologies, which are as useful to pressure politicians as they are to advertise to constituents.

Fiorina postulates that these factors—government expansion, plus the rise of activists and citizens' groups—culminated in "the hijacking of American democracy."[27] Fiorina concedes that the basis of politics is conflict; that the changes in American politics he describes have sometimes led to great progress, as in areas of race and gender; and that sometimes extremists are right, as in the example of the abolitionists. Nevertheless, he argues, more often these changes have led to extremist control of the political agenda:

> The political order that now exists in the United States creates unnecessary conflicts and indulges itself in conflicts that are the concern of relatively small numbers of unrepresentative people. Often this comes at the expense of attention to conflicts that concern larger numbers of people and leads to inattention to policy solutions that would be widely viewed as progressive.[28]

The problem with political participation in America is that few people participate. Attending evening meetings, writing checks, and working in campaigns are the province of the few. And the few who do participate hold intense, if not extreme, views about an issue or some complex of issues, says Fiorina. Thus not only is participation narrowly distributed, but the extremes are overrepresented and the center underrepresented in the political arena.

As we discussed in chapter 4 the terms of the abortion debate are set by the 10 percent or so of the population who occupy each tail of the distribution of abortion attitudes, while the three-quarters of the population of "pro-choice buts" goes largely unheard. Extremists march, work in campaigns, give money, and otherwise push their views more strongly than do moderates.[29]

Furthermore, Fiorina emphasizes that the issues that are attended to are often not those that interest most people:

> Most citizens want a secure country, a healthy economy, safe neighborhoods, good schools, affordable healthcare, and good roads, parks, and other infrastructure. Such issues do get discussed, of course, but a disproportionate amount of attention goes to issues like abortion, gun control, the pledge of allegiance, medical marijuana, and other narrow issues that simply do not motivate the great bulk of the American people.[30]

To Fiorina, the operating styles of extremists differ from the styles of most people:

> They are completely certain of their views: they are right and their opponents are wrong. Moreover, their opponents are not just misguided or misinformed, but corrupt, stupid, evil, or all three. There can be no compromise because truth does not compromise with error. Their issues are too serious to permit any levity to enter the discussion. Angry attacks substitute for reasoned discussion.[31]

In sum, polarization continues and activists and candidates do not opt for moderation because a political class does most of the participating. That class is largely out of touch with the world of most Americans, societal issues and community problems that concern ordinary Americans are frequently not debated, extreme policy solutions are often proposed for the issues and problems that do get debated, and often the behavior of the political class causes disengagement for many Americans.

To Jacob Hacker and Paul Pierson, the polarization that Fiorina investigates can best be laid at the feet of the Republican Party, for which the "returns on extremism" have been beneficial.[32] To Kurt Andersen, who is searching for a middle- ground, or "purple," party:

> We are people without a party. We open-minded, openhearted moderates are alienated from the two big parties because backward-looking ideologues and p.c. hypocrites are effectively in charge of both. We are appalled by the half-cynical half-medieval mistrust and denial of science —the crippling of stem-cell research, the refusal to believe in man-made climate change.[33]

Still, he adds: "demagoguery is endemic to both parties, but when it comes to exploiting fundamentally irrelevant issues (such as the medical condition of Terri Schiavo), the GOP takes the cake."[34]

Following Fiorina's analysis, political analyst E. J. Dionne writes:

> If one looks primarily at the extremes of opinion . . . of course there is a deep cultural conflict in the United States. It is waged between the 15 to 20 percent of the country that is both profoundly religious and staunchly conservative and the 15 to 20 percent that is profoundly secular and staunchly liberal. . . . they regularly toss epithets across their divide. The godly attack the ungodly. The tolerant attack the intolerant. The cosmopolitan attack the parochial. The rooted attack the rootless. Moralists attack the permissive.[35]

To Dionne, like Fiorina, those most engaged in the culture war do not constitute a majority of Americans: "The rest of the population watches the battle from the sidelines, sometimes with sympathy for one camp or the other, but without anything like engagement or commitment of the true warriors."[36] Quoting Fiorina, he spotlights those who are "moderate in their views and tolerant in their manner."

Elsewhere, other scholars have viewed the values voters episode as a contradictory reading to changes that were already under way in America. In *Moral Freedom,* social scientist Alan Wolfe "sees American moving en masse away from social conservatism and toward a moderate form of moral freedom."[37]

Admittedly, Fiorina is at odds with some political scientists, who believe that he understates the level of polarization in America. For example, James Q. Wilson takes issue with *Culture War?* He argues that polarization has indeed spread beyond political elites to "the opinions of many ordinary Americans."[38] John D. Donahue of the John F. Kennedy School of Government at Harvard, the author of *Disunited States*,[39] also offers a different interpretation than Fiorina: "We have fairly intense cleavages in values, preferences, points of view across the population, and in some of these areas they do cluster state by state."[40]

One answer to continued polarization lies in a 2004 article (written shortly before that year's election) by some Harvard scholars who propose that there has been a definite return to extremism.[41] What might be called "the redder the better" argument proposes that, despite the logic that political parties emphasize centrist policies when seeking the "median voter," the mechanism of polarization described by Fiorina is not illogical, in that turnout of core voters and contributions are enhanced by such displays of extremism. This would not come as a surprise to those who grow impatient with repeated mention of same-sex marriage when more pressing domestic and global issues present themselves.

Reading Morality Issues: Taking "Third Ways"

Building from analyses like Fiorina's, some progressives and Democratic strategists have emphasized the need for their party to embrace a "third way" in bringing back disaffected voters who do not necessarily respond to ideological appeals on a range of issues. In particular on the morality war issues presented in this book, this group discussed these issues in their "culture project" and especially emphasized the importance of the "abortion grays"—those moderate and ambivalent Americans who favor keeping *Roe v. Wade* and its protections, but who also are in favor of parental consent laws, see themselves as opposing late term abortion, and may be ambivalent about the entire abortion issue.

One reason for this emphasis has been that not all progressive analysts believed that the values voters phenomenon was a misreading. William Galston and Elaine Kamarck underscore these findings with their interpretation, based on focus group data, of how the "moral issues" superseded other concerns in the 2004 vote:

A recently completed series of focus groups among non-college rural and red state voters underscores the growing salience of morally laden cultural themes. Participants reported broad dissatisfaction with the

Bush Administration on three issues—the lack of progress in Iraq, economic stagnation and job insecurity, and soaring health care costs—and indicated support for some progressive initiatives in these areas, which they believed Democrats would be more likely to offer. But as the summary of these focus groups goes on to note, "the introduction of cultural themes—specifically gay marriage, abortion, the importance of the traditional family unit, and the role of religion in public life—quickly renders [these progressive issues] almost irrelevant in terms of electoral politics at the national level."[42]

As they sorted through the aftermath of the 2004 election, considering these morality war issues, and with an eye especially turned toward religious affiliation and voting behavior, Galston and Kamarck argued for better ways for the Democratic Party to regain its electoral edge:

Before Democrats jettison long-held principles on issues such as abortion and tolerance for gays, they should be aware that when Catholic voters are asked to define moral values in an open-ended question, they are much more likely to emphasize personal integrity, family solidarity, and the social compact than to mention specific positions on abortion, gay marriage, belief in God, or the Ten Commandments. Catholics are also more likely to endorse tolerance than are the evangelical Protestants who form the base of the Republican Party.[43]

Missouri Senate candidate Claire McCaskill, then a Democrat in a close race for a contested Republican seat (and now a newly elected U.S. senator), emphasized that the Democratic Party had to reestablish itself as a party that could connect with voters in the red states, and certainly the purple states, stating: "I think it's a tone thing. It's the 'We know better' thing. . . . there's a critical number of Missourians who believe that people from the East Coast or West Coast don't think that people in the heartland are smart."[44]

Longtime Democratic senator Joseph Biden suggested that the acceptance of religion after 2004 had much to do with the reframing:

I think the problem with a lot of élites in the Democratic Party, quite frankly, is that they communicate that they don't respect people's faith. People out there don't want them to believe like they believe, but they want to know that they respect them. We have too many élites in our party who look down their nose on people of faith. The people of faith don't want us to share their view, they just want to know we respect them. That's the big problem with my party.[45]

Mark Warner, former governor of Virginia and 2008 Democratic presidential hopeful, whose record has been mentioned as a corrective to the elite nature of recent candidates—explained: "Part of this is just showing respect. Respect for culture, faith, values."[46]

Senator Barack Obama of Illinois has gone so far as to assert that his Democratic Party needs to court the evangelical vote, and to give ground on some elements of the separation of church and state issues, saying: "I think we make a mistake when we fail to acknowledge the power of faith in people's lives . . . and I think it's time that we join a serious debate about how to reconcile faith with our modern, pluralistic democracy."[47]

Framing Wars

Other approaches, such as that of George Lakoff, specifically reject the notion of moderation and argue for progressives to focus their efforts on winning the "framing wars," at which social conservatives have succeeded dramatically in the last decade. Rather than modifying views or reaching out to embrace new constituencies, Lakoff argues that the natural responsiveness of large parts of the American public will come about when progressives have framed their values in ways that resonate.

In the past few years, Lakoff has become that most unusual of persons: an academic whose academic work has entered the national political debate. Lakoff, whose more disciplinary work deals with cognitive linguistics, is best known for his 2002 book, *Moral Politics*,[48] which develops in detail his ideal types of liberals and conservatives and their methods of successfully framing moral issues of our time.

While sociologists like David Snow have focused our attention on the processes and strategies of framing, and generated numerous empirical studies utilizing his framework,[49] Lakoff has focused on the use of framing in a specific political context: the ability of American conservatives to evaluate issues through their "strict father" morality model.

While Lakoff is not the first to crystallize these worldviews in such ways (think Kristin Luker and her "constellation of values," as apt an explanatory vehicle for appreciating abortion politics in 2007 as it was when published in 1984),[50] he certainly has the most fully developed approach.

Don't Think of an Elephant can justifiably be called a primer of Lakoff's moral politics work as applied to the 2004 elections.[51] Read against Santorum, it is meant as a clarion call to Democrats and progressives to establish a strategy to effectively counter the Republican dominance on framing issues—moral and otherwise—to its advantage. In this way Lakoff echoes Wallis: "The right knows how to talk about values. We need to talk about values."[52]

In the preface to his book (admittedly penned so close to the November 2004 election that he would not have seen the debunking of the "value voter" hypothesis), Lakoff actually embraces the values voters argument: "The [2004] exit polls revealed what this book predicted, that moral values were more important than any particular issue— more important than terrorism, the war, the economy, health care, or education.[53]

Lakoff is prescriptive, and a major thrust of his message is that "reframing is social change." What is remarkable about Lakoff is the emphasis on the work of cognitive scientists and other social scientists to "reframe the full range of public policy issues from a progressive perspective." His advice turns on the notion that progressive values are the "best of traditional American values."

Lakoff is direct in his analysis: "The right wing is attempting to impose a strict father ideology on America, and, ultimately, the rest of the world. . . . God is the original strict father. . . . preserving and extending the conservative moral system (strict father morality) is the highest priority."

On the issues of most interest to morality warriors—reproductive rights and gay rights—Lakoff uses his model to display how frames can be changed for progressive ends. On same-sex marriage, for example, he writes:

> In arguing against same-sex marriage, the conservatives are using two powerful ideas: definition and sanctity. We must take them back. . . . Progressives need to reclaim the moral high ground—of the grand American tradition of freedom, fairness, human dignity, and full equal-

ity under the law. If they are pragmatic liberals, they can talk this way about the civil unions and material benefits. If they are idealistic progressives, they can use the same language to talk about the social, cultural and material benefits of marriage.[54]

In a later book, however, Lakoff expresses his lack of belief in the concept of the "purple center" and its possibility as a rallying place to challenge the extremes of the culture war. He thus challenges the conclusions of Fiorina, Kamarck and Galston, and Third Way: "Let's put to rest the notion of the political or ideological 'center'—it doesn't exist."[55] Instead of the depiction of those who are ambivalent as being "cross-pressured," Lakoff views those persons who find that their values are in conflict as being "biconceptual." Lakoff further argues: "Biconceptuals are not to be confused with 'moderates.' There is no moderate worldview, and very few people are genuine moderates."[56] He thinks instead there are "partial conservatives" and "partial progressives."

Addressing the matters that make up the heart of this book, Lakoff argues: "Many cases are yes-or-no matters. No scales. . . . Should abortion be legal? What does it mean to speak of abortion in moderation? Assisted suicide? What does moderation mean?"[57]

The next section will identify where we differ with Lakoff, as we argue that there are many points along the morality contest continuum, that ambivalence about these issues is real, and that its resolution shapes the development of American laws and policies. We also identify how these polarization-centered analyses can be understood as contributing to our concept of problematic normalization.

Problematic Normalization and Theoretical Considerations

This book has its roots in an earlier tradition when scholars in the 1960s and 1970s placed police treatment of gays and lesbians, gambling, and abortion in the same framework, in order to understand the legal enforcement of personal morality. Looking across the issues of gambling, abortion, gay rights (marriage), assisted suicide, and stem cell research helps regenerate a broad systematic social science study of personal morality and the law, and offers an effective sociolegal framework for studying the culture wars.

In our earlier work on assisted suicide, we analyzed the various parties' competition over relative moral standing. In this book as well, our focus has followed a line of study in which legal activities to produce or block moral reform are analyzed as one way through which "a cultural group acts to preserve, defend, or enhance the dominance and prestige of its own style of living within the total society."[58]

A major focal point for such studies of collective definition has to do with the processes through which, and conditions under which, particular deviance categories develop and change. Schur identified continuing struggles over competing social definitions in terms of power:

> At all levels, deviance situations reflect some people's response to other people's behavior as being troublesome, offensive, problematic, or unsettling—as being, in one way or another, personally or socially threatening. . . . The perceived threat may be direct or indirect, patently economic or largely symbolic, and grounded in rational assessment, irrational response, or mistake. What is most important . . . is the perception itself.[59]

In that prior work, we echoed Schur's assertion that "deviance is always a social construction, brought about through a characteristic process of social definition and reaction,"[60] and his further dictum that the sociologist's endeavor in explaining the collective definition of a social problem, and the commencement of a political movement, is to determine who feels threatened, and whose interests are at stake.

Two approaches drawn from sociolegal studies have also informed our "middle range" theory of the culture wars and personal morality. First, our case studies are situated as models of law and social change. The case of gambling offers a model of widespread reform success. Abortion is situated as a model wherein reformers achieve a grand victory, only to be faced with relentless opposition leading to incremental legal and cultural shifts against the practice. The case of gay rights offers a third model—one where reforms are obtained through challenging discriminatory practices, such as in housing, employment, and even political campaigns. Eventually, the focus on equality shifts and builds on those successes and turns to reforming the laws of marriage. Representing a fourth model, pressure for reform of laws governing death and dying has led to broad changes from within the medical profession itself. Finally, it is too early for us to call whether laws and policies involving conflicts over stem cell research will evolve into a distinct model of law and social change, but our chapter on stem cell research has discussed the similarities and differences developing around that topic.

Our second approach to studying the law and politics of personal morality since the 1970s entails identifying and analyzing key sociolegal factors that seem to drive the controversies we detail. Across our case studies, we observe American federalism impacting both the choices reformers make about where and how to press claims for change and the outcomes of reform campaigns. Thus, in the gambling model, state and local jurisdictions that want to liberalize gambling laws benefit from the state and local nature of gaming markets. The impact of federalism has been far different in the case of abortion, where nationalizing the issue by making it a federal constitutional matter has galvanized a national antiabortion movement. In the case of gay rights, on the other hand, until recently state and local reform successes have been met with conservative efforts to nationalize the issue. Yet after the U.S. Supreme Court outlawed state antisodomy laws, conservatives have looked to the states to pass defense-of-marriage legislation. In the assisted suicide scenario, the Supreme Court rejected efforts to nationalize the issue but has nevertheless defended states' rights to experiment with novel social policies. Finally, with the developing controversy over embryonic stem cell research, some states are coming up with their own funding policies to counter President Bush's severe limitations on federal funding.

A second key sociolegal factor analyzed across our case studies is the differing roles of courts, legislatures, and voter ballot initiatives. Gambling and gay rights reform strategies have centered on local ordinances and state legislative activities, although the Supreme Court has handed gay rights reformers both their greatest defeat and their greatest victory, and gay marriage is being fought out in courts and through voter ballot initiatives. In the abortion model, legislatures are used to pass laws that are intended to be fought out in courts. With assisted suicide, the most highly publicized reform efforts have played out through voter ballot initiatives, although most of the actual changes in end-of-life care have come about through legislation and court decrees. Finally, President Bush's executive order has played the most prominent role in restricting stem cell research, but many state legislatures have passed their own laws, and California's huge funding program was enacted by voters.

Normalization Yet Contestation

Across these issues, we have identified how normalization has occurred in all these areas over the past three decades, but also how that normalization has been problematic, challenged, and resisted. One of our earliest responses to the values voters frame of the 2004 election was an article written within weeks of the election, challenging the dominant frame that a shift in moral leanings had shaped the election, and suggesting a future that would retrench on many of the liberalization strides that were being made in these areas in that time period.[61]

In chapter 1, we presented the issue of the problematic normalization of victimless crime in America over the past thirty years. We emphasized the enduring issues of ambivalence and have used the intervening chapters to describe a situation in which increased liberalization of attitudes has coexisted alongside an often fervent series of morality contests that have fluctuated across thirty years and have even crested in the past six years. In this section, we elaborate on the theoretical meaning of this situation and what it means for other issues in law and social change.

One paradox we identified earlier regarding the state of victimless crimes in America is that of "problematic normalization." While many American states and the federal system have largely moved toward new legal forms in the past thirty years, this has been done in various forms, and not all have resulted in a consensual acceptance of American liberalization. This has resulted in continuing and ever energized morality contests.

For many of these issues, America has a checkerboard pattern of laws, in some ways reflecting our federalism and emphasis on states' rights, or on the diversity of our large population and the strength of views of the "blue" America and the "red" America, representing the Democratic and Republican leanings of various states in presidential elections. But it can also be described as a stubborn ambivalence, a stalled movement toward the 1960s clarion call for liberalization of laws controlling personal morality, and the enactment of decriminalization laws in the 1970s.

We wrote in chapter 1 that the culture wars of the 1980s and 1990s were a result of the advances made in reproductive rights, anti–gay discrimination measures, drug decriminalization, and general changes in gender relations in American society. We are not alone in observing that the advances have led to backlash movements. A focus on the backlash to such advances and a visceral reaction to such moralization is common throughout treatments of the social and conservative Right.[62] Some portions of what we could call the "rollback coalition" are propelled by what Svend Ranulf identified and examined decades ago as "moral resentment."[63] The urgent call to protect "traditional values" created countermovements specifically designed to thwart the movement toward tolerance and creation of new rights in the personal sphere.

As the Society for the Study of Social Problems said in its materials for its 1997 annual meeting: "The same processes that have brought such striking partial successes have also unleashed an increasingly powerful backlash, as both cause and consequences of status insecurities, real and imagined 'culture wars.'"

Numerous scholars have emphasized the raising of rights consciousness and its translation into effective social movement strategies for legal reform.[64] Others have emphasized the presence of ambivalence. For instance, Goldberg-Hiller explains the nature of the majority response to the possibility of legal same-sex marriage in Hawaii:

> The first is a reaction against the fast-growing visibility of gays and lesbians and the forms of knowledge and political presentation of the self under which the demand for civil rights has been made. . . . I explore a second, related reason for the vitality of this politics. The rhetorical tactics used to retain the privilege of marriage for non-gays have combined formerly diverse, contradictory, and sometimes dormant American discourses into mutual coherence, amplifying their effects.[65]

While we differ with Goldberg-Hiller's explanation of "pluralistic intolerance," we nonetheless appreciate his focus on the backlash elements that converge with Frank's analysis, as an explanation of the vitality of the culture wars.

For one, we have an asymmetrical pattern where the drivers of change are very involved—and polarized—movement players and true believers, neither of which represent a plurality of the population. Meanwhile, the moderate majority of Americans have become more tolerant, more protective of autonomy. The culture wars have masked this process, which is why the reaction to the Schiavo episode came as such a surprise to those who were orchestrating it, as an example of overreach.[66]

We have emphasized the contestation over the proper legal treatment of five central morality issues, for which the criminal law had been the primary recourse until recent years. It is the struggle for the reframing and legal reclassification of these activities—the movements and the countermovement they inspire—that informs this research. And an underlying question asked above it all is: What can be said about the state of American beliefs and attitudes in this area in 2007?

Meanwhile, one key assertion of our approach is that this backlash, while it raised the profile of the issues contested in the morality wars—think protests at abortion clinics, all night vigils outside Terri Schiavo's hospital, "God Hates Fags" banners at Matthew Shepard's funeral—nonetheless masked the growing tolerance of Americans and support for concepts of autonomy. In this way, a new American electorate has chosen to embrace tolerance—more of a liberalization approach than legalization (which would equate to support for same-sex marriage)—and to turn away from framings such as that of Gary Bauer when he writes of how "militant homosexual groups are demanding a litany of special rights."[67]

Importance of Autonomy

When Schur, Kadish, Packer, Skolnick, Geis,[68] and others wrote about the proper use of the criminal law in the 1960s, they used a variety of arguments that followed from John Stuart Mill's nineteenth-century writings on the limits of law to compel individual morality.[69] While the central feature of Mill's argument was for individual autonomy (and the limits of valid state intrusion into that sphere), other arguments about harm to sanctioned and incarcerated individuals, the fiscal costs to society, the symbolic cost to the legitimacy of the law, and varying elements of futility were relied upon to argue for liberalization of the laws governing personal reality or "victimless crimes." Over time, the many-headed movement for liberalization of law in the victimless crime area sought to design and implement laws that would be more humane and respectful of individual autonomy in the area of reproductive rights, drug use, and sexual behavior.

The discussion of the value of compassion over time has also framed some of the debates of the topics in this book. For instance, at one time abortion reform or abortion law liberalization relied greatly on this dimension.[70] It continues to be a significant contributor to the discussions on end-of-life issues and underpins the stem cell research debate.

In the chapters that preceded this one, our book has located the central driving principle of societal support for liberalization in the concept of personal autonomy. The driving force has not been that of the concept of compassion, as Schur and others might have predicted, or the concept of futility. In both those cases, we would see greater success with alternative drug policies, and we have seen only incomplete and stalled decriminalization in that area. Instead, the changes that have taken place have followed the model of reproductive rights and have stressed autonomy—a core Millian principle—at the center of their argument. It is indeed these arguments and these movements that have generated the greatest backlash from social and religious conservatives.

On key argument of this book is that the rise of the Moral Majority as a force within the Republican Party has masked the simultaneous growth of a libertarian impulse among many of that party's members. It is among the political moderates—in the purple area of the American political and social landscape—that many of these changes can best be seen.

Autonomy has been a contested value nonetheless. Central among these has been the debate over the extent of autonomy of women, as the various debates within the realm of reproductive rights have unfolded. In the case of gay and lesbian rights, the nature of the rights discussion has naturally taken on the dimensions of a minority rights discourse. It is in this context that the notion of a majority deciding what sort of rights the other group might have has taken place. It is clear that this consideration for now has stopped short of allowing the full rights and name of marriage to apply, as Goldberg-Hiller has argued.[71] Alternatively, an examination of the age gradation of approval of same-sex marriage suggests that there may be a gradual waning of this opposition over time, and a withering of the same-sex marriage issue.

One offsetting variable on that issue may be the increasing liberalization among younger cohorts on issues of sexual orientation and the recognition of same-sex marriage. While it remains to be seen whether these attitudes will stay at the current level as the cohorts' age, one scholar has observed: "This is really the most socially liberal generation since (scientific public-opinion) polling began. This is a highly tolerant generation."[72] Recent polling of the Pew Research Center for the People and the Press agrees:

> Today's younger Americans are more liberal than the country as a whole on many social issues. . . . The youngest generation is most distinctive on social issues, notably questions about gay marriage and interracial dating. For example, a Pew poll in March found 58 percent of those ages 18–29 favor allowing gays and lesbians to adopt children. Among no other age group did as many as half favor this. Similarly, 48% in a July 2005 Pew poll supported gay marriage, significantly more than in any other age group.[73]

Rereading Religion and Its Role in the Paradox

A third element of our theorizing has been a necessary rereading of religion that accompanies the analysis and interpretation of the interior chapters of this book. Following Michael Lerner and Rev. Jim Wallis (to be discussed shortly), we pose the dominant academic consideration of religion in American life as a misreading that overexplains American morality contests as a dominance of religious concepts in the political sphere. Often, religion is read as a fairly monolithic, homogeneous element of society.

Thus, one of the themes of this book has been that of the necessary reevaluation of religion in American society, a consideration that is central to any contemporary sociolegal theorizing about how American society treats issues of personal morality and the legal system in 2007.

One strand of thought has equated religiosity with the conservative and single-issue orientation of the Moral Majority and other similar forces since they helped elect President Ronald Reagan in 1980. To these theorists, the battle has been between an increasingly secular America that has also enshrined the primacy of personal autonomy over such religiosity. We disagree, and think that the turn toward moderation and rejection of the values voters frame is not a rejection of religion, but the sign of a more heterogeneous religious profile in America, with its resulting implications for sociolegal theory in this area.

For those who were treating their psychic wounds after the November 2004 elections, and in particular those who thought that the Democrats had painted themselves into a corner as an overly secular party in a decidedly religiously observant America, Rev. Jim Wallis offered a welcome voice in 2005. With the release of *God's Politics,* which rose to heights on the *New York Times* best-seller list,[74] and Wallis's book-signing and speaking tour, his numerous appearances on national talk shows, and his contributions to political journals, he offers a critique of Santorum and other social conservatives, and prophetically offers a religious alternative. Wallis is an American anomaly precisely because he does not argue for a critique of conservative programs and ideology based on an appeal to secular values. Instead, his appeal is to challenging the conservative religious regime with a contrasting set of progressive religious values.

Wallis may be best viewed as the "anti-Falwell," engaging the values debate on a similar level as Santorum, neither denying its vitality nor shirking from its discussion: "I welcome the discussion of 'moral values.' And I believe the values debate should be the future of American politics. Of course, the questions are, 'Which values and whose values?' "[75] While welcoming a focus and national dialogue on values, Wallis challenges the exit poll analysis, noting that shortly after the 2004 election, a Zogby poll found that the specific "moral" issue that most voters identified as influencing their vote was overwhelmingly "the war in Iraq," and far more mentioned greed and materialism, or poverty and economic justice, as troublesome moral values than mentioned abortion or same-sex marriage.[76] Wallis emphasizes that there are progressive people of faith, even progressive evangelicals, as well as socially conservative yet religious African Americans, who would rally around themes of peace, poverty, and social justice.

On a 2005 book tour, Wallis found welcome respondents for his interpretations and approach:

Those divisions were illustrated on his most recent book tour, Wallis said, when he encountered people who seemed there not so much to get a book signed but to find alternatives to the narrow national debate.

He met many people from a variety of faiths who felt left out of the national religious dialogue, including Jews, Muslims, evangelical Christians who didn't share the concerns of those who had the national ear, Catholics who felt that bishops who focused only on abortion didn't speak for them, leaders of black churches who had been left out, youth who described themselves as "spiritual but not religious," and people who feel that religion doesn't have a monopoly on morality.[77]

Parallel to Wallis, Michael Lerner, the political theorist and rabbi who edits the progressive Jewish journal *Tikkun,* has organized the Network of Spiritual Progressives, whose goal is to challenge the misuse of religion, God, and spirit by the religious Right. In his 2005 book, *The Left Hand of God,* Lerner offers his views for the need and the path for those who are religious (or spiritual) but also progressives to challenge the assumptions and policies of the religious Right.[78]

As opposed to Frank, Lerner is concerned with spiritual issues, beyond material issues. Unlike George Lakoff (discussed later in this chapter), he is willing to direct progressives to addressing some of the issues raised by social conservatives rather than relying on strategizing and successful reframing.[79] Contrasted with Santorum, he offers a progressive view for mobilizing the country around deeply held moral issues for the transformation of society. Similar to Wallis, he relies on biblical traditions but offers a more sweeping progressive critique. He is certainly far from megachurch pastor and best-selling author Rick Warren in his prescriptions for living the purposeful life. Lerner is closer to Bill Moyers, who even uses terminology similar to Santorum's when he says, "We need a strong moral ecology."[80] Lerner also discusses something that is both delicate and critical for societal resolution of these morality battles—the role of religion in American society. And while he, Wallis, and others open up the discussion by displaying alternatives to the notion that all religious beliefs necessarily reinforce social conservative positions, Americans nonetheless offer a complicated social and legal landscape in which to promote change.

Are Americans Now Millians? Exploring the Paradox of Liberalization with Contestation

Social scientist and policy expert Mark Kleiman addresses the question of "Who won the culture wars?" and presents an answer that fits the thrust of this chapter—we have an apparent inconsistency in that we have a higher level of tolerance for the morality war issues in American society, but an active morality war that truly affects elections:

> The Blue Team won. When a "victory" by cultural conservatives consists of preventing some states, but not others, from recognizing gay

marriage, and when they don't even contest the abolition of the laws against gay sex, and when the live question about reproductive choice is whether minors can have abortions without their parents' consent rather than whether married couples can buy contraceptives, it's clear that this war is being fought deep inside Red territory.[81]

Kleiman goes on to conclude that the rapidity of such change—one of the themes of this book, as it pertains to the consciousness of social conservatives and their attempts to preserve "traditional" family values —has also created the backlash that Frank dwells upon. He explains the paradox of increased societal tolerance at the same time as there are engaged morality battles and electoral consequences (before November 2006): "Precisely because the rate of cultural change has been so fast, the median voter tends to be for slowing things down rather than speeding things up. So the Blue Team won the culture war, but the Red Team has been winning the elections."[82]

To many observers, the Schiavo case demonstrated in a surprising manner the extent to which the zone of privacy has expanded. A year later, a 2006 Gallup poll disclosed that "Americans are divided as to whether the government should attempt to promote moral values, and are less accepting of government involvement in this area than they were in 1996."[83]

Democratic National Committee chair Howard Dean responded to this theme when he said in October 2005:

> This administration continually wants to insert themselves into family business. The Terri Schiavo case, that's the family business, not the government's business. All these abortion cases, that's a family's personal business. That's not the government's business. And we'd like to keep the government out of people's private, personal lives.[84]

The American response has not been to totally reject the legal moralism of a different time, nor to fully embrace a sense of autonomy that would privilege the individual in a Millian sense, but to exemplify in these different areas various versions of a project partly done—a path that Schur and others indicated we start on forty years back.

When pitted against each other, in the contest between autonomy versus intrusiveness as the guiding principles in American treatment of personal morality concerns, the resolution has come down on the side of autonomy.

Into the Future: 2007 and Beyond

We did not need the midterm congressional elections of November 2006 to bring this book to an effective end, but they do serve as a coda for many of the themes presented here. While there were many contributing factors for the Republicans' loss of the two houses of Congress, one finding among these for our purposes is the receding of the values voters concept as a dominant construct for the American electorate or public.

Until late 2006, very little had been written or conjectured about the post–George W. Bush era. There have been inklings—as happens soon after an election—about what face the Republican Party will present in 2008, and how the results of 2006, after the values voters frame of 2004, affect this selection process. The resounding Republican defeat in the 2006 elections was called a "thumping" in which the party lost both houses of Congress.[85]

The strategy of the 2006 elections spoke at least indirectly to the vitality of the values voters construct as an organizing tool and motivating force. In attempting to reprise a successful strategy, White House adviser Karl Rove had advised in May 2006 that painting the Democrats as the party of "gay marriage" and "secularism," among other things, would once again rally the social conservative base of the Republican Party and prove successful in 2006: "America is a center-right country, and the Republican party is a center-right party."[86]

Morality issues had also accounted for three of the ten items on the agenda of the Republican House Study Committee in 2006: "5. Pass a marriage protection amendment to keep marriage the union of one man and one woman; 8. Ban human cloning and promote ethical adult stem cell research; and 9. Pass protections for religious freedom."[87]

However, when the Democrats in June 2006 announced their plans for that year's campaign, they included a "morality war" subject among them:

Their plan, presented at a news conference, included promises to raise the minimum wage, make college tuition tax deductible, eliminate subsidies for oil and gas companies, negotiate lower drug prices for the prescription plan passed last year, increase stem cell research and restore a pay-as-you-go policy for federal budgets.[88]

Indeed, as CNN political analyst Candy Crowley observed on election night in 2006: "As we traveled the country, stem cell seems to be the new issue—and it breaks for independents and democrats, it seems to be the perfect issue to put out there for Democrats because it divides Republicans."[89]

In a preelection analysis assessing where the Republicans had lost their power as governing majority party, former House leader Dick Armey argued about the missteps of the Republican Party that followed the years of the Newt Gingrich–led congressional revolution he helped lead:

> Rather than rolling back government, we have a new $1.2 trillion Medicare prescription drug benefit, and non-defense discretionary spending is growing twice as fast as it had in the Clinton administration. Meanwhile, Social Security is collapsing while rogue nations are going nuclear and the Middle East is more combustible than ever. Yet Republican lawmakers have taken up such issues as flag burning, Terri Schiavo and same-sex marriage.[90]

Critiques of the religious right came from moderate places within even the Republican Party. Former senator John Danforth, himself an ordained Episcopal minister, followed an influential *New York Times* op-ed piece with a book that offered a stinging critique of where the Republican Party had gone in the years since he was a power in the U.S. Senate:

> That the federal government could intervene in the Schiavo case was a threat to all the families who had seen their loved ones suffer through terminal illness. It was a threat to people who were terrified that their own lives might someday be artificially extended in nightmarish circumstances. It was a threat to some of our most heartfelt values. It was Big Brotherism in the extreme, an exercise of the raw and awesome power of the federal government.[91]

Adding to the consternation and disarray for the Republican Party were the charges leveled in a book by a former official with the Office of

Faith-Based Programs that the Bush administration had largely paid lip service to the real desires of evangelicals. David Kuo, arguing for a step back to an earlier position of evangelicals in the political world, argued for a "fast" from politics, and a step away from the overidentification of evangelicals with electoral and partisan politics:

> Despite strong Republican majorities, and his own pro-life stands, Mr. Bush settled for the largely symbolic partial-birth abortion restriction rather than pursuing more substantial change. Then there were the forgotten commitments to give faith-based charities the resources they needed to care for the poor. Evangelicals are not likely to fall for such promises in the future.[92]

Realignment?

Observers, analysts, and partisans agreed that public dissatisfaction with the Iraq War was the leading concern of voters in November 2006, along with concerns about the government's incompetent and insensitive reaction to Hurricane Katrina in 2005, and the issue of corruption —both financial corruption that drove out Republican political leaders and a cover-up of liaisons between a closeted gay Republican representative and congressional pages.

Still, the rejection of the values voters agenda was on the mind of some analysts: "From the country's heartland, voters sent messages that altered America's culture wars and dismayed the religious right—defending abortion rights in South Dakota, endorsing stem cell research in Missouri, and, in a national first, rejecting a same-sex marriage ban in Arizona."[93]

Reflecting on the defeat of the draconian abortion law in South Dakota, the head of Planned Parenthood in that state offered this observation: "This was really a rebellion in the heart of red-state, pro-life America—the heart of the northern Bible belt."[94]

An official of the Human Rights Campaign lauded the Arizona rejection of the Defense of Marriage Act initiative: "It's the end of an era for divisive, gay-bashing politics—at least in the minds of the American people."[95]

To one conservative commentator, "The right managed to win seven more anti–gay marriage resolutions across the country, but it was repudiated on Iraq, immigration and excessive religiosity."[96] This perspective was also given weight eventually by moderates who thought that the collaboration with the religious Right to emphasize moral purity as a key tenet of Republican Party platforms and politics may have been a Faustian deal.

A prominent Democratic strategy firm (Greenberg Quinlan Rosner Research) found that there was a defection of upscale men from the Republican base in 2006. The same group dispelled the notion that the results could be read as an increase in support for liberals. Using their measure, they found that the "warmth" rating for liberals did not increase demonstrably from 1994 to 2006, but there had been a cooling off of public consideration of conservatives in 2006.[97] To an ABC news reporter, "The Reagan Democrats have returned home."[98]

Many analysts—including those hoping and working for electoral change—stopped short of concluding that the American public had switched in a liberal direction. To William Galston, who has argued for Democrats finding a more moderate coalition, a different conclusion can be drawn: "The election was de-aligning rather than re-aligning. Millions of moderates and independents divorced the Republican Party." Ideological composition of the electorate remains consistent, with 47 percent moderates (32 conservative, 20 liberal). "The American people are looking for a congress that is more effective and less polarized."[99]

Pollster and political analyst Andrew Kohut concurred, after looking at the poll data, that the changes embraced also proved more of a "de-alignment: "There is no evidence the country is moving culturally or ideologically to the left."[100]

Instead of support for the liberals—and in agreement with Kohut and the Greenberg group—another analyst suggests that there may be opportunities for more coalescence in the future between liberals and libertarians—and the emergence of hybrid voters such as "liberaltarians." Bruce Bartlett suggests that one of the eventual outcomes of the realignments after the 2006 vote will be the desertion of libertarians from the Republican Party, chased away by the moralists.[101]

CNN's Jeff Greenfield, who had reflected on the moral dissatisfaction of voters in 2004, asked on election night 2006 whether the American West—where Senate and House seats switched to Democratic representation—was turning blue or purple.[102] Even Republican partisans placed the blame for the defeat in the social and religious conservative tack of the party:

The real answer to this election is found not in what the Democrats did but why the Republican majority crumbled. First, there were three broad policy issues that hurt Republicans on the margins . . . 2) Schiavo & Stem cells: Fairly or unfairly, the perception that religious beliefs were trumping individual family choices, science and medical research hurt Republicans with moderates, independents and libertarian-leaning conservatives.[103]

Political analyst E. J. Dionne concurred that it was indeed moderates who influenced the 2006 election, but they were "angry moderates."[104] He later considered that 2006 might be a "hinge year," in which the readings of the 2004 elections, with values voters and NASCAR dads, was changing.[105]

Political writer Joe Klein, who had trumpeted the vitality of the "radical middle" in his *Time* columns and 2006 book,[106] called the election "the end of George W. Bush's radical experiment in partisan governance."[107]

Political analyst Chuck Todd concludes:

Forget "red" and "blue." The country is basically divided into *four* voting blocs: the Democratic Northeast, the Republican South, the populist Midwest and the libertarian West. Democrats probably have a decent grip on those populist Midwest voters for a while (at least until the area transforms completely into a new economy). As for the libertarian West (home of the first state—Arizona—to reject a gay marriage ban), this is a region that is more up for grabs than it should be. And it's because the Republican Party has grown more religious and more pro-government which turns off these "leave me alone," small-government libertarian Republicans.[108]

Moderates in the Republican Party blamed the Bush administration's Iraq war policy, but also the focus on morality issues at the expense of more serious accomplishments during the 109th Congress. As one Pennsylvania-based activist wrote after the elections, describing as well the loss of Rick Santorum's Senate seat:

You can't spend six years opposing everything from life saving stem cell research to contraception, and expect moderates to continue to support you. The final straws for most in the moderate majority were the bone thrown to the far right with the veto of stem cell research and injecting big government in the middle of the Terry [sic] Schiavo battle, both of which imposed personal, religious and moral beliefs on the American people.[109]

This same group identified social and religious conservatives, and their dependence on a message of morality, as the culprit in the loss of majority support in the election:

> When asked by Alan Colmes if he wanted the GOP to be known as the "Big Tent Party," far-right Focus on the Family Founder James Dobson replied "I don't want to be in the big tent. . . . I think the party ought to stand for something." It's time to tell Dobson and his cohorts that we do stand for something—we stand for personal freedom, liberty, tolerance and fairness, and we're also standing up today to take our Party back from their grasp.[110]

Reading the returns, Republican moderate senator Arlen Specter, also from Pennsylvania, argued, "The GOP should return to the 1964 advice of Barry Goldwater, who would be left of center by today's standards, to get the government off our backs, out of our pocketbooks and out of our bedrooms."[111]

Conclusion

The events of the past few years have raised the question for us: What has become of Americans in the law and morality area in the past forty years? Certainly there is greater support for personal autonomy in intensively private life-and-death decisions, but also a mistrust of these issues as political items represented by an active lobbying presence, left and right. The center, such as it is, has moved leftward in a historical sense—who could have dreamed in 1966 of the debates we are engaged in now on same-sex marriage, the morning after-pill, and stem cell research?

Even as law professor Alta Charo talks about the "endarkenment" as she analyzes the politics of stem cell research,[112] and political writer Kevin Phillips explores the "cultural antimodernism" of the social and religious conservatives,[113] the end of the 2004–2006 period may have signaled that America may be experiencing the dulling of the power of wedge issues, as some political commentators claimed.[114]

We assert that autonomy is ascendant over government intrusions; that is one of the key lessons from the Schiavo affair and the 2006 elections. In a contest between two philosophical approaches, the Millian position is favored more and more by Americans, despite the distractions of the contests. When pitted against each other, in the contest between autonomy versus intrusiveness as the guiding principles in American treatment of personal morality concerns, the resolution has come down on the side of autonomy.

Does this mean we are seeing the waning of the culture war? Or is it merely an interlude? Can it ever be revved up again? What would be the conditions under which it would be vital again? We assert, and the previous chapters demonstrate, that we are a country growing more tolerant and more protective of personal autonomy.

In 2007, having just celebrated the bicentennial of the birth of British philosopher John Stuart Mill, it may be most accurate to say that America has become decidedly more tolerant of liberalized positions and has moved along the lines that Mill argued for, and which legal scholars and activists have been fighting for from the 1950s onward.

But 2006 also marked the fiftieth anniversary of the ministry of the late Rev. Jerry Falwell, whose Moral Majority organization encouraged the political involvement of evangelicals over the last twenty-five years, and who was in large part responsible for the vitality of the morality wars.[115]

Which vision will prevail? As Arlene Skolnick observes,[116] the morality wars reach a flash point soon after we think we have moved past them and can address more important and systemic issues in a national discussion. Will the next decade hold in store more battles in the morality wars as these issues are used to increase polarization in ways that dramatically shape our politics? Or perhaps, following the words of former Republican attorney general Edward Levi in 1973, before the rise of the Moral Majority,[117] we are growing in wisdom enough to adopt the laws and policies of a mature society on the issues contained in these morality battles.

Notes

NOTES TO CHAPTER 1

1. *Hardball* 2004.
2. NBC News' *Meet the Press* 2004.
3. Seelye 2004.
4. Foreman 2003.
5. Frank 2004c.
6. Seelye 2004.
7. Kalb 2004.
8. Barone 2004.
9. Pew Research Center 2004b.
10. Kohut 2004.
11. Nagourney 2005b.
12. Reynolds 2005b.
13. Catholic Answers 2004.
14. Lester 2004.
15. Nagourney and Elder 2004b.
16. *Mother Jones* 2005.
17. Lyons 2004.
18. Langer 2004.
19. Guth et al. 1991.
20. Jones 2004.
21. D'Emilio 2000.
22. Luker 1984.
23. Glick 1992.
24. *Business Week* 1978.
25. Carter 1977.
26. "Quick Fixes for Web Info-Junkies" 2004.
27. Skolnick and Dombrink 1978.
28. DiChiara and Galliher 1994.
29. Craig and O'Brien 1993; Reagan 1997.
30. Frank 2004b.
31. Phillips 2006:100, 103.

32. Schur 1980.
33. Mill 1859, 1956.
34. Committee on Homosexual Offences and Prostitution 1957.
35. Kadish 1967.
36. Schur 1965.
37. Skolnick 1968.
38. Geis 1979.
38. Packer 1968.
40. Devlin 1965:23.
41. Geis 1979; Schur 1965.
42. Schur 1965.
43. Becker 1963; Goffman 1963; Lemert 1967; Tannenbaum 1938.
44. Schur 1965:8.
45. Schur 1965:v.
46. Schur 1965.
47. Cook 1988.
48. Conrad and Schneider 1992.
49. Conrad and Schneider 1992:12.
50. Reagan 1997.
51. Cook 1988.
52. McConahay 1988:32.
53. Sullivan 1995.
54. Schur 1965.
55. Sutherland and Cressey 1960.
56. Schur 1980:24.
57. Schur 1980:6.
58. Schur 1980:7.
59. Jenness 1993.
60. Jenness 1993; Loseke and Best 2003.
61. Schur 1980.
62. Schur 1980:5, 8.

63. Meier and Geis 1997.
64. Mill 1859/1956:6.
65. Devlin 1965:13.
66. Schur 1980.
67. Skolnick 1988.
68. Frank 2004c.
69. Christian Exodus 2005.
70. Lester 2006.
71. Dobson 2005.
72. http://www.ouramericanvalues.org.
73. Bauer 2006e.
74. Garafoli 2005; O'Reilly 2006.
75. Bull and Gallagher 1996.
76. Kazin 2005; Pew Research Center 2005b.
77. Casanova 1994; Reed 1996.
78. Shockley 2004.
79. Princeton University 2000.
80. www.godhatesfags.com.
81. Alvarez 2006.
82. *New York Times* 2004; Sheldon 2004.
83. Pew Forum on Religion and Public Life 2003.
84. Pew Forum on Religion and Public Life 2003.
85. Lugo 2004.
86. Smith 2003.
87. Anti-Defamation League 2005.
88. Currie 1998; Tonry 2004.
89. Ahrens 2004.
90. Ahrens 2004:3.
91. Ahrens 2004:3–11.
92. Safire 1998.
93. Reagan 1997; Staggenborg 1991.
94. D'Emilio 2000; Vaid 1995.
95. Schur 1965.
96. Massing 1998a.
97. Frank 2004c.
98. Calavita 1996; Edelman 1985.
99. Weisberg 1999:41.
100. Skolnick 2004.
101. Obama 2004.
102. Wallis 2005.
103. Pew Research Center 2005b.

104. Broder 2006.
105. Skolnick 1988.

NOTES TO CHAPTER 2

1. Alter and Green 2003.
2. Bennett 1996.
3. Bennett 1992.
4. Bennett 1995:12.
5. Kinsley 2003.
6. *American Prospect* 2006.
7. Burkeman 2003.
8. Cooper 2004:3.
9. Lambert 2002; Reith 2003.
10. American Gaming Association 2006; Christiansen Capital Advisors 2001.
11. Cooper 2004.
12. Peterson 2004.
13. Morain 2004a.
14. Eadington 2006.
15. Baker 2004.
16. Dao 2004.
17. Rose 1980.
18. Dombrink 1990.
19. Eadington 1990.
20. Mangione and Fowler 1979.
21. Geis 1979.
22. Commission on the Review of the National Policy toward Gambling 1976.
23. Dombrink and Thompson 1990.
24. Frey 1992.
25. Clotfelter and Cook 1989.
26. Eadington 1990.
27. Christiansen Capital Advisors 1999.
28. March Madness 2006; Morsch 2005.
29. McManus 2003.
30. Gros 2005:4.
31. Lambert 2002; Skolnick 2003:313.
32. Fahrenkopf 2005:14.
33. Rothman 2003; Skolnick 1978.
34. *Business Week* 1978.
35. Thompson 1998:2.
36. Earley 2000; Martinez 2005.

37. *Reno Gazette-Journal* 2006.
38. Bellin 2002.
39. Ferrari 2005:6.
40. Feldman 2006.
41. Skolnick 2003:313.
42. Gallup Poll 2006; Lambert 2001.
43. Dombrink and Thompson 1990.
44. Clotfelter and Cook 1989.
45. Committee on the Social and Economic Impact of Pathological Gambling 1999.
46. Molica 2003:4.
47. Loveman 2002:38.
48. American Gaming Association 2006; Williams 2006.
49. Morain 2004b.
50. Darian-Smith 2005.
51. Stevens 2004:108.
52. Eadington 1990.
53. Bailey 2004.
54. Lazarus 2003:2.
55. Morain 2004b.
56. Moneymaker 2005.
57. O'Brien 2006:7.
58. Lederer 2003.
59. Duke 2005.
60. Bass 1985; Mezrich 2002.
61. American Gaming Association 2006.
62. McManus 2003; Moneymaker 2005.
63. State of Nevada, State Gaming Control Board, "Gaming Revenue Report," Year Ending December 31, 2004.
64. Eadington 2005; McMillen 1996.
65. Thompson 2003.
66. Clotfelter and Cook 1989; Committee on the Social and Economic Impact of Pathological Gambling 1999.
67. American Gaming Association 1998.
68. Clotfelter and Cook 1989.
69. Goodman 1995.
70. Reith 2003:12.
71. Lambert 2002:4–5.

72. National Gambling Impact Study Commission 1999:7–19, 7–20.
73. Responsible Gaming Association of New Mexico 2005.
74. Eadington 2006.
75. Hills 2003.
76. Open Letter 2002.
77. Dobson 1999.
78. Messerian and Derevensky 2004:1.
79. Dombrink and Thompson 1990.
80. Dahlburg 2005.
81. No Casinos 2005.
82. Stone 2004.
83. Center for Responsive Politics 2006.
84. Skolnick 2003.
85. Kramer 1987; Kushner 1993, 1994; Shilts 1987.
86. Dombrink and Thompson 1990; Rose 1980.
87. Geis 1979.
88. Gray 2001; MacCoun and Reuter 2001.
89. Eadington 2006.
90. Pew Research Center 2006a.
91. Pew Research Center 2006a:2.
92. Carruthers 2006.
93. Eadington 2006.
94. *USA Today* 2006.

NOTES TO CHAPTER 3

1. Biskupic 2005.
2. Biskupic 2005:270.
3. Biskupic 2005:271–272.
4. Michelman 2005b:109.
5. Schneider 1992.
6. Newport and Carroll 2005.
7. Lester 2004.
8. Limbaugh 1992.
9. CNN 2005a.
10. Jones 2005a.
11. Transcript 2005b.
12. Corn 2005.
13. Stolberg 2005b.

14. Transcript 2005c.
15. Stolberg and Bumiller 2005.
16. Fund 2005.
17. Reynolds and Hamburger 2005:A15.
18. Reynolds and Wallsten 2005.
19. Bumiller and Kirkpatrick 2005: A18.
20. Bauer 2005.
21. Coulter 2005a.
22. Gingrich 2005.
23. Yoo 2005.
24. http://redstate.org.
25. Deignan 2005.
26. Coulter 2005b:44.
27. Blankley 2005.
28. Neas 2005.
29. Bauer 2005.
30. Bork 2005.
31. Dickerson 2005.
32. *Alito's America* 2005.
33. Focus on the Family 2006.
34. Goldstein and Babington 2006.
35. Mears 2006.
36. Bauer 2006b.
37. Press 2006a; Press 2006b.
38. Luker 1984.
39. Garrow 1994.
40. Garrow 1994; Luker 1984.
41. Craig and O'Brien 1993:75.
42. Reagan 1997.
43. Ginsburg 1993; Risen and Thomas 1998.
44. Luker 1984.
45. Casanova 1994.
46. Joffe 2005.
47. Ginsburg 1993; Risen and Thomas 1998.
48. Reed 1996.
49. Guth et al. 1991.
50. Tribe 1992.
51. Risen and Thomas 1998; Flory 2005.
52. Flory 2005.
53. Winn 2005b; *Ayotte v. Planned Parenthood of Northern New England*, U.S.

Supreme Court, 04–1144 (2005); Greenhouse 2006b.
54. Page 2006.
55. Greenhouse 2006b.
56. Hausknecht 2006.
57. Smith 2006b.
58. Rosenberg 2004.
59. Joffe 2005.
60. Tumulty 2006:51.
61. Biskupic 2005:274.
62. Saletan 2004.
63. Gitlin 2005:39.
64. Dionne 2004; Moore 2004; PollingReport.com 2007.
65. Saad 2006a.
66. Ponnuru 2006a:19.
67. Ponnuru 2005a.
68. Pew Research Center 2004.
69. PollingReport.com 2007.
70. Baldassare 2002; DiCamillo and Field 2006b.
71. Benac 2006.
72. Fiorina 2006.
73. Conley 2005.
74. Turley 2005.
75. Bonavoglia 2005:144.
76. DiIulio 2006.
77. Dominus 2005.
78. Gorney 2004:35.
79. Gorney 2004.
80. Gorney 2004:41.
81. Gorney 2004:28.
82. Gorney 2004:34.
83. Gorney 2004.
84. Gorney 2004:40.
85. Rainey and LaGanga 2004; Rosenberg, 2004.
86. Feldt 2004:3.
87. Page 2005.
88. Feuerherd 2004:1.
89. Joffe 2005; A. Skolnick 2005; Dionne 2004; Dombrink 2005a.
90. Laser, 2006a:6; Laser 2006a:1.
91. Goldberg 2006:71.
92. Laser 2006a:2.
93. Shorto 2006:51.

94. GAO 2005.
95. Shorto 2006:51.
96. NARAL 2006c.
97. Page 2006.
98. FDA News 2006; Harris 2006.
99. Steinbrook 2006:1110.
100. Steinbrook 2006: 1110.
101. UPI 2005.
102. Specter 2006.
103. Maugh 2005.
104. FDA 2006.
105. Brown 2006.
106. *New York Times* 2006a.
107. Page 2006.
108. Press 2006b.
109. National Abortion Federation 2006.
110. Press 2006a; Press 2006b.
111. Napoli 2006.
112. NARAL 2006b.
113. Jurist 2006.
114. Page 2006:145.
115. Taylor 2002.
116. Ponnuru 2006b.
117. Rosen 2006.
118. Gorney and Greenman 2006.
119. Biskupic 2005:313.
120. Hirshman 2005.
121. Dominus 2005.
122. Kleiman 2005a.
123. Joffe 2005.
124. Laser 2006b.
125. Davey 2006b.
126. NARAL 2006a.
127. Goldschein 2006.
128. Greenhouse 2006a; United States Supreme Court 2006.
129. Stout 2007.
130. Opinion, *Gonzales v. Carhart*, 550 U.S. xxx (2007) at 1–39.
131. Ginsburg, J., et al., dissenting, *Gonzales v. Carhart*, 550 US xxx (2007) at 1–25.
132. Bauer 2007.
133. NARAL 2007a; NARAL 2007b.
134. Lithwick 2007.
135. Charo 2007; Drazen 2007.
136. Associated Press 2007; MSNBC 2007.
137. Garrow 2007; Wittes 2007.

NOTES TO CHAPTER 4

1. Dolan and Romney 2004:A1.
2. Hubler 2004.
3. Woman Vision 2003.
4. Walters 2001.
5. "Phyllis Lyon and Del Martrin Make History Again" 2004.
6. *The Times of Harvey Milk* (1984).
7. National Center for Lesbian Rights 2003.
8. Meeker, Dombrink, and Geis 1985.
9. Rubin and Anton 2004.
10. Ricci and Biederman 2004.
11. FitzGerald 1986:36–37.
12. Moats 2004.
13. FitzGerald 1986:27.
14. Bayles 2004
15. "Bush Calls for Ban on Same-Sex Marriages" 2004.
16. NGLTF 2004a; Ricci and Biederman 2004.
17. Nagourney and Elder 2004a.
18. Nagourney and Elder 2004b.
19. National Council of State Legislatures 2007; NGLTF 2006.
20. http://www.traditionalvalues.org; Truthwinsout.org 2006.
21. *Ballot Measure 9* 1995; Price 2006.
22. Hagerty 2006.
23. Bauer 2006c.
24. Bauer 2006d.
25. American Family Radio 2006.
26. Simon 2005.
27. Coulter 2006.
28. Rich 2005b; Trebay 2005.
29. Flynnfile.com 2006; Trebay 2005.
30. Simon 2006:A1.
31. Skolnick 1997.
32. Santorum 2005; *USA Today* 2003.

33. Bauer 2006f.

34. *Bowers v. Hardwick*, 478 U.S. 186 (1986).

35. Opinion, *Lawrence v. Texas*, 539 U.S. 558 (2003) at 13.

36. Greenhouse 2003.

37. Rostow 2003.

38. Richards 2005:88

39. D'Emilio 2000.

40. Smyth 2004.

41. Duberman 1991: 94, 105, 92.

42. Vaid 1995:52.

43. Vaid 1995:52.

44. Meeker, Dombrink, and Geis 1985.

45. NGLTF 2004.

46. Meeker, Dombrink, and Geis 1985.

47. Vaid 1995.

48. Smyth 2004.

49. D'Emilio 2000.

50. Vaid 1995:54.

51. Smyth 2004.

52. Vaid 1995.

53. Rich 2005b.

54. Griffiths, Weyers, and Bood 1998.

55. Greenberg, 1988:478–480; Marty and Appleby 1992.

56. D'Emilio 2000:41.

57. Richman 2003.

58. Dworkin 1996; Keen and Goldberg 1998.

59. NGLTF 1998.

60. D'Emilio 2000; Keen and Goldberg 1998.

61. Altman 1982.

62. Rich 2004.

63. See, for example, Wallis 2005 and Lerner 2005; and Green, Schmidt, and Kellstedt 2005.

64. BBC News 2006.

65. Congregation for the Doctrine of the Faith 2003.

66. http://www.dignityusa.org.

67. http://www.dignityusa.org.

68. Wilkinson 2005.

69. Bauer 2006g.

70. Talbot 2004:44.

71. Religious Coalition for Marriage 2006.

72. Banerjee 2006a.

73. http://www.stillspeaking.com; MSNBC 2004.

74. Bull and Gallagher 1996.

75. Banerjee 2005.

76. Banerjee 2006d.

77. Banerjee 2006b.

78. Banerjee 2006c; Boyer 2006.

79. Polgreen 2005.

80. Kelley 2006.

81. Goodstein 2006.

82. va4marriage 2006.

83. http://www.traditionalvalues.org.

84. Graff 2006:42.

85. South Carolina Equality Coalition 2006.

86. Schweitzer 2005.

87. Moats 2003.

88. *New York Times* 2005a.

89. Jackson 2006.

90. Nagourney and Elder 2004.

91. Pew Forum on Religion and Public Life 2004.

92. Human Rights Campaign 2006.

93. Dobson 2006.

94. Religious Coalition for Marriage 2006.

95. Bauer 2006.

96. Hook 2006.

97. Fox News Sunday 2006.

98. CNN Late Edition 2006.

99. Bush 2006.

100. Citizen Link 2006; MSNBC 2006.

101. NGLTF 2006.

102. Pew Research Center, 2006b:1.

103. Stolberg 2006b; White House 2006.

104. Mansnerus 2006.

105. Johnson 2006.

106. Davey 2006.

107. Chen 2006a.

108. Saad 2006c.

109. Skolnick 1997.

110. National Marriage Project 2004.

111. Gallup Poll 2006a.
112. http://huffingtonpost.com 2006.
113. Crystal 2006.
114. Ponnuru 2006a.

NOTES TO CHAPTER 5

1. Hulse 2005:1.
2. Hulse 2005.
3. Hulse 2005:1.
4. Fagan 2005.
5. Hulse 2005:2.
6. Hulse 2005:2.
7. Caplan 2005.
8. Hillyard and Dombrink 2001.
9. Kohut 2005.
10. Colby 2005.
11. Klein 2005.
12. Ponnuru 2006a; *Wall Street Journal* 2005.
13. Noonan 2005.
14. Noonan 2005.
15. Hook 2005:A12.
16. Simon and Reynolds 2005.
17. Hook 2005.
18. Ginsburg 1993.
19. Terry 2005.
20. Hook 2005.
21. Quill 2005.
22. Hagerty 2005.
23. O'Reilly 2005.
24. Operation Rescue 2005.
25. Hentoff 2005.
26. Brownstein 2005; Simon and Hook 2005.
27. Langer 2005.
28. Reynolds 2005b.
29. Ireland 2005.
30. Brooks 2005.
31. Beutler 2006:11.
32. Boyce 2005.
33. Hentoff 2005.
34. Schiavo 2006; Schindler and Schindler 2006.
35. Tisch 2006.

36. CNN/*USA Today* Gallup Poll 1996; Glick 1992.
37. Quill 1996; Williams 1958.
38. Williams 1957.
39. Hillyard and Dombrink 2001.
40. Reagan 1997.
41. Quill 1991.
42. Dworkin 1996.
43. Reagan 1997.
44. Meier and Geis 1997.
45. van Alestyn 2005.
46. Hillyard and Dombrink 2001.
47. John Paul II 2004.
48. Gilmore and Simon 1991.
49. O'Keefe 1994a, 1994b.
50. Doerflinger 1999.
51. Limbaugh 2005.
52. Smith 1997:109.
53. Smith 1997:88.
54. Bagdikian 2004.
55. Ponnuru 2006a.
56. Smith 2005c.
57. Smith 2005b.
58. Smith 2004c.
59. Ashcroft 1998.
60. BBC News 2001.
61. Verhovek 2001.
62. Hillyard and Dombrink 2001:2.
63. Hillyard and Dombrink 2001.
64. Coombs Lee 2004.
65. 66 *Fed. Reg.* 56, 607 (2001); November 6, 2001, Memorandum of John Ashcroft, Attorney General, to Asa Hutchinson, Administrator, the Drug Enforcement Administration: "Dispensing of Controlled Substances to Assist Suicide."
66. Amici Curiae Not Dead Yet et al. 2005:7.
67. AUTONOMY and Cascade AIDS Project 2005:4.
68. United States Catholic Conference et al., 2005:4–5.
69. Americans United for Life 2005:2.
70. Christian Medical Association et al., 2005:3.
71. U.S. Congress Members 2005:3.

72. National Legal Center for the Medically Dependent and Disabled 2005:3.

73. Catholic Medical Association 2005:2.

74. International Task Force on Euthanasia and Assisted Suicide 2005:2.

75. Pro-Life Legal Defense Fund, Inc., et al. 2005:2.

76. Thomas More Society 2005:7.

77. Battin et al. 2005:2.

78. Battin et al. 2005:3.

79. Battin et al. 2005:4.

80. Mental Health Professionals 2005:8.

81. Healthlaw Professors 2005:4.

82. American College of Legal Medicine 2005:2.

83. American College of Legal Medicine 2005:2.

84. Religious Organizations and Leaders 2005:4.

85. Religious Organizations and Leaders 2005:5.

86. Surviving Family Members 2005: 1–2.

87. Surviving Family Members 2005:24.

88. American Public Health Association 2005:2.

89. American Public Health Association 2005:3.

90. American Public Health Association 2005:3.

91. Cato Institute 2005:1.

92. Cato Institute 2005:3.

93. Law Professors 2005:4.

94. *Washington v. Glucksberg,* 521 U.S. 702, 735 (1997).

95. *Cruzan v. Missouri Department of Health,* 101497 U.S. 261 (1990).

96. American Civil Liberties Union 2005:2.

97. Amici States 2005:2.

98. Transcript 2005a:22.

99. Transcript 2005a:23.

100. Transcript 2005a:25–26.

101. Transcript 2005a:28.

102. Transcript 2005a:28.

103. Transcript 2005a:28.

104. Transcript 2005a:9.

105. Transcript 2005a:10.

106. Transcript 2005a:18.

107. Transcript 2005a:22.

108. Transcript 2005a:47.

109. Transcript 2005a:31.

110. Transcript 2005a:50.

111. Transcript 2005a:56.

112. Transcript 2005a:53.

113. Transcript 2005a:53.

114. Transcript 2005a:54.

115. Transcript 2005a:60.

116. Transcript 2005a:16.

117. *Washington v. Glucksberg,* 521, U.S. 702, 735 (1997).

118. *Gonzales v. Oregon,* 546 U.S. No. 04–623, 7 (2006).

119. 546 U.S. No. 04–623, 3 (2006).

120. 546 U.S No. 04–623, 19 (2006).

121. "Oregon Wins—without Roberts" 2006.

122. Associated Press 2006a; U.S. Newswire 2006.

123. National Right to Life 2006.

124. National Catholic Bioethics Center 2006.

125. Foust 2006.

126. Smith 2006b.

127. Hillyard and Dombrink 2001.

128. California Healthline 2005a; 2005b; 2005c.

129. DiCamillo and Field 2005.

130. Hillyard and Dombrink 2001.

131. DiCamillo and Field 2005.

132. Vogel 2006.

133. Smith 2006a.

134. Emmanuel et al., 2000; Meier et al., 1998; Wolfe et al., 1999.

135. Danforth 2006:75.

136. Kondracke 2006.

137. Armey 2006.

138. Stockman 2006.

139. Hillyard and Dombrink 2001.

NOTES TO CHAPTER 6

1. Missouri Coalition 2006f.
2. See *Webster v. Reproductive Health Services*, 492 U.S. 490, 1989.
3. Castillo 2006.
4. Angel 2006.
5. Gillespie 2006.
6. Angel 2006.
7. Missouri Coalition 2006c.
8. www.nocloning.org, 2006.
9. Kraske 2006.
10. Hananel 2006.
11. Missouri Coalition 2006g.
12. Danforth 2005.
13. Townsend 2005.
14. CNN 2005b.
15. Burke 2005.
16. U.S. Conference of Catholic Bishops (2005).
17. Missouri Coalition 2006e.
18. Cardetti 2006.
19. Fox 2006.
20. Mehlman 2006.
21. *New York Times* 2006b; Sollars 2006.
22. Bush 2001.
23. President's Council on Bioethics 2004:chap. 2.
24. Bonnicksen 1989; President's Council on Bioethics 2004.
25. Bonnicksen 1989:81.
26. Bonnicksen 1989.
27. Devitt 1998.
28. President's Council on Bioethics 2004.
29. Bonnicksen 1989:81.
30. Fletcher 1999:34.
31. Bonnicksen 2002:67.
32. New York State Task Force on Life and the Law 1998.
33. *Congressional Record* 2001:H2925.
34. Bonnicksen 2002; Broder and Pollack 2004.
35. Nisbet, Brossard, and Kroepsch 2004.

36. *Congressional Record* 1998, S323.
37. *Congressional Record* 1998, S428.
38. Bonnicksen 2002:57–58.
39. Nobel Laureates 1999.
40. Perry 2000.
41. CBS News 2001; Nisbet 2004.
42. Shehzad 2001.
43. Davis 2001b; Hatch 2001.
44. Meyer 2005:18.
45. Keen 2001.
46. Davis 2001a; Haley 2001; Shehzad 2001; Weiss 2001a, 2001b.
47. Davis 2001b; Hatch 2001.
48. Davis 2001b.
49. Davis 2001a:2.
50. Bruni 2001.
51. Nisbet 2004.
52. Nisbet, Brossard, and Kroepsch 2004.
53. Nisbet, Brossard, and Kroepsch 2004.
54. Seelye 2001.
55. Lacayo 2001:1–2.
56. Keen 2001.
57. Bruni 2001; Lacayo 2001.
58. Lacayo 2001.
59. Connolly and Weiss 2001.
60. Allen 2001.
61. Bruni 2001:2.
62. Milbank 2001.
63. Bruni 2001.
64. Henderson Blunt 2001.
65. Saletan 2002.
66. CNN 2001.
67. Connolly and Weiss 2001.
68. Henderson Blunt 2001; Lacayo 2001.
69. Meyer 2005.
70. Lacayo 2001:2.
71. Allen 2001.
72. Lacayo 2001.
73. Shehzad 2001.
74. Meyer 2005:19.
75. *Christianity Today* 2001.
76. Lacayo 2001:2.
77. Mooney 2001.

78. Goodstein 2001.
79. Goodstein 2001.
80. Goodstein 2001.
81. Seelye 2001.
82. Goodstein 2001.
83. BBC News 2001.
84. Manier 2001.
85. Goldstein and Allen 2001.
86. Manier 2001.
87. Meyer 2005:20.
88. Coalition for Stem Cell Research and Cures 2004c; Coalition for Stem Cell Research and Cures 2004b.
89. Coalition for Stem Cell Research and Cures 2004a.
90. Mathews and Garvey 2004.
91. California Healthline 2005c.
92. International Society for Stem Cell Research 2004.
93. California Healthline 2005a.
94. Morrison 2005; PARADE/Research!America Health Poll 2005.
95. Pew Forum on Religion and Public Life: 2004.
96. Center for Genetics and Society 2006.
97. Coalition for the Advancement of Medical Research 2005.
98. Kalb and Rosenberg 2004; Results for America 2004.
99. BBC News Online 2004.
100. Missouri Coalition 2006b.
101. Skocpol 1995.
102. Cameron 2005.
103. Ponnuru 2006a:1.
104. Catholic Answers 2004.
105. Catholic News Service 2004.
106. Vargo 2005.
107. Vargo 2005.
108. CBS/AP 2005.
109. Focus on the Family 2005a.
110. Focus on the Family 2005b.
111. Ehrenhalt 2005.
112. Hwang et al. 2004; Moon 2005.
113. National Academy of Sciences 2005.

114. Citizen Link 2005b.
115. http://handsoffourovaries.com.
116. Downs 1989.
117. Beeson 2006.
118. Danforth 2005.
119. Mulkern 2005.
120. Stolberg 2005d.
121. *New York Times* 2005b.
122. Cameron 2005.
123. Family Research Council 2005; Winn 2005.
124. Hatch 2005.
125. Reagan 2006.
126. Kellman 2006b.
127. Talev 2006:131.
128. Kessler 2006.
129. Reid 2006.
130. *Scientific American* 2006.
131. Chen 2006a.
132. Limbaugh 2006.
133. Smith 2006.
134. Solo and Pressberg 2006.
135. *Congressional Record* 2007; *New England Journal of Medicine* 2007; White House 2007.

NOTES TO CHAPTER 7

1. Frank 2004c.
2. Moyers 2005a.
3. Frank 2005c.
4. A. Skolnick 2005.
5. Simon 2006.
6. Dionne 2006c.
7. Santorum 2005.
8. Clinton 1996.
9. Santorum 2005:4.
10. Santorum 2005:5.
11. Santorum 2005:6.
12. Santorum 2005:235.
13. Santorum 2005:426.
14. Schwartz and Blumstein 1983; A. Skolnick 1992.
15. Santorum 2005:427.
16. Santorum 2005:428.

17. Santorum 2005:424.

18. Cohen 2001; Griffiths, Weyers, and Bood 1998; MacCoun and Reuter 2001; Punch 1996.

19. Pew Research Center 2006b.

20. Fiorina 2006:xiii.

21. Fiorina 2006:88.

22. Fiorina 2006:94.

23. Fiorina 2006:94.

24. Fiorina 2006:95.

25. Fiorina 2006:96.

26. Fiorina 2006:98.

27. Fiorina 2006:99.

28. Fiorina 2006:103.

29. Fiorina 2006:100.

30. Fiorina 2006:101.

31. Fiorina 2006:102.

32. Hacker and Pierson 2005.

33. Andersen 2006:28.

34. Andersen 2006:28.

35. Dionne 2006c.

36. Dionne 2006c.

37. Wolfe 2001.

38. Wilson 2005a.

39. Donahue 1997.

40. Belluck 2006:4.

41. Glaeser, Ponzetto and Shapiro 2004.

42. Galston and Kamarck 2005:43.

43. Galston and Kamarck 2005:35.

44. Goldberg 2006:65.

45. Biden 2006.

46. Goldberg 2006:70.

47. Espo 2006; Obama 2006:3.

48. Lakoff 2002.

49. Snow et al. 1986.

50. Luker 1984.

51. Lakoff 2004.

52. Lakoff 2004:29.

53. Lakoff 2004:xvi.

54. Lakoff 2004:46, 49–50.

55. Lakoff 2006:22.

56. Lakoff 2006:23.

57. Lakoff 2006:21.

58. Gusfield 1972; Hillyard and Dombrink 2001.

59. Schur 1980:229.

60. Schur 1980:18.

61. Dombrink 2005a.

62. Frank 2004c.

63. Ranulf 1938/1964.

64. McCann 1994.

65. Goldberg-Hiller 2002:7.

66. Mickthelwait and Wooldridge 2004.

67. Bauer 2006h.

68. Geis 1979; Kadish 1967; Packer 1968; Schur 1965; Skolnick 1968.

69. Mill 1859/1956.

70. Garrow 1994; Reagan 1997; Schur 1965.

71. Goldberg-Hiller 2002.

72. Melendez 2006.

73. Keeter 2006a.

74. Wallis 2005.

75. Wallis 2005:xvii.

76. Wallis 2005:xv–xvii.

77. Powell 2005.

78. Lerner 2005.

79. Lakoff 2004.

80. Moyers 2005a.

81. Kleiman 2006b.

82. Kleiman 2006b.

83. Jones 2006:1.

84. MSNBC 2005a, 2005b.

85. Nagourney 2006c, 2006d.

86. Rove 2006.

87. Bauer 2006c.

88. Zernicke 2006.

89. Crowley 2006.

90. Armey 2006.

91. Danforth 2006:75.

92. Kuo 2006b.

93. Crary 2006a.

94. Crary 2006a.

95. Crary 2006b.

96. Kondracke 2006.

97. Greenberg Quinlan Rosner Research 2006:66.

98. Halpin 2006.

99. Galston 2006.

100. Kohut 2005.

101. Bartlett 2006.

102. Greenfield 2006.
103. McIntyre 2006.
104. Dionne 2006a.
105. Dionne 2006b.
106. Klein 2006a.
107. Klein 2006b.
108. Todd 2006.
109. Real Republican Majority 2006.
110. Real Republican Majority 2006.
111. Specter 2006.
112. Charo 2006.
113. Phillips 2006.
114. Legum et al. 2006.
115. Inskeep 2006.
116. Skolnick, A. 2005.
117. Levi 1973.

References

Abowitz, Richard (2006) "Gangstas as Poker Enemy No. 1." *Los Angeles Times,* March 12, E26.

Abramowitz, Alan I. (1995) "It's Abortion, Stupid: Policy Voting in the 1992 Presidential Election." *Journal of Politics* 57 (1): 176–186.

Abt, Vickie, James Smith, and Eugene Martin Christiansen (1985) *The Business of Risk: Commercial Gambling in Mainstream America.* Lawrence: University Press of Kansas.

Ackley, Kate (2002) "Storming the Hill." *Global Gaming Business,* December 1, 16–21.

Ader, Jason (2002) "That's the Ticket: Worldwide Lottery Sales Hit $125.6 Billion, and the Growth Potential Is Still Abundant." *Global Gaming Business,* October 1, 12.

Agne, Karl, and Stan Greenberg (2005) "The Cultural Divide and the Challenge of Winning Back Rural and Red State Voters." Memo, Washington, D.C.: Democracy Corps, August 9.

Ahrens, Dan (2004) *Investing in Vice: The Recession-Proof Portfolio of Booze, Bets, Bombs and Butts.* New York: St. Martin's Press.

Alito's America (2005) Video, www.alitosamerica.org. Accessed on December 8.

Allen, Mike (2001) "Pope Tells Bush Views on Embryos; Pontiff Opposes Use for Research." *Washington Post,* July 24, A1.

Alter, Jonathan, and Joshua Green (2003) "The Man of Virtues Has a Vice." *Newsweek,* May 2.

Altman, Dennis (1982) *The Homosexualization of America: The Americanization of the Homosexual.* New York: St. Martin's Press.

Altman, Lawrence K. (2005) "Doctors Support a Childhood Vaccine for a Sex-Related Virus." *New York Times,* October 28, 2005.

Alvarez, Lizette (2006) "Outrage at Funeral Protests Pushes Lawmakers to Act." *New York Times,* April 17.

American Civil Liberties Union (2005) Brief of the American Civil Liberties Union and the ACLU of Oregon as Amici Curiae in Support of Respondents, *Gonzales v. Oregon,* in the Supreme Court of the United States, July 18.

American College of Legal Medicine (2005) Brief of American College of Legal Medicine, as Amicus Curiae in Support of Respondents, *Gonzales v. Oregon,* in the Supreme Court of the United States, July 15.

American Family Radio (2006) Broadcast of American Family Radio's AFA Report, March 8.

American Gaming Association (1998) *Responsible Gaming Resource*

Guide. 2nd ed. Washington, D.C.: The Responsible Gaming Task Force of the American Gaming Association. June.

American Gaming Association (2006) *State of the States: The AGA Survey of Casino Entertainment.* Washington, D.C.: American Gaming Association.

American Prospect (2006) "Bill Bennett Forecasts the New Baseball Season," April 8.

American Public Health Association (2005) Brief of the American Public Health Association as Amicus Curiae in Support of Respondents, *Gonzales v. Oregon,* in the Supreme Court of the United States, July 18.

Americans United for Life (2005) Brief of Amicus Curiae Americans United for Life in Support of Petitioners, *Gonzales v. Oregon,* in the Supreme Court of the United States, May 9.

Amici Curiae Not Dead Yet et al. (2005) Brief for Amici Curiae Not Dead Yet, ADAPT, Center on Disability Studies, Law and Policy at Syracuse University, Center for Self-Determination, Hospice Patients Alliance, May 9.

Amici States (2005) Brief of the States of California, Mississippi, Missouri, Montana, and the District of Columbia as Amici Curiae in Support of Respondent State of Oregon, *Gonzales v. Oregon,* in the Supreme Court of the United States, July 21.

Andersen, Kurt (2006) "Introducing the Purple Party." *New York,* April 24.

Angel, Traci (2006) "Scientists Seek Assurance from State for Stem Cell Research." *Columbia Missourian,* April 27. columbiamissourian.com/related/story.php?ID=19644. Accessed on April 27, 2006.

Ansolabehere, Stephen, Jonathan Rodden, and James M. Snyder Jr. (2005) "Purple America." Unpublished manuscript, Massachusetts Institute of Technology, September.

Anti-Defamation League (2005) "Poll: Americans Believe Religion Is 'Under Attack'—Majority Says Religion Is 'Losing Influence' in American Life." New York: Anti-Defamation League, November 21.

Armey, Dick (2006) "Where We Went Wrong." Washington Post, October 29.

Arnold, Wayne (2006) Las Vegas Sands to Build Casino in Singapore." *New York Times,* May 26.

Ashcroft, John (1998) *Lessons from a Father to a Son.* Nashville, Tenn.: Thomas Nelson Books.

Associated Press (2005) "Bush Signs Schiavo Legislation." March 21.

Associated Press (2006a) "Backers of Assisted Suicide Law Applaud Ruling." *Spokane Spokesman-Review.* http://www.deathwithdignity.org/news/news/spokanespokesmanreview.01.18.06.asp. Accessed on January 17, 2006.

Associated Press (2006b) "Mass. Wal-Marts Told to Sell Morning-After Pill." *Los Angeles Times,* February 15, A22.

Associated Press (2006c) Nancy Reagan Again Takes Lead on Stem Cells, May 15.

Associated Press (2006d) "Poll: On Abortion, Americans Agree to Disagree." MSNBC.com, March 12.

Associated Press (2007) "Reactions to Court's Abortion Decision." *Sacramento Bee,* http://www.sacbee.com, April 18.

AUTONOMY and Cascade AIDS Project (2005) Brief of Autonomy, Inc. and Cascade AIDS Project as Amici Curiae Supporting Respondents, *Gonzales v. Oregon,* in the Supreme Court of the United States, July 21.

Ayala, Francisco (2006) "Religious Concern about Stem Cells." Presentation at "Stem Cells and Society: A Series of Dialogues." Schools of Biological Sciences and Humanities, University of California, Irvine, April 26.

Ayotte v. Planned Parenthood of Northern New England. U.S. Supreme Court, 04-1144 (2005).

Bagdikian, Ben H. (2004) *The New Media Monopoly.* Boston: Beacon Press.

Bailey, Eric (2004) "Weighing Casino Cash v. Problems." *Los Angeles Times,* July 7, B1.

Baker, Al (2004) "New York Begins to Cash In with Video Lottery Terminals." *New York Times,* March 12.

Baker, Wayne E. (2005) "Voting Your Values and Moral Visions." Paper prepared for the annual meetings of the American Sociological Association.

Baldassare, Mark (2002) "Political Winds Favor Democrats." *San Diego Union Tribune,* November 3.

Baldonado, Ronald R. (2005) "Indian Gaming, Public Opinion, and Policy in California." Honor's thesis, Department of Criminology, Law and Society, University of California, Irvine.

Balestra, Mark (2002) "The European Plan." *Global Gaming Business,* December 15, 30–32.

Balkin, Jack M. (2005) "*Roe v. Wade:* An Engine of Controversy." In Jack M. Balkin, ed., *What* Roe v. Wade *Should Have Said: The Nation's Top Legal Experts Rewrite America's Most Controversial Decision.* New York: NYU Press.

Balko, Radley (2006) "Anti-gambling Crusade a Bad Bet." Arizona Republic, March 12.

Ballot Measure 9 (1995) Documentary, Fox Lorber Studios. Directed by Heather MacDonald.

Banerjee, Neela (2005) "Methodist Divisions over Gays Intensify." *New York Times,* October 21.

Banerjee, Neela (2006a) "Black Churches' Attitudes toward Gay Parishioners Is Discussed at Conference." *New York Times,* January 21.

Banerjee, Neela (2006b) "Church Urges Its Dioceses Not to Elect Gay Bishops." *New York Times,* June 22.

Banerjee, Neela (2006c) "Episcopal Leader Retiring amid Divisive Debate on Sexuality of Bishops." *New York Times,* June 11.

Banerjee, Neela (2006d) "Woman Is Named Episcopal Leader." *New York Times,* June 19.

Barfield, Chet (2004) "Indian Casinos' Payout to State Spurs Debate." *San Diego Union-Tribune,* October 10.

Barone, Michael (2004) Panel discussion, "Values, Religion, Politics and the Media." Harvard University, John F. Kennedy School of Government, November 15.

Bartels, Larry M. (2005) "What's the Matter with *What's the Matter with Kansas?*" Unpublished manuscript, Department of Politics and Woodrow Wilson School of Public and International Affairs, Princeton University.

Bartlett, Bruce (2006) "Libertarian GOP Defection?" Real Clear Politics, http://www.realclearpolitics.com, December 12.

Bartlett, Donald, and James Steele (2002) "Wheels of Misfortune: Look Who's Cashing In at Indian Casinos." *Time,* December 16.

Bass, Thomas A. (1985) *The Eudaemonic Pie.* Boston: Houghton Mifflin.

Battin, Margaret P., et al. (2005) Brief of Amici Curiae (Margaret P. Battin, Tom L. Beauchamp, Dan W. Brock, and Edward Lowenstein; S. James Adelstein, Anita L. Allen-Castellitto, Marcia Angell, Robert Arnold, John D. Arras, Charles H. Baron, Howard Brody, Robert V. Brody, Allen Buchanan, Norman L. Cantor, Arthur L Caplan, Christine K. Cassel, Eric J. Cassell, R.

Alta Charo, Robert Cook-Deegan, Norman Daniels, Nancy Neveloff Dubler, Ronald Dworkin, Ruth Faden, Daniel D. Federman, Joel E. Frader, Leslie Pickering Francis, John M. Freeman, Bernard Gert, Samuel Gorovitz, Jeffrey Kahn, Yale Kamisar, Jerome P. Kassirer, Sylvia Law, Robert S. Lawrence, Robert J. Levine, Charles F. McKhann, Alan Meisel, David Orentlicher, Timothy E. Quill, Arnold S. Relman, Ben A. Rich, John A. Robertson, Thomas M. Scanlon, Lawrence J. Schneiderman, Anita Silvers, Peter Singer, Bonnie Steinbock, Jeremy Sugarman, Judith J. Thomson, Robert D. Truog, Sidney H. Wanzer, Richard A. Wasserstrom, William J. Winslade, and Peter M. Winter) in Support of Respondents, *Gonzales v. Oregon,* in the Supreme Court of the United States, July 18.

Bauer, Carol (2006) "Prayer Alert." American Values, http://www.americanvalues.org, May 25.

Bauer, Gary (2005) "Second Thoughts Anyone?" American Values, http://www.americanvalues.org, October 26.

Bauer, Gary (2006a) "End of Day." American Values, http://www.americanvalues.org, February 1.

Bauer, Gary (2006b) "End of Day." American Values, http://www.americanvalues.org, February 2.

Bauer, Gary (2006c) "End of Day." American Values, http://www.americanvalues.org, March 1.

Bauer, Gary (2006d) "End of Day." American Values, http://www.americanvalues.org, March 21.

Bauer, Gary (2006e) "End of Day." American Values, http://www.americanvalues.org, March 24.

Bauer, Gary (2006f) "End of Day." American Values, http://www.americanvalues.org, April 24.

Bauer, Gary (2006g) "Fighting for Our Values." American Values, http://www.americanvalues.org, March 13.

Bauer, Gary (2006h) "We Need You." American Values, http://www.americanvalues.org, December 14.

Baumgartner, Frank R., and Bryan D. Jones (1993) *Agendas and Instability in American Politics.* Chicago: University of Chicago Press.

Bayles, Fred (2004) "Gay-Marriage Debate Quiet for Now." usatoday.com, June 16.

BBC News (2001) "Profile: John Ashcroft." January 16. http://news.bbc.co.uk/1/hi/world/americas/1120440.stm. Accessed on May 29, 2006.

BBC News (2005a) "Evangelist Says Voters Reject God." http://www.bbcnews.com, November 10.

BBC News (2005b) "Pope Warns against 'DIY' Religion." http://www.bbcnews.com, August 21.

BBC News Online (2001) "Companies Cheer Bush Stem Cell Move," August 10. http://news.bbc.co.uk/1/low/business/1483722.stm. Accessed on September 1, 2001.

BBC News Online (2004) "Nancy Reagan Plea on Stem Cells." May 10.

BBC News Online (2005) "Schroeder Urges Stem Cell Easing." June 14.

Becker, Howard (1963) *Outsiders: Studies in the Sociology of Deviance.* New York: Free Press.

Beeson, Diane (2006) "On Common Ground": An interview with M. L. Tina Stevens and Diane Beeson, *Center for Bioethics and Culture Network,* January 31, http://www.cc-network.org.

Bellin, Andy (2002) *Poker Nation: A High-Stakes, Low-Life Adventure into the Heart of a Gambling Country.* New York: HarperCollins.

Belluck, Pam (2006) "The Not So United-States." *New York Times,* April 23, 4.

Belson, Ken, and Gary Rivlin (2005) "The Perils of Casinos That Float." *New York Times,* September 7, C1.

Benac, Nancy (2006) "Americans Consistent but Conflicted in Abortion Views: Poll Suggests Most in Middle on Issue." *Boston Globe,* March 13.

Bennett, William J. (1992) *The De-valuing of America: The Fight for Our Culture and Our Children.* New York: Summit Books.

Bennett, William J. (1995) *The Moral Compass: Stories for a Life's Journey.* New York: Simon and Schuster.

Bennett, William J. (1996) *The Book of Virtues: A Treasury of Great Moral Stories.* Parsippany, N.J.: Silver Burdett.

Beutler, Brian (2006) "Sour Mashed." *American Prospect,* November, 11–13.

Biden, Joseph (2006) Remarks of United States Senator (D-Delaware) on *Real Time with Bill Maher,* HBO, April 7.

Bing, Jonathan (2003) "Films, Books, Magazines Beat Path to Las Vegas." *Toronto Star,* March 15.

Binkley, Christina, Jon E. Hilsenrath, and Charles Forelle (2003) "States Confronting Budget Deficits Make Long-Shot Bets on Gambling." *Wall Street Journal,* March 14, A1.

Biskupic, Joan (2005) *Sandra Day O'Connor: How the First Woman on the Supreme Court Became Its Most Influential Justice.* New York: ecco/HarperCollins.

Blankley, Tony (2005) "Bush on the Edge." RealClearPolitics, http://www.realclearpolitics.com, October 26.

Bolton, Alexander (2005) "Angst on Right over Frist." *The Hill,* December 7.

Bonfadelli, Heinz, Urs Dahinden, and Martina Leonarz (2002) "Biotechnology in Switzerland: High on the Public Agenda, but Only Moderate Support." *Public Understanding of Science* 11:113–130.

Bonnicksen, Andrea L. (1989) *In Vitro Fertilization: Building Policy from Laboratories to Legislatures.* New York: Columbia University Press.

Bonnicksen, Andrea L. (2002) *Crafting a Cloning Policy: From Dolly to Stem Cells.* Washington, D.C.: Georgetown University Press.

Bork, Robert (2005) "Slouching towards Miers: Bush Shows Himself to Be Indifferent, If Not Hostile, to Conservative Values." *Wall Street Journal,* October 19.

Boyce, David (2005) "Gov. Jeb Bush Ends Schiavo Inquiry." Associated Press, July 8.

Boyer, Peter (2006) "A Church Asunder," *New Yorker,* April 17, 54–65.

Braiker, Brian (2005) " 'No Moral Sense.' " *Newsweek,* http://www.msnbc.msn.com/id/7276850/site/newsweek/.

Broder, John (2004) "As Schwarzenegger Tries to Slow It, Gambling Grows." *New York Times,* October 10.

Broder, John (2006) "The 2006 Elections; Democrats Take Senate." *New York Times,* November 10.

Broder, John M., and Andrew Pollack (2004) "Californians to Vote on Stem Cell Research Funds." *New York Times,* September 20, A1.

Brookings Institution (2006) "American Politics and the Religious Divide." Washington, D.C.: Brookings Institution, September 26.

Brooks, David (2005) "Reining in the G.O.P.'s Parade." *New York Times,* April 9.

Brown, David (2006) "HPV Vaccine Advised for Girls." *Washington Post,* http://www.washingtonpost.com, June 30.

Brownstein, Ronald (2005a) "Americans

Remain Polarized over Bush." *Los Angeles Times,* January 19, A1.

Brownstein, Ronald (2005b) "Conservatives' Challenges, Gains Clear in Schiavo Case." *Los Angeles Times,* March 29.

Bruce, Steve (2002) *God Is Dead: Secularization in the West.* Oxford: Blackwell.

Bruni, Frank (2001) "Unexpected Priority: Stem Cell Research's Rise as a Test for Bush." *New York Times,* July 14, A10.

Bull, Christopher, and John Gallagher (1996) *Perfect Enemies: The Religious Right, the Gay Movement, and the Politics of the 1990s.* New York: Crown.

Bumiller, Elisabeth, and David D. Kirkpatrick (2005) "Bush Fends Off Sharp Criticism of Court Choice." *New York Times,* October 5, A1.

Burke, Archbishop Raymond L. (2005) "Safeguarding Human Life: The Very Beginning." *St. Louis Review Online,* November 11. http://www.stlouisreview.com/abpcolumn.php?abpid=9557. Accessed on November 27, 2005.

Burkeman, Oliver (2003) "Voice of Morality Exposed as Chronic Casino Loser." *Guardian,* May 6.

Burns, Gene (2005) *The Moral Veto: Framing Contraception, Abortion, and Cultural Pluralism in the United States.* New York: Cambridge University Press.

Bush, George W. (2001) "Stem Cell Science and the Preservation of Life." *New York Times,* August 12, D13.

Bush, George W. (2006) "President Discusses Marriage Protection Amendment." http://www.whitehouse.com, June 5.

"Bush Calls for Ban on Same-Sex Marriages" (2004) www.cnn.com.

"Bush Keeps Woman Alive" (2005) news24.com, South Africa, March 21.

Business Week (1978) "Special Report: Gambling: The Newest Growth Industry." June 26, 110–129.

Butterfield, Fox (2003) "With Cash Tight, States Reassess Long Jail Terms." *New York Times,* November 10.

Butterfield, Fox (2005) "As Gambling Grows, States Depend on Their Cut to Bolster Revenues." *New York Times,* March 31.

Calavita, Kitty (1996) "The New Politics of Immigration: 'Balanced Budget Conservatism' and Prop 187." *Social Problems* 43:284–305.

California Healthline (2005a) "Group Files Lawsuit against Stem Cell Agency." June 14.

California Healthline (2005b) "More Than Two-Thirds of State Residents Support Physician-Assisted Suicide, Poll Finds." March 2.

California Healthline (2005c) "Other States Observing Implementation of California Stem Cell Initiative." February 14.

California Lottery (1999) "Thanks a Million, Make That $10 Billion for Our Schools since 1985." Pamphlet. Sacramento, Calif.: California State Lottery.

California Lottery (2003) "18 Winning Years!" Sacramento, Calif.: California State Lottery, October.

California State Association of Counties (2004) "CSAC Fact Sheet on Proposition 70: Tribal Fair Share Act of 2004." August 23.

Cameron, Nigel (2005) "Dr. Frist's Dilemma." *Christianity Today,* October 11.

Cameron, Nigel (2006) "Poaching Eggs: The Latest Sad Story from the Korean Soap Opera—and a Lack of Talent in Missouri." February 17. http://www.christianitytoday.com/ct/2006/107/53.0.html. Accessed on February 24, 2006).

Caplan, Arthur, M.D. (2005) "Dahlia Lathwick Indicts the Palm Sunday Compromise." http://blog.bioethics.net, March 22.

Cardetti, Jack (2006) Spokesman for the

Missouri Democratic Party. Telephone interview with Daniel Hillyard, February 9.

Carruthers, David (2006) "Don't Bet Against Online Gambling." *Los Angeles Times,* March 14.

Carter, Bill (2004) "Many Who Voted for 'Values' Still Like Their Television Sin." *New York Times,* November 22, A1.

Carter, Jimmy (1977) "Drug Abuse Message to the Congress." August 2.

Casanova, Jose (1994) *Public Religions in the Modern World.* Chicago: University of Chicago Press.

Casey, Doug (2005) "What We Now Know." howestreetresearch.com, November 8.

Castillo, David, III. (2006) "Stem cell issue on costly trek toward ballot." *Columbia Missourian,* April 26. http://columbia missourian.com/news/print.php?ID= 19599. Accessed on April 27, 2006.

Catholic Answers (2004) http://www .catholic.com, September 14.

Catholic Medical Association (2005) Brief Amicus Curiae of the Catholic Medical Association in Support of Petitioners and in Support of Reversal, *Gonzales v. Oregon,* in the Supreme Court of the United States, May 11.

Catholic News Service (2004) "Survey shows support for nonembryonic stem-cell research." http://www.catholic_ news.com, August 24.

Cato Institute (2005) Brief for the Cato Institute as Amicus Curiae in Support of Respondents, *Gonzales v. Oregon,* in the Supreme Court of the United States, July 18.

CBS (2006) Interview with stem cell researcher Dr. Hans Keirstad, *60 Minutes,* February 25.

CBS/AP (2005) "Bush Vows Stem Cell Veto." May 20.

CBS News (2001) "Stem Cell Support." June 27, http://www.cbsnews.com/ stories/200(1/06/27/tech/printable 298611.shtml. Accessed on July 27, 2001.

Center for American Progress (2006) "Voters Deeply Concerned about Rising Materialism and Self-Interest in American Society; Desire Government Focused on the Common Good and Basic Decency and Dignity of All." Memorandum, Washington, D.C.: Center for American Progress, http://www .americanprogress.org.

Center for Genetics and Society (2006) "New Directions for Stem Cell Research?" *Genetic Crossroads.* Oakland, Calif.: Center for Genetics and Society, November 15.

Center for Responsive Politics (2006) "Money in Politics: Casinos/Gambling: Long-Term Contribution Trends." Washington, D.C.: Center for Responsive Politics, http://www.opensecrets.org.

CHA (2005) "Response to Issues Relating to the Terri Schiavo Situation: Talking Points." Catholic Health Association of the United States. http://www.chausa .org, March 23.

Chapman, Steve (2005) "For Those Who Believe in the Sanctity of Life: Why Morning-After Pill Is Pro-life and Not Abortion in Disguise." *Chicago Tribune,* November 17.

Charo, R. Alta (2006) "Stemming the Tide: Politics, Policy and Regenerative Medicine." Sixteenth Annual Howard A. Schneiderman Memorial Bioethics Lecture, University of California, Irvine, October 3.

Charo, R. Alta (2007) "The Partial Death of Abortion Rights." *New England Journal of Medicine,* http://www.nejm .org, April 23.

Chauncey, George (2004) *Why Marriage? The History Shaping Today's Debate over Gay Equality.* New York: Basic Books.

Chaves, Mark (2004) *Congregations in America.* Cambridge, Mass.: Harvard University Press.

Chayes, Matthew (2006) "Stem Cell Issue Is Causing Headaches for GOP." *Chicago Tribune.* http://pqasb.pqarchiver .com/chicagotribune/access/996526941 .html. Accessed on March 4, 2006.

Chen, David W. (2006a) "New Jersey Lawmakers Pass Stem-Cell Bill." *New York Times,* December 14.

Chen, David W. (2006b) "Ruling on Same-Sex Marriage: New Jersey Court Backs Full Rights for Gay Couples." *New York Times,* October 26.

Christian Coalition (2005) "Christian Coalition Condemns Supreme Court's 10 Commandments Decision." Christian Coalition of America, http://www.cc .org, June 28. Christian Defense Coalition (2005) "White House Fails to Understand the Demoralizing Impact the Miers Nomination Has Had on Grassroots Activists around the Country— Many Feel Betrayed and Let Down by President Bush." Washington, D.C.: Christian Communication Network, October 25.

Christian Exodus (2005) "Welcome to the Christian Exodus." http://www.christian exodus.org. Accessed on August 31, 2005.

Christian Medical Association et al. (2005) Brief Amici Curiae of Christian Medical Association, American Association of Pro-Life Obstetricians and Gynecologists, Union of Orthodox Jewish Congregations of America, National Association of Evangelicals and Christian Legal Society in Support of Petitioner, *Gonzales v. Oregon,* in the Supreme Court of the United States, May 9.

Christianity Today (2001) "Two Cheers: President Bush's Stem-Cell Decision Is Better Than the Fatal Cure Many

Sought." August 10. http://www .christianitytoday.com/ct/2001/011/ 32.42.html. Accessed on March 12, 2005.

Christiansen Capital Advisors, LLC (1999) "The Gross Annual Wager of the United States, 1998." http://www.cca-i.com.

Christiansen Capital Advisors, LLC (2001) "The Gross Annual Wager of the United States, 2000: Waiting to Exhale." http://www.cca-i.com.

Cicerone, Ralph (2005) "Supporting Science by Communicating It." *InFocus,* Washington, D.C.: National Academies of Science, Vol. 5, No. 3, Fall.

Citizen Link (2005a) "Show-Me State Governor Vows to Fight for Pro-Life Issues." Colorado Springs: Focus on the Family, November 1.

Citizen Link (2005b) "South Korean Researcher Pays for Human Eggs." Colorado Springs: Focus on the Family, November 28.

Citizen Link (2006) "*USA Today Marriage-Protection Ads to Target Sens. McCain and Clinton.*" Colorado Springs: Focus on the Family, June 2.

Clift, Eleanor (2005) "Widening Rift: With Republicans Already Battling Each Other, Stem-Cell Research Threatens to Split the Party Further Apart." *Newsweek.com,* October 21.

Clinton, Hillary Rodham (1996) *It Takes a Village: And Other Lessons Children Teach Us.* New York: Simon and Schuster.

Clotfelter, Charles, and Philip Cook (1989) *Selling Hope: State Lotteries in America.* Cambridge, Mass.: Harvard University Press.

CNN (2001) "Bush to Allow Limited Stem Cell Funding." http://archives.cnn.com/ 2001/ALLPOLITICS/08/09/stem.cell.bus h/index.html. Accessed on September 1, 2001.

CNN (2004a) "California High Court

Voids Same-Sex Marriages." http://www.cnn.com, August 13.

CNN (2004b) News Report on Defense of Marriage Law Passing in Georgia, March 2.

CNN (2005a) Critics, Supporters Battle over Roberts. http://www.cnn.com, August 25.

CNN (2005b) "Priests Urge Stem Cell Opposition." November 28. http://www.cnn.com/2005/US/11/27/stemcell.sermons.ap/#. Accessed on November 30, 2005.

CNN Late Edition with Wolf Blitzer (2006) Interview with Bill Frist, May 14. http://www.cnn.com.

CNN/*USA Today* Gallup Poll (1996) "Should a Doctor Aid Suicide?"

Coalition for Stem Cell Research and Cures (2004a) "Fox 2." Television advertisement, aired October 20.

Coalition for Stem Cell Research and Cures (2004b) "Keith Black." Television advertisement, aired October 26.

Coalition for Stem Cell Research and Cures (2004c) "Nobel Interview" Television advertisement, aired October 20.

Coalition for the Advancement of Medical Research (2005) "Survey: More Americans Support Stem Cell Research, with Even Wider Backing Seen for Bipartisan Federal Bill, State Pushes." http://camradvocacy.org, February 15.

Cohen, Eric (2005) "Editorial: The Bioethics Agenda and the Bush Second Term." *New Atlantis: A Journal of Technology and Society*, no. 7 (Fall 2004/Winter 2005): 11–18.

Cohen, Peter (2001) Testimony before Canadian Senate. Proceedings of the Special Committee on Illegal Drugs, Issue 3—Evidence for May 28—Morning Session. Ottawa: Canadian Senate. http://www.cedro-uva.org/lib/cohen.senate.html. Accessed on December 15, 2006.

Colby, Bill (2005) "5 Minutes That Can Spare a Family Years of Pain." *USA Today.com*, March 7.

Collins, Peter (2006) "UK Gambling Law Reform: 1999 to the Present—An Overview." Address to the Thirteenth International Conference on Gambling and Risk Taking, Lake Tahoe, May 22–26.

Columbia Daily Tribune (2005) "Stem-Cell Research Is Pro-life, Danforth Says." *Columbia Daily Tribune*, November 19.

Commission on the Review of the National Policy toward Gambling (1976) Gambling in America. Final Report. Washington, D.C.: U.S. Government Printing Office.

Committee on Homosexual Offences and Prostitution (1957) *Report of the Committee on Homosexual Offences and Prostitution*. London: Her Majesty's Stationery Office.

Committee on the Social and Economic Impact of Pathological Gambling (1999) *Pathological Gambling: A Critical Review*. Committee on Law and Justice, National Research Council. Washington, D.C.: National Academy Press.

Condit, Celeste Michelle (1990) *Decoding Abortion Rhetoric: Communicating Social Change*. Champaign: University of Illinois Press.

Congregation for the Doctrine of the Faith (1986) "Letter to the Bishops of the Catholic Church on the Pastoral Care of Homosexual Persons." Rome, October 1.

Congregation for the Doctrine of the Faith (2003) "Considerations Regarding Proposals to Give Legal Recognition to Unions between Homosexual Persons." Rome, June 3.

Congressional Record (1998–2001) Washington, D.C.

Congressional Record (2007) Vol. 153, no. 58, April 11, 54368.

Conley, Dalton (2005) "A Man's Right to Choose." *New York Times,* December 1.

Connolly, Ceci, and Rick Weiss (2001) "Stem Cell Research Divides Administration; Thompson Expresses Optimism That a Compromise Will Be Reached Soon." *Washington Post,* June 12, A8.

Conrad, Peter, and Joseph Schneider (1992) *Deviance and Medicalization: From Badness to Sickness.* Philadelphia: Temple University Press.

Cook, Philip (1988) "An Introduction to Vice." *Law and Contemporary Problems* 51:1–8.

Coombs Lee, Barbara (2004) "Compassion President Gratified by Ruling but Wary of Future." http://www.compassionindying.org/news_breaking.php. Accessed on May 31, 2004.

Cooper, Marc (2001) "Fifth Lady Down: The Death of the Desert Inn. Is This the End of Vegas Cool?" *LA Weekly,* November 28.

Cooper, Marc (2004) *The Last Honest Place in America: Paradise and Perdition in the New Las Vegas.* New York: Nation Books.

Cooperman, Alan (2004) "Liberal Christians Challenge 'Values Vote.'" *Washington Post,* November 10, A7.

Cooperman, Alan (2006) "The House's Catholic Democrats Detail Role Religion Plays." *Washington Post,* washingtonpost.com, March 1.

Corn, David (2005) "Democrats Split on Roberts Nomination." http://www.thenation.com, September 21.

Coulter, Ann (2005a) Comments of guest on *Real Time with Bill Maher,* October 7.

Coulter, Ann (2005b) *How to Talk to a Liberal (If You Must).* Updated edition. New York: Three Rivers Press, 2005.

Coulter, Ann (2005c) "Where's That Religious Fanatic We Elected?" In Coulter, 2005b.

Coulter, Ann (2006) "Speaking Truth to Dead Horses: My Oscar Predictions." http://www.frontpagemag.com, March 2.

Craig, Barbara Hinkson, and David M. O'Brien (1993) *Abortion and American Politics.* Chatham, N.J.: Chatham House.

Crary, David (2006a) "Losses on Ballot Measures Jolt Religious." Associated Press, November 8.

Crary, David (2006b) "Rejected Measures: Arizona Gay Marriage Ban, South Dakota Abortion Ban." Canadian Press, canada.com, November 8.

Crowley, Candy (2006) cnn.com, November 7.

Crystal, Billy (2005) *700 Sundays.* New York: Warner Books.

Crystal, Billy (2006) *700 Sundays.* Performance at Wilshire Theatre, Los Angeles, January.

Currie, Elliott (1998) *Crime and Punishment in America.* New York: Henry Holt.

Dahlburg, John-Thor (2005) "Ballot Offers a Vegas Vice for Miami." *Los Angeles Times,* March 8, A10.

Danforth, John C. (2005) "In the Name of Politics." *New York Times,* March 30. http://www.nytimes.com/2005/03/30/opinion/30danforth.html. Accessed on May 28, 2006.

Danforth, John (2006) *Faith and Politics: How the "Moral Values" Debate Divides America and How to Move Forward Together.* New York: Viking.

Danner, Mark (2005) "How Bush Really Won." *New York Review of Books,* January 13.

Dao, James (2004) "Two States Trying to Keep Gambling at Home." *New York Times,* March 22.

Darian-Smith, Eve (2005) "Paris, Diamonds, and Champagne: Casinos on Reservations and the New 'Rich Indian' Identity." Paper presented at the Meeting of the Law and Society Association, Las Vegas, June.

Darwin, Charles (1859/1995) *The Origin of Species.* New York: Gramercy.

Davey, Monica (2006a) "Sizing Up the Opposing Armies in the Coming Abortion Battle." *New York Times,* February 26, sec. 4, p. 3.

Davey, Monica (2006b) "The 2006 Elections: Ballot Measures; South Dakotans Reject Sweeping Abortion Ban." *New York Times,* November 8.

Davey, Monica (2006c) "The 2006 Elections: Voter Initiatives; Liberals Find Rays of Hope on Ballot Measures." *New York Times,* November 9.

Davis, Mathew (2001a) "Coalition for the Advancement of Medical Research Formed to Press the Case for Federal Support of Embryonic Stem Cell Research." *Washington Fax,* March 26. http://www.washingtonfax.com/p1/frarchive.html. Accessed on May 14, 2005.

Davis, Matthew (2001b) "High Profile Republicans Show Support for Embryonic Stem Cell Research." *Washington Fax,* June 25. http://www.washingtonfax.com/p1/frarchive.html. Accessed on May 14, 2005.

Deignan, Paul (2005) "Birds of a Feather." info-theory.blogspot.com, October 19. Accessed on October 11, 2005.

D'Emilio, John (2000) "Cycles of Change, Questions of Strategy: The Gay and Lesbian Movement after Fifty Years." In Craig Rimmerman et al., eds., *The Politics of Gay Rights.* Chicago: University of Chicago Press.

Democracy Corps (2006) Public Poll Analysis, January 20.

Devitt, Terry (1998) "Wisconsin Scientists Culture Elusive Embryonic Stem Cells."

http://www.news.wisc.edu/packages/stemcells/3327.html. Accessed on March 20, 2005.

Devlin, Patrick (1965) *The Enforcement of Morals.* London: Oxford University Press.

DiCamillo, Mark, and Mervin Field (2005) "By a Large Margin Californians Still Support the Concept of Doctor-Assisted Suicide." The Field Poll, March 2.

DiCamillo, Mark, and Mervin Field (2006a) "Continued Support for Doctor-Assisted Suicide." The Field Poll. Release no. 2188. March 15.

DiCamillo, Mark, and Mervin Field (2006b) "Two-Thirds of Californians Remain Pro-Choice." San Francisco: The Field Poll, Release no. 2187, March 14.

DiChiara, Albert, and John F. Galliher (1994) "Dissonance and Contradictions in the Origins of Marihuana Decriminalization." *Law and Society Review* 28, no. 41.

Dickerson, John (2005) "Gods vs. Geeks: GOP Evangelicals Fight Intellectuals over Harriet Miers." Slate.com, October 5.

DiIulio, John (2006) "The Catholic Voter: A Description with Recommendations." *Commonweal,* March 24. http://www.commonwealmagazine.org.

Dionne, E. J., Jr. (2004) Panel Discussion, "How the Faithful Voted: Political Alignments and the Religious Divide in Election 2004." Washington, D.C.: Pew Forum on Religion and Public Life and the Brookings Institution, November 17.

Dionne, E. J., Jr. (2006a) "Busting This Year's Election Myths." *Washington Post,* November 14.

Dionne, E. J., Jr. (2006b) "2006: A Hinge Year." realclearpolitics.com, December 19.

Dionne, E. J., Jr. (2006c) "Why the Culture War Is the Wrong War." *Atlantic Monthly,* January/February.

Dobson, James (1999) "Going for Broke." Dr. Dobson's Newsletter, Focus on the Family, http://www.family.org, July.

Dobson, James (2005) "Religious Values under Attack in the Courts." Focus on the Family Action, June 28.

Dobson, James (2006) Letter, Colorado Springs: Focus on the Family Action, May 16.

"Doctor-Assisted Suicides Up Slightly under Law" (2004) *Los Angeles Times,* March 11, A13.

Doerflinger, Richard M. (1999) Testimony of Richard M. Doerflinger on behalf of the National Conference of Catholic Bishops in support of H.R. 2260, the Pain Relief Promotion Act of 1999. United States House of Representatives, House Judiciary Subcommittee on the Constitution.

Dolan, Maura, and Lee Romney (2004a) "High Court Halts Gay Marriages." *Los Angeles Times,* March 12, A1.

Dolan, Maura, and Lee Romney (2004b) "S.F. Wedding Planners Are Pursuing a Legal Strategy." Los Angeles Times, February 22.

Dombrink, John (1990) "Gambling's Status among the Vices, 1990—A Comparative View." Paper presented at the Eighth International Conference in Risk and Gambling. London, August 15–17.

Dombrink, John (2005a) "Red, Blue, and Purple: American Views on Personal Morality and the Law." *Dissent,* Spring, 87–92.

Dombrink, John (2005b) "Terri Schiavo and the 'Purple' Public." *Orange County Register,* April 5.

Dombrink, John (2006) "Deepening Reds, Contrasting Blues, and Various Purples." Review essay in "A Symposium on Morality Battles." *Contemporary Sociology,* June.

Dombrink, John, and William N. Thompson (1990) *The Last Resort: Success and Failure in Campaigns for Casinos.* Reno: University of Nevada Press.

Dominus, Susan (2005) "The Mysterious Disappearance of Young Pro-choice Women." *Glamour,* August, 200–219.

Donahue, John D. (1997) *Disunited States: What's at Stake as Washington Fades and the States Take the Lead.* New York: Basic Books.

Downs, David Alexander (1989) *The New Politics of Pornography.* Chicago: University of Chicago Press.

Drazen, Jeffrey M. (2007) "Government in Medicine." Editorial, *New England Journal of Medicine.* http://www.nejm.org, April 23.

Duberman, Martin (1991) *Cures: A Gay Man's Odyssey.* New York: Dutton.

Duffner, Paul A., O.P. (1993) "Cafeteria Catholics." *Rosary Light and Life,* July–August.

Duke, Annie (2005) *How I Raised, Folded, Bluffed, Flirted, Cursed and Won Millions at the World Series of Poker.* New York: Hudson Street Press.

Dworkin, Ronald (1996) "Sex, Death and the Court." *New York Review of Books,* August 8, 44–50.

Eadington, William R (1990) *Indian Gaming and the Law.* Reno: University of Nevada Press.

Eadington, William R (2003a) "Values and Choices: The Struggle to Find Balance with Permitted Gambling in Modern Society." In Gerda Reith, ed., *Gambling: Who Wins? Who Loses?* Amherst, N.Y.: Prometheus Books.

Eadington, William R. (2003b) "Where Commercial Gambling Will Take Us in the Future." Luncheon speaker, Twelfth International Conference on Gambling and Risk Taking. Vancouver, May.

Eadington, William R. (2005) "Current Trends in Gambling Industries Worldwide." http://www.unr.edu/gaming, September 15.

Eadington, William R. (2006) "Ten Challenges: Issues That Are Shaping the Future of Gambling and Commercial Gaming." Address to the Thirteenth International Conference on Gambling and Risk Taking, Lake Tahoe, Nevada, May 23.

Earley, Pete (2000) *Inside the "New" Las Vegas.* New York: Bantam.

Eaton, Leslie (2006) "Tax Revenues Are a Windfall for Louisiana." *New York Times,* June 26.

Edelman, Murray (1985) *The Symbolic Uses of Politics.* Champaign: University of Illinois Press.

Ehrenhalt, Alan (2005) "A Tent Divided." *New York Times,* November 13.

Elster, Peter, Lork Halman and Rund de Moor (1993) *The Individualizing Society: Value Change in Europe and North America.* Tilburg, the Netherlands: Tilburg University Press.

Emmanuel, Ezekiel J., Diane Fairclough, Brian C. Clarridge, Diane Blum, Eduardo Bruera, Charles Penley, Lowell E. Schnipper, and Robert J. Mayer (2000) "Attitudes and Practices of U.S. Oncologists Regarding Euthanasia and Physician-Assisted Suicide." *Annals of Internal Medicine* 133:527–532.

Engel, Mary (2006) "Reality Check for Stem Cell Optimism." *Los Angeles Times,* December 3.

Espo, David (2006) "Obama: Democrats Must Court Evangelicals." *Sacramento Bee,* June 28.

Faces (1994) Television advertisement for Measure 16, Oregon Death with Dignity.

Fagan, Amy (2005) "Congress OKs Schiavo Bill." Washington Times, March 21.

Fahrenkopf, Frank (2005) "A Fine State of Affairs." *Global Gaming Business* 4, no. 4 (May 1): 14.

Family Research Council (2005) Statement of Director Tony Perkins, July 29. http://www.frc.org

Farmer, Ronald L. (2005) "Homosexuality and the Bible: A Study of Relevant Texts as Part of the Open and Affirming Process." Chapman University, Orange, California. Notes prepared for Neighborhood Congregational Church, Laguna Beach, California, October.

Farrell, Mark G. (2006) Address to the Thirteenth International Conference on Gambling and Risk Taking, Lake Tahoe, Nevada, May 24.

FDA (2006) "FDA Licenses Quadrivalent Human Papillomavirus (Types 6, 11, 16, 18) Recombinant Vaccine (Gardasil) for the Prevention of Cervical Cancer and Other Diseases in Females Caused by Human Papillomavirus." Washington, D.C.: Office of Oncology Drug Products, July 20.

FDA News (2006) "FDA Approves Over-the-Counter Access for Plan B for Women 18 and Older; Prescription Remains Required for Those 17 and Under." Press release. Washington, D.C.: U.S. Food and Drug Administration, August 24.

Feinberg, Joel (1988) *The Moral Limits of the Criminal Law.* Vol. 4, *Harmless Wrongdoing.* New York: Oxford University Press.

Feldman, Alan (2006) Luncheon address to the Thirteenth International Conference on Gambling and Risk Taking, Lake Tahoe, Nevada.

Feldman, Noah (2005) *Divided by God: America's Church-State Problem—and What We Should Do about It.* New York: Farrar, Straus and Giroux.

Feldt, Gloria (2004) *The War on Choice: The Right-Wing Attack on Women's Rights and How to Fight Back.* New York: Bantam.

Ferrari, Michelle, with Stephen Ives (2005)

Las Vegas: An Unconventional History.
New York: Bulfinch Press.

Feuerhard, Joe (2004) "Democrats and
the Politics of Abortion." http://www
.nationalcatholicreporter.com.

Fineman, Howard (2006a) "Evangelicals
Fed Up with GOP?" *Newsweek,*
msnbc.com, October 16.

Fineman, Howard (2006b) "Rove's
Revamp." *Newsweek,* May 10.

Fiorina, Morris P., with Samuel J. Abrams
and Jeremy C. Pope (2006) *Culture
War? The Myth of a Polarized America.*
2nd ed. New York: PearsonLongman.

Fischer, Claude S., and Michael Hout
(2006) "How Americans Prayed: Religious Diversity and Change." In *Century of Difference: How America
Changed in the Last Hundred Years.*
New York: Russell Sage Foundation.

Fisher, Ian (2005) "What Wasn't Said Is
Focus as Italy Debates Gay Rights."
New York Times, September 18.

Fitcher, Pam (2006) President of Missouri
Right to Life. Telephone interview with
Daniel Hillyard, February 6.

FitzGerald, Frances (1986) *Cities on a
Hill: A Journey through Contemporary
American Cultures.* New York: Simon
and Schuster.

Fletcher, John C. (1999) "Deliberating
Incrementally on Pluripotential Stem
Cell Research." http://www.georgetown
.edu/research/nrcbl/nbac/briefings/
may99/fletcher.pdf. Accessed on March
15, 2004.

Flory, Josh (2005) "The Burke Factor."
January 30. http://www.showmenews
.com/2005/Jan/20050130Pers001.asp.
Accessed on November 27, 2005.

Flynnfile.com (2006) January 17.

Focus on the Family (2004) "Position
Statement on Human Embryonic Stem
Cell Research." A Focus on the Family
Position Statement, December 10.

Focus on the Family (2005a) "Stem Cell

Research." http://www.family.org/
socialissues.

Focus on the Family (2005b) "What the
Media Won't Tell You about Stem Cell
Research." Colorado Springs: Focus
on the Family, http://www.family.org,
July 12.

Focus on the Family (2006) "Greetings
from Colorado Springs." January 16.

Foreman, Matt (2003) "A Future of Promise and Peril." *Advocate,* July 29.

Foust, Michael (2006) "Supreme Court
Ruling Gives Boost to Doctor-Assisted
Suicide." *Baptist Press News.* http://
www.baptistpress.org/bpnews.asp?
ID=22462. Accessed on January 17,
2006.

Fox, Sam (2006) St. Louis businessman
and influential GOP contributor. In-
person comments to Daniel Hillyard.
Kansas City, Missouri, February 4.

Fox News Sunday (2006) "Senate Majority Leader Frist on 'FNS.'" http://www
.foxnews.com. May 28.

Francis, David R. (2006) "Gambling:
Where the Money Goes." *Christian
Science Monitor,* June 19.

Franck, Matt (2006) "Stem Cell Proponents Claim Razor-Thin Victory."
St. Louis Post-Dispatch, November 8.

Frank, Thomas (2004a) "American
Psyche." *New York Times Book Review,*
November 28, 21–22.

Frank, Thomas (2004b) "What's the
Matter with Kansas?" Speech, Decem-
ber 6, Washington, D.C., broadcast on
CSPAN.

Frank, Thomas (2004c) *What's the Matter
with Kansas? How Conservatives Won
the Heart of America.* New York: Henry
Holt.

Frank, Thomas (2004d) "Why They
Won." *New York Times,* November 5.

Frank, Thomas (2005a) Speech, University
of California, Irvine.

Frank, Thomas (2005b) "What's the

Matter with Liberals?" *New York Review of Books,* May 12.

Franke-Ruta, Garance (2005) "Liberal Concerns about Abortion: Multiple Choice." *New Republic,* November 25.

Frey, James H. (1992) "Gambling on Sport: Policy Issues." *Journal of Gambling Studies* 8 (4): 351–360.

Fromson, Brett Duval (2003) *Hitting the Jackpot: The Inside Story of the Richest Indian Tribe in History.* New York: Atlantic Monthly Press.

Fund, John (2005) "Judgment Call: Did Christian Conservatives Receive Assurances That Miers Would Oppose *Roe v. Wade?" Wall Street Journal,* October 17.

Gallagher, John, and Chris Bull (1996) *Perfect Enemies: The Religious Right, the Gay Movement and the Politics of the 1990s.* New York; Random House.

Gallup Poll (2006a) "Homosexual Relations." Gallup's Pulse of Democracy, Gallup Poll, May 31. http://www.gallup.com.

Gallup Poll (2006b) Values and beliefs survey, May 8–11. http://www.gallup.com.

Galston, William (2006) "De-alignment." *Democratic Strategist,* December 4.

Galston, William A., and Elaine C. Kamarck (2005) "The Politics of Polarization." Washington, D.C.: The Third Way Middle Class Project, October.

GAO (2005) "Food and Drug Administration: Decision Process to Deny Initial Application for Over-the-Counter Marketing of the Emergency Contraceptive Drug Plan B Was Unusual." U.S. Government Accountability Office, GAO-06-109, November 14.

Garafoli, Joe (2005) "Falwell Fighting for Holy Holiday: He Threatens to Sue, Boycott Groups That Subvert Christmas." *San Francisco Chronicle,* November 20.

Garrow, David J. (1994) *Liberty and Sexuality: The Right to Privacy and the Making of Roe v. Wade.* New York: Macmillan.

Garrow, David J. (2007) "Don't Assume the Worst." *New York Times,* April 21.

Garvey, Megan (2004) "California Stem Cell Project Energizes Other States to Act." *Los Angeles Times,* November 22.

Gaylin, Willard (1972) "The Frankenstein Myth Becomes Reality—We Have the Awful Knowledge to Make Exact Copies of Human Beings." *New York Times Magazine,* March 5.

Geis, Gilbert (1979) *Not the Law's Business: An Examination of Homosexuality, Abortion, Prostitution, Narcotics, and Gambling in the United States.* New York: Schocken Books.

Gelman, Andrew, Boris Shor, Joseph Bafumi, and David Park (2005) "Rich State, Poor State, Red State, Blue State: What the Matter with Connecticut?" Unpublished paper, Department of Statistics and Department of Political Science, Columbia University.

Gibson, John (2005) *The War on Christmas: How the Liberal Plot to Ban the Sacred Christian Holiday Is Worse Than You Thought.* New York: Penguin.

Gillespie, Kelly (2006) Executive director of the Missouri Biotechnology Association. In-person comments to Daniel Hillyard. Kansas City, Missouri. February 4.

Gilmore, Susan, and Jim Simon (1991) "Death, Abortion, and Catholics— Church's Political Thrust Debated." *Seattle Times,* November 10, B1.

Gingrich, Newt (2005) "Conservatives Can Trust in Miers." *Baltimore Sun,* October 7.

Ginsburg, Faye (1993) "Saving America's Souls: Operation Rescue's Crusade against Abortion." In Martin E. Marty and R. Scott Appleby, eds., *Fundamentalisms and the State: Remaking Polities,*

Economies, and Militance. Chicago: University of Chicago Press.

Girvan, Paul, and Tom Zitt (2002) "Winners and Losers: Election 2002 Fallout for the U.S. Gaming Industry." *Global Gaming Business*, December 1, 24–28.

Gitlin, Todd (2005) "A Gathering Swarm." *Mother Jones*, January/February, 37–39, 74+.

Glaeser, Edward L., Giacomo A. M. Ponzetto, and Jesse M. Shapiro (2004) "Strategic Extremism: Why Republicans and Democrats Divide on Religious Values." Cambridge, Mass.: Harvard Institute of Economic Research, Harvard University, Discussion paper 2044, October.

Glick, Henry R. (1992) *The Right to Die: Policy Innovation and Its Consequences.* New York: Columbia University Press.

Goffman, Erving (1963) *Stigma: Notes on the Management of Spoiled Identity.* Englewood Cliffs, N.J.: Prentice-Hall.

Goldberg, Jeffrey (2006) "Central Casting." *New Yorker*, May 29, 62–71.

Goldberg-Hiller, Jonathan (2002) *The Limits to Union: Same-Sex Marriage and the Politics of Civil Rights.* Ann Arbor: University of Michigan Press.

Goldschein, Sondra (2006) "South Dakota Abortion Ban Defeated!!" http://blog .aclu.org, November 8.

Goldstein, Amy, and Mike Allen (2001) "Bush Backs Partial Stem Cell Funding." *Washington Post,* August 10.

Goldstein, Amy, and Charles Babington (2006) "Alito Leaves Door Open to Reversing 'Roe.'" *Washington Post,* January 12, A1.

Golway, Terry (2004) "Racino: Get to Know the Word." *New York Times,* August 5.

Goodman, Robert (1995) *The Luck Business: The Devastating Consequences and Broken Promises of America's Gambling Explosion.* New York: Free Press.

Goodstein, Laurie (2001) "Abortion Foes Split over Bush's Plan on Stem Cells." *New York Times.* http://query.nytimes .com/gst/fullpage.html?sec=health&res= 990CE7D7103FF931A2575BC0A9679 C8B63. Accessed on March 13, 2005.

Goodstein, Laurie (2005) "Schiavo Case Highlights Catholic-Evangelical Alliance." *New York Times,* March 24.

Goodstein, Laurie (2006) "Episcopalians Shaken by Division in Church." *New York Times,* July 2.

Gordon, Daniel (2003) "Moralism, the Fear of Social Chaos: The Dissent in *Lawrence* and the Antidotes of *Vermont* and *Brown.*" *Texas Journal on Civil Liberties and Civil Rights* 9 (Winter).

Gorney, Cynthia (2004) "Gambling with Abortion: Why Both Sides Think They Have Everything to Lose." *Harper's,* November, 33–46.

Gorney, Cynthia (2006) "Reversing *Roe.*" *New Yorker,* June 26, 46–53.

Gorney, Cynthia, and Ben Greenman (2006) "A Choice in South Dakota." *New Yorker Online,* http://www.newyorker.com, June 19.

Graff, E. J. (2006) "Marital Blitz." *American Prospect* 17, no. 3. http://www .prospect.org, May 10.

Gray, James P. (2001) *Why Our War on Drugs Has Failed and What We Can Do about It: A Judicial Indictment.* Philadelphia: Temple University Press.

Green, John C. (2004) "The American Religious Landscape and Political Attitudes: A Baseline for 2004." Pew Charitable Trusts, September 10.

Green, John, Corwin Schmidt, and Lyman A. Kellstedt (2005) "The American Religious Landscape and the 2004 Presidential Vote: Increased Polarization." Pew Forum on Religion and Public Life, February 3.

Greenberg, David F. (1988) *The Construction of Homosexuality.* Chicago: University of Chicago Press.

Greenberg, Stan, and Bob Borosage (2004) "Re: What Mandate? A Report on the Joint National Post-election Survey." Memo, Washington, D.C.: Democracy Corps, November 11.

Greenberg, Stan, and James Carville (2006) "Getting Heard: Points of Engagement for a Change Election." Washington, D.C.: Democracy Corps, July 28.

Greenberg, Stan, and Matt Hogan (2005) "Reclaiming the White Catholic Vote." Memo, Washington, D.C. Democracy Corps, March 29.

Greenberg, Stan, and Matt Hogan (2006) "Cracks in the Two Americas: Republican Loyalists and Swing Blocs Move toward the Democrats." Memo, Washington, D.C.: Democracy Corps, March 3.

Greenberg Quinlan Rosner Research (2006) "America's New Direction: Democracy Corps and Campaign for America's Future Post-Election Poll." Washington, D.C.: Greenberg Quinlan Rosner Research, November 13.

Greenfield, Jeff (2004) Panel discussion, "Values, Religion, Politics and the Media." Harvard University, John F. Kennedy School of Government, November 15.

Greenfield, Jeff (2006) "Greenfield: What to Watch for—Hour by Hour." cnn.com, November 7.

Greenhouse, Linda (2003) "Supreme Court Paved Way for Marriage Ruling with Sodomy Law Decision." *New York Times,* November 19.

Greenhouse, Linda (2006a) "Justices Hear Arguments on Late-Term Abortion." *New York Times,* November 9.

Greenhouse, Linda (2006b) "Roberts Is at Court's Helm, But He Isn't Yet in Con-

trol." *New York Times,* July 2, sec. 1, p. 1.

Griffiths, John, Heleen Weyers, and Alex Bood (1998) *Euthanasia and Law in the Netherlands.* Amsterdam and Ann Arbor: Amsterdam University Press and University of Michigan Press.

Grinols, Earl L., and David B. Mustard (2006) "Casinos, Crime, and Community Costs." *Review of Economics and Statistics* 88 (1): 28–45.

Gros, Roger (2005) "Editor's Letter: A Pause for Poker." *PokerBiz,* Spring, 4.

Gusfield, Joseph R. (1972) *Symbolic Crusade: Status Politics and the American Temperance Movement.* Chicago: University of Illinois Press.

Guth, James L., John C. Green, Corwin E. Smidt, and Margaret M. Poloma (1991) "Pulpits and Politics: The Protestant Clergy in the 1988 Presidential Election." In James L. Guth and John C. Green, eds., *The Bible and the Ballot Box: Religion and Politics in the 1988 Election.* Boulder, Colo.: Westview Press.

Guthrie, Stan (2005) "Q & A: Nigel M. de S. Cameron." *Christianity Today,* October.

Hacker, Jacob S., and Paul Pierson (2005) *Off Center: The Republican Revolution and the Erosion of American Democracy.* New Haven, Conn.: Yale University Press.

Hadaway, C. Kirk, Penny Long Marler, and Mark Chaves (1993) "What the Polls Don't Show: A Closer Look at Church Attendance." *American Sociological Review* 58:741–752.

Hagerty, Barbara Bradley (2006) Marriage Plays Starring Role in Politics . . . Again." NPR Morning Edition, February 15.

Hagerty, Margaret (2005) "Schiavo Case Is Grayest of Gray Areas." NPR, March 25.

Haley, Shirley (2001) "Over 100 University Presidents Join Higher Education Associations in Letter Supporting NIH-Funded Embryonic Stem Cell Research." March 27. *Washington Fax,* March 26. http://www.wasgingtonfax.com/p1/frarchive.html. Accessed on May 14, 2005.

Halpin, John (2006) "Election Results a Victory for Progressive Movement: Bush Rove Policy Dealt a Blow." www.abcnews.com, November 8.

Hananel, Sam (2006) "Stem-Cell Research Divides GOP in Missouri." *Sacramento Bee,* www.sacbee.com, February 6.

Hardball (2004) *Hardball with Chris Matthews.* MSNBC, December 2.

Hardball (2006) *Hardball with Chris Matthews.* MSNBC, June 7.

Harris, Gardiner (2006) "F.D.A. Approves Broader Access to Next-Day Pill." *New York Times,* August 25.

Hatch, Orrin G. (2001) Letter to the President of the United States. http://www.stemcellfunding.org/fastaction/presletter1.asp. Accessed on July 27, 2005.

Hatch, Orrin G. (2005) "Hatch Introduces Human Cloning Ban, Stem Cell Research Act." Web site of United States Senator Orrin Hatch (R-Utah), http://hatch.senate.gov, April 21. Accessed on July 1, 2006.

Hausknecht, Bruce (2006) "Watch the Guy on the Left." *Citizen,* March.

Healthlaw Professors (2005) Brief of Amici Curiae Healthlaw Professors in Support of Respondents for Affirmance of the Court and Opinion Below, Gonzales v. *Oregon,* in the Supreme Court of the United States, June 10.

Hebblethwaite, Peter, Margaret Hebblethwaite, and Peter Stanford (2005) "Pope John Paul II." *Guardian Weekly,* April 8–14, 17–18.

Heielemann, John (2006) "Show Me Purple." *New York,* November 6, http://nymag.com/news/politics/powergrid/23782/index.html.

Henderson Blunt, Sheryl (2001) "Embryos Split Prolifers." *Christianity Today.* http://www.christianitytoday.com/global/printer.html?/ct/2001/011/15.23.html. Accessed on March 12, 2005.

Hentoff, Nat (2005) " 'Judicial Murder' and Terri Schiavo." *Washington Times,* July 11.

Herper, Matthew, and Aude Lagorce (2004) "The Best Places to Die." *Forbes,* forbes.com, August 18.

Hills, Chad (2003) *The National Gambling Impact Study Commission (NGISC) Report.* Citizen Link: Focus on Social Issues. Colorado Springs: Focus on the Family, November 26.

Hillyard, Daniel, and John Dombrink (2001) *Dying Right: The Death with Dignity Movement.* New York: Routledge.

Hillygus, D. Sunshine, and Todd G. Shields (2005) "Moral Issues and Voter Decision Making in the 2004 Elections." *PS: Political Science and Politics* 38:201–210.

Hirshman, Linda R. (2005) "America's Stay-at-Home Feminists." *American Prospect,* November 24.

Hook, Janet (2005) "Some in GOP Fear Effort May Alienate Voters." *Los Angeles Times,* March 22, A12.

Hook, Janet (2006) "A Restive Base Throws the GOP Off Balance." *Los Angeles Times,* May 22, A1.

Hope Along the Wind (2001) *Hope Along the Wind: The Life of Harry Hay.* Eric Slade, producer and director.

Horowitz, Jason (2005) "Pope Denounces Gay Marriage." *New York Times,* January 11.

Hubler, Shawn (2004) "Hotels Are Hoping to Capitalize on a Gay

Marriage Boom." *Los Angeles Times,* March 28, C1.

Hudson, Kathy L., Joan Scott, and Ruth Faden (2005) "Values in Conflict: Public Attitudes on Embryonic Stem Cell Research." Genetics and Public Policy Center, Johns Hopkins University, October.

huffingtonpost.com (2006) http://www.huffingtonpost.com, June 4.

Hulse, Carl (2005) "The Medical Turns Political." *New York Times.* March 19, A1.

Human Rights Campaign (2006) "New Polling Shows Opposition to Congress' Focus on Federal Marriage Amendment." May 9. http://www.hrc.org.

Hunter, James Davison (1991) *Culture Wars: The Struggle to Define America.* New York: Basic Books.

Huxley, Aldous (1932) *Brave New World.* New York: HarperCollins.

Hwang, Woo Suk, et al. (2004) "Evidence of a Pluripotent Human Embryonic Stem Cell Line Derived from a Cloned Blastocyst." *Science* 303:169–174.

Inskeep, Steve (2006) "Religion, Politics a Potent Mix for Jerry Falwell." National Public Radio, http://www.npr.org, June 29.

International Society for Stem Cell Research (2004) "International Society for Stem Cell Research Supports California Proposition 71." Press release, August 25.

International Society for Stem Cell Research (2005) "The International Society for Stem Cell Research Salutes Members of Congress for Passing Bill H.R. 810." Press release, May 27.

International Task Force on Euthanasia and Assisted Suicide (2005) Brief Amicus Curiae of the International Task Force on Euthanasia and Assisted Suicide in Support of Petitioners, *Gonzales*

v. Oregon, in the Supreme Court of the United States, May 9.

Ireland, Doug (2005) "In Our Misery: The Right to Die Faces a Big Test in Congress." *LA Weekly,* April 8–14.

Jackson, Henry C. (2006) "Family Group Says Iowa Lawmakers Trying to Quash Gay Marriage Debate, Vote." WCFcourier.com, March 17.

Jacoby, Susan (2005) "Reason before Religion." In Jim Wallis and Susan Jacoby, "With God on Our Side?" *American Prospect,* August 1.

Jenkins, Philip (2006) *Decade of Nightmares: The End of the Sixties and the Making of Eighties America.* New York: Oxford University Press.

Jenness, Valerie (1993) *Making It Work: The Prostitutes' Rights Movement in Perspective.* New York: Aldine De Gruyter.

Jenness, Valerie (2004) "Explaining Criminalization: From Demography and Status Politics to Globalization and Modernization." *Annual Review of Sociology* 30:147–171.

Jenness, Valerie, David S. Meyer, and Helen Ingram (2005) "Social Movements: Public Policy, and Democracy: Rethinking the Nexus." In David S. Meyer, Valerie Jenness, and Helen Ingram, eds., *Routing the Opposition: Social Movements, Public Policy and Democracy.* Minneapolis: University of Minnesota Press.

Joffe, Carole (2005) "It's Not Just the Abortion, Stupid." *Dissent,* Winter.

John Paul II (1998) "Bishops Must Stand Firmly on the Side of Life, against the Culture of Death—Encouraging Those Who Defend It." *Ad limina* address of the Pope John Paul II to U.S. Bishops of California, Nevada, and Hawaii, October 2. http://www.wf-f.org/JPII-Bishops-Life-Issues.html. Accessed on January 14, 2006.

John Paul II (2004) "Address of John Paul II to the Participants in the International Congress on Life-Sustaining Treatments and Vegetative State: Scientific Advances and Ethical Dilemmas." March 20. http://www.vatican.va/holy_father/john_paul_ii/speeches/2004/march/.

Johnson, Kirk (2006) "The 2006 Campaign; Gay Marriage Losing Punch as Ballot Issue." *New York Times,* October 14.

Jones, Jeffrey M. (2004) "Gambling a Common Activity for Americans." Gallup National Report. March 24.

Jones, Jeffrey M. (2005) "Most Americans Engaged in Debate about Evolution, Creation." Gallup Poll, October 13.

Jones, Jeffrey M. (2006) "Americans Divided on Whether Federal Government Should Promote Moral Values." Gallup Poll, June 22.

Jones, Susan (2005a) "Abortion Activists Turn Thumbs Down." http://www.cnsnews.com, July 20.

Jones, Susan (2005b) "Vatican Bans Most Homosexuals from Catholic Seminaries." cnsnews.com.

Jurist (2006) "South Dakota Abortion Ban Going on November Ballot." *Jurist Legal News and Research,* http://www.jurist.law.pitt.edu, June 19.

Kadish, Sanford (1967) "The Crisis of Overcriminalization." *Annals of the American Academy of Political and Social Science,* no. 374:157–170.

Kalb, Claudia, and Debra Rosenberg (2004) "Nancy's Next Campaign." *Newsweek,* June 14.

Kalb, Marvin (2004) Panel discussion, "Values, Religion, Politics and the Media." Harvard University, John F. Kennedy School of Government, November 15.

Kang, K. Connie (2006) "Episcopal Leader Calls for Move Past Gay Debate." *Los Angeles Times,* June 20, A5.

Kaplan, Esther (2005) *With God on Their Side: George W. Bush and the Christian Right.* New York: New Press.

Kaufman, Marc (2006) "Plan B Battles Embroil States: Proposals Mirror Red-Blue Divide." *Washington Post,* February 27, A1.

Kazin, Michael (2005) "Life of the Party." *Mother Jones,* January/February, 37–39, 74+.

Kearney, Melissa Schettini (2005) "The Economic Winners and Losers of Legalized Gambling." Working paper. Washington, D.C.: Brookings Institution, February.

Keen, Judy (2001) "Reading, Reflection Brought Bush to Decision." *USA Today,* August 10. http://www.usatoday.com/news/washington/august01/2001-08-10-bush-stem-reading.htm. Accessed on May 14, 2005.

Keen, Lisa, and Suzanne B. Goldberg (1998) *Strangers to the Law: Gay People on Trial.* Ann Arbor: University of Michigan Press.

Keeter, Scott (2006a) "Politics and the 'DotNet' Generation." Washington, D.C.: Pew Research Center for the People and the Press, May 30.

Keeter, Scott (2006b) "Will White Evangelicals Desert the GOP?" Washington, D.C.: Pew Research Center, May 2.

Kelley, Tina (2006) "Gay Episcopal Priest Named as Possible Newark Bishop." *New York Times,* June 29.

Kellman, Laurie (2006a) "Bush Rallies Gay Marriage Opponents." abcnews.com, June 5.

Kellman, Laurie (2006b) "Sen. Bill Frist Revives Stem Cell Bill." Associated Press, June 29.

Kessler, E. J. (2006) "Stem-Cell Issue Viewed as Pitfall for Republicans." *Forward,* February 17.

Kessler, Jim (2005) "The Demographics of Abortion: The Great Divide between Abortion Rhetoric and Abortion Reality." The Third Way Culture Project. Washington, D.C.: Third Way, August 30.

Kessler, Jim, and Jessica Dillon (2005) "Who Is Winning the Abortion Grays?" The Third Way Culture Project. Washington, D.C.: Third Way, August.

Kingdon, John W. (1995) *Agendas, Alternatives and Public Policies.* 2nd ed. New York: HarperCollins College Publishers.

Kinsley, Michael (2003) "Bill Bennett's Bad Bet: Extremism in Defense of Virtue Can't Absolve His Own Vice." Slate.com, May 4.

Kirkpatrick, David (2005) "Some Democrats Believe the Party Should Get Religion." *New York Times,* November 17.

Kirkpatrick, David D., and Carl Hulse (2005) "G.O.P. Reaches to Other Party on Supreme Court Pick." *New York Times,* November 1.

Kleiman, Mark (2006a) "Sex, Science and the Bush Administration." The Reality-Based Community, http://www.samefacts.org, March 9.

Kleiman, Mark (2006b) "Who Won the Culture Wars?" The Reality-Based Community, http://www.samefacts.com, May 16.

Klein, Joe (2006a) *Politics Lost: How American Democracy Was Trivialized by People Who Think You're Stupid.* New York: Doubleday.

Klein, Joe (2006b) "Reaching for the Center." *Time,* November 12.

Klein, Rick (2003) "Massachusetts Lawmaker Suggests Turning Boston Convention Center into Casino." *Boston Globe,* March 17.

Klein, Rick (2005) "Feeding Tube Case Heads to US Court: Congress Votes to Let Judge Decide; Bush Endorses Bill." *Boston Globe,* boston.com, March 21.

Kohut, Andrew (2004) Panel discussion, "How the Faithful Voted: Political Alignments and the Religious Divide in Election 2004." Washington, D.C.: Pew Forum on Religion and Public Life and the Brookings Institution, November 17.

Kohut, Andrew (2005) A Political Victory That Wasn't." *New York Times,* March 23.

Kondracke, Mort (2006) "Moderates Fed Up with Polarization." *RollCall,* rollcall.com, November 9.

Kramer, Larry (1987) *The Normal Heart.* London: Methuen.

Kraske, Steve (2006) "Opposition to Stem-Cell Ballot Consistent, Talent Says." *Kansas City Star,* May 3, http://www.kansascity.com.

Krauthammer, Charles (2005) "The Matter with Kansas." *Washington Post,* November 18.

Kristof, Nicholas (2005) "Time to Get Religion." *New York Times,* November 6.

Kuo, David (2006a) *Tempting Faith: An Inside Story of Political Seduction.* New York: Free Press.

Kuo, David (2006b) "Why a Christian in the White House Felt Betrayed." *Time,* October 16.

Kushner, Tony (1993) *Angels in America, Part One: Millennium Approaches.* New York: Theatre Communications Group.

Kushner, Tony (1994) *Angels in America, Part Two: Perestroika.* New York: Theatre Communications Group, 1996

Kuttner, Robert (2005) "True West: At the Democratic Party's Western States Caucus in Montana, Evidence Abounds of a Region 'Red on the Outside, Blue on the Inside.'" *American Prospect,* July 3.

Lacayo, Richard (2001) "How Bush Got There." *Time,* August 20. http://www.time.com/time/archive/preview/

0,10987,170839,00.html. Accessed on March 16, 2005.

Lakoff, George (2002) *Moral Politics: How Liberals and Conservatives Think.* Chicago: University of Chicago Press.

Lakoff, George (2004) *Don't Think of an Elephant: Know Your Values and Frame the Debate.* White River Junction, Vt.: Chelsea Green.

Lakoff, George (2006) *Talking Points: Communicating Our American Values and Vision, A Progressive's Handbook.* New York: Farrar, Straus and Giroux.

Lambert, Craig (2002) "Trafficking in Chance." *Harvard Magazine,* July–August.

Langer, Gary (2004) "Public Backs Stem Cell Research; Most Say Government Should Fund Use of Embryos." abcnews.com, June 26.

Langer, Gary (2005) "Poll: No Role for Government in Schiavo Case." ABC News, abcnews.go.com, March 21.

Laser, Rachel (2006a) *Winning the Abortion Grays.* The Third Way Culture Project. Washington, D.C.: Third Way.

Laser, Rachel (2006b) *A Defining Moment from South Dakota: Abortion Ban Presents Opportunity to Reframe the Debate.* Third Way Culture Project, www.thirdway.com.

Laser, Rachel (2006c) *A New Direction on Abortion for Progressives: Winning the Battle of Reasonableness.* Washington, D.C.: Third Way Culture Project, September 14.

Late Night with Conan O'Brien (2004) NBC, Show 1823, November 19.

Law Professors (2005) Brief for Professors of Law Richard Briffault, William N. Eskridge, Jr., Philip P. Frickey, Elizabeth Garrett, Jerry L. Mashaw, Edward Rubin, David L. Shapiro, Peter L. Strauss, and Ernest A. Young as Amici Curiae Supporting Respondents,

Gonzales v. Oregon, in the Supreme Court of the United States, July 18.

Lawrence, Jerome, and Robert E. Lee (1955) *Inherit the Wind.* New York: Ballantine Books.

Layman, Geoffrey, Thomas Carsey, John Green, and Richard Herrera (2005) "Party Polarization and 'Conflict Extension' in American Politics: The Case of Party Activists." Paper prepared for presentation at the University of Maryland, October 5.

Lazarus, Edward (2003) "One Reason Why Arnold Won: His Attack Ads Involved Indian Gaming, and Their Larger Context and Significance." http://www.findlaw.com October 16.

Lears, Jackson (2003) *Something for Nothing: Luck in America.* New York: Viking.

Lederer, Katy (2003) *Poker Face: A Girlhood among Gamblers.* New York: Crown.

Lee, Sam (2006) Director of Campaign Life Missouri. Telephone interview with Daniel Hillyard, February 6.

Legum, Judd, Faiz Shakir, Nico Pitney, Mipe Okunseinde, and Christy Harvey (2005) "Stem Cell: The Final Hurdles." The Progress Report. Washington, D.C.: American Progress Action Fund, July 14.

Legum, Judd Faiz Shakir, Nico Pitney, Amanda Terkel, and Payson Schwin (2006) "Election 2006: A Progressive Analysis." Center for American Progress, November 9.

Lemert Edwin M. (1967) *Human Deviance, Social Problems, and Social Control.* Englewood Cliffs, N.J.: Prentice-Hall.

Lerner, Michael (2005) *The Left Hand of God: Taking Back Our Country from the Religious Right.* New York: HarperSanFrancisco.

Lester, Will (2004) "New Poll: Americans

Want Roe v. Wade Upheld." Associated Press, November 29.

Lester, Will (2006) "DeLay Says Justices 'Don't Get' Criticism." Associated Press, March 26.

Levi, Edward H. (1973) "The Collective Morality of a Maturing Society." *Washington and Lee Law Review* 30:399.

Limbaugh, Rush (1992) *The Way Things Ought to Be.* New York: Pocket Books.

Limbaugh, Rush (2005) Rush Limbaugh, syndicated radio talk show, October 5.

Limbaugh, Rush (2006) "Michael J. Fox Is Not Infallible; He's Just the Latest Victim Used by the Democrats." http://www.rushlimbaugh.com, October 24.

Limerick, Patricia Nelson (2005) "Hope and Gloom Out West." *New York Times*, June 22.

Lindsey, Brink (2006) "Liberaltarians: A Progressive Manifesto." *New Republic* online, December 4, tnr.com.

Lithwick, Dahlia (2005) "Activist Legislators." *Slate.* March 21. http://slate.msn.com/id/2115124/. Accessed on March 21, 2005.

Lithwick, Dahlia (2007) "Father Knows Best: Dr. Kennedy's Magic Prescription for Indecisive Women." *Slate*, April 19. http://www.slate.com.

Long, Mark (2005) "Federal Judge Nixes Schiavo's Feeding Tube." *Durant Daily Democrat*, http://www.durantdemocract.com, March 25.

Lopez, Steve (2005) "The Right to Die Is a Personal Matter." Points West. *Los Angeles Times*, March 23, B1.

Lorenzi, Riossella (2005) "Italy's Embryo Law Remains." *Scientist*, June 14.

Loseke, Donileen R., and Joel Best (2003) *Social Problems: Constructionist Readings.* New York: Aldine de Gruyter.

Lovell-Badge, Robin (2005) "The Regulation of Embryo and Stem Cell Research in a Pluralistic Society." The Fifteenth Annual Howard Schneiderman Bioethics Lecture, University of California, Irvine, March 29.

Loveman, Gary (2002) "Casino Communications: Q & A." *Global Gaming Business,* October 1.

Lovett, Benjamin J., and Alexander H. Jordan (2005) "Moral Values, Moralism, and the 2004 Presidential Election." *Analyses of Social Issues and Public Policy* 5 (1): 165–175.

Lowry, Rich (2006) "The Democrats' Abortion Problem." *Fallon Star Press,* May 12.

Lugo, Luis (2004) "Religion as Political Issue Extends beyond Bible Belt." *Atlanta Journal-Constitution,* January 30.

Luker, Kristin (1984) *Abortion and the Politics of Motherhood.* Berkeley: University of California Press.

Lynne, Dianne (2006) "After Schiavo: Religious Right 'Using Terri'?—Part II." worldnetdaily.com, March 28.

Lyons, Linda (2004) "Public Grapples with Legality, Morality of Euthanasia." The Gallup Organization, July 13.

MacCoun, Robert J., and Peter Reuter (2001) *Drug War Heresies: Learning from Other Vices, Times and Places.* New York: Cambridge University Press.

Mallaby, Sebastian (2006) "A Split in the GOP Tent." *Washington Post,* December 4.

Mangione, Thomas W., and Floyd J. Fowler Jr. (1979) "Enforcing the Gambling Laws." *Journal of Social Issues* 35 (3): 115–128.

Manier, Jeremy (2001) "Bush OKs Some Stem Cell Funding." *Chicago Tribune,* August 10, 1.

Mansnerus, Laura (2006) "Legislators Vote for Gay Unions in N.J. ." *New York Times,* December 15.

March Madness (2006) "March Madness Spawns Gambling Madness." http//www.accountingWeb.com, March 17.

Martin, Allie, and Jody Brown (2006) "Bishop Jackson: Marriage Amendment Presents Political Vote on a Biblical Issue." June 1. http://headlines.agapepress.org.

Marty, Martin E., and E. Scott Appleby (1992) *The Glory and the Power: The Fundamentalist Challenge to the Modern World.* Boston: Beacon Press.

Massey, Douglas S. (2005) *Return of the "L" Word: A Liberal Vision for the New Century.* Princeton, N.J.: Princeton University Press.

Massing, Michael (1998a) *The Fix.* New York: Simon and Schuster.

Massing, Michael (1998b) "Strong Stuff." *New York Times Magazine,* March 22.

Mathews, Joe, and Megan Garvey (2004) "Schwarzenegger Backs Stem Cell Study." *Los Angeles Times,* October 19.

Maugh, Thomas H., II (2005) "Vaccine Blocks Most Cancer of the Cervix." *Los Angeles Times,* October 7.

Mauro, Tony (2004) "Another High Court Look at Gay Rights Likely." *Law.com,* February 9 at http://www.sodomylaws.org/lawrence/lwnews099.htm. Accessed on April 25, 2004.

McCain, John (2006) Senator John McCain's Straight Talk America, http://www.straighttalkamerica.com, Liberty University Commencement Address, May 13.

McCann, Michael W. (1994) *Rights at Work: Pay Equity Reform and the Politics of Legal Mobilization.* Chicago: University of Chicago Press.

McConahay, John (1988) "Pornography: The Symbolic Politics of Fantasy." *Law and Contemporary Problems* 51:31–70.

McIntyre, John (2006) "Election 2006: What Happened and What Does It Mean?" Realclearpolitics, November 16.

McManus, James (2003) *Positively Fifth Street: Murderers, Cheetahs, and Binion's World Series of Poker.* New York: Picador.

McMillen, Jan, ed. (1996) *Gambling Cultures: Studies in History and Interpretation.* London: Routledge.

Meacham, Jon (2006) "God, the GOP and Election Day: The Theological Reason Evangelicals May Not Turn Out to Vote." *Newsweek,* msnbc.com, October 9.

Mears, Bill (2006) "Consensus Is Roberts' Rule of Order." www.cnn.com, June 2.

Meeker, James W., John Dombrink, and Gilbert Geis (1985) "State Law and Local Ordinances in California Barring Discrimination on the Basis of Sexual Orientation." *University of Dayton Law Review* 10 (3): 745–765.

Mehlman, Ken (2006) National Republican Party chairman. In-person comments to Daniel Hillyard, Kansas City, Missouri, February 4.

Meier, Diane E., Carol-Ann Emmons, Sylvan Wallenstein, Timothy Quill, R. Sean Morrison, and Christine Cassel (1998) "A National Survey of Physician-Assisted Suicide and Euthanasia in the United States." *New England Journal of Medicine* 338:1193–1201.

Meier, Robert F., and Gilbert Geis (1997) *Victimless Crimes? Prostitution, Drugs, Homosexuality, Abortion.* Los Angeles: Roxbury.

Melendez, Michele M. (2006) "Young Americans More Likely to Support Gay Marriage, Polls Suggest." *Newhouse News Service,* August 31.

Menand, Louis (2004) "Permanent Fatal Errors." *New Yorker,* December 6, 54–60.

Mental Health Professionals (2005) Brief of Amicus Curiae Coalition of Mental Health Professionals in Support of Respondents, *Gonzales v. Oregon,* in the Supreme Court of the United States, July 21.

Messerlian, Carmen, and Jeffrey L. Derevensky (2005) "Youth Gambling: A Public Health Perspective." *Journal of Gambling Issues,* no. 14, September.

Meyer, David S. (2005) "Social Movements and Public Policy: Eggs, Chicken, and Theory." In David S. Meyer, Valerie, Jenness, and Helen Ingram, eds., *Routing the Opposition: Social Movements, Public Policy, and Democracy.* Minneapolis: University of Minnesota Press.

Meyerson, Harold (2003) "Too Much a Gray Matter." *Washington Post,* October 9.

Mezrich, Ben (2002) *Bringing Down the House: The Inside Story of Six M.I.T. Students Who Took Vegas for Millions.* New York: Free Press.

Michelman, Kate (2005a) "This Time, Alito, It's Personal." *Los Angeles Times,* November 13, M3.

Michelman, Kate (2005b) *With Liberty and Justice for All.* New York: Hudson Street Press.

Mickthelwait, John, and Adrian Wooldridge (2004) *The Right Nation: Conservative Power in America.* New York: Penguin Press.

Milbank, Dana (2001) "Clear Break from the Right May Be Brief." *Washington Post,* August 10, A1.

Mill, John Stuart (1859/1956) *On Liberty.* Indianapolis: Bobbs-Merrill.

Miller, Ronald B., M.D. (2006) "Ethical Issues in Stem Cell Research, Therapy, and Public Policy." Unpublished manuscript, University of California, Irvine.

Missouri Coalition (2006a) "Dr. Danforth." Television advertisement, the Missouri Coalition for Lifesaving Cures. Kirkwood, Missouri. http://www .missouricures.com.

Missouri Coalition (2006b) "Dr. F. Sessions Cole." Television advertisement, the Missouri Coalition for Lifesaving Cures. Kirkwood, Missouri. http:// www.missouricures.com.

Missouri Coalition (2006c) "Dr. Maureen Dudgeon." Television advertisement, the Missouri Coalition for Lifesaving Cures. Kirkwood, Missouri. http://www .missouricures.com.

Missouri Coalition (2006d) "Jeff." Television advertisement, the Missouri Coalition for Lifesaving Cures. Kirkwood, Missouri. http://www.missouricures .com.

Missouri Coalition (2006e) "Pastor Cleaver." Television advertisement, the Missouri Coalition for Lifesaving Cures. Kirkwood, Missouri. http://www .missouricures.com.

Missouri Coalition (2006f) "Renee and Austin." Television advertisement, the Missouri Coalition for Lifesaving Cures. Kirkwood, Missouri. http://www .missouricures.com.

Missouri Coalition (2006g) "Sen. Danforth Pro-Life." Television advertisement, the Missouri Coalition for Lifesaving Cures. Kirkwood, Missouri. http://www.missouricures.com.

Missouri Coalition (2006h) "The Stem Cell Initiative." Television advertisement, the Missouri Coalition for Lifesaving Cures. Kirkwood, Missouri. http://www.missouricures.com.

Moats, David (2004) *Civil Wars: Gay Marriage in America.* San Diego: Harcourt.

Molica, Anthony S. (2003) "Celebrating 18 Years of Fun and Games." *Lotto People,* October.

Moneymaker, Chris (2005) *Moneymaker: How an Amateur Poker Player Turned $40 into $2.5 Million at the World Series of Poker.* New York: Harper-Entertainment.

Moon, Shin-Yong (2005) "Embryonic Stem Cell Research: Present and Future." The Howard A. Schneiderman and

Audrey R. Schniederman Distinguished Lecture in Modern Biology, University of California, Irvine, November 4.

Mooney, Chris (2001) "Irrationalist in Chief." *American Prospect,* October 8. http://www.prospect.org/print/V12/17/mooney-c.html. Accessed on May 31, 2005.

Moore, David W. (2004) "Abortion Sentiment Affected by Rating Scale" Gallup news briefing, June 15.

Morain, Dan (2004a) "California on Path to Become Nation's Gambling Capital." *Los Angeles Times,* August 25, A1.

Morain, Dan (2004b) "Tribal Casinos Should Ante Up, Voters Say." *Los Angeles Times,* April 24, B1.

Morford, Mark (2004) "Down with Fancy Book Learnin': What's It Mean That the Big Cities and College Towns of America All Voted Blue?" *San Francisco Chronicle,* http://www.sfgate.com, November 12.

Morrison, Micah (2005) "Who's Leading the Way?" *Parade,* July 10.

Morsch, Linda (2005) "Gambling Plays Big in Daily Workplace." http://www.officebuilder.com, April 27.

"Most Pessimistic about U.S. Morality, Poll Finds" (2003) *Los Angeles Times,* June 14, B15.

Mother Jones (2005) January–February, 76.

Moyers, Bill (2005a) "Moyers on America." Speech, University of California, Irvine, November 14.

Moyers, Bill (2005b) *Moyers on America: A Journalist and His Times.* New York: Anchor Books.

Moyers, Bill (2005c) "9/11 and the Sport of God." CommonDreams.org, September 9.

MSNBC (2005a) "Dean Discusses Alito, Abortion, Libby and Iraq." *Hardball,* November 1.

MSNBC (2005b) "First Glance." *First Read.* http://www.msnbc.com, March 21.

MSNBC (2007) "Abortion Ruling Reaction." http://www.msnbc.msn.com, April 18.

Mulkern, Anne C. (2005) "Stem-Cell Shift 'An Earthquake,' " *Denver Post,* July 30.

Mulkern, Anne C. (2006) "Anti-gay Nuptials Ad Targets Salazar." *Denver Post,* May 31.

Murray, Yxta Maya (1999) *What It Takes to Get to Vegas.* New York: Grove Press.

Myers, Dennis (2002) "A Land Rush toward New Gambling." *Las Vegas Business Press,* November 25.

Nagourney, Adam (2005a) "In a Polarizing Case, Jeb Bush Cements His Political Stature." *New York Times,* March 25.

Nagourney, Adam (2005b) "So What Happened in That Election, Anyhow?' *New York Times,* January 2.

Nagourney, Adam (2006a) "In Address, McCain Gives Avid Defense of Iraq War." *New York Times,* May 14.

Nagourney, Adam (2006b) "Looking to Win in November with a 2-Year-Old Playbook." *New York Times,* April 16, sec. 4, p. 1.

Nagourney, Adam (2006c) "The Nation: Early Returns; Now, the Tape Measure for Those Other Drapes." *New York Times,* November 12.

Nagourney, Adam (2006d) "The 2006 Elections: The Overview; Democrats Take House." *New York Times,* November 8.

Nagourney, Adam, and Janet Elder (2004a) "Americans Still Concerned about Bush Agenda, Poll Shows." *New York Times,* November 22.

Nagourney, Adam, and Janet Elder (2004b) "Nation's Direction Prompts Voters' Concern, Poll Finds." *New York Times,* March 16.

Napoli, Bill (2006) South Dakota State Senator Bill Napoli (R-Rapid City) on *The News Hour with Jim Lehrer,* March 3.

NARAL (2006a) "Elections 2006: You Acted! You Voted! We Won!" NARAL Pro-Choice America, May 25.

NARAL (2006b) "A Rallying Cry from South Dakota." NARAL Pro-Choice America, May 25.

NARAL (2006c) "Wal-Mart Agrees to Carry Emergency Contraception in ALL Stores."

NARAL (2007a) "Supreme Court Upholds Federal Abortion Ban. For the First Time since *Roe,* This Ban Makes No Exception for a Woman's Health." NARAL Pro-Choice America. http://www.naral.org, April 18.

NARAL (2007b) "Shocking Statements from Presidential Candidates." NARAL Pro-Choice America. http://www.prochoiceaction.org, May 8.

NARAL News, NARAL Pro-Choice America, March 20.

National Abortion Federation (2006) "Abortion-Care Education Is Deficient in U.S. Health Professional Training." Press release, May 9.

National Academy of Sciences (2005) "Guidelines for Human Embryonic Stem Cell Research." Committee on Guidelines for Human Embryonic Stem Cell Research, National Catholic Bioethics Center (2006) "Statement on *Gonzales, Attorney General, et al., v. Oregon et al.*" http://www.ncbcenter.org, January 18.

National Research Council and Institute of Medicine of the National Academies, Washington, D.C.: National Academy Press, April 26.

National Center for Lesbian Rights (2003) "The Evolution of California's Domestic Partnership Law: A Timeline." September 19, 2003, http://www.nclrights.org, March 20.

National Center for Responsible Gaming (2002) NCRG Annual Report 2001. Kansas City, Mo.: National Center for Responsible Gaming.

National Council of State Legislatures (2007) "Same Sex Marriage." http://www.ncst.org.

National Gambling Impact Study Commission (1999) *Final Report.* Washington, D.C.: National Gambling Impact Study Commission.

National Gay and Lesbian Task Force (2004) "Recent National Polls on Same-Sex Marriage and Civil Unions." Washington, D.C.: National Gay and Lesbian Task Force, http://www.ngltf.org.

National Legal Center for the Medically Dependent and Disabled (2005) Brief of Amicus Curiae National Legal Center for the Medically Dependent and Disabled, Inc., in Support of Petitioners, *Gonzales v. Oregon,* in the Supreme Court of the United States, May 9.

National Marriage Project (2003) The State of Our Unions, 2003: The Social Health of Marriage in America. Piscataway, N.J.: Rutgers University, National Marriage Project, June.

National Organization for Women (2005) "Dear Friend of Women's Rights." www.thetruthaboutgeorge.org, December.

National Research Council (1999) *Pathological Gambling: A Critical Review.* Washington, D.C.: National Academy Press.

National Right to Life (2006) "National Right to Life Responds to Ruling on *Gonzales v. Oregon.*" http://www.nrlc.org/pressrelease, January 17.

NBC News' *Meet the Press* (2004) November 28.

NBC News/*Wall Street Journal* Poll (2004) June 25–28.

Neas, Ralph (2005) Statement of Executive Director of People for the American Way, October 27, http://www.pfaw.org.

Neuhaus, Richard John (2006) *Catholic Matters: Confusion, Controversy and the Splendor of Truth.* New York: Basic Books.

New England Journal of Medicine (2007) Audio Interview: Expanding Federal Funding for Embryonic Stem-Cell Research, with Senator Orrin G. Hatch. Vol. 356:e18.

New York State Task Force on Life and the Law (1998) "Executive Summary of Assisted Reproductive Technologies: Analysis and Recommendations for Public Policy." http://www.health.state.ny.us/nysdoh/taskfce/execsum.htm. Accessed on March 19, 2005.

New York Times (2004) "National Briefing, South: South Carolina: Bush Urged to Use Mandate." November 12.

New York Times (2005a) "Civil Unions in Connecticut." Editorial, *New York Times,* March 7.

New York Times (2005b) "Senator Frist's Stem Cell Shift." Editorial, July 30.

New York Times (2006a) "New Hampshire: Cancer Vaccine to Be Free for Girls." November 30.

New York Times (2006b) "Stem Cell Proposal Splits Missouri GOP." March 12.

Newport, Frank (2006) "American Teenagers Split on Gay Marriage." The Gallup Poll, March 9.

Newport, Frank, and Joseph Carroll (2005) "Choosing a New Supreme Court Justice." The Gallup Organization, July 6.

NGLTF (1998) "Issue Maps: Sodomy Map, the Right to Privacy in the United States." National Gay and Lesbian Task Force, http://www.ngltf.org.

NGLTF (2004a) "Issue Maps: Nondiscrimination Laws." National Gay and Lesbian Task Force, www.thetaskforce.org.

NGLTF (2004b) "Recent National Polls on Same-Sex Marriage and Civil Unions." Washington, D.C.: National Gay and Lesbian Task Force, http://www.thetaskforce.org.

NGLTF (2006) "Marriage Action Center: Fighting against the Federal Marriage Amendment." National Gay and Lesbian Task Force, www.thetaskforce.org. Accessed on June 2.

Nickel, Philip (2006) "How Can We Conduct Human Embryonic Stem Cell Research Responsibly?" Presentation at "Stem Cells and Society: A Series of Dialogues." Schools of Biological Sciences and Humanities, University of California, Irvine, April 26.

Nieves, Evelyn (2006) "South Dakota Abortion Ban Takes Aim at National Stage." *Washington Post,* washingtonpost.com, February 23.

NIGC (2006) National Indian Gambling Commission, http://www.nigc.gov.

Nisbet, Mathew C. (2004) "Public Opinion about Stem Cell Research and Human Cloning." *Public Opinion Quarterly* 68 (1): 131–154.

Nisbet, Matthew C., Dominique Brossard, and Adrianne Kroepsch (2004) "Framing Science: The Stem Cell Controversy in an Age of Press/Politics." *Harvard International Journal of Press/Politics* 9:11–37.

No Casinos (2005) Advertisement. http://www.nocasinosfl.com.

Nobel Laureates (1999) Letter to the President of the United States and Members of the United States Congress. http://www.ascb.org/news/vo122n04/policy.htm. Accessed on July 26, 2005.

Noll, Mark A., and Carolyn Nystrom (2005) *Is the Reformation Over? An Evangelical Assessment of Contempo-*

rary Roman Catholicism. Grand Rapids, Mich.: Baker Academic.

Noonan, Peggy (2005) "Don't Kick It: If Terri Schiavo Is killed, Republicans Will Pay a Political Price. " *Wall Street Journal,* March 18.

Obama, Barack (2004) "Transcript: Illinois Senate Candidate Barack Obama." Keynote speech at Democratic Party Convention, *Washington Post,* July 27.

Obama, Barack (2006) "The Connection between Faith and Politics." Speech by United States Senator (D-Ill.) to "Call for Renewal" Conference, June 30. realclearpolitics.com, June 30.

O'Brien, Timothy (2006) "Is Poker Losing Its First Flush?" *New York Times,* April 16, sec. 3, p. 1.

O'Connell, Sue (2006) "The Money behind the Marriage Amendments." Helena, Mont.: Institute on Money in State Politics, January 24.

O'Keefe, Mark (1994a) "Catholic Church Plans to Fight Suicide Measure." *Oregonian,* September 9, A1.

O'Keefe, Mark (1994b) "Catholic Leaders to Use Pulpit to Fight Initiative." *Oregonian,* September 10, A1.

Open Letter (2002) "An Open Letter from 200 Religious Leaders to the President and Congress on the Spread of Gambling." *Roll Call,* May 6.

Operation Rescue (2005) "Voice for Terri." http://www.operationrescue.org, March.

Opinion Research Corporation (2005) "American Views on Stem Cell Research: Summary of Survey Findings." Prepared for Results for America: A Project of Civil Society Institute, February 15

Oregon Department of Health Services (2006) "Eighth Annual Report on Oregon's Death with Dignity Act." Office of Disease Prevention and Epidemiology, March 19.

"Oregon Wins—without Roberts" (2006) *Oregonian,* editorial, January 18. http://www.oregonlive.com/editorials/oregonian/index.ssf?/base/editorial/1137549314247060.xml&coll=7. Accessed on January 18, 2006.

O'Reilly, Bill (2005) "A Solution to the Schiavo Case." *The O'Reilly Factor,* March 24.

O'Reilly, Bill (2006) *Culture Warrior.* New York: Broadway Books.

Pacheco, Patrick (2005) "Rescripting the Strip." *Los Angeles Times,* September 11, E52.

Packer, Herbert (1968) *The Limits of the Criminal Sanction.* Stanford, Calif.: Stanford University Press.

Page, Clarence (2005) "Hillary and Crew Delivering Shout-outs to the Center." *Chicago Tribune,* February 16.

Page, Cristina (2006) *How the Pro-choice Movement Saved America: Freedom, Politics and the War on Sex.* New York: Basic Books.

PARADE/Research!America Health Poll (2005) "Taking Our Pulse: The PARADE/Research!America Health Poll." The Charlton Research Company, July 10.

Pasadena Star-News (2004) "Don't Change State Gaming." October 9.

Perry, Daniel (2000) "Patients' Voices: The Powerful Sound in the Stem Cell Debate." *Science* 287:1423.

Peterson, Iver (2002) "And They're Off, as States Race to Add Gambling Sites." *New York Times,* November 18, B1.

Peterson, Iver (2004) "Atlantic City's Casinos Say They Fear No Lemons from Pennsylvania's Slots." *New York Times,* August 15.

Peterson, Kavan (2004) "Battle over Gay Marriage Goes to Voters." *Infozine .com,* April 24, at http://www.infozine .com/news/stories/op/storiesView/sid/2107/. Accessed on April 24, 2004.

Pew Forum on Religion and Public Life (2003) "Religion and Politics: Contention and Consensus." July 24.

Pew Forum on Religion and Public Life (2004) "The American Religious Landscape and Politics, 2004." Pew Charitable Trusts, September 10.

Pew Forum on Religion and Public Life (2006a) "In Pursuit of Values Voters: Religion's Role in the 2006 Election." October 11

Pew Forum on Religion and Public Life (2006b) "Is There a Culture War?" Event transcript, Key West, Florida, May 23.

Pew Forum on Religion and Public Life (2006c) "Judicial Showdown: The Supreme Court Returns to the Abortion Debate." Event transcript, Washington, D.C.: Pew Forum on Religion and Public Life, November 2.

Pew Research Center (2004a) "Morals Values: How Important?" Washington, D.C.: Pew Research Center for the People and the Press, November 11.

Pew Research Center (2004b) "Religion and the Presidential Vote: Bush's Gains Broad-Based." Washington, D.C.: Pew Research Center for the People and the Press, December 6.

Pew Research Center (2005a) "Abortion, the Court and the Public." Washington, D.C.: Pew Research Center for the People and the Press, October 3.

Pew Research Center (2005b) "Public's Agenda Differs from President's." Washington, D.C.: Pew Research Center for the People and the Press, January 13.

Pew Research Center (2005c) "Reading the Polls on Evolution and Creationism." Washington, D.C.: Pew Research Center for the People and the Press, September 28.

Pew Research Center (2005d) "Religion a Strength and Weakness for Both Parties: Public Divided on Origins of Life."

Washington, D.C.: Pew Research Center for the People and the Press, August 30.

Pew Research Center (2006a) "Gambling: As the Take Rises, So Does Public Concern." Washington, D.C.: Pew Research Center for the People and the Press, May 23.

Pew Research Center (2006b) "Less Opposition to Gay Marriage, Adoption and Military Service: Only 34% Favor South Dakota Abortion Ban." Washington, D.C.: Pew Research Center for the People and the Press, March 22.

Phillips, Kevin (2006) *American Theocracy: The Peril and Politics of Radical Religion, Oil and Borrowed Money in the 21st Century.* New York: Viking.

"Phyllis Lyon and Del Martin Make History Again" (2004) http://www.now.org, February 13.

Pickler, Nedra (2006) "Sen. Reid: Ethics, Stem Cells Top Agenda." Associated Press, November 28.

Planned Parenthood v. Gonzales (2006) No. 04-16621.

Polgreen, Linda (2005) "Nigerian Anglicans Seeing Gay Challenge to Orthodoxy." *New York Times,* December 18.

PollingReport.com (2007) "Abortion and Birth Control." Taken April 21.

Ponnuru, Ramesh (2005a) "Bad News for Pro-Lifers." nationalreview.com, October 12.

Ponnuru, Ramesh (2005b) "Why Conservatives Are Divided." *New York Times,* October 16.

Ponnuru, Ramesh (2006a) *The Party of Death: The Democrats, the Media, the Courts, and the Disregard for Human Life.* Washington, D.C.: Regnery.

Ponnuru, Ramesh (2006b) "What If *Roe* Is Overturned: Half-Life? *New Republic* online, April 13.

Powell, Alvin (2005) "Reclaiming Religion from the Right: Religious Activist Outlines Path for New National Dialogue." *Harvard University Gazette,* September 29.

President's Council on Bioethics (2004) "Monitoring Stem Cell Research." http://bioethicsprint.gov/reports/stemcell/ chapter2.html. Accessed on October 14, 2004.

Press, Eyal (2006a) "Abortion, from a Distance." *New York Times,* March 12.

Press, Eyal (2006b) Absolute Convictions: My Father, a City, and the Conflict That Divided America. New York: Henry Holt.

Price, Caleb (2006) "Do Gays Really Want 'Marriage'?" *Citizen* magazine, June.

Princeton University (2000) "Study on Religion and Politics Finds Widespread Interest in Progressive Issues." Press release, Office of Communications, May 3.

Pro-Life Legal Defense Fund, Inc., et al. (2005) Brief of Amici Curiae Pro-Life Legal Defense Fund, Legal Center for Defense of Life, and University Faculty for Life in Support of Petitioners, *Gonzales v. Oregon,* in the Supreme Court of the United States, May 9.

Prose, Francine (2003) *Gluttony: The Seven Deadly Sins.* New York: New York Public Library and Harvard University Press.

Provance, Michael, and Michael Pfarrer (2006) "When Institutions Collide: A Model of Institutional Rivalry from the Gambling Industry." Paper presented at the Thirteenth International Conference on Gambling and Risk Taking, Lake Tahoe, Nevada, May 25.

Punch, Maurice (1997) "The Dutch Criminal Justice System: A Crisis of Identity." *Security Journal* 9:177–184.

"Quick Fixes for Web Info-Junkies" (2004) Technology and You: Online Extra. *Business Week,* May 24.

Quill, Timothy E. (1991) "Death and Dignity: A Case of Individualized Decision

Making." *New England Journal of Medicine* 324:693.

Quill, Timothy E. (1993) *Death and Dignity: Making Choices and Taking Charge.* New York: Norton.

Quill, Timothy E., (1996) *A Midwife through the Dying Process.* Baltimore: Johns Hopkins University Press.

Quill, Timothy E., (2005) "Terri Schiavo—A Tragedy Compounded." *New England Journal of Medicine,* http:// www.nejm.org, March 22.

Rafferty, Jim (2002) "Mega Trends: Issues That Will Impact Your Casino in the Coming Years." *Global Gaming Business,* December 1, 30.

Rainey, James, and Maria L. LaGanga (2004) "Abortion Issue Pushes Kerry's Faith to Fore." *Los Angeles Times,* April 24, A20.

Ranulf, Svend (1938/1964) *Moral Indignation and Middle Class Psychology: A Sociological Study.* New York: Schocken Books.

Reagan, Leslie (1997) *When Abortion Was a Crime: Women, Medicine and Law in U.S., 1867–1973.* Berkeley: University of California Press.

Reagan, Nancy (2006) Letter to Senator Orrin Hatch, May 1, http://www .camradvocacy.org/resources/Nancy_ Reagan.pdf, June 6, 2006.

Real Republican Majority (2006) "Battle to Bring the GOP Back to the Center Begins—The Real Republican Majority Demands Change." realrepublican majority.org, November 9.

Reed, Ralph (1996) *Active Faith: How Christians Are Changing the Soul of American Politics.* New York: Basic Books.

Reid, Harry (2006) Statement of Nevada Senator and Senate Minority Leader on Senate Floor. *Congressional Record* 152, no. 70, June 6.

Reith, Gerda (2003) "Pathology and

Profit: Controversies in the Expansion of Legal Gambling." In Gerda Reith, ed., *Gambling: Who Wins? Who Loses?* Amherst, N.Y.: Prometheus Books.

Religion and Ethics Newsweekly (2005) "Poll: Americans Idealize Traditional Family, Even as Nontraditional Families Are More Accepted." PBS, October 19.

Religious Coalition for Marriage (2006) "A Letter from America's Religious Leaders in Defense of Marriage." http://www.religiouscoalitionformarriage.com.

Religious Organizations and Leaders (2005) Amici Curiae Brief of 52 Religious and Religious Freedom Organizations and Leaders in Support of Respondents, *Gonzales v. Oregon,* in the Supreme Court of the United States, July 18.

RenewAmerica (2005) "Sin and Responsibility." RenewAmerica Forum, http://www.renewamerica.us, October 23.

Reno, Ronald A. (1999) "The National Gambling Impact Study Commission Report: What Does It Say? What Does It Mean?" Citizen Link: A Web Site of Focus on the Family. http://www.family.org.

Reno Gazette-Journal (2006) "Las Vegas: Sin City Still King of Colossal Conventions." www.rgj.com, May 1.

Responsible Gaming Association of New Mexico (2005) http://rganm.org.

Results for America (2004) "American Views on Stem Cell Research in the Wake of the Death of Ronald Reagan." http://222.resultsforamerica.org, June 16.

Reynolds, Maura (2005a) "After Schiavo, GOP's Push on End-of-Life Issues Fades." *Los Angeles Times,* April 7, A17.

Reynolds, Maura (2005b) "Kennedy Calls on Left to Keep Faith." *Los Angeles Times,* January 13, A10.

Reynolds, Maura, and Tom Hamburger (2005) "GOP Doubts Build over Court Choice." *Los Angeles Times,* October 6, A1.

Reynolds, Maura, and Peter Wallsten (2005) "Key Conservatives Demur on Miers." *Los Angeles Times,* October 7, A20.

Ricci, James, and Patricia Ward Biederman (2004) "Acceptance of Gays on Rise, Polls Show." *Los Angeles Times,* March 31.

Rich, Frank (2004) "The Joy of Gay Marriage." *New York Times,* February 29.

Rich, Frank (2005a) "A Culture of Death, Not Life." *New York Times,* April 10.

Rich, Frank (2005b) "Two Gay Cowboys Hit a Homerun." *New York Times,* December 18, sec. 4, p. 13.

Richards, David A. J. (2005) *The Case for Gay Rights: From Bowers to Lawrence and Beyond.* Lawrence: University Press of Kansas.

Richman, Kimberly (2003) "Judicial Narratives in Custody Cases Involving Gay and Lesbian Parents, 1952–1999: A Study of Indeterminacy and Meaning Making in Legal Rationales and Outcomes." Ph.D. diss., University of California, Irvine.

Rimmerman, Craig A., Kenneth D. Wald, and Clyde Wilcox, eds. (2000) *The Politics of Gay Rights.* Chicago: University of Chicago Press.

Risen, James, and Judy Thomas (1998) *Wrath of Angels: The American Abortion War.* New York: Basic Books.

Robinson, Paul (2005) *Queer Wars: The New Gay Right and Its Critics.* Chicago: University of Chicago Press.

Roe v. Wade. 410 U.S. 13 (1973).

Rome, Jim (2004) Radio sports talk show, XTRA, Los Angeles, March 17.

Rose, I. Nelson (1980) "The Legalization and Control of Casino Gambling." *Fordham Law Review* 8:245–300.

Rose, I. Nelson (2002) "Is It Bingo, or a

Slot Machine?" *Gambling and the Law,* Column, 82, December.

Rose, I. Nelson, and Martin D. Owens (2005) *Internet Gaming Law.* New Rochelle, N.Y.: Mary Ann Liebert.

Rosen, Jeffrey (2006) "The Day after *Roe.*" *Atlantic Monthly,* June, 56–66.

Rosenberg, Debra (2004) "Anxiety over Abortion: Pro-choice Democrats Eye a More Restrictive Approach to Abortion as One Way to Gain Ground at the Polls." *Newsweek,* December 20.

Rostow, Ann (2003) "Supreme Court Strikes Down Sodomy Law." *Gay.com/ PlanetOut.com Network,* June 26, http://www.sodomylaws.org/lawrence/ lwnews048.htm. Accessed on April 25, 2004.

Rothman, Hal (2003) *Neon Metropolis: How Las Vegas Started the Twenty-first Century.* New York: Routledge.

Rounders (1998) Miramax Films, Joel Stillerman, Producer. Written by David Levien and Brian Koppelman, Directed by John Dahl.

Rove, Karl (2006) Speech of presidential adviser at American Enterprise Institute, Washington, D.C., May 15. Transcript, http://washingtonpost.com, May 15.

Rubin, Edward L., ed. (1999) *Minimizing Harm: A New Crime Policy for Modern America.* Boulder, Colo.: Westview Press.

Rubin, Joel, and Mike Anton (2004) "Gay Enclave Is Iffy on Marriage." *Los Angeles Times,* March 2, B1.

Saad, Lydia (2006a) "Abortion Views Reviewed as Alito Vote Nears." Gallup Poll, January 20.

Saad, Lydia (2006b) "Americans at Odds over Gay Rights." Gallup Poll, May 31.

Saad, Lydia (2006c) "Morality Ratings the Worst in Five Years: Americans Becoming More Pessimistic about Morals." Gallup Poll, May 25.

Safire, William (1998) "The Syntax of Sin Tax." *New York Times,* April 13.

Safire, William (2002) "Tribes of Gamblers." *New York Times,* December 12, A35.

Saletan, William (2002) "Supple Frist: The Wily New Senate Majority Leader." Slate. http://slate.msn.com/toolbar.aspx? action=print&id=2075911. Accessed on July 29, 2005.

Saletan, William (2004) *Bearing Right: How Conservatives Won the Abortion War.* Berkeley: University of California Press.

Saletan, William (2006) "Three Decades after Roe, a War We Can All Support." *New York Times,* January 22.

Sandler, Craig (2005) "Poll: Citizens Approve of Romney But Question His Job Plan, Stem Cell Stance." Weekly News Roundup, State House News Service, March 3.

Santorum, Rick (2005) *It Takes a Family: Conservatism and the Common Good.* Wilmington, Del.: ISI Books.

Scheer, Robert (2004) "The Invisible Hand Holds the Remote." *Los Angeles Times,* November 30.

Schiavo, Michael (2006) *Terri: The Truth.* New York: Dutton.

Schindler, Mary, and Robert Schindler (2006) *A Life That Matters: The Legacy of Terri Schiavo—A Lesson for Us All.* New York: Warner Books.

Schneider, William (1992), "The Battle for Saliency: The Abortion Issue in This Campaign." *Atlantic Monthly,* October.

Schur, Edwin (1965) *Crimes without Victims.* Englewood Cliffs, NJ: Prentice-Hall.

Schur, Edwin (1980) *The Politics of Deviance.* Englewood Cliffs, N.J.: Prentice-Hall.

Schwartz, Pepper, and Philip Blumstein (1983) *American Couples: Money,*

Work, and Sex. New York: William Morrow.

Schweitzer Sarah (2005) "Conn. Approves Gay Civil Unions: Advocates and Opponents Criticize Compromise Law." *Boston Globe,* April 21.

Scientific American (2006) "Con Men in Lab Coats." Editorial, March.

Seelye, Katharine Q. (2001) "Bush Backs Federal Funding for Some Stem Cell Research." *New York Times,* August 10, A1.

Seelye, Katharine Q. (2004) "Moral Values Cited as a Defining Issue of the Election." *New York Times,* November 4.

Shaffer, Howard, and Rachel Kidman (2003) "Shifting Perspectives on Gambling and Addiction." *Journal of Gambling Studies* 19 (1): 1–6.

Shanks, Pete (2005) *Human Genetic Engineering: A Guide for Activists, Skeptics, and the Very Perplexed.* New York: Nation Books.

Sharlet, Jeff (2006a) "Faith, Reason, and Murder." Review of Eyal Press, *Absolute Convictions, Columbia Journalism Review,* March/April.

Sharlet, Jeff (2006b) "God's Senator." *Rolling Stone,* www.rollingstone.com, January 25.

Shehzad, Nura (2001) "President Is Not 'Pro-life' If He Allows Embryonic Stem Cell Research, American Life League States." *Washington Fax,* August 6, 1–2.

Sheldon, Louis P. (2004) "Schwarzenegger Is Blind to the Values Mandate in Urging a Broader Party." *Los Angeles Times,* December 29.

Shelley, Mary (1818/1993) *Frankenstein.* New York: Barnes and Noble Books.

Shepard, Gary (2006) "It's Going to Get Ugly." Citizen Link, Focus on the Family, March 9.

Shepard, Stuart (2005) "The Linguistics of Abortion and Politics." Colorado Springs: Focus on the Family, http://www.citizenlink.org, December 21.

Shilts, Randy (1987) *And the Band Played On: Politics, People and the AIDS Epidemic.* New York: St. Martin's Press.

Shockley, Madison (2004) "Since When Does Conflict Turn Off the Networks?" *Los Angeles Times,* December 3, B13.

Shorto, Russell (2005) "What's Their Real Problem with Gay Marriage? It's the Gay Part." *New York Times Magazine,* June 19.

Shorto, Russell (2006) "Contra-Contraception" *New York Times Magazine,* May 7, 48+.

Simon, Laurence (2006) Thisblogisfullof crap. http://www.isfullofcrap.com, June 5.

Simon, Richard, and Janet Hook (2005) "Case Proves Politically Touchy." *Los Angeles Times,* March 25.

Simon, Richard, and Maura Reynolds (2005) "Frist Treads a Delicate Path in Citing Medical Background." *Los Angeles Times,* March 22, A12.

Simon, Stephanie (2005) "A Voice That Carries: Millions of People Hang on the Advice of Evangelical Psychologist James C. Dobson." *Los Angeles Times,* October 7.

Simon, Stephanie (2006) " 'Ex-Gays' Seek a Say in Schools." *Los Angeles Times,* May 28.

Skidmore, Max (2006) Professor of political science at University of Missouri–Kansas City. Interview with Daniel Hillyard. Kansas City, Missouri, February 3.

Skocpol, Theda (1995) *Social Policy in the United States: Future Possibilities in Historical Perspective.* Princeton, N.J.: Princeton University Press.

Skolnick, Arlene (1992) *Embattled Paradise: The American Family in an Age of Uncertainty.* New York: Basic Books.

Skolnick, Arlene (1997) "Family Values: The Sequel." *American Prospect* 8 (32).

Skolnick, Arlene (2004) Special Series. "Rethinking the Politics of the Family." *Dissent*, Fall, 116–118.

Skolnick, Arlene (2005) "Rethinking the Politics of the Family: Part IV." *Dissent*, Summer, 63–64.

Skolnick, Arlene S., and Jerome H. Skolnick (1999) *Family in Transition*. 10th ed. New York: Longman.

Skolnick, Jerome H. (1968) "Coercion to Virtue: The Enforcement of Morals." *Southern California Law Review* 41:588.

Skolnick, Jerome H. (1978) *House of Cards: Legalization and Control of Casino Gambling*. Boston: Little, Brown.

Skolnick, Jerome H. (1988) "The Social Transformation of Vice." *Law and Contemporary Problems* 51:9–29.

Skolnick, Jerome H. (1992) "Rethinking the Drug Problem." *Daedalus: Journal of the American Academy of Arts and Sciences* 121:133–159.

Skolnick, Jerome H. (2003) "Regulating Vice: America's Struggle with Wicked Pleasure." In Gerda Reith, ed., *Gambling: Who Wins? Who Loses?* Amherst, N.Y.: Prometheus Books.

Skolnick, Jerome H., and John Dombrink (1978) "The Legalization of Deviance." *Criminology* 16 (2): 193–208.

Skube, Michael (2004) "We're Saved. You Lost. Now What?" *Los Angeles Times*, November 7, M1.

Smelser, Neil J. (1998) "The Rational and the Ambivalent in the Social Sciences: 1997 Presidential Address." American Sociological Review 63 (1): 1–16.

Smiley, Jane (2004) *A Year at the Races: Reflections on Horses, Humans, Love, Money and Luck*. New York: Knopf.

Smith, Christian (2003) "Introduction: Rethinking the Secularization of American Public Life." In Christian Smith, ed., *The Secular Revolution: Power, Interests and Conflict in the Secularization of American Public Life*. Berkeley: University of California Press.

Smith, Garry J. (2006) "Gambling Studies, Examples of Social Science Methods Used in." *Encyclopedia of Social Measurement*. Burlington, Mass.: Elsevier.

Smith, J. Donald (2002) *Right-to-Die Policies in the American States: Judicial and Legislative Innovation*. New York: LFB Scholarly Publishing.

Smith, Rod (2002) "Heavy Regulation of Gambling Has Helped Casinos Avoid Corporate Scandals." *Las Vegas Journal Review*, November 17.

Smith, Wesley J. (1997) *Forced Exit: The Slippery Slope from Assisted Suicide to Legalized Murder*. New York: Times Books.

Smith, Wesley J. (2004) *Consumer's Guide to a Brave New World*. San Francisco: Encounter Books.

Smith, Wesley J. (2005a) "The Case Heard round the Web: How Terri Schiavo Became a Household Name." *Weekly Standard*, April 4. http://www.discovery .org/scripts/viewDB/index.php? command=view&id=2483. Accessed on May 27, 2006.

Smith, Wesley J. (2005b) "Human Nonperson: Terri Schiavo, Bioethics, and Our Future." *National Review Online*, March 29. http://www.discovery.org/ scripts/viewDB/index.php?command= view&id=2488. Accessed on May 27, 2006.

Smith, Wesley J. (2005c) "Prescription for Chaos: Understanding the Lethal Oregon Case That's Hitting the Supreme Court." *National Review Online*, February 23. http://www.discovery.org/scripts/ viewDB/index.php?command=view&id= 2428. Accessed on May 27, 2006.

Smith, Wesley J. (2006a) "Stem Cell

Research, Cloning and Euthanasia: Bioethics Year in Review." lifenews.com,
December 11.

Smith, Wesley J. (2006b) "U.S. Supreme
Court Rules in Favor of Oregon: Sec-
ondhand Smoke." www.wesleyjsmith
.org, January 17.

Smyth, Michael (2004) "Queers and Pro-
vocateurs: Hegemony, Ideology and the
Doctrine of Provocation." Unpublished
paper, Department of Criminology, Law
and Society, University of California,
Irvine.

Smyth, Michael (2006) "Queers and Pro-
vocateurs: Hegemony, Ideology and the
Homosexual Advance Defense." *Law
and Society Review* 40 (4): 903–930.

Snow, David, E. Burke Rochford, Steven
K. Worden, and Robert D. Benford
(1986) "Frame Alignment Processes,
Micromobilization, and Movement
Participation." *American Sociological
Review* 51:464–481.

Solinger, Rickie (2005) *Pregnancy and
Power: A Short History of Reproductive
Politics in America.* New York: NYU
Press.

Solo, Pam, and Gail Pressberg (2006) *Stem
Cell Research: Promise and Politics.*
New York: Praeger.

Solter, Davor, et al. (2003) *Embryo
Research in Pluralistic Europe.* Berlin:
Springer.

South Carolina Equality Coalition (2006)
"What's at Stake." http://www
.scequality.org.

Specter, Arlen (2006) "Republicans Can
Win by Picking Up 'Vital Center.'"
Philadelphia Inquirer, philly.com,
November 14.

Specter, Michael (2006) "The President
and the Scientists." *New Yorker,*
March 13.

Sperling, John, Suzanne Helburn, Samuel
George, John Morris, and Carl Hunt
(2004) *The Great Divide: Retro vs.*

Metro America. Sausalito, Calif.: Poli-
Point Press.

Spilde, Kate (2004) "Negotiating Fairness
in California." *Global Gaming Business,*
October, 114–116.

Staggenborg, Suzanne (1991) *The Pro-
choice Movement: Organization and
Activism in the Abortion Conflict.* New
York: Oxford University Press.

State of Nevada, Gaming Control Board
(2005) *Gaming Revenue Report.*
Year ending December 31, 2004.
Carson City, Nev.: Gaming Control
Board.

Steinbrook, Robert, M.D. (2006) "The
Potential of Human Papillomavirus
Vaccines." *New England Journal of
Medicine* 354:1109–1112.

Steinfels, Peter (2003) *A People Adrift:
The Crisis of the Roman Catholic
Church in America.* New York: Simon
and Schuster.

Steinfels, Peter (2004a) "Beliefs." *New
York Times,* October 23, A15.

Steinfels, Peter (2004b) "The 'Moral
Values' Issue." *New York Times,*
November 6.

Steinfels, Peter (2006) "Beliefs: Abortion
Has Returned to Center Stage, but
Should the Dialogue Be Changed? And
If So, How?" *New York Times,* Febru-
ary 25.

Steinhoff, Patricia G., and Milton Dia-
mond (1977) *Abortion Politics: The
Hawaii Experience.* Honolulu: University of Hawaii Press.

Stepp, Laura Sessions (2004) "Simple Science: Kids and Religion." *Los Angeles
Times,* March 29, E11.

Stevens, Ernest, Jr. (2004) "The Rising
Tide: Indian Gaming Is Bringing Oppor-
tunity to All Americans." *Global
Gaming Business,* October, 108–109.

Stockman, Jennifer (2006) "Battle to Bring
the GOP Back to the Center Begins—
The Real Republican Majority Demands

Change." realrepublicanmajority.org, November 12.

Stolberg, Cheryl Gay (2005a) "Changes Are Weighed on Stem Cells." *New York Times,* April 7.

Stolberg, Cheryl Gay (2005b) "Democratic Leader Intends to Vote against Roberts." *New York Times,* September 20.

Stolberg, Cheryl Gay (2005c) "Schiavo's Case May Reshape American Law." *New York Times,* April 1.

Stolberg, Cheryl Gay (2005d) "Senate's Leader Veers from Bush over Stem Cells." *New York Times,* July 29.

Stolberg, Cheryl Gay (2006a) "Nancy Reagan Supports Stem Cell Bill." *New York Times,* May 16.

Stolberg, Cheryl Gay (2006b) "The 2006 Campaign; G.O.P. Moves Fast to Reignite Issue of Gay Marriage." *New York Times,* October 27.

Stolberg, Cheryl Gay, and Elisabeth Bumiller (2005) "Senate Confirms Roberts as 17th Chief Justice." *New York Times,* September 30, A1.

Stollars, Stella (2006) Kansas City Republican ward committeewoman. Interview with Daniel Hillyard, Kansas City, Missouri, February 3.

Stone, Peter (2004) "Ralph Reed's Other Cheek." *Mother Jones,* November/December.

Stout, David (2007) "Supreme Court Upholds Ban on Abortion Procedure." *New York Times,* April 28.

Stricherz, Mark (2005) "Goodbye Catholics: How One Man Reshaped the Democratic Party." *Commonweal,* November 4.

Sturgeon, Will (2005) "Tech's Big Gamble: Las Vegas Cheat-Busting: The Truth about Tech Detection." www.silicon .com, August 19.

Sullivan, Amy (2006) "When Would Jesus Bolt?" *Washington Monthly,* April.

Sullivan, Andrew (1995) *Virtually Normal: An Argument about Homosexuality.* New York: Vintage Books.

Surviving Family Members (2005) Brief of Amici Curiae Surviving Family Members in Support of Respondents, *Gonzales v. Oregon,* in the Supreme Court of the United States, July 20.

Sutherland, Edwin, and Donald R. Cressey (1960) *Principles of Criminology.* 6th ed. Philadelphia: Lippincott.

Swarns, Rachel L. (2006) "Rift on Immigration Widens for Conservatives and Cardinals." *New York Times,* March 19.

Talbot, Margaret (2004) "The Struggle." *New Yorker,* November 8.

Talev, Margaret (2006) "Republicans Walk a Fine Line for Bipartisan Stem Cell Push." *Sacramento Bee,* April 3, http:// www.sacbee.com.

Tannenbaum, Frank (1938) *Crime and the Community.* Boston: Glinn.

Taylor, Brett (2004) "Where Playboy and 'Will and Grace' Reign." *New York Times,* November 21.

Taylor, Stuart, Jr. (2002) "Political Pulse: A Popularity Contest." *Atlantic Monthly,* November 19.

Teixeira, Ruy (2005) "It's Definitely a Pro-choice, Pro–Roe v. Wade Country 'Donkey Rising.' " www.emerging democraticmajorityweblog.com, November 11.

Terry, Jennifer (2006) "Reproductive Rights and Stem Cell Research." Presentation at "Stem Cells and Society: A Series of Dialogues." Schools of Biological Sciences and Humanities, University of California, Irvine, April 26.

Terry, Randall (2003) "Saving Terri Schiavo: How an Avalanche of Media and Sympathy Won Her Reprieve." Society for Truth and Justice, http:// www.societyfortruthandjustice.com, October 26.

Terry, Randall (2005) "Judicial Decrees Are Not 'The Rule of Law.' " http://www.theconservativevoice.com. March 17.

Thavis, John (2005) "Vatican Official: Norms Not Aimed at Transitory Homosexual Episodes." Catholic News Service, November 29.

Thomas, Rev. John H. (2006) "The IRS, the IRD, and the Red State/Blue State Religion." Address by United Church of Christ General Minister and President, Gettysburg College, March 12.

Thomas More Society (2005) Brief Amicus Curiae of the Thomas More Society in Support of Petitioners, *Gonzales v. Oregon,* in the Supreme Court of the United States, May 9.

Thompson, William N. (1998) "Uncertain Futures with Proven Entertainment Formulas: Las Vegas Approaches the Millennium." Unpublished paper, University of Nevada, Las Vegas, September 2.

Thompson, William N. (2003) "The Social Costs of Gambling: Old Questions and New Answers from a Las Vegas Survey." On panel, "Social Costs of Gambling." Twelfth International Conference on Gambling and Risk Taking, Vancouver, British Columbia, May 26–30.

The Times of Harvey Milk (1984) A film by Rob Epstein and Richard Schmeichen.

Tisch, Chris (2005) "A Fate Unclear, a Legacy Assured." *St. Petersburg Tines Online, Tampa Bay,* February 27.

Tisch, Chris (2006) "Schiavo-Inspired Laws Mostly Fail." *St. Petersburg Times,* March 27.

Todd, Chuck (2006) "Congress Gets a Case of the Blues." NationalJournal.com, November 8.

Tollison, Jeanne (2003) "Explain This to Me Again: If We Protect the Right to Intimate Sexual Relations, We Can't Protect the Right to Abortion? Justice Scalia's Implausible Dissent in *Lawrence v. Texas." Western State University Law Review* 31:163–183.

Tonry, Michael (2004) *Thinking about Crime: Sense and Sensibility in American Penal Culture.* New York: Oxford University Press.

Townsend, Tim (2005) "Catholic Clergy Will Oppose Embryonic Cell Research from Pulpit." *St. Louis Post-Dispatch,* November 4. http://www.stltoday.com/stltoday/news/stories.nsf/religion/story/294E9B64D99D1274862570C4001B3D84?OpenDocument. Accessed on November 25, 2005.

Transcript (2005a) Official Transcript of Oral Arguments, *Gonzales v. Oregon,* in the Supreme Court of the United States, October 5

Transcript (2005b) "Transcript: Day Two of the Roberts Confirmation Hearings." September 13. http://www.washingtonpost.com.

Transcript (2005c) "Transcript: Day Three of the Roberts Confirmation Hearings." September 14. http://www.washigntonpost.com.

Trebay, Guy (2005) "Cowboys, Just Like in the Movie." *New York Times,* December 18, sec. 9, p. 1.

Tribe, Laurence (1992) *Abortion: The Clash of Absolutes.* 2nd ed. New York: Norton.

Tribe, Laurence (2004) "*Lawrence v. Texas:* The 'Fundamental Right' That Dare Not Speak Its Name." *Harvard Law Review* 117:1893.

truthhwinsout.org (2006) truthhwinsout.org.

Tumulty, Karen (2006) "Where the Real Action Is . . ." *Time,* January 30, 50–53.

Turley, Jonathan (2005) "A Parent's Right to Know." *USA Today,* December 5.

United Church of Christ (2004) "All the People." http://www.stillspeaking.com.

UPI (2005) "Doctors Willing to Give Teens STD Vaccine." October 28.

Urban, Nancy, Alyssa Wulf, and Anat Shenker-Osorio (2006) "The Value of Values." Berkeley, Calif.: Rockridge Institute. www.rockridgeinstitute.com, March 24.

U.S. Catholic Conference et al. (2005) Brief Amici Curiae of the United States Conference of Catholic Bishops, California Catholic Conference, Oregon Catholic Conference, Washington State Catholic Conference; Catholic Health Association of the United States, and Lutheran Church-Missouri Synod in Support of Petitioners, *Gonzales v. Oregon*, in the Supreme Court of the United States, May 9.

U.S. Conference of Catholic Bishops (2005) Secretariat for Pro-Life Activities, May 16.

U.S. Congress Members (2005) Amicus Curiae Brief of Senators Rick Santorum, Tom Coburn, M.D., James N. Inhofe, Jim Demint, Christopher S. Bond, Larry Craig, Judd Craig, and Sam Brownback, and Representatives Steve Chabot, Chris Smith, Jack Kingston, John Shimkus, Joseph R. Pitts, Henry Hyde, Mark Green, Todd Akin, Roscoe Bartlett, Jeff Miller, Steve King, Thomas Petri, Mark E. Souder, Pete King, Paul Ryan, Virgil H. Goode, Jr., Gene Taylor, John N. Hostettler, and Ralph Hall in Support of Petitioners, *Gonzales v. Oregon*, in the Supreme Court of the United States, May 11.

U.S. Newswire (2005) "LULAC: AB 654 Advocates Are Misleading the Public." May 11. http://www.usnewswire.com. Accessed on June 19, 2006.

U.S. Newswire (2006) "Department of Justice Statement on Supreme Court's Decision in *Gonzales v. Oregon*" Press release, January 17. http://www.usdoj .gov/opa/pr/2006/January/06_opa_018 .html. Accessed on January 17, 2006.

U.S. Supreme Court (2006) *Gonzales v. Carhart*. No. 05-380, transcript of oral arguments, November 8.

USA Today (2003) "Excerpt from Santorum Interview." http://www.usatoday .com, April 23.

USA Today (2006) "Lottery Results." April 28.

USA Today/CNN/Gallup Poll (1996) "Should a Doctor Aid Suicide?" http:// www.usatoday.com.

Vaid, Urvashi (1995) *Virtual Equality: The Mainstreaming of Gay and Lesbian Liberation*. New York: Anchor Books.

van Aelstyn, Nicholas, et al. (2005) Brief for Patient-Respondents in *Gonzales v. Oregon*. United States Supreme Court, No. 04-623.

Vargo, Dianne (2005) "Connecting the Dots: Stem Cells and Human Cloning." Citizen Link, Colorado Springs: Focus on the Family.

va4marriage (2006) http://www .va4marriage.org, Official Website of Supporters of the Virginia Marriage Amendment.

Verhovek, Sam Howe (2001) "Federal Agents Are Directed to Stop Physicians Who Assist Assisted Suicides." *New York Times*, November 7.

Vestal, Christine (2006) "States Probe Limits of Abortion Policy." http://www .stateline.org, June 22.

Vogel, Nancy (2006) "Assisted-Suicide Measure Falls a Vote Short." *Los Angeles Times*, June 28.

Volberg, Rachel (2001) *When the Chips Are Down: Problem Gambling in America*. New York: Century Foundation Press.

Walker, Doug (2006) "Different Perspectives on Estimating the Social Costs of Gambling." Paper presented at the

Thirteenth International Conference on Gambling and Risk Taking, Lake Tahoe, Nevada, May 25.

Wall Street Journal (2005) "Terri Schiavo and the Law: The Case for Life." Editorial, March 21.

Wallis, Jim (2005) *God's Politics: Why the Right Gets It Wrong and the Left Doesn't Get It.* San Francisco: HarperSanFrancisco.

Walters, Suzanna Danula (2001) *All the Rage: The Story of Gay Visibility in America.* Chicago: University of Chicago Press.

Warren Rick (2002) *The Purpose-Driven Life: What on Earth Am I Here For?* Grand Rapids, Mich.: Zondervan.

Weiner, Jonathan (2004) *His Brother's Keeper: One Family's Journey to the Edge of Medicine.* New York: ecco/ HarperCollins.

Weisberg, Jacob (1999) "The Governor-President." *New York Times Magazine,* January 17, 30+.

Weiss, Rick (2001a) "Nobel Laureates Back Stem Cell Research." *Washington Post,* February 22, A2.

Weiss, Rick (2001b) "Scientists Use Embryos Made Only for Research." *Washington Post,* July 11, A1.

The White House (2006) "Remarks by the President at Georgia Victory 2006 Rally." http://www.whitehouse.gov, October 30.

The White House (2007) "Statement by the President on Stem Cell Research." http://www.whitehouse.gov, April 11.

Wilkinson, Tracy (2005) "Vatican Document Bans Active Gays as Priests." *Los Angeles Times,* November 30.

Williams, Glanville (1957) *The Sanctity of Life and the Criminal Law.* New York: Knopf.

Williams, Glanville (1958) "Euthanasia Legislation: A Rejoinder to the Nonreligious Objections." *Minnesota*

Law Review 43:134–147. Reprinted in A. B. Downing, ed., *Euthanasia and the Right to Death: The Case for Voluntary Euthanasia.* London: Peter Owen, 1969.

Williams, Juliet (2006) "American Indian Casinos Now a $23 Billion-a-Year Industry." Associated Press, http:// news.lp.findlaw.com.

Wilmut, Ian, and Roger Highfield (2006) *After Dolly: The Uses and Misuses of Human Cloning.* New York: Norton.

Wilson, James Q. (2005a) "Politics and Polarization." Tanner Lecture. Cambridge, Mass.: Harvard University, November 4.

Wilson, James Q. (2005b) "Religion and Polarization." Tanner Lecture. Cambridge, Mass.: Harvard University, November 5.

Winn, Pete (2005a) "Court Issues 'Dangerous' Decisions on Ten Commandments." citizenlink.org. Colorado Springs: Focus on the Family, June 27.

Winn, Pete (2005b) "Frist Backs Embryonic Stem-Cell Bill" Colorado Springs: Focus on the Family, July 29.

Winn, Pete (2005c) "Supreme Court Hears Two Key Abortion Cases." citizenlink.org. Colorado Springs: Focus on the Family, December 1.

Winn, Pete (2006) " 'Values Voter Summit' Set for Fall." citizenlink.org. Colorado Springs: Focus on the Family, May 2.

Winn, Pete, and Jessica Headley (2006) "Episcopal Leader: Homosexuality Not a Sin." Colorado Springs: Focus on the Family. http://www.citizenlink.com.

Winseman, Albert L. "U.S. Government Loses Public's Blessing to Promote Values." Gallup Poll, October 25.

Wittes, Benjamin (2007) "Winner Takes Some: The Supreme Court's Shift on Abortion Is Not What You Think." *New Republic,* April 30.

Wolfe, Alan (1998) *One Nation, after All: How the Middle-Class Americans*

Really Think About: God, Country, Family, Racism, Welfare, Immigration, Homosexuality, Work, the Right, the Left, and Each Other. New York: Viking.

Wolfe, Alan (2001) *Moral Freedom: The Search for Virtue in a World of Choice.* New York: Norton.

Wolfe, Alan (2004) "Faith, Freedom and Toleration." in E. J. Dionne Jr. et al., eds., *One Electorate under God: A Dialogue on Religion and American Politics.* Washington, D.C.: Brookings Institution Press.

Wolfe, Joanne, Diane L. Fairclough, Brian R. Clarridge, Elisabeth R. Daniels, and Ezekiel J. Emanuel (1999) "Stability of Attitudes Regarding Physician-Assisted Suicide and Euthanasia among Oncology Patients, Physicians, and the General Public." *Journal of Clinical Oncology* 17:1274–1279.

Wolfson, Evan (2004) *Why Marriage Matters: America, Equality, and Gay People's Right to Marry.* New York: Simon and Schuster.

Woman Vision (2003) "No Secret Anymore: The Times of Del Martin and Phyllis Lyon." http://woman-vision.org.

Wuthnow, Robert (2004) *Saving America: Faith-Based Services and the Future of Civil Society.* Princeton, N.J.: Princeton University Press.

Wuthnow, Robert (2005) *America and the Challenges of Religious Diversity.* Princeton, N.J.: Princeton University Press.

www.nocloning.org (2006) Missourians against Human Cloning. Radio advertisement.

Yoo, John (2005) "Opportunity Squandered." *Washington Post,* October 4.

Zernicke, Katie (2006) "Democrats Outline a Platform for the Fall." *New York Times,* June 17.

Zweynert, Astrid (2006) "British Parliament Blocks Assisted Suicide Law." Reuters, May 12.

Index

three "A's," 29
"five nonnegotiables," 6, 29
7-Eleven stores, 52
60 Minutes (television show), 140, 186
700 Sundays (Crystal), 93, 126
1980 presidential election, 70, 246
1992 presidential election, 70
2000 presidential election, 79, 187
2002 midterm elections, 79
2004 presidential election, 1–6; abortion, 5, 70–71, 247; Bush (George W.) and, 1, 2, 4–5, 22, 53, 66, 74, 82, 125, 187, 204; Catholics, 204; contestation of personal morality after, 82; Democratic Party, 5–6, 246–247; Dobson and, 2; Falwell and, 1–2; gay marriage, 5, 6, 97, 120; Iraq War, 5, 247; Kerry and, 4, 6, 70–71, 74; moral values, 5; *New York Times,* 2, 4–5; same-sex marriage, 121, 247; stem cell research, 210; value voters, 10, 53, 61, 82, 226, 228, 235–236, 238, 242
2006 midterm elections, 250–256; abortion, 252; de-alignment during, 253; Democratic Party, 29, 250–251, 254; Dionne on, 254; Iraq War, 252; liberalization, 256; Missouri, 211, 213, 222–223; political moderates, 254; Reagan Democrats, 253; Republican Party, 180–181, 250–252, 253–255; same-sex marriage, 252; Schiavo case, 181, 222; social conservatives, 250, 255; stem cell research, 221, 222–224, 251, 252; value voters, 226, 250, 252–253; Western states, 253

ABC (network), 26
ABC News poll, 74, 136, 212
ABC News/*Washington Post* poll, 76
abortion, 53–92; 2004 presidential election, 5, 70–71, 247; 2006 midterm elections, 252; "abortion grays," 83–84, 235; abortion providers, 87–88; "absolute right" framing, 71–72; ambivalence about, 53, 56–57, 73–78, 212; American Medical Association, 16; antiabortion activists, 198, 208–209; attitudes toward, 13, 15–16, 19; autonomy, 85; Bush (George W.) and, 205; cartoons/graphic depictions of, 79–80; Catholic Church, 71, 78, 113, 194; Catholics, 75–76; Christian Coalition, 70; Christian Right, 24, 69–70; compassion, 244–245; contestation of, 70; counties lacking abortion providers, 87; courts, 241; criminalization of, 16, 90, 141; culture wars, 68; Democratic Party, 77, 82–84; demography, 15–16; "Dilation and Extraction for Late Second Trimester Abortion" (Haskell), 79; federalism, 241; government intrusion into family affairs, freedom from, 222; incest, 87; judicial activism, 72–73; late-term/"partial birth" abortions, 56, 57, 70, 76, 78–82, 90–92; legal shifts against, 240; liberalization of abortion laws, 69; life of the mother, 87; litmus test on, 70; Louisiana, 88; Medicare funding, 56; Ohio, 88; parental consent, 78, 85, 235; Partial-Birth Abortion Act, 82; pragmatism about, 185; pre-*Roe v. Wade* years, 68–69; primary users, 85; privacy, 85; pro-choice movement, 57, 75, 76–77, 78, 86–87, 89, 90; pro-life movement, 57, 68, 70, 71, 75, 78–79; Protestants, 75–76; public support for legal abortion, 53, 57, 69, 73–78, 89; rape, 87; Reagan Democrats, 70; reduction in number of, 90; *Roe v. Wade* (see *Roe v. Wade*); Schiavo case, 133; social conservatives, 98, 126; "Sodomized Religious Virgin Exception," 88; South Dakota 2006 law, 53, 87–88, 90, 252; stability regarding, period of, 70; stem cell research, 190, 220–222; teenage access, 56; vacuum aspiration, 80; woman's health, 57, 81–82, 85, 91; young women, 89
Abramoff, Jack, 49
abstinence, 86

ACLU (American Civil Liberties Union), 90, 161
ACT UP, 25, 108, 109
activists, rise of, 231–232
ADAPT, 153
ADL (Anti-Defamation League), 24
advance directives, 140
African Americans, gay rights and, 115–116
African Church, 117
AGA. *See* American Gaming Association
Ahrens, Dan, 25–26
Akin, Todd, 155
Akinola, Peter, 117
Alito, Samuel A., Jr.: Bauer and, 65; *Casey v. Pennsylvania*, 65; Clinton (Hillary) and, 92; confirmation hearings, 65–68, 76, 228; *Griswold v. Connecticut*, 66–67; late-term/ "partial birth" abortions, 91; O'Connor and, 66; *Planned Parenthood v. Casey*, 67; *Roe v. Wade*, 66–67; Specter and, 66
Allen, Bill, 146
Allen, George, 137
Alliance for Justice, 58
Altman, Dennis, 111
AMA. *See* American Medical Association
ambivalence: about 1960s style liberalization, 242; about abortion, 53, 56–57, 73–78, 212; about change, 29; about gay rights, 95, 120; about homosexuality, 120; about legal gambling, 45–46, 52; about legislating personal morality, 29–30; about safeguarding individuals, 183, 184; about same-sex marriage, 115; about stem cell research, 195, 203; of Americans, 225, 230–231
American Academy of HIV Medicine, 161
American Academy of Pain Management, 161
American Academy of Pediatrics, 84
American Association for the Advancement of Science, 200
American Association of Pro Life Obstetricians and Gynecologists, 155
American Banker (newspaper), 26
American Center for Law and Justice, 177
American Civil Liberties Union (ACLU), 90, 161
American College of Legal Medicine, 158
American College of Obstetricians and Gynecologists, 84
American Enterprise Institute, 75, 95
American Episcopal Church, 116–117
American Family Association, 98, 100
American Football Conference, 35
American Gaming Association (AGA): campaign contributions, 49; poker playing, 43;

president, 36; problem gambling, 45, 46; public support for legal gambling, 36
American Geriatrics Society, 161
American Life League, 201, 207
American Medical Association (AMA): abortion, 16; assisted suicide, 155, 174, 179
American Prospect (magazine), 208
American Public Health Association (APHA), 160
American Society for Cell Biology, 202
American Society for Reproductive Medicine, 199
American Values (group): anti–gay rights sentiment, 98; Bauer (Gary) and, 20; Bush's 2006 State of the Union address, 121; Santorum and, 229
Americans United for Life, 155
Anderson, Kurt, 234
Anglican Church, 117
Anti-Defamation League (ADL), 24
APHA (American Public Health Association), 160
Arizona, defense of marriage act (DOMA) in, 125, 252
Arlington Group, 98
Armey, Dick, 181, 251
Aron, Nan, 58
artificial nutrition and hydration, 140
Ashcroft, John: assisted suicide, 147; assisted suicide, prescription of drugs for, 165; Bush (George W.) and, 148; Clinton (Bill) and, 147; *Gonzales v. Oregon*, 152, 154, 155; home state, 187; *Lessons from a Father to a Son*, 147; Missouri governor race (2000), 147–148; Oregon Death with Dignity Act (ODDA/DWDA), 147–148, 150–151, 152, 157, 160–161, 167 (see also *Gonzales v. Oregon*); pain management, 160; ratings of, 147
assisted suicide, 127–185; abuses against sick and vulnerable, 144; advancements in end-of-life care, 179–180; American Medical Association (AMA), 155, 174, 179; Ashcroft and, 147; attitudes toward, 13; California, 140, 178–179, 180; Catholic Church, 143–144; Christian Right, 24, 183; compatibility with medicine's aims, 154–155, 156–157, 174, 180; criminalization of, 141, 182; criminalization of physicians prescribing pain relief for terminal patients, 150; *Cruzan v. Director, Missouri Department of Health*, 161, 170, 180; decriminalization of, 140–141, 142; as elite liberal movement, 127; Family Research Council, 155; federal commerce power, 175; *Gonzales v. Oregon* (see *Gonzales v.*

Oregon); harm reduction, 141–142; high-profile controversies, 180; impaired judgment of patients wanting, 157; "legitimate medical purpose," 152, 158, 165, 173, 182; Limbaugh on, 145; Maine, 140, 178; Michigan, 140, 177–178; nationalization of the issue, 241; opposition to, 142–148, 214; Oregon, 184 (*see also* Oregon Death with Dignity Act); pain management, 155; physician movement for reform, 138–139; physicians' willingness to prescribe medication, 179–180; prescription of drugs for, 150, 152, 165–166, 171, 174–175, 179–180; public support for, 6, 7, 146, 178, 179; Rehnquist on, 172, 174; sacredness of life argument, 142–144; Schiavo case (*see* Schiavo, Michael; Schiavo, Terri); slippery slope argument, 144–146, 169; spread of laws supporting, 177–178; states' right to experiment with, 241; *Vacco v. Quill*, 153; Vermont, 179; voter ballot initiatives, 241; *vs.* tried-and-true methods of suicide, 145; Washington State, 140, 142, 143–144; *Washington v. Glucksberg* (see *Washington v. Glucksberg*). *See also* death with dignity movement
Associated Press, 6, 56
Association of American Medical Colleges, 202–203
Association of American Universities, 202
Atkinson, Robert M., 166–170
Atlanta Journal-Constitution (newspaper), 23–24
Atlantic City, New Jersey, 11, 34
Atwater, Lee, 29
AUTONOMY, Inc., 154
autonomy (personal/individual): abortion, 85; contestation of, 245; death and dying, 138, 139, 159; government intrusion into family affairs, freedom from, 249–250; Mill and, 14, 244, 245, 249; moderate Americans, 243; personal morality, 249–250, 256; public support for, 244, 245, 255–256; Schiavo case, 7, 243
Ayotte v. Planned Parenthood of Northern New England, 71

Baird, Douglas, 129
Baldassare, Mark, 77
Banks, Amanda, 220
Barnes, Fred, 146
Barone, Michael, 5
Barr Pharmaceuticals, 84
Barron's (newspaper), 26
Bartle, Matt, 188–189
Bartlett, Bruce, 253

Bartlett, Roscoe, 155
Bass, Thomas, *Eudaemonic Pie*, 43
Bauer, Carol, 122
Bauer, Gary: Alito and, 65; American Values, 20; anti-gay rights sentiment, 98; Bush's 2006 State of the Union address, 121; federal marriage protection amendment, 102–103; on homosexuals, 20–21, 244; late-term/"partial birth" abortions, 91; Miers nomination, 61, 63–64; pro-family movement, 115; same-sex marriage, 93, 99–100; Schiavo case, 134; Supreme Court vacancies, 68; traditional marriage, 99–100
Becker, Howard, 15
Beeson, Diane, 217
Belgium, same-sex marriage in, 96
Bellin, Andy, *Poker Nation*, 37
Benedict XVI, Pope, 113, 114–115
Bennett, William (Bill): *Book of Virtues*, 31; *De-valuing of America*, 31; gambling habit, 2, 9, 31–32, 45; moral education, 32
Berg, Paul, 210
"biconceptuals," 239
Biden, Joseph, 59, 236–237
Biotechnology Industry Organization, 199, 202, 209
birth control: abortion (*see* abortion); abstinence, 86; contraception, 86, 87; morning-after pill (Plan B), 84–86, 90
Blackmun, Harry A.: *Roe v. Wade*, 54, 55, 69; trimester system, 54
Blagojevich, Rod, 189
Blankley, Tony, 63
Blumenauer, Earl, 160
Blunt, Matt, 191, 195
Bonavoglia, Angela, 78
Bond, Christopher S., 155
Bonnicksen, Andrea L., 196, 198, 200
Boogie Nights (film), 101
Book of Virtues (Bennett), 31
Bopp, James, Jr., 71–72, 144–145
borderline crimes, 15, 16
Bork, Robert, 64
Bowers v. Hardwick: *Lawrence v. Texas*, 104, 110–111; sodomy laws upheld, 103, 110; Stevens and, 73
Bowman, Karlyn, 75
Boxer, Barbara, 76
Boy Scouts, 73
Breyer, Stephen, in *Gonzales v. Oregon*, 167–168, 169, 171, 172
Bringing Down the House (Mezrich), 43
Brokeback Mountain (film), 9, 93, 100–101
Brooks, David, 136–137
Brown, Judie, 207

Brown, Willie, 10, 93
Brownback, Sam, 79, 137, 155
Bryant, Anita, 108
Buchanan, Patrick, 1, 100
Buckley, William F., 146
Bureau of Narcotics and Dangerous Drugs, 152
Burke, Raymond L., 71, 192–194
Burkeman, Oliver, "Voice of Morality Exposed as Chronic Casino Loser," 31
Bush, George H. W.: funding of research involving human embryos, 196–197; no-new-taxes pledge, 205, 206; Roberts and, 58
Bush, George W.: 2000 presidential election, 79, 187; 2004 presidential election, 1, 2, 4–5, 22, 53, 66, 74, 82, 125, 187, 204; 2006 State of the Union address, 121; abortion, 205; administration of (see Bush administration, George W.); Ashcroft and, 148; federal marriage protection amendment, 123; funding of research involving human embryos, 206, 207, 241; John Paul II and, 206; performance and priorities, 29; pro-life movement, 208; pro-life principles, 62; Roe v. Wade, 62; same-sex marriage, 96, 125; social conservatives, 64–65; stem cell research, 148, 191, 195, 197, 201, 202, 203, 204–209, 215–216, 221, 222; supporters, 22; Supreme Court nominations, 6, 57, 59–60, 62–63, 64, 109; value voters, 4–5, 225, 228
Bush, Jeb: legal gambling in Florida, 48; Schiavo case, 128–129, 131, 137
Bush, Laura, 62
Bush administration, George W.: Armey on, 250–251; dissatisfaction with, 235–236; intrusion into family business/private affairs, freedom from, 249; O'Connor's retirement, 55; Oregon Death with Dignity Act (ODDA/DWDA), 150, 179; Protestants, evangelical, 252; stem cell research, 186, 218, 221
Business Week (magazine), 11

Cabazon. See California v. Cabazon Band of Mission Indians
California: abortion, decriminalization of, 10; assisted suicide, 140, 178–179, 180; death with dignity movement, 10–11; defense of marriage act (DOMA), 125; domestic partner law (AB 205, 2003), 95; "ex-gay movement," 101; gay and lesbian teachers, 9, 11; gay rights, 111; Indian casinos, 40–42; living will legislation, 10; Moscone Act (1976), 10; Natural Death Act (1976), 10–

11, 131, 138; pro-choice electorate, 76–77; pro-life movement, 211; Proposition 5 (1998), 40; Proposition 68 (2004), 42; Proposition 70 (2004), 42; Proposition 71 (2004), 186, 210–211, 215, 216, 217; sodomy, decriminalization of, 10, 11; stem cell research, 8, 10, 187, 210–211, 222; textbooks, gays and lesbians in, 101; Tribal Government Gaming and Economic Self-Sufficiency Act (1998), 40
California Institute of Regenerative Medicine (CIRM), 222
California Lottery, 38
California v. Cabazon Band of Mission Indians, 34, 35, 41, 52
Callahan, Daniel, 208
campaign finance, 231
Campaign Life Missouri, 191
Canada, same-sex marriage in, 96, 103
Caplan, Arthur, 130, 132, 209
Capote, Truman, 101
Capote (film), 101
Card, Andy, 205
Carnahan, Mel, 147–148
Carter, Jimmy, 11–12
Carville, James, "Getting Heard" (with Greenberg), 225
Casanova, Jose, 22, 70
Cascade AIDS Project, 154
Casey v. Planned Parenthood, 65. See also Planned Parenthood v. Casey
Castle, Mike, 219
Catholic Church: abortion, 71, 78, 113, 194; assisted suicide, 143–144; banning of homosexuals from the priesthood, 114–115; believers (see Catholics); death penalty, 113; end-of-life issues, 135; euthanasia, 71, 113, 194; federal marriage protection amendment, 114, 121; "five nonnegotiables," 6, 29; gay rights, 113–115; Gonzales v. Oregon, 158; human cloning, 71, 194; Kerry and, 71, 193–194; Oregon Death with Dignity Act (ODDA/DWDA), 144; same-sex marriage, 71, 194; stem cell research, 71, 113, 191–194; views of, 24–25; Washington State, 143–144
Catholic Health Association of the United States, 154
Catholic Healthcare Association, 143
Catholics: 2004 presidential election, 204; abortion, 75–76; "purpleness" of, 78; tolerance, 236
Cato Institute, 160
CBS (network), 26
CBS poll, 89
CBS News poll, 134, 201

CDC (Centers for Disease Control), 86
Center for American Progress, 83
Center for Genetics and Society, 212
Center for Self-Determination, 154
Center on Disability Studies, Law, and
  Human Policy, 153
Centers for Disease Control (CDC), 86
Chabot, Steve, 155
Charlton Associates, 212
Charo, Alta, 255
Cheney, Dick, 146, 205
Cheney, Mary, 122
Christian Coalition: abortion, 70; anti–gay
  rights sentiment, 98; antidiscrimination
  laws affecting gays and lesbians, 25;
  Ashcroft and, 147; backlash against liber-
  alization, 27, 50; Bush's stem cell stance,
  208; in Christian Right, 22; drug laws, 27;
  executive director, 22; gay rights, 109;
  Reed and, 49; Santorum and, 229
Christian Exodus, 20
Christian Legal Society, 155
Christian Medical and Dental Association,
  177
Christian Medical Association, 155
Christian Right: abortion, 24, 69–70; as-
  sisted suicide, 24, 183; gay rights, 24, 108,
  111; organizations in, 22; power of, 22–
  23; Republican Party, 231; Schiavo case,
  185; stem cell research, 24, 190–191
Christianity Today (newspaper), 208
Christiansen, Eugene, 33
Christmas season, 21
Christopher Reeve Paralysis Foundation, 202
CIRM (California Institute of Regenerative
  Medicine), 222
Cities on a Hill (FitzGerald), 96
civil rights, gay rights and, 114, 116
Civil Rights for Families Initiative, 118
civil unions for same-sex couples: American
  attitudes toward, 97; Connecticut, 119;
  gay marriage, 119; Massachusetts, 119;
  New Jersey, 125; public support for, 6, 7,
  97–98, 120, 124, 212, 230; states allowing, 7; Vermont, 96, 97, 113, 119. *See also*
  gay marriage; same-sex marriage
Clarkson, Kelly, 211
Clement, Paul D.: *Gonzales v. Oregon,* 162–
  166, 167–168, 170–171; *Washington v.
  Glucksberg,* 164
Clinton, Bill: 1992 presidential election, 70;
  administration of (*see* Clinton administration); adultery by, 28; Ashcroft and, 147;
  defense of marriage acts (DOMAs), 117–
  118; "Don't Ask, Don't Tell" policy, 110;
  funding of research involving human embryos, 197, 200; gays in the military, 204–
  205; *Planned Parenthood v. Casey,* 55; sex
  scandal, 3
Clinton, Hillary: Alito and, 92; federal marriage protection amendment, 124; Focus
  on the Family, 124; *It Takes a Village,* 228;
  morning-after pill (Plan B), 84–85; pro-life
  Democrats, outreach to, 82, 83; Roberts
  and, 92; *Roe v. Wade,* 92; Schiavo case,
  133; South Dakota 2006 abortion law, 90
Clinton administration: on-defense discre-
  tionary spending, 251; Oregon Death with
  Dignity Act (ODDA/DWDA), 148, 150
cloning: Dolly (cloned sheep), 190, 198–199;
  human cloning (*see* human cloning);
  Korean scandal, 216, 221; stem cell
  research, 188, 189, 190, 214, 216
Clotfelter, Charles, 45
CNN (network), 26
CNN poll, 96–97
CNN/USA Today/Gallup poll, 212
Coalition for the Advancement of Medical
  Research, 202, 213
Coalition for Urgent Research, 209
Coburn, Tom, 155
Colmes, Alan, 255
Colorado: Amendment 2 (1992), 110
"Come Death" (Davis), 159
Commission on the Review of the National
  Policy Toward Gambling, 34, 44, 52
compassion, 244–245
Compassion and Choices, 138
Comprehensive Drug Abuse Prevention and
  Control Act (1970), 151
Concerned Women for America: *Brokeback
  Mountain,* 101; Bush's stem cell stance,
  209; Crouse and, 101; *Gonzales v. Ore-
  gon,* 177; Santorum and, 229
Congressional Biomedical Ethics Advisory
  Committee, 145
Conley, Dalton, 77–78
Connecticut: civil unions for same-sex
  couples, 119; gay rights, 119
"Connecting the Dots" (Vargo), 186
Conrad, Peter, 15
Constantine, Thomas A., 165
constructivist approach to social problems,
  17
contraception, 86, 87
Controlled Substances Act (CSA), 160–166,
  169–177; administration of, 156, 171; attorney general's authority under, 151, 155–
  156, 173; consistency in interpreting, 165;
  enactment, 151, 160, 166, 172–173; GHB
  (drug), 163; *Gonzales v. Oregon,* 155–
  156, 157, 162–163, 165, 166, 169–170,

Controlled Substances Act (*continued*)
171, 173; intent of, 155, 160, 161, 166; judgment of the medical community, 171; "legitimate medical purpose," determination of a drug's, 176, 177; "legitimate medical purpose" of prescribing drugs for assisted suicide, 152, 165, 173; Oregon Death with Dignity Act (ODDA/DWDA), 150–152, 155–156, 164, 165, 175; prescriptions under, 152, 165–166; provisions, 151–152; states's authority to regulate medical practice, 161, 170, 173, 174

Cook, Philip, 15–16, 45

Cooper, Marc, 32, 33

Cornyn, John, 7

Coulter, Ann, 61, 63, 100–101

Council on Education, 202

Craig, Judd, 155

Craig, Larry, 155

creationism: public support for, 24

Crenson, Mathew, 191

Crimes without Victims (Schur), 15

criminal law: personal morality, 182–183, 184, 239–241, 244; private behavior, 14–15, 27; reach of, 27; social change, 240–241; victimless crime, 17–18. *See also* criminalization; decriminalization

criminal laws: assisted suicide, 177–178

criminalization: of abortion, 16, 90, 141; of assisted suicide, 141, 182; of marijuana, 27; of physicians prescribing pain relief for terminal patients, 150; of sodomy (see *Bowers v. Hardwick*); of stem cell research, 188, 189, 199, 201

Cromartie, Michael, 115

Crouse, Janice, 101

Crowley, Candy, 251

Cruzan v. Director, Missouri Department of Health, 161, 170, 180

Crystal, Billy: *700 Sundays*, 93, 126

CSA. See Controlled Substances Act

"cultural antimodernism," 12, 255

"culture of life," 130, 215

Culture of Life Foundation, 177

Culture War? (Fiorina), 225, 230–235

culture wars: abortion, 68; causes, 27, 242–243; central features, 12–13, 18; combatants in, 234; de-religionizing of American society, 21; "middle range" theory of, 240; social problems, discussion of, 227; waning of, 256; "Weapons of Mass Distraction," 227–228; winner of, 248–249

Cures (Duberman), 106

Danforth, John: on Republican Party, 251; Schiavo case, 181; stem cell research, 191, 218

Darian-Smith, Eve, 39

Daughters of Bilitis, 26, 94, 106

Davis, Gray, 40–41, 111

Davis, Jim, 130

Davis, Norma, "Come Death," 159

De-valuing of America (Bennett), 31

DEA (Drug Enforcement Administration), 150, 152, 165

Dean, Howard: pro-life Democrats, outreach to, 82; on Republican Party, 249; Schiavo case, 131, 133

death and dying: advance directives, 140; advancements in end-of-life care, 139–140, 179–180; American attitudes, 131–135; artificial nutrition and hydration, 140; assisted suicide (*see* assisted suicide); autonomy in dying, 138, 139, 159; death with dignity (*see* death with dignity movement); do-not-resuscitate orders (*see* do-not-resuscitate orders); end-of-life bills, 138; end-of-life issues, 135, 170, 244–245; harm reduction, 141–142; immunization from criminal/civil liability, 184; institutionalized death and dying, 179; living will statues (*see* living will statues); medical powers of attorney, 182, 184; natural death acts, 10–11, 131, 138, 184; Oregon (*see* Oregon Death with Dignity Act); physicians aiding dying patients, 140–141, 150; politics of, 183; reform of laws governing, 240–241; right-to-die, public support for, 138; right-to-die legislation, 184; right-to-die movement, 133, 139–141, 180–181; "right-to-life" issue, 133; safe harbor provisions, 184; scheduled drugs, 164; surrogate decision making, 140; "terminal sedation," 184; treatment withholding and withdrawal, 140; "wink and a nod" for rich patients, 141, 150

death penalty, Catholic Church and, 113

death with dignity movement: California, 10–11; impetus for, 138–139; institutionalized attention to palliative care and training, 179; Oregon (*see* Oregon Death with Dignity Act); public support for, 7, 10. *See also* assisted suicide

decriminalization: of abortion, 10, 16, 141, 183; of assisted suicide, 140–141, 142; of gambling, 183; gay rights and, 183–184; of marijuana, 11–12, 25, 148; of sodomy, 10, 11, 25, 103, 107 (see also *Lawrence v. Texas*); of suicide, 139; of victimless crime, 183

DeFazio, Peter, 160
defense of marriage acts (DOMAs): Arizona, 125, 252; California, 125; Clinton (Bill) and, 117–118; Republican Party, 118; social conservatives, 117–120; states voting for (2004), 3, 98; "super-DOMAs," 120
DeLay, Tom, 20, 49, 136
D'Emilio, John, on gay rights movement, 9, 106, 107–108, 110–111
Demint, Jim, 155
Democracy Corps, 83
Democratic National Committee, 249
Democratic Party: 2004 National Convention, 8, 29; 2004 presidential election, 5–6, 246–247; 2006 midterm elections, 29, 250–251, 254; abortion, 77, 82–84; American Gaming Association, 49; "Church gap," 2; "culture of life," 130; elites in, 236–237; liberalism, 231; Limbaugh on, 57; people of faith, 236–237; red state voters, 236; Roberts nomination, 59; Schiavo case, 130, 131, 133, 136; secularization, 246–247; stem cell research, 194, 250–251; "third way," 235
Department of Health, Education, and Welfare (DHEW), 196–197
Department of Health and Human Services (DHHS), 196, 197, 199
Derevensky, Jeffrey, 48
Deukmejian, George, 76
deviance, 15–18, 240
Devlin, Patrick, 14, 18
DiCamillo, Mark, 178
Dickerson, John, 64
Dignity (group), 113–114
"Dilation and Extraction for Late Second Trimester Abortion" (Haskell), 79
Dionne, E. J., Jr.: 2006 midterm elections, 254; public support for legal abortion, 74; "Weapons of Mass Distraction," 227–228, 234
disabilities rights movement, 153–154
Disunited States (Donahue), 235
do-not-resuscitate orders: acceptance of, 170; honoring of, 182; immunization from criminal/civil liability, 184; participation in, 179
Dobson, James: 2004 presidential election, 2; "big tent" Republican Party, 255; Bush's stem cell stance, 208; federal marriage protection amendment, 121; Focus on the Family, 20; on judicial tyranny, 20; Miers nomination, 60; National Gambling Impact Study Commission, 47; stem cell research, 219
Doe v. Bolton, 62

Doerflinger, Richard, 144, 208–209, 214–215
Dolly (cloned sheep), 190, 198–199
DOMAs. *See* defense of marriage acts
domestic partnerships: American attitudes toward, 97; California law (AB 205, 2003), 95; health benefits, 112; recognition of, 111
Dominus, Susan, 79, 89
Donahue, John D., *Disunited States*, 235
Don't Think of an Elephant (Lakoff), 238–239
Dowd, Maureen, 64
"Down with Fancy Book Learnin'" (Morford), 1
Drug Enforcement Administration (DEA), 150, 152, 165
drug laws, 19, 27
Duberman, Martin, *Cures*, 106
Dudgeon, Maureen, 189
Duke, Annie, 43
Durbin, Richard, 66, 124
DWDA. *See* Oregon Death with Dignity Act
Dworkin, Ronald, 150
Dying Right (Hillyard and Dombrink), 131

EAB (Ethics Advisory Board), 196–197
Eadington, Bill: gambling as entertainment, 33; mainstreaming of gaming organizations, 51, 52; problem gambling, 46
EC-help.org, 85
Eggan, Kevin, 189
elections: 1980 presidential election, 70, 246; 1992 presidential election, 70; 2000 presidential election, 79, 187; 2002 midterm elections, 79; 2004 presidential election (*see* 2004 presidential election); 2006 midterm elections (*see* 2006 midterm elections)
Enzi, Mike, 136
Episcopal Church, 116–117, 158
Ethics Advisory Board (EAB), 196–197
Ethics and Public Policy, 115
Eudaemonic Pie (Bass), 43
euthanasia: Catholic Church, 113, 194; England, 138; "euthanasia by omission," 142–143; Schiavo case, 133, 137
evangelicalism, secularization and, 24
Evangelicals in Public Life, 115
Evangelium Vitae (encyclical), 193
"ex-gay movement," 99, 101
extremists, political, 233–234

Fahrenkopf, Frank, 26
false consciousness: emphasis on, 4; morality contests, 226–227; *What's the Matter with Kansas?*, 3, 20, 29, 226–227

Falwell, Jerry: 2004 presidential election, 1–2; the "anti-Falwell," 247; anti–gay rights sentiment, 98; Bush's stem cell stance, 208; Christmas, 21; on "God Is Still Speaking Campaign," 116; political involvement of evangelicals, 256; Wallis and, 2
Family Foundation of Virginia, 99
Family Policy Network, 122
Family Research Council: abstinence, 86; anti–gay rights sentiment, 98; Bush's stem cell stance, 209; in Christian Right, 22; Frist and, 219; *Gonzales v. Oregon,* 155; Perkins and, 61; Santorum and, 229; stem cell research, 216
family values, attitudes toward, 3–4
FDA (Food and Drug Administration), 84–85, 86, 199
federal marriage protection amendment (FMPA): Bauer and, 102–103; Bush (George W.) and, 123; Catholic Church, 114, 121; Clinton (Hillary) and, 124; Dobson and, 121; Focus on the Family, 123, 124; Frist and, 122–123; gay rights, 102–103, 114, 120–124; National Gay and Lesbian Task Force, 124; Reid and, 123–124; Republican Party, 221, 250; Specter and, 124
Federal Register (newspaper), 152
federalism, 241, 242
Feinberg, Joel, 50
Feinstein, Dianne, 76, 130
Feldbaum, Carl, 209
Feldman, Alan, 38
Feldt, Gloria, 82
Felos, George, 130
feminazis, 57
feminists and stem cell research, 216–217
Financial Times (newspaper), 26
Fiorina, Morris: *Culture War?,* 225, 230–235; on "ideological moderates," 77–78; Lakoff and, 239
FitzGerald, Frances, 95–96
Fletcher, John, 198
Florida, legal gambling, 48
FMPA. *See* federal marriage protection amendment
Focus on the Family: Alito nomination, 65–66; anti–gay rights sentiment, 98, 100; Bopp and, 145; Christian Right, 22; Clinton (Hillary) and, 124; Dobson and, 20, 255; federal marriage protection amendment, 123, 124; founder, 255; gay rights, 99, 119–120; *Gonzales v. Oregon,* 155; National Gambling Impact Study Commission, 46–47; Santorum and, 229; stem cell research, 215–216, 220–221

Food and Drug Administration (FDA), 84–85, 86, 199
Forced Exit (Smith), 145–147
Fosburgh, Lacey, 95
Fox, Michael J., 200, 210, 223
Fox, Sam, 194
Fox News (network), 21, 135
Foxman, Abraham, 24
framing wars, 237–239
Frank, Thomas: backlash against liberalization, 243; rapidity of social change, 249; on the Right in America, 12; *What's the Matter with Kansas?* (see *What's the Matter with Kansas?*)
Frey, James, 11, 35
Frist, Bill: Family Research Council, 219; federal marriage protection amendment, 122–123; presidential aspirations, 137; Reagan (Nancy) on, 218; Schiavo case, 134, 137; stem cell research, 191, 205, 218–220

Gallup polls: abortion, 74–75; death with dignity, 7; gambling, 33, 38; gay marriage, 125; government intrusion into family business/private affairs, freedom from, 249; homosexuality, 120, 126; *Roe v. Wade,* 55
Galston, William, 235–236, 239, 253
gambling: books about, 42–43; as criminal activity, 34, 50–51; decriminalization of, 183; federalism, 241; Internet gambling, 52; lack of attention to, 50; legal gambling (*see* legal gambling); local ordinances, 241; morality of, 38; as "normal vice," 36, 38, 56; normalization of, 50–52; office betting pools, 35; organized crime, 38; poker, 36, 43; political corruption, 38; problem gambling, 38, 45–48; reform success, 240, 241; social conservatives, 50; state legislative activities, 241; youth gambling, 45
"Gambling with Abortion" (Gorney), 79–81
Gandy, Kim, 94–95
GAO (General Accounting Office), 84
Garner, Tyron, 103
Garrow, David J., 69
gay marriage: 2004 presidential election, 5, 6, 97, 120; American attitudes toward, 97; civil unions for same-sex couples, 119; constitutional amendment opposing, 97; courts, 241; legalization, 9–10; Massachusetts, 96; opposition to, 125, 230; public support for, 95, 96–97, 120, 124, 125; Rove and, 66; Scalia on, 100; voter ballot initiatives, 241; Wolfson on, 93; young Americans, 246. *See also* civil unions for same-sex couples; same-sex marriage

gay rights, 93–126; 1950s groups, 26; adoption, 246; African Americans, 115–116; ambivalence about, 95, 120; anti–gay rights sentiment, 98–103; antidiscrimination ordinances, 107, 111, 240; attitudes toward, 13, 19; backlash against, 98; *Bowers v. Hardwick* (see *Bowers v. Hardwick*); California, 111; Catholic Church, 113–115; Christian Coalition, 109; Christian Right, 24, 108, 111; civil rights, 109, 114, 116; Connecticut, 119; dangerousness of gays, 108–109; decriminalization and, 183–184; deterioration of traditional family, 102; domestic partnerships, 95, 97, 111, 112; "ex-gay movement," 99, 101; federal marriage protection amendment, 102–103, 114, 120–124; federalism, 241; Focus on the Family, 99, 119–120; fourth stage of, 9; "gay agenda," 111; gay and lesbian teachers, 9, 11; gender equality, 109; history of, 105–112; *Lawrence v. Texas* (see *Lawrence v. Texas*); "life-style choice," 99; Massachusetts, 95; minority rights, 245; modern era (1993 on), 106, 110–112; normalization of laws related to, 9, 26; overturning of state sodomy laws, 103; post-Stonewall/AIDS era (1980s), 106, 108–110; pre-Stonewall era (1950s–1969), 106–107; "predator" image of gays, 107–108; Protestants, evangelical, 115–116; Protestants, mainline, 113, 116–117; public support for, 6–7, 95, 120, 212, 246; reforms through challenging discrimination, 240; religion, 112–117; Republican Party, 218; Santorum and, 228–229; school curricula/textbooks, 101, 111; social conservatives, 98, 109, 111, 112; sodomy laws, 10, 11, 25, 103, 107 (see also *Bowers v. Hardwick*; *Lawrence v. Texas*); Stevens and, 73; Stonewall era (1970s), 106, 107–108; Supreme Court, 241; Vermont, 95; Wisconsin, 95

Geis, Gilbert: activities not the law's business, 14; gambling as criminal activity, 34, 50–51; liberalization of laws pertaining to victimless crime, 19; proper use of law, 244

General Accounting Office (GAO), 84

"Getting Heard" (Greenberg and Carville), 225

GHB (drug), 163

Gingrich, Newt, 61, 228, 251

Ginsburg, Faye, 70

Ginsburg, Ruth Bader: *Gonzales v. Oregon*, 163–164, 169, 172; late-term/"partial birth" abortions, 91

Gitlin, Todd, 74

Global Gaming Business (magazine), 36

Glover, Joe, 122

"God Hates Fags" campaign, 23, 112, 244

"God Is Still Speaking Campaign," 116

God's Politics (Wallis), 247–248

Goffman, Erving, 15

Goldberg, Jackie, 152, 154, 155; Atkinson

Goldberg-Hiller, Jonathan, 243, 245

Goldwater, Barry, 255

Gonzales, Alberto, 152

Gonzales v. Carhart, 92

Gonzales v. Oregon, 150–177; amici curiae (friend-of-the-court briefs), 153–162; Ashcroft and, 152, 154, 155; Atkinson and, 166–170; attorney general's authority under Controlled Substances Act, 151, 155–156, 173; Breyer and, 163–166, 167–168, 169, 171, 172; brief submitted by surviving family members, 158–159; Clement and, 162–166, 167–168, 170–171; compatibility of assisted suicide with medicine's aims, 154–155, 156–157, 174; Controlled Substances Act (CSA), 155–156, 157, 162–163, 165, 166, 169–170, 171, 173; criminalization of assisted suicide, 182; democracy and shared authority, 160–161, 174; disabilities rights movement, 153–154; dissenting opinions, 175–176; federal government's power to regulate controlled substances, 171; friend-of-the-court briefs (amici curiae), 153–162; future impact, 178; Ginsburg and, 163–164, 169, 172; impaired judgment of patients wanting assisted suicide, 157; judicial tyranny theme, 177; Kennedy (Anthony M.) and, 167–170, 171, 172, 173; "legitimate medical purpose," determination of a drug's, 176, 177; "legitimate medical purpose," enshrinement of assisted suicide as, 182; "legitimate medical purpose" of prescribing drugs for assisted suicide, 152, 158, 165, 173; Limbaugh on, 145; meaning/significance of, 182, 184–185; narcotics addiction, 163; Not Dead Yet, 153; O'Connor and, 165–166, 169, 172; ODDA opponents, arguments of, 153–157; ODDA supporter, arguments of, 157–162; oral arguments, 151, 162–172; pain management, 160; preemption doctrine, 166, 168–169; public support for right-to-die, 142; religious and spiritual beliefs, 158; Roberts and, 162, 169, 170, 171, 172; ruling in, 172–177, 179; Scalia and, 168–169, 170, 171, 172, 175, 177; scheduled drugs, 164; significance/meaning of, 182, 184–185; Smith (Wesley J.) on,

Gonzales v. Oregon (continued)
73; Souter and, 162–163, 164, 166, 169–170, 171–172; state immunization of physicians from federal control, 156; state's right to determine which medical practices are legitimate, 171; state's authority to regulate medical practice, 161, 170, 174; Stevens and, 170, 171–172; Thomas and, 172, 175–176; usurpation of federal authority, 164; *Washington v. Glucksberg*, 153, 161–162, 163–164
Gonzales v. Reich, 170, 176
Goode, Virgil H., Jr., 155
Goodman, Robert, 45
Goodrich v. Department of Public Health, 177
Goodwin, Peter, 182
Gordon, Phil, 43
Gorney, Cynthia, 79–81, 88–89
government: expansion of, 231–232; intrusion into family business/private affairs, freedom from, 49, 222, 249–250, 251, 254–255, 256
Green, Mark, 155
Greenberg, Stan, "Getting Heard" (with Carville), 225
Greenberg Quinlan Rosner Research, 253
Greenfield, Jeff, 253
Greer, George, 128–129
Gregg, Judd, 124
Grey, Tom, 49
Griffiths, John, 110
Griswold v. Connecticut, 66–67, 110
Gros, Roger, 36
Guth, James L., 8
Gutmacher Institute, 57

Hacker, Jacob, 233–234
Hagel, Chuck, 124
Hall, Ralph, 155
Hanks, Tom, 112
Hardball (television show), 1–2
Hart, Peter, 49
Harvard University, 202
Haskell, Martin, "Dilation and Extraction for Late Second Trimester Abortion," 79
Hatch, Orrin, on stem cell research, 201, 202–203, 219–220, 224
Hawaii, same-sex marriage in, 243
Hay, Harry, 126
Hentoff, Nat, 135, 137
Hill, Anita, 219
Hoffman, Philip Seymour, 101
homosexuality: acceptance of, 124, 125–126; ambivalence about, 120; banning of homosexuals from the priesthood, 114–115; gay marriage (*see* gay marriage); gay rights (*see* gay rights); John Paul II on, 113
Hooley, Darlene, 160
Hospice Patients Alliance, 154
Hostettler, John N., 155
House of Cards (Skolnick), 36
HPV vaccine, 86–87, 90
Huffington, Arianna, 126
Huffman, Felicity, 101
Hughes, Karen, 204, 205
Hulse, Carl, 129–130
human cloning: Catholic Church, 71, 194; clinics for, 199; pro–stem cell, anticloning position, 205; Republican Party, 250; stem cell research, 71, 194, 199
Human Cloning Ban and Stem Cell Research Protection Act (2005), 220
Human Life International, 209
Human Rights Campaign, 26, 120, 124
Hwang, Woo-Suk, 221
Hyde, Henry, 155

ICOC (Independent Citizens' Oversight Committee), 211, 222
"ideological moderates," 77–78
IGRA (Indian Gaming Regulatory Act, 1988), 34, 35, 40, 41
In re Quinlan, 180
In Vitro Fertilization (Bonnicksen), 198
Incapacitated Person's Legal Protection Act, 136
Independent Citizens' Oversight Committee (ICOC), 211, 222
Indian Gaming Regulatory Act (IGRA, 1988), 34, 35, 40, 41
individual autonomy. *See* autonomy
individualism, personal morality and, 183
Inhofe, James N., 155
International Anti-Euthanasia Task Force, 145
International Gambling Conference (2003), 45
International Society for Stem Cell Research, 210–211
International Task Force on Euthanasia and Assisted Suicide, 156
Internet gambling, 52
interracial dating, 246
Iraq War: 2004 presidential election, 5, 247; 2006 midterm elections, 252; protests at funerals of Iraq War veterans, 23
Ireland, Doug, 136
Islam and end-of-life issues, 135
It Takes a Family (Santorum), 228–230
It Takes a Village (Clinton), 228
"It's Going to Get Ugly" (Shepard), 53

"It's Not Just the Abortion, Stupid" (Joffe), 53
Ives, Stephen, 37
Ivey, Phil, 43

Joffe, Carole: ambivalence about abortion, 73; contestation of personal morality issues, 82; "It's Not Just the Abortion, Stupid," 53; Reagan Democrats, 70; South Dakota 2006 abortion law, 90
John Paul II, Pope: Bush (George W.) and, 206; "culture of life," 215; death, 136; "euthanasia by omission," 142–143; *Evangelium Vitae,* 193; funding of research involving human embryos, 206; on homosexuality, 113
Johns Hopkins University, 198
Johnson, Randy, 43
Jones, Bob, III, 23
Judaism and end-of-life issues, 135
Judeo-Christian values, personal morality and, 183
judicial-made law, 72
Justice Sunday, 98
Justice Sunday III, 228
Juvenile Diabetes Research Foundation, 202, 203, 213

Kadish, Sanford, 14, 19, 244
Kalb, Marvin, 5
Kamarck, Elaine, 235–236, 239
Kass, Leon, 208
Kazin, Michael, 22
Keirstad, Hans, 186
Kennedy, Anthony M.: *Gonzales v. Oregon,* 167–170, 171, 172, 173; late-term/"partial birth" abortions, 91; *Lawrence v. Texas,* 72, 104–105; *Planned Parenthood v. Casey,* 54, 72, 104; social conservatives, 72; in Supreme Court film, 168
Kennedy, Edward, 6, 219
Kerry, John: 2004 presidential election, 4, 6, 70–71, 74; Bauer on, 64; Catholic Church, 71, 193–194; pro-life Democrats, outreach to, 82
Kertz, Molly, 192
Kevorkian, Jack, 140, 164–165
King, Peter, 155
King, Steve, 155
Kingston, Jack, 155
Kinsley, Michael, 32
Kleiman, Mark, 90, 248–249
Klein, Joe, 254
Knowing When to Stop (documentary film), 46
Kohut, Andrew, 5, 132, 253

Kondracke, Mort, 181
Kramer, Larry, 108
Kristol, William, 146
Kuo, David, 252

Ladder (magazine), 106
Lakoff, George, 88, 237–239
Land, Richard, 60, 126
Las Vegas, legal gambling in, 31, 34, 36–38, 44
Laser, Rachel, 83–84
law. *See* criminal law
Lawrence, John, 103–104
Lawrence v. Texas: Bowers v. Hardwick, 104, 110–111; consequences of, 112; judicial tyranny theme, 177; Kennedy (Anthony M.) and, 72, 104–105; National Gay and Lesbian Task Force, 3; O'Connor and, 104; privacy rights, 105; same-sex marriage, 104; Stevens and, 73
League of Conservation Voters, 147
Leahy, Patrick, 58–59
Lederer, Katy, *Poker Face,* 434
Lee, Ang, 101
Lee, Sam, 191
Left Hand of God (Lerner), 248
Legal Center for Defense of Life, 156
legal gambling, 31–52; acceptance as entertainment, 13, 18, 33, 49–50; ambivalence about, 45–46, 52; Atlantic City, 11, 34; backlash against, 50, 52; *Cabazon* ruling, 34, 35, 41; corporate involvement, 49; economic development, 45, 51; first casino outside Nevada, 11; Florida, 48; gaming stock analysts, 11, 26; gaming stocks, 26; government intrusion into private life, freedom from, 49; Indian casinos, 11, 26, 34, 39–42, 49; Indian Gaming Regulatory Act, 34, 35, 40, 41; lack of successful opposition, 51; Las Vegas, 31, 34, 36–38, 44; "loophole legalization," 34; New Hampshire, 8, 11, 33; New York State, 33; opposition/impediments to, 45–49; poker, 36, 43; problem gambling, 38, 45–48; public education, 38; public support for, 6, 8–9, 34, 36, 41, 52; racinos, 33, 40; regressive taxation, 38, 45; revenues, 8, 32–34, 35, 37, 39, 44; riverboats, 34; "sin taxes" on, 26; slot machines, 44; social benefits, 38–39; sports betting, 11, 35; spread of, 8–9, 11, 26, 34–35, 36, 40, 50–52; state encouragement of, 36, 51; state-run lotteries, 11, 26, 33, 35; uncoupling from other vices, 51
Lemert, Edwin, 15
Lerner, Michael, 83, 246, 248

Lessons from a Father to a Son (Ashcroft), 147
Levi, Edward, 256
Lewinsky, Monica, 28
liberalization, 9–13, 242–246; 2006 midterm elections, 256; ambivalence about, 242; backlash against, 19, 27, 50, 243–244; with contestation, 248–249; of laws about abortion, 69; of laws about victimless crime, 9–13, 19; legalization, 244; Mill and, 256; morality contests, 242–244; public support for, 245; tolerance of, 256; young Americans, 245–246
libertarians and Republican Party, 245, 253, 254
Liberty Counsel, 21, 98
Limbaugh, Rush: on Democratic Party, 57; drug problem, 2; feminazis, 57; Miers nomination, 60; stem cell research, 223; tried-and-true methods of suicide, 145
living will statues: acceptance of, 170; California, 10; first statute, 140; immunization from criminal/civil liability, 184; use of, 179
Lopez, Steve, 127
Los Angeles Times (newspaper): abortion, 76; banning of homosexuals from the priesthood, 114–115; on Bush's (George W.'s) performance and priorities, 29; on fundamentalist Christianity, 23; Indian casinos, 39, 42
Louisiana, in, 88
Lugo, Luis, 23–24
Luker, Kristin, 68, 69–70, 238
Luntz, Frank, 49
Lyon, Phyllis, 94

Mabon, Lon, 99
Mack, Connie, 202–203
Maher, Bridget, 86
Maine, assisted suicide in, 140, 178
"March Madness," 35
marijuana: Carter and, 11–12; criminalization of, 27; decriminalization of, 11–12, 25, 148; medical marijuana laws, 170–171, 172, 175–176; Oregon, 148
Martin, Del, 94
Massachusetts: gay marriage, 96; gay rights, 95; same-sex marriage, 9, 94, 109–110
Mattachine Society, 26, 106–107, 126
Matthews, Chris, 1–2
Mazzaschi, Tony, 202–203
McCain, John, 92, 124
McCaskill, Claire, 190, 223, 236
McConahay, John, 16
McDevitt, Michael, 192

medical powers of attorney, 182, 184
Meet the Press (television show), 2
Mehlman, Ken, 124, 194
Methodist Church, 116
Meyer, David S., 201–202
Meyers, Hardy, 148
Mezrich, Ben, *Bringing Down the House,* 43
Michelman, Kate, 54–55, 65, 80
Michigan, assisted suicide in, 140, 177–178
"middle range" theory, 240
Miers, Harriet, 60–64
Milk, Harvey, 9–10, 11, 95
Mill, John Stuart: harm, concern with, 50–51; individual autonomy, 14, 244, 245, 249; liberalization, 256; *On Liberty,* 14; power, rightful use of, 18; zone of privacy, 14, 25, 29
Miller, Jeff, 155
Missouri: 2006 midterm elections, 211, 213, 222–223; abortion-rights opposition, 73–74; as bellwether state, 187; pro-life movement, 190, 211; *Roe v. Wade,* 187; stem cell research, 8, 187–195, 222–223
Missouri Baptist Convention, 190
Missouri Biotechnology Association, 189
Missouri Catholic Conference, 188, 190
Missouri Coalition for Lifesaving Cures, 188
Missouri Right to Life, 190
Missourians Against Human Cloning, 189–190
Moneymaker (Moneymaker), 43
Montana, Joe, 43
Moore, Mary Tyler, 200
Moore, Michael, 64
moral education, Bennett on, 32
Moral Freedom (Wolfe), 234
Moral Majority: antidiscrimination laws affecting gays and lesbians, 25; backlash against liberalization, 50; in Christian Right, 22; political involvement of evangelicals, 256; religiosity equated with, 246; Republican Party, 245
Moral Politics (Lakoff), 237–238
moral pragmatism, 182–185
"moral resentment," 243
moral values: 2004 presidential election, 5; liberalization of laws related to, 9–13, 19; overemphasis on, 227
morality contests: false consciousness, 226–227; liberalization, 242–244; overemphasis on, 227; religion in politics, 246, 248; Schur on, 16–17; as "wedge issues," 226
Morford, Mark, "Down with Fancy Book Learnin'," 1
morning-after pill (Plan B), 84–86, 90
Moscone, George, 95

Moscone Act (California, 1976), 10
Mouth (magazine), 154
Moyers, Bill, 227, 248
MSNBC (network), 133
Murdoch, Rupert, 146
Murray, Patty, 84–85
Muslims and end-of-life issues, 135

Nagourney, Adam, 5–6
NARAL (National Abortion Rights Action League): late-term/"partial birth" abortions, 91; morning-after pill (Plan B), 85; president, 54; pro-choice movement in California, 77; South Dakota 2006 abortion law, 53, 88, 90; vice president, 80
National Abortion Rights Action League. *See* NARAL
National Academy of Science, 216
National Association for the Advancement of Preborn Children, 211
National Association of Evangelicals, 155
National Association of Pro-Life Nurses, 154–155
National Association of State Universities and Land-Grant Colleges, 202
National Bioethics Advisory Commission, 144, 198, 199
National Catholic Bioethics Center, 177
National Coalition Against Legalized Gambling, 49
National Collegiate Athletic Association (NCAA) basketball tournament, 35
National Council of Catholic Bishops, 203
National Council on Independent Living, 153
National Council on Problem Gambling, 46
"national Disenlightenment," 12
National Football Conference, 35
National Gambling Impact Study Commission (NGISC), 46–47, 52
National Gay and Lesbian Task Force: antidiscrimination laws affecting gays and lesbians, 25; federal marriage protection amendment, 124; *Lawrence v. Texas*, 3; "super-DOMAs," 120
National Institutes of Health (NIH), 144, 199
National Legal Center for the Medically Dependent and Disabled, 145, 155–156
National Organization for Women (NOW), 65, 94–95, 147
National Public Radio (NPR), 135, 203
National Review (magazine), 146
National Right to Life Committee: assisted suicide, 142; Bopp and, 71, 145; Bush's stem cell stance, 208; *Gonzales v. Oregon*, 177
National Science Foundation, 189

National Spinal Cord Injury Association, 154
Natural Death Act (California, 1976), 10–11, 131, 138
Neas, Ralph, 58, 63
Neaves, William, 188
Nebraska, late-term/"partial birth" abortions in, 81
Netherlands, same-sex marriage in, 96
Network of Spiritual Progressives, 248
New England Journal of Medicine, 91–92, 140, 224
New Hampshire: HPV vaccine, 87; legal gambling, 8, 11, 33
New Jersey: civil unions for same-sex couples, 125; same-sex marriage, 124–125; stem cell research, 187, 222
New York State, legal gambling in, 33
New York Times (newspaper): 2004 presidential election, 2, 4–5; civil unions for same-sex couples, 119; gaming stocks, 26; physicians aiding dying patients, 150; Republican Party, 251; same-sex marriage, 111–112; same-sex partners in "Style" section, 97; Schiavo case, 181; stem cell research, 191, 218, 219; "values voters," 4–5
New York Times Magazine, 28
New York Times–CBS poll, 97, 120
News Corporation, 146
Newsom, Gavin, 9–10, 93–94, 111
Newsweek (magazine), 106, 108
NGISC (National Gambling Impact Study Commission), 46–47, 52
NIH (National Institutes of Health), 144, 199
NIH Human Fetal Tissue Transplantation Research Panel, 145
NIH Revitalization Act, 197
Nisbet, Mathew C., 203
Nixon, Richard M., 151
No Secret Anymore (documentary film), 94
Noonan, Peggy, 133–134
Not Dead Yet, 153
NOW (National Organization for Women), 65, 94–95, 147
NPR (National Public Radio), 135, 203

Obama, Barack, 29, 92, 237
O'Connor, Sandra Day: abortion rulings, 54, 81; affirmative action, 54, 55; appointment to Supreme Court, 54; gay rights, 55; *Gonzales v. Oregon*, 165–166, 169, 172; *Lawrence v. Texas*, 104; "O'Connor seat," 59–60; *Planned Parenthood v. Casey*, 54, 55, 89; replacement for, 66; resignation from Supreme Court, 53–55; retirement, 55, 56, 57; right-wingers, 63; *Roe v. Wade*, 54, 55, 74, 89; social conservatives, 55, 63;

O'Connor, Sandra Day (*continued*)
as swing vote, 54; *Webster v. Reproductive Health Services,* 54
ODDA. *See* Oregon Death with Dignity Act
Office of Faith-Based Initiatives, 78, 251–252
Ohio, abortion in, 88
On Liberty (Mill), 14
One (magazine), 106
Operation Rescue: emergence of, 70; founder/leader, 129, 134; Schiavo case, 135
Oregon: anti–gay rights initiative (1994), 99; assisted suicide, 184 (*see also* Oregon Death with Dignity Act); citizen initiatives, 148; marijuana, decriminalization of, 148; Measure 9 (1992), 110
Oregon Citizens Alliance, 99
Oregon Death with Dignity Act (ODDA/DWDA, 1994), 147–166; administration of prescribed drugs, 171; Ashcroft and, 147–148, 150–151, 152, 157, 160–161, 167 (see also *Gonzales v. Oregon*); Bopp and, 145; brief submitted by surviving family members, 158–159; Bush (George W.) administration, 150, 179; Catholic Church, 144; changes in medicine and law, 179, 182; Clinton administration, 148, 150; compatibility of assisted suicide with medicine's aims, 154–155, 156–157; Controlled Substances Act (CSA), 150–152, 155–156, 164, 165, 175; court challenges in Oregon, 149; disabilities rights movement, 153–154; effective date, 149; first death under, 149; *Gonzales v. Oregon* (see *Gonzales v. Oregon*); immunity from criminal and civil liability, 184; impetus for, 138–139; moral opponents of, 151; narcotics addiction, 163; Ninth Circuit Court of Appeals, 151; opponents of, arguments of, 153–157; passage, 149; physicians' responsibilities, 149–150, 174–175, 178; prescriptions under, 152, 165–166, 171, 174–175; Reno and, 165; repeal effort, 132, 149; Republican Party, 150; scheduled drugs, 164; Smith (Wesley) and, 147; supporters of, arguments of, 157–162; uniqueness of, 7; usage, 150
Oregon Family Council, 144
Oregon Hospice Association, 161
Oregonian (newspaper), 176
O'Reilly, Bill, 21, 135

Packer, Herbert, 14, 19, 244
Page, Cristina, 87, 88
pain management: Ashcroft directive, 160; assisted suicide, 154, 155; criminalization

of physicians prescribing pain relief for terminal patients, 150
Parade (magazine), 211–212
Parkinson's Action Network, 202
Partial-Birth Abortion Act (2003), 82
Party of Death (Ponnuru), 146
Passion of the Christ (film), 101
Pataki, George, 33
People for the American Way, 58, 63
Perkins, Tony, 61
personal autonomy. *See* autonomy
personal morality: autonomy, 249–250, 256; contestation after 2004 elections, 82; criminal law, 182–183, 184, 239–241, 244; individualism, 183; Judeo-Christian values, 183; legislating, 29–30, 229–230; "middle range" theory of, 240; social conservatives, 226
Peter D. Hart Research Associates, 120–121, 193
Petri, Thomas, 155
Pew Forum on Religion and Public Life, 23, 193
Pew Research Center polls: 2004 presidential election, 5; abortion, 57, 75–76, 212; Bush voters in 2004 election, 22; death and dying issues, 132; domestic priorities, 29; gay marriage, 124, 246; gay rights, 212; homosexuality, 120; legal gambling, 51–52; same-sex marriage, 212; stem cell research, 212; "values voters," 4, 5; venture capitalists, 221–222; young Americans, 246
Phelps, Fred: "God Hates Fags" campaign, 23, 112, 244; protests at funerals of Iraq War veterans, 23
Philadelphia (film), 112
Phillips, Kevin, 12, 255
physician-assisted suicide. *See* assisted suicide
Physicians for Compassionate Care Educational Foundation, 154–155
Pierson, Paul, 233–234
Pitts, Joseph R., 155
Plan B (morning-after pill), 84–86, 90
Planned Parenthood of America: Bopp on, 71; frames used by, 85; president, 82; Sioux City clinic, 88
Planned Parenthood v. Casey: Alito and, 65, 67; Clinton (Bill) and, 55; Kennedy (Anthony M.) and, 54, 72, 104; Miers and, 62; O'Connor and, 54, 55, 89; public support for, 74; Roberts and, 58; *Roe v. Wade*, 72; Souter and, 54; stability regarding abortion, 70; stare decisis, 67
poker, 36, 43
Poker Face (Lederer), 434

Poker Nation (Bellin), 37
PokerBiz (magazine), 36
polarization in American politics: elite polarization, 231; level of, 234–235; political
class *versus* most Americans, 233–234;
"problematic normalization," 239; Republican Party, 233–234; value voters, 225–
226
Political Action to Restore Personal Freedoms
and Individual Rights (Terri PAC), 137
political compromise, rejection of, 231
political extremists, 233–234
political moderates, 239, 254
political participation, 231–233
Politics of Deviance (Schur), 16–17
Ponnuru, Ramesh: overturning of *Roe v.
Wade,* 88; *Party of Death,* 146; public
support for abortion, 75; stem cell
research, 214–215
pornography, 16
Portland, Oregon, same-sex marriage in,
94
prayer in public schools, 24
President's Committee on Mental Retardation, 145
Press, Eyal, 87
Pressberg, Gail, 224
privacy: abortion, 85; *Lawrence v. Texas,*
105; Mill and, 14, 25, 29; *Roe v. Wade,*
110; Schiavo case, 249
private behavior and criminal law, 14–15, 27
Pro-Life Legal Defense Fund, 156
pro-life movement: Bush (George W.) and,
208; California, 211; Missouri, 190, 211;
stem cell research, 186, 191, 195, 201, 208
"problematic normalization": polarization in
American politics, 239; of victimless crime,
13, 18–19, 28–30, 242–243
prostitution, 19
Protestants: abortion, 75–76; Bush administration, George W., 252; evangelicals, 3,
20, 22, 64, 75–76, 115–116, 236, 252;
gay rights, 113, 115–116, 116–117;
mainline, 75–76, 113, 116–117, 193;
Republican Party, 3, 20, 22, 64, 236; stem
cell research, 193; views of, 24–25
public sector, expansion of, 232
"purple": American Catholics as, 78; Americans as, 3, 29, 132, 182; Lakoff on, 239;
meaning of, 230–231; Schiavo case, 132,
182

Queer Eye for the Straight Guy (television
show), 1, 126
Quill, Timothy, 135, 138, 140
Quinlan, Karen, 140

racinos, 33, 40
Ranulf, Svend, 243
Reagan, Leslie, 68–69, 141
Reagan, Nancy: on Frist, 218; "rollback
coalition," 27; stem cell research, 8, 186,
191, 213, 218, 219, 220
Reagan, Ron, Jr., 8, 213, 219
Reagan, Ronald: 1976 presidential election,
12; 1980 presidential election, 70, 246;
Bopp and, 145; conservative jurists, 70,
72; death, 8, 213; decriminalization of
abortion, 10; funding of research involving
human embryos, 196–197; litmus test on
abortion, 70; O'Connor and, 54; Roberts
and, 58
Reagan Democrats: 2006 midterm elections,
253; abortion, 70, 227; Republican Party,
70; *What's the Matter with Kansas?,* 22
Real Time with Bill Maher (television show),
61
Reed, Ralph, 22, 49
Reeve, Christopher, 200, 210, 223
Reform Judaism, 158
Rehnquist, William H.: on assisted suicide,
172, 174; death, 59; Roberts and, 57
Reid, Harry: federal marriage protection
amendment, 123–124; Roberts and, 59;
Schiavo case, 133; stem cell research, 221
Reith, Gerda, 45
religion: in American life, 246–248; end-of-
life issues, 135; gay rights, 112–117; religiosity, 19, 21–25; religious freedom, 250;
religious symbols in public buildings, 24;
secularization (*see* secularization)
Religious Coalition for Marriage, 115
Renew America, 98
Reno, Janet, 150, 165
Reno Gazette-Journal (newspaper), 31
Republican Party: 2006 midterm elections,
180–181, 250–252, 253–255; African
Americans, 115; American Gaming Association, 49; base, 22; as a "big tent," 194–
195, 255; business leaders, 191; as center-
right party, 250; Christian Right, 231;
church activism, responsiveness to, 218;
criminalization of physicians prescribing
pain relief for terminal patients, 150;
"culture of life," 130; Danforth on, 251;
Dean on, 249; defense of marriage acts
(DOMAs), 118; federal marriage protection amendment, 221, 250; gay rights,
218; Goldwater's advice to, 255; human
cloning, 250; libertarians, 245, 253, 254;
moderates in, 254; Moral Majority, 245;
Oregon Death with Dignity Act (ODDA/
DWDA), 150; polarization in American

Republican Party (*continued*)
politics, 233–234; pro-business pro-choice Republicans, 77; Protestants, evangelical, 3, 20, 22, 64, 236; Reagan Democrats, 22, 70; Reed and, 49; religious freedom, 250; "right-to-life" issue, 133; right wing of, 63; *Roe v. Wade,* 88–89; Schiavo case, 130, 131, 133, 136, 137, 181, 218, 234; social conservatives, 221, 253–254; stem cell research, 130, 191, 194, 202–203, 216, 217–218, 220; upscale men, defection of, 253; value voters, 228
Research!America, 212
Resorts International Hotel, 11
Responsible Gaming Association of New Mexico, 46
Results for America, 213
Rich, Frank, 109, 111–112
Richards, David, 105
right-to-die, public support for, 138
right-to-die legislation, 184
right-to-die movement, 133, 139–141, 180–181
"right-to-life" issue, 133
Risen, James, 70
Roberts, John G., Jr.: church-state separation, 58; Clinton (Hillary) and, 92; confirmation hearings, 57–59, 76; environmental protections, 58; *Gonzales v. Oregon,* 162, 169, 170, 171, 172; late-term/"partial birth" abortions, 91; "minimalist" judicial philosophy, 68; Neas on, 58; *Planned Parenthood v. Casey,* 58; as political appointee, 58; Rehnquist, 57; Reid and, 59; *Roe v. Wade,* 58, 59; Scalia and, 58; school desegregation, 58; Specter and, 58; voting rights for African Americans, 58; women's reproductive rights, 58
Robertson, Pat, 208
Robinson, Gene, 116
Roe v. Wade: "abortion grays," 235; abortion prior to, 68–69; aftermath, 196; Alito and, 66–67; anniversary of, 172; backlash against, 69–70; Blackmun and, 54, 55, 69; Bush (George W.) and, 62; Bush (Laura) and, 62; Clinton (Hillary) and, 92; decriminalization of abortion, 16; funding of research involving human embryos, 196; judicial activism, 72; judicial tyranny theme, 177; medicine, changes in, 19; Miers and, 62; Missouri, 187; O'Connor and, 54, 55, 74, 89; overturning of, 88–89; *Planned Parenthood v. Casey,* 72; post-*Roe* era, predictions concerning, 87–92; privacy rights, 110; public support for, 6, 55, 56–57, 74, 75, 76, 230; reexamination

of, 81; Republican Party, 88–89; Roberts and, 58, 59; stare decisis, 58, 66–67; test case state against, 187; threats to, 53; trimester system, 54; undercutting of, 56, 70; young women, 89
"rollback coalition," 27, 243
Romer v. Evans, 110
Romney, Mitt, 137
Rose, Nelson, 50
Rosen, Jeffrey, 88
Rounders (film), 31
Rove, Karl, 66, 204, 250
Ryan, Paul, 155

Saad, Lydia, 74–75
Safire, William, 26
St. Louis Post-Dispatch (newspaper), 191–192, 194
Salazar, Ken, 123
Saletan, William, 74
Salk, Jonas, 220
same-sex marriage: 2004 presidential election, 121, 247; 2006 midterm elections, 252; AIDS epidemic, 111–112; ambivalence about, 115; American attitudes toward, 97; Bauer on, 93, 99–100; box turtle comparison, 7; Bush (George W.) and, 96, 125; Catholic Church, 71, 194; constitutional amendment against, opposition to, 6, 7, 230 (*see also* federal marriage protection amendment); Hawaii, 243; *Lawrence v. Texas,* 104; legalization of, 111; Massachusetts, 9, 94, 109–110; National Organization for Women, 94–95; New Jersey, 124–125; opposition to, 245; Portland, Oregon, 94; public support for, 7, 212; San Francisco, 9, 93–96; social conservatives, 121, 124–125, 126; Western countries, 96; younger cohorts, 245–246. *See also* civil unions for same-sex couples; gay marriage
San Francisco, 9, 93–96
Santorum, Rick: deterioration of traditional family, 102; gay rights, 228–229; *Gonzales v. Oregon,* 155; individualism to, 229; *It Takes a Family,* 228–230; judicial tyranny theme, 228; Justice Sunday III, 228; legislating personal morality, 229–230; loss of his Senate seat, 254–255; moral decline of America, 230; overturning of state sodomy laws, 103; presidential aspirations, 137; Wallis and, 247
"Save Our Children" crusade, 108
Scalia, Antonin: gay marriage, 100; *Gonzales v. Oregon,* 168–169, 170, 171, 172, 175, 177; late-term/"partial birth" abortions, 91; Roberts and, 58

Schiavo, Michael: Congressional involvement in wife's case, 130; lawyer for, 130; public support for, 131; remarriage, 137; right-to-die claims, 133; Smith (Wesley) on, 146; *Terri: The Truth*, 138; as Terri's guardian, 128–129, 146; "Terri's Law," 128–129

Schiavo, Terri, 127–138; 2006 midterm elections, 181, 222; abortion, 133; assisted suicide laws, 178, 182; autonomy in personal/family matters, 7, 243; autopsy, 137; Bush (Jeb) and, 128–129, 131, 137; Christian Right, 185; Congressional involvement, 130, 134, 136, 137; "culture of life" issue, 130; Democratic Party, 130, 131, 133, 136; Eleventh Circuit Court, 130; end-of-life bills, 138; euthanasia, 133, 137; Florida Senate, 128; Frist and, 134, 137; government intrusion into family affairs, freedom from, 222, 249, 251, 254–255, 256; Greer and, 128; guardian, 128, 146; media coverage, 132, 133–134, 135, 181; "Palm Sunday Compromise," 130; parents (Bob and Mary Schindler), 128–129, 130, 131; persistent vegetative state, 128; politicians' withdrawal from the case, 135–136, 180; "purple" Americans, 132, 182; religious conservatives, 134; religious views of end-of-life issues, 135; removal of feeding tube, 128–129; removal of feeding tube, public support for, 131, 134, 135, 136–137; Republican Party, 130, 131, 133, 136, 137, 181, 218, 234; right-to-die movement, 140; "right-to-life" issue, 133; significance of her case, 131–138; stem cell research, 185; Supreme Court, 131; "telemisdiagnosis" of, 137; "Terri's Law," 128–129; vigils at hospital, 244; zone of privacy, 249

Schindler, Bob and Mary (Terri Schiavo's parents), 128–129, 130, 131

Schneider, Joseph, 15

Schneider, William, 74

Schur, Edwin: borderline crimes, 16; compassion, 245; *Crimes without Victims*, 15; criminal law, reach of, 27; deviance situations, 240; individual autonomy, 249; liberalization of laws pertaining to victimless crime, 19; *Politics of Deviance*, 16–17; proper use of law, 244; "stigma contests," 13; victimless crimes, 14

Schwartz, Pepper, 229

Schwarzenegger, Arnold: Indian casinos in California, 42; stem cell research, 8, 210; Wildmon and, 23

Science (magazine), 198, 200

Scientific American (magazine), 221

secondary crime, 15

secularization: of America/U.S., 21, 23–24; Christmas season, 21; de-religionizing of American society, 21; Democratic Party, 246–247; evangelicalism, 24; political parties, 25; religiosity and, 19, 21–25

Self-Advocates Becoming Empowered, 154

Sensenbrenner, James, 130

Shaffer, Howard, 26

Sheldon, Louis, 110, 118

Shepard, Gary, "It's Going to Get Ugly," 53

Shepard, Matthew, 244

Shimkus, John, 155

Shockley, Madison, 23

"sin," 4

"sin taxes," 26

Skidmore, Max, 191

Skocpol, Theda, 214

Skolnick, Arlene: ambivalence/anxiety about change, 29; contestation of personal morality issues, 82; diversity of American families, 229; "fragmented families," 125; morality wars, 256; on overemphasis on moral values, 227; proper use of law, 244; social conservatives, 102

Skolnick, Jerome: coercion of virtue, 14; gambling as "normal vice," 36, 38, 56; *House of Cards*, 36; legislating personal morality, 30; personal morality issues, 19

Skube, Michael, "We're Saved. You Lost. Now What?," 225

Slate (online magazine), 32

slot machines, 44

Smith, Chris, 79, 155

Smith, Christian, 24

Smith, Gordon, 202

Smith, Jeff, 71

Smith, Wesley J.: on assisted suicide, 127; assisted suicide in California, 179; *Forced Exit*, 145–147; *Gonzales v. Oregon*, 177; on *Gonzales v. Oregon*, 73; judicial tyranny theme, 177; slippery slope argument, 169; stem cell research, 215, 223

Smyth, Michael, 106, 107, 108–109

Snow, David, 237

social conservatives: 2006 midterm elections, 250, 255; abortion, 98, 126; abstinence, 86; backlash against liberalization, 19, 27, 50, 243–244; Bush (George W.) and, 64–65; business leaders, 191; contraception, 86, 87; defense of marriage acts (DOMAs), 117–120; deterioration of traditional family, 102; framing wars, 237; Frist and, 219; gambling, 50; gay rights, 98, 109, 111, 112; HPV vaccine, 86; judicial tyranny theme, 20, 177; Kennedy (Anthony M.)

social conservatives (*continued*)
    and, 72; Miers nomination, 60–64; "national Disenlightenment," 12; National Gambling Impact Study Commission, 46–47; O'Connor and, 55, 63; personal morality, 226; Phillips on, 12; religious beliefs and, 248; Republican Party, 221, 253–254; right-to-die legislation, 184; same-sex marriage, 121, 124–125, 126; stem cell research, 195, 216, 221–222; Supreme Court, composition of, 68; venture capitalists, 221–222
Society for Adolescent Medicine, 84
Society for Disability Studies, 154
Society for the Study of Social Problems, 243
Society for Truth and Justice, 134
"Sodomized Religious Virgin Exception," 88
sodomy: criminalization of (see *Bowers v. Hardwick*); decriminalization of, 10, 11, 25, 103, 107 (see also *Lawrence v. Texas*)
Solinger, Rickie, 69
Solo, Pam, 224
Souder, Mark E., 155
Souter, David H.: *Gonzales v. Oregon*, 162–163, 164, 166, 169–170, 171–172; *Planned Parenthood v. Casey*, 54
South Carolina Equality Coalition, 119
South Dakota 2006 abortion law, 53, 87–88, 90, 252
South Dakota Campaign for Healthy Families, 88
Southern Baptist Convention, 126
Southern Baptist Ethics and Religious Liberty Commission, 177
Specter, Arlen: Alito and, 66; federal marriage protection amendment, 124; Goldwater's advice to Republican Party, 255; Roberts and, 58; stem cell research, 203
Stand Up for California, 41–42
stem cell research, 186–224; 2004 presidential election, 210; 2006 midterm elections, 221, 222–224, 251, 252; abortion, 190, 220–222; abortion opponents, 185; adult stem cell research, 193, 216; alternatives to, 214, 216; ambivalence about, 195, 203; antiabortion activists, 208–209, 214–215; assisted suicide opponents, 214; attitudes toward, 13; autonomy arguments, 213–214; Bush administration, George W., 186, 218, 221; Bush (George W.) and, 148, 191, 195, 197, 201, 202, 203, 204–209, 215–216, 221, 222; California, 8, 10, 187, 210–211, 222; California Proposition 71 (2004), 186, 210–211, 215, 216, 217; Catholic Church, 71, 113, 191–194; Christian Right, 24, 190–191; cloning,

188, 190, 214, 216; cloning, human, 71, 194, 199; compassion, 244–245; criminalization of, 188, 189, 199, 201; Danforth and, 191, 218; Democratic Party, 194, 250–251; destruction of embryos, 186, 214; Dolly (cloned sheep), 190, 198–199; economic development, 210, 214; embryonic stem cell research, 193; emergence as an issue, 195; federalism, 241; feminists, 216–217; Frist and, 191, 205, 218–220; funding of research involving human embryos, 196–199, 200, 205, 206, 207, 241; harvesting embryos, 215; Hatch and, 201, 202–203, 219–220, 224; lobbying favoring, 199–200; media coverage, 200, 203; Missouri, 8, 187–195, 222–223; mobilization of interested parties, 199–203, 207, 209; morality of, 199, 200; New Jersey, 187, 222; opponents of, 189–195, 209, 214–217; politics of, 255; potential benefits/cures/discoveries, 195, 199, 210–211, 213, 214, 215; pro-life movement, 186, 191, 195, 208; pro–stem cell, anticloning position, 205; profit motive of biotech industry, venture capitalists, 214, 216, 221; proponents of, 202–203; Protestants, mainline, 193; public awareness, 200–201; public support for, 6, 8, 185, 190, 201, 203, 211–213, 217–218, 218, 223–224; Reagan (Nancy) and, 8, 186, 191, 213, 218, 219, 220; Reagan (Ron, Jr.) and, 8, 213, 219; reproductive cloning, 188, 189; Republican Party, 130, 191, 194, 202–203, 216, 217–218, 220; sanctity of life, 195; scandal, Korean, 216, 221; scandals, 214; Schiavo case, 185; Schwarzenegger and, 8, 210; science of stem cells, 198–199, 207; slippery slope argument, 189, 214–215; social conservatives, 195, 216; somatic cell nuclear transfer, 188, 215; Specter and, 203; state competitiveness, 189; state legislatures, 241; states allowing, 189, 195; states banning, 195; therapeutic cloning, 188, 189; University of Wisconsin, 198, 202, 205, 207; as wedge issue, 220–221
Stevens, John Paul, 72–73, 170, 171–172
"stigma contests," 13
stigmatization, 17
Stowers, Jim and Virginia, 188
suicide, 139, 145
Super Bowl, 35
"super-DOMAs," 120
surrogate decision making, 140
Sutherland, Edwin, 16
"symbolic politics," 27

Talent, Jim, 190–191, 195
Tannenbaum, Frank, 15
TASH (formerly Association for Persons with Severe Handicaps), 154
Taylor, Gene, 155
Taylor, Stuart, 88
"terminal sedation," 184
Terri: The Truth (Schiavo), 138
Terri PAC (Political Action to Restore Personal Freedoms and Individual Rights), 137
Terry, Randall, 129, 134
Third Way, 239
Third Way Culture Project, 83, 90
"third way" for Democratic Party, 235–237
Thomas, Clarence: *Gonzales v. Oregon,* 172, 175–176; *Gonzales v. Reich,* 176; late-term/"partial birth" abortions, 91; medical marijuana laws, 175–176; nomination hearings, 219
Thomas, Judy, 70
Thompson, Tommy, 205
Thompson, William N., 37, 45
Thurmond, Strom, 2, 202
Tikkun (journal), 248
Tilghman, Shirley, 209
Time (magazine), 106
Times of Harvey Milk (documentary film), 95
Todd, Chuck, 254
tolerance, 95–96, 236, 256
Traditional Values Coalition (TVC): anti-gay rights sentiment, 98; Bush's stem cell stance, 209; in Christian Right, 22; Civil Rights for Families Initiative, 118; Santorum and, 229; sex education, opposition to, 110; Wildmon and, 23
Transamerica (film), 101
Tribal Government Gaming and Economic Self-Sufficiency Act (California, 1998), 40
Tucker, Kathryn, 169
Tumulty, Karen, 73–74
Turley, Jonathan, 78
TVC. *See* Traditional Values Coalition

Union of Orthodox Jewish Congregations of America, 155
Unitarian Universalist Association of Congregations, 158
United Church of Christ, 2, 116, 158
U.S. Catholic Conference, 135
U.S. Conference of Catholic Bishops: assisted suicide, 142; compatibility of assisted suicide with medicine's aims, 154; deputy director, 144; stem cell research, 215
University Faculty for Life, 156

University of Wisconsin in stem cell research, 198, 202, 205, 207
USA Today (newspaper), 21, 52, 124

Vacco v. Quill, 153, 184
Vaid, Urvashi, 107, 108
values voters: 2004 presidential election, 10, 53, 61, 82, 226, 228, 235–236, 238, 242; 2006 midterm elections, 226, 250, 252–253; Bush (George W.) and, 4–5, 225, 228; out-of-stepness of, 234; polarization, 225–226; rejection of, 246; Republican Party, 228
Vargo, Diane, "Connecting the Dots," 186
Vermont: assisted suicide, 179; civil unions for same-sex couples, 96, 97, 113, 119; gay rights, 95
victimless crime: first paradox of, 19, 21–25; second paradox of, 19, 25–26; third paradox of, 19, 27; fourth paradox of, 28; attitudes toward, 4, 15–16; checkerboard pattern of laws, 19, 28, 242; consensual nature, 15; conservative backlash, 19, 27, 243–244; crimes characterized as, 14; criminal law, 17–18; decriminalization of, 183; enforcement, 16; judicial-made law, 72; law's reach in, 19, 25–26; liberalization of laws related to, 9–13, 19; morality contests, 16–17; "problematic normalization" of, 13, 18–19, 28–30, 242–243; secondary crime, 15; stigmatization, 17
"Voice for Terri" coalition, 135
"Voice of Morality Exposed as Chronic Casino Loser" (Burkeman), 31

Wagoner, James, 80
Wal-Mart, 85
Wall Street Journal (newspaper): gaming stocks, 26; Miers nomination, 60; on Schiavo case, 133–134; stem cell research, 202
Wallis, Jim: Falwell and, 2; *God's Politics,* 247–248; religion in American life, 83, 246; talk about values, 238
Walters, Suzanna, 94
Warner, Mark, 83, 237
Warren, Earl, 72
Warren, Rick, 248
Washington Post (newspaper), 202
Washington State, assisted suicide in, 140, 142, 143–144
Washington University in St. Louis, 202
Washington v. Glucksberg: assisted suicide, 153, 164; Clement and, 164; compatibility of assisted suicide with medicine's aims, 155; exploration of approaches to

Washington v. Glucksberg (continued)
end-of-life issues, 161; *Gonzales v. Oregon*, 153, 161–162, 163–164; Not Dead Yet amicus brief, 153
Waxman, Henry A., 130
Weaver, John, 192
Weber, Larry, 188
Webster v. Reproductive Health Services, 54, 70
"wedge issues," 4, 220–221, 226
Weekly Standard (magazine), 146
Weisberg, Jacob, 28
"We're Saved. You Lost. Now What?" (Skube), 225
West Wing (television show), 1
Westberg, Jenny, 79–80
What's the Matter with Kansas? (Frank): false consciousness, 3, 20, 29, 226–227; Reagan Democrats, 22; Santorum's response to, 228; working-class evangelicals, 3
White, Byron, 70
White, Dan, 95
White House Conference on Aging, 145

Why Marriage Matters (Wolfson), 93
Wildmon, Donald, 23, 100
Williams, Glanville, 138–139
Wilson, James Q., 234–235
Wilson, Pete, 76–77, 111
Wisconsin, gay rights in, 95
Wolfe, Alan, *Moral Freedom*, 234
Wolfson, Evan, *Why Marriage Matters*, 93
Wood, Susan, 86
World Institute on Disability, 154
World Series of Poker, 36, 43
Wright, Wendy, 209
Wu, David, 160, 176–177
Wuthnow, Robert, 23
Wyden, Ron, 160, 176
Wynn, Steve, 38

Yoo, John, 61
young Americans, 245–246

Zogby poll, 247
zone of privacy: Mill and, 14, 25, 29; Schiavo case, 249

About the Authors

John Dombrink is Professor of Criminology, Law & Society at the University of California, Irvine, and co-author of a book on gambling policy, *The Last Resort*. Daniel Hillyard is an Assistant Professor in the Center for the Study of Crime, Delinquency, and Corrections, at Southern Illinois University, Carbondale. Together they are the authors of *Dying Right: The Death with Dignity Movement*.